The handbook of project-based management

Second Edition

Other books by the author

Also published by McGraw-Hill

THE COMMERCIAL PROJECT MANAGER
Managing owners, sponsors, partners, supporters, stakeholders, contractors and consultants
J. Rodney Turner   ISBN 0-07-707946-9

THE PROJECT MANAGER AS CHANGE AGENT
Leadership, influence and negotiation
J. R. Turner, K. V. Grude and L. Thurloway   ISBN 0-07-707741-5

The handbook of project-based management

Improving the processes for achieving strategic objectives

Second Edition

J. Rodney Turner

The McGraw-Hill Companies

London · New York · Chicago · St Louis · San Francisco
Auckland · Bogotá · Caracas · Lisbon · Madrid · Mexico
Milan · Montreal · New Delhi · Panama · Paris · San Juan
São Paulo · Singapore · Sydney · Tokyo · Toronto

Published by
McGRAW-HILL Publishing Company
Shoppenhangers Road, Maidenhead, Berkshire, SL6 2QL, England
Telephone: +44 (0)1628 502500
Fax: +44 (0)1628 770224
Website address: http://www.mcgraw-hill.co.uk

British Library Cataloguing in Publication Data
A catalogue record for this book is available from the British Library

ISBN 0-07-709161-2

Publisher: Alfred Waller
Development Editor: Elizabeth Robinson
Produced by: Steven Gardiner Ltd
Cover by: Aricot Vert Design

McGraw-Hill

A Division of The McGraw-Hill Companies

2 3 4 5 BB 3 2 1

Printed and bound in the United Kingdom by Bell & Bain Ltd., Glasgow

To Edward:
who was conceived and born at the same time
as the material on which this book is based

Contents

Foreword to the second edition

Since the publication of the first edition in 1993, project management has continued its rapid development towards full professional standing and recognition, and this second edition reflects the changes in emphasis and practice which have occurred in the last five years. Project management is now not only fully recognized, but more significantly regarded by client and top management alike as the first essential for their projects. There are now clients appointing a project manager before any other appointment, a rare occurrence five years ago, and much to be welcomed.

Furthermore high standards of training and achievement are demanded in project management, and rather less emphasis is placed on the technology in which it is practised. The new edition takes account of these significant shifts in approach, for example the sections on the management of risk, quality, and audits are either addded or enhanced.

As the use and availability of information technology expands, so the importance of achieving success in information systems projects increases. These projects remain among the most difficult, and I think it is right that they are now specifically included in a section on the application of project-based management. Small projects can be very challenging, either alone or in multi-projects, and a new section on multi-project management, including programme management, fills a long-standing gap.

The new edition of the *Handbook* is a practical reference text to take us into the next century of project-based management.

Eric Gabriel
Vice-President, Association for Project Management

Foreword to the first edition

Books about project management give a static impression, a feeling that the book proposes to encapsulate a fund of knowledge and experience, a body of knowledge, which can be absorbed to give the capability of managing a project effectively.

After reading these books, I am usually disappointed – not because useful information and insights are not given – but because expectations are not realizable in practice. Dr Turner's handbook gives at once a touch of realism. It is about new approaches to general management based on projects. It is about managing change – a very challenging and dynamic endeavour. It is about managing that change through projects, the emerging idea that widens the scope of project management.

Project management has developed quite markedly over the last 20 years, from a systems-oriented methodology, through 'goal orientation', to project-based management. From a topic in which computers were pre-eminent, to one in which people, interpersonal and intergroup relationships predominate.

There has been a broadening of the definition of projects, and a broadening of the scope of project management. Management by projects, the theme of the IPMA World Congress in Vienna in 1990, was a signpost to the new directions in which project management was moving.

Dr Turner's book, *The Handbook of Project-Based Management*, catches the tide of development trends. It is current, relevant and timely.

I was pleased to see that the single point contact – the emphasis on the project manager – is maintained. Having gone through the mistaken phase myself of believing that systems would, in the end, make the role of the project manager redundant, I support the unified theory, which Turner quotes from Exodus 20.3 'Thou shalt have no other gods before me', indicating that the reality of the matrix organization has been anticipated, but the prime authority always remained with the Great Project Manager in the Sky.

Quality is given a welcome and effective treatment. This is an area requiring great care and attention, and is a high risk area for a project manager, as quality issues almost always involve cost and time effects.

I find the concept of 'zero defects' difficult, partly because one person's defect may be acceptable to others, and partly because 'customer requirements' are not fixed, nor easily defined. Sufficient to remember that 'The best is the enemy of the good'. Nevertheless, the section on quality includes the salient issues and will be found very useful.

The sections on management procedures come towards the end of the book, in Part 4, and this is the right emphasis for the new century. This implies the view, which I support strongly, that if one gets the issues in Parts 1, 2 and 3 wrong, the best systems in the world will not work. If these issues are right, the Part 4 matters will not constitute a problem in themselves.

I was particularly pleased to read the section on international projects in Part 5, and the inclusion of cultural factors researched by G. Hofstede. This is required reading by everyone involved in international projects and change projects across cultural boundaries – very relevant in today's changing world.

The book includes a fund of information across the whole spectrum of contemporary project management as applied to the management of change. The material is presented without pedantry or oversimplification, yet in a form that makes it easily assimilated. It is readable page after page, holding the interest – a rare quality for a book with this depth and breadth of information, which could so easily have become superficial or academic. Key issues, checklists and practical comments are readily found on any topic for reference.

The book has much for anyone engaged in the management of change and management of projects. It will help experienced project managers to understand more fully what they often do by instinct, and hence improve their performance.

Aspiring project managers, on the other hand, will be helped to understand the basics of the subject – and most importantly – to get the priorities right.

It will be valuable, too, for all involved in the provision of project management services; in the vital areas of planning and scheduling, cost control, cost engineering, materials management, contracts management and so many others, helping them to understand the role of the project manager, and advising on how to improve the quality of the information and of the service which they supply.

The book will be on my bookshelf and is required reading for all involved and interested in the management of change and the emerging concepts for effective management in the new century.

Eric Gabriel
Vice-President, Association for Project Management

Preface to the second edition

In writing this second edition, I have maintained the basic approach of the book, writing a book that people can either read through from start to finish, or dip into as they wish to remind themselves of how to approach a particular issue. I have retained the structure of the book:

Part 1 dealing with the context of projects

Part 2 describing the five functions of management, scope, organization, quality, cost and time

Part 3 describing the stages of the project life cycle

Part 4 covering administrative techniques

Part 5 giving applications and illustrating how project-based management is adapted to different circumstances.

Some chapters are fundamentally unchanged, (except the numbers are different because there are fewer chapters). Those that are unchanged are the chapters dealing with the strategy of the parent organization (2), the parties involved (3), managing scope, organization, cost and time (5, 6, 8 and 9), and the three stages of the life cycle (11, 12 and 13). Other chapters have been updated to incorporate new research in developing areas of project-based management. These include the chapters dealing with project success and strategy (4), managing quality and risk (7 and 10), and the project manager (17). I took a new approach in Part 4, having a chapter dealing with programme management (14), procedures and systems (15), and health checks and audits (16). I also took a different approach in Part 5. Although I do not disagree with what I did in the first edition, I am not so sure any more that the categorization of projects I gave leads to useful differences. I therefore have a single chapter on types of project from both the product life cycle and types of discipline. I dropped the section on engineering projects, because I do not think that gave new insights. The section on design projects has been incorporated into Chapter 12. I added new sections on concurrent engineering and business process reengineering. I have substantially extended the chapter on international projects (19). Overall the book is three chapters shorter, which I hope makes it even more focused.

Throughout the book I have tried to give up-to-date references, even where I have not substantially changed the text.

Rodney Turner
East Horsley, Surrey
June 1998

Preface to the first edition

The first book in The Henley Management Series (Paul Thorne, *The New General Manager*, McGraw-Hill, 1989) identified the rapid, structural changes taking place within modern organizations, and how this is leading to a new brand of general manager. This rapid change has been brought about by an explosion in the rate of change of technology and communication, and the access of managers to information. The second book in the series (Tony Knight and David Silk, *Managing Information*, McGraw-Hill, 1990), explained the key role of information to business success.

Both these books identified a parallel development, driven by rapid change in modern organizations: management by projects has become the new general management. The bureaucratic organization, introduced in the nineteenth century to provide efficiency through permanence, can no longer respond to the competitive environment of modern business. Organizations must be flexible to respond quickly and effectively to changing circumstance, and this requires new general managers who are able to manage change through projects, involving them in:

- the management of a portfolio of projects, through a team of project managers working for them;
- the management of individual projects, as project manager, through teams of people who do not normally respond directly to them;
- the management of the interface between these projects, the rest of the organization, and the external environment.

This change is not limited to small organizations. British Telecom has identified that half its operations are project based. Translate this to the economy as a whole, and the annual spend on projects in the United Kingdom is £300 billion, and this consumes 27 million man-years of effort.

The management of projects has therefore become a skill which the general manager requires in his portfolio of skills alongside more traditional disciplines, such as accounting and finance, marketing and strategic management. This book aims to provide a comprehensive guide to the discipline for the general manager, and will enable them to:

– define projects required to achieve their business objectives
– manage the work and organization required to achieve them
– achieve their objectives to the required specification, and at a time and price which make the investment worth while
– undertake the work at different stages of a project
– ensure timely and effective completion of the project
– understand their role as manager of the project in building and maintaining the team
– compare the application of project management in different circumstances.

It describes a structured approach to the management of projects, and is illustrated throughout by reference to real examples of projects with which I have been associated. It is designed to be read through to provide an overview of the approach, or to be referred to as a handbook to give specific advice on how to manage certain aspects of projects, and the tools and techniques to use. The overall model of the approach (in Chapter 1), together with the contents page, should help readers to find their way around the book, and to dip into specific chapters. The book is intended for busy managers, as well as for more formal study by students on programmes leading to an MBA or an MSc in a project-related subject.

The Introduction defines projects, and introduces the structured approach to project management described in the book. Part 1 deals with context of projects. It defines projects, describes why companies undertake them and the impact they have on the organization, and explains how to adopt strategies for successful projects. Part 2 describes the first set of methods of the approach: the objectives of project management, i.e. how to define the projects required to achieve your business objectives, and how to manage the scope of work required, the project organization to deliver them, the constraints of quality, cost and time, and the risk inherent in projects. Part 3 describes a second set of methods of the approach: the management processes required to undertake projects. It follows the project management life cycle, and shows how each of the objectives is managed at each stage. Part 4 introduces further tools and techniques covering specific management systems and procedures, including project administration, the use of computer systems, and the role and skills of the project manager.

Part 5 concludes the book by describing some specific applications of the management of projects. It covers projects from different stages of the product life cycle, various industries and sectors, different size of project, and projects involving international collaboration.

Rodney Turner
Wargrave, Berkshire
October 1991

manuscripts. Their comments and advice have been very valuable.

As great as the contribution of all these people has been, it is small compared to that of Kristoffer Grude, Tor Haug and Erling Andersen. Their book, *Goal Directed Project Management*, the English edition of which I wrote, provided the embryonic structure and approach of this book. However, their contribution has gone further: a section of Chapter 3 is derived from a paper I wrote jointly with Tor, and I have spent many hours with Kristoffer sharing his experience and philosophy of project management. To acknowledge the direct contribution of these authors would require repeated statements in Chapters 2, 4, 5, 6, 7, 14 and 18. To acknowledge their indirect contribution would require statements on almost every page.

Finally, I would like to thank the following people who have contributed to this book in their own way: Beverley, my wife, who gave me the space to work on my projects; John Logan, who provided the opportunity to develop the material of my previous book into the present structure; and David Birchall, since without my liaison with Henley I would not have had the opportunity to develop the material or approach.

Rodney Turner
Wargrave, Berkshire
October 1991

Acknowledgements to the first edition

The content of this book is based largely on my experience as a project manager and consultant. I am grateful to the organization that provided my experience, including my employers (ICI, Coopers & Lybrand, Henley Management College), and those whom I have advised as a consultant. Through Henley, I have had contact with many practising project managers and organizations such as the European Construction Institute and the Association for Project Management, all of whom have provided insights. My clients I cannot mention, both because they are too many and because I need to preserve their confidence. However, I should like to thank Steve Kenny for the pleasure of working on his projects, and for providing the model on which the running case study in this book is based. (Although the case study is based on a project on which I worked, the company in which it is set is totally fictitious.)

I also wish to thank the people mentioned below, who contributed distance learning material – through course material or through articles written jointly – for courses at Henley Management College: John Dingle (Oxford College of Petroleum Studies); Lynn Thurloway, Frances Clark, Alex Lord, Mahen Tampoe, Debbie Carlton, Susan Foreman, Padma Nathan and Svine-Arne Jessen (Henley Management College); Peter Morris (Bovis and Templeton College, Oxford); Julie Hartley (University of Central England); Alan Oliver (SD-Scion); Simon Bissel (British Aerospace); Bob Thomas (W.S. Atkins); Morten Fangel (Management Consultant); Nick Aked and Roger Sharp (Coopers & Lybrand); Paddy Lewis and Martin Samphire (Nichols Associates); Richard Morreale (Life Cycle Management Systems); Jancie Light and Gordon Edge (Scintific Generics Ltd); David Topping (Peter Brett Associates); Steven Kirk (Brown & Root Vickers) and Anne French (Farnborough College). Their contributions have, with acknowledgement, been incorporated to a greater or lesser extent into corresponding chapters in this book.

I should like to thank all the people who have given support and advice while I have been writing the text, and in particular Kate Allen the editor and the reviewers whom McGraw-Hill asked to peruse early proposals and

Acknowledgements to the second edition

My main thanks in writing this second edition go to the 15 000 people who have bought copies of the first edition, and who therefore make this second edition a worthwhile proposal. I should also like to thank those people who have provided advice and encouragement over the five years since the first edition appeared, and who have made me think this second edition will be welcomed.

I should like to thank the people with whom I have worked over the last five years, developing new material incorporated into this book, including Robert Cochrane (Coopers & Lybrand), Lynne Crawford (University of Technology, Sydney), Mike Hougham (consultant), John Payne (Line Management Group Ltd), Arnon Speiser (IBM), and John Wateridge (Bournemouth University).

I should also like to thank Alison Pyper and Billy Meehan, my partners in EuroProjex, for their support, allowing me time to work on my books, while they run the business, and Kristoffer Grude for his continued friendship and advice. I must also thank Alison for helping with the preparation of the manuscript. We have had role reversal, with my doing the typing, and Alison the proofreading.

And finally I must thank my family for putting up with all the travel that spreading the good word of Project Management seems to entail.

Rodney Turner
East Horsley, Surrey
June 1998

1
Projects and their management

1.1 Managing change through projects

Projects touch all our lives, in working and social environments. However, traditionally most managers have not been directly involved in the management of projects. Bureaucracies have been viewed as providing an efficient, stable and certain environment in which to conduct business.[1] Change was mistrusted. Managing change was limited to specialist, technical functions, and its introduction was carefully controlled. That has now changed.[2] Change is endemic, brought on by an explosion in the development of technology and communications. Rather than being the preferred style of management, bureaucracies are viewed as restricting an organization's ability to respond to change, and thereby maintain a competitive edge.

The last 40 years characterized this changing emphasis. The 1960s were a decade of mass production. Manufacturing companies strove to increase output. Production methods and systems were introduced to facilitate that process. High production rates were achieved, but at the expense of quality. During the 1970s, to differentiate themselves companies strove for quality. By imposing uniformity, and restricting their product range, managers could achieve quality while maintaining high production. In the 1980s, the emphasis shifted to variety. Every customer wanted their purchase to be different from their neighbours'. No two motor cars coming off the production line were the same, and non-smokers would rather have a coin-tray in place of the ash-tray. Companies introduced flexible manufacturing systems to provide variety, while maintaining quality and high production. In the 1990s, customers wanted novelty. No one buying a new product wanted last year's model. Product development times and market windows shrank, requiring new products to be introduced quickly and effectively.

Organizations must adopt flexible structures to respond to the changing environment. Now, at the start of the new century, in order for organizations to gain competitive advantage, that is not enough. Organizations need to be in an almost constant state of flux to improve their ways of working and business processes.[3,4] Many clients expect to make every product bought an individual bespoke design, and so every product becomes a mini project.

The project-based organization is becoming common,[5,6] and project-based management is becoming the new general management. Project management is a skill all managers require in their portfolio of skills. The Management Charter Initiative has identified that of the UK's four million managers, one million, at least, work in project-oriented companies.[7] This book provides the general manager in the project-oriented company with a structured approach to the management of projects.

In this chapter, I describe the structured approach and its three dimensions: the project, the process of managing the project and the levels over which it is managed. I then explain the importance of the process approach and introduce a model for the strategic management of projects. Next, I cover two issues, one dealing with the nature of projects, and one the nature of project management. The first is a classification of projects based on how well defined are the project's goals and the methods of achieving those goals, which influences the choice of strategy for managing the project. The second is an analogy of project management as sailing a yacht, which challenges traditional concepts of management. I end the chapter by explaining the overall structure of the book.

1.2 Definitions

Projects come in many guises. There are traditional major projects from heavy engineering, or WETT, industries: water, energy, transport and telecommunications. These are significant endeavours involving large dedicated teams, often requiring the collaboration of several sponsoring organizations. On the other hand, most projects with which most of us are involved are smaller. Projects at work include: engineering or construction projects to build new facilities; maintenance of existing facilities; implementation of new technologies or computer systems; research, development and product launches; or management development or training programmes. Projects from our social lives include: moving house; organizing the local church fete; or going on holiday. So what do we understand by projects and project management? In spite of our thinking that we understand what projects are, it proves very difficult to give a definition on which people can agree, even people working in the traditional engineering industries. Previously, I derived the following definition of a project which most people find acceptable (except see Example 1.1):

A project is an endeavour in which human, financial and material resources are organized in a novel way to undertake a unique scope of work, of given specification, within constraints of cost and time, so as to achieve beneficial change defined by quantitative and qualitative objectives.

I had a student on the MBA programme at Henley Management College who took exception to my definition. He worked on projects, he said, which were repetitive, and neither unique nor novel. They were maintenance projects in British Telecom. He said my definition was wrong; he did not have the humility to see that his application of the word might be wrong. Of course that was not the point; his maintenance projects had some features of projects and some of routine operations, and therefore needed a hybrid management approach. He did not see that the purpose of a definition is to aid understanding, not to be precise and prescriptive.

Example 1.1 Maintenance 'projects' in BT

However, the modern style is not to attempt a precise definition for something which is not precise. It is more common to identify those features of the endeavour we plan to undertake which differentiate it from the features of other endeavours, routine operations. In the process, we recognize that rather than having either projects or routine operations, we have a spectrum of endeavours ranging from the routine to the unique, novel and transient. As we move along that spectrum we use management approaches designed for the routine or the unique, novel and transient, or something in between. Jain[8] at a conference in St Petersburg in 1995 gave the following definition of project management:

Project management is the art and science of converting vision into reality.

I find this neat, because it is imprecise, and from it I can derive the features of projects and their management, and the three dimensions of project management which form the structured approach of this book. Converting vision into reality requires us to do work, and that endeavour, being based on a new vision, will be different from anything done previously, and being different, or unique, will require people to develop novel working relationships. Further, the endeavour will be transient, having a beginning, middle and end, as we will want our output within a certain time. The process of conversion implies a life cycle, in which we take our vision, and convert it first into a mission (a definition of business objectives, or things we would practically like to achieve), then into project objectives (things the project will produce which we can operate to achieve our mission), and then into objectives and tasks for teams and individuals to undertake to deliver the higher level objectives. Finally, to complete the conversion process, we must ensure the work is brought to a conclusion, which means we must ensure the work is finished, that the project outputs are achieved, and that the mission and vision are delivered. In this process we have also defined a hierarchy of objectives, vision, mission, deliverables, team and individual goals. The above discussion implies many of the traditional definitions of projects. The following were given in the previous edition of this book:

> a human endeavour which creates change, is limited in time and scope, has mixed goals and objectives, involves a variety of resources and is unique;

> a complex effort to achieve a specific objective, within a schedule and budget target, which typically cuts across organizational lines, is unique and is usually not repetitive within the organization;

> a one-time unique endeavour by people to do something that has not been done that way before.

Other definitions talk about managing a complex sequence of activities. Project management is about managing people to deliver results, not managing work. These definitions all emphasize this.

1.3 The three dimensions of project-based management

I now describe the three dimensions of project management derived above, and the features of projects and their management to show how the management of people in novel relationships to deliver novel results is different from the management of people in routine ways to deliver routine results.

The project

It is annoying when project managers try to grab the moral high ground by saying projects are about delivering objectives within constraints of time, cost and quality. All of business, all of life, is about trying to deliver objectives within constraints of time, cost and quality. By trying to grab the moral high ground in this way project managers do themselves no favours, because they fail to focus on what is special about their discipline, the uniqueness, novelty, transience and implied risk. In business there are repeat objectives, which require us to do repetitive things, and there are new objectives which require us to do unique, novel and transient things. With unique, novel and transient things, it is just more difficult to achieve the constraints of time, cost and quality, because there is less previous experience on which to base our plans, and therefore greater risk of failure.

FEATURES

Thus we derive the essential features of projects, Table 1.1. A project is an endeavour, a package of work, designed to produce some novel, unitary objective from which we expect to derive new benefit. The endeavour is unique, novel and transient. The transience creates urgency, a need to complete the work and obtain the benefit to repay the money spent. The novelty requires us to create new ways of working, and hence to integrate the working of people from across established organization structures. The uniqueness creates uncertainty; you cannot predict the future, and therefore you cannot be certain that the planned ways of working will deliver the objectives you want.

Now this uncertainty creates the first dilemma of project management: how much planning to do. There are those that say there is no point doing any planning, you cannot predict the future, so you might as well start and knife-and-fork your way through the project. Well, there are two little sayings about those who use this approach, the second credited to the managing director of a French pharmaceutical company:

> if you fail to plan, then plan to fail;

> we never seem to have time to plan our projects, but we always have time to do them twice.

You must have a plan; you need a framework within which to coordinate people's activities, the delivery of materials and the use of resources, including money. However, the one thing you can guarantee about your plan is that it is wrong, that is not the way the project will turn out. You must have it as the framework for coordination, but you must be ready and willing to change it as the project progresses. There are those, on the other hand, who think they can eliminate all uncertainty by planning in minute detail, that by developing a highly detailed plan, they can cover every eventuality, that they can predict the future. There are two problems with this approach. The first is it costs time and effort to plan. There is an empirical rule, that says if a certain amount of effort, x, is required to produce a plan of a given accuracy, then to double the accuracy requires

Table 1.1   The features of projects

Goal	Features	Pressures	The plan
Unitary	Unique	Uncertainty	Flexible
Beneficial	Novel	Integration	Goal oriented
Change	Transient	Urgency	Staged

four times as much effort, $4x$, and to double it again requires four times as much effort again, $16x$. Further and further planning gives decreasing return, less value for the effort, and you eventually reach a point where you are putting more effort into planning than the value of the information you get out. You eventually have to stop planning and start managing the risk (and this is what is so special about projects – the risk). The second problem is you cannot eliminate the risk and uncertainty, you cannot predict the future, but if you make the plan too complicated, too sophisticated, then it becomes inflexible and less able to respond to changes as they occur.

So we must have a plan, we must accept that it will not be completely accurate and so will need to be flexible and to change. To make the plan flexible we will see later that it must be goal oriented.

PROJECT, FACILITY, PURPOSE

Jain's definition implied a hierarchy of objectives, and the simplest way of viewing that is shown in Figure 1.1. The project itself is an endeavour, the work to be done. But we do not do it for its own sake, we do it to achieve some output (called 'the facility' throughout this book). The facility may be a new building, manufacturing plant, computer system, organization structure or ways of working, design, etc. It is something we want. However, we do not produce the facility for its own sake; we make it to

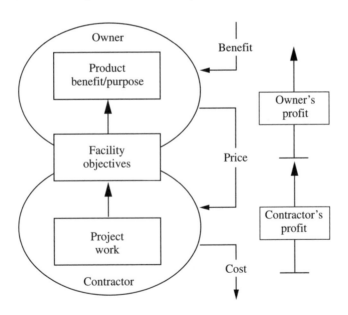

Figure 1.1   Project, facility, purpose

operate to satisfy some purpose or produce some benefit. Now, this is the same for routine operations, the plant is operated to produce product, which is sold to produce benefit. However, here the two differ again. In the routine operation, the plant is operated today to produce product tomorrow, which is sold the next day. Here we have instant feedback about how well we are doing, and we can make minor changes to the plant, small touches on the tiller, to bring the process back on course and to achieve the profit we want. On a project we do the work today, to produce the facility next year, and achieve the benefit the year after. By the time we achieve the benefit, the project team is disbanded, and it is not possible to put the work right to achieve the benefit we actually wanted. This reemphasizes the risk, and encourages people all the more to plan in great detail. Rather than focusing on the work, on a project you must focus on the desired results, continually reminding yourself of the purpose of what you are doing, to try to ensure that all the work done delivers essential project objectives which are necessary to achieve the purpose or expected benefit.

Figure 1.1 also illustrates that there are two groups of people involved on the project, called here the owner and the contractor. The owner pays the contractor to do the work, and in the process buys the facility. They then operate it to achieve the benefit. They make their profit from the difference between the benefit they receive from operating the facility, and the price they pay the contractor. The contractor does the work of the project. They receive money from the owner to do the work, and make their profit from the difference between the price they receive and the costs they pay to do the work. Here we see for the first time that different people working on the project can have conflicting objectives, different views about what constitutes success. The owner increases their profit if they can get the price down, and the contractor can increase theirs if they get the price up. If the owner and contractor are ICI and Foster Wheeler, respectively, we understand that conflict. Its resolution is part of the making of the contract between the two parties. However, if they are both part of the same parent organization, the production and engineering departments of ICI, say, then you may assume that they are all part of the same organization and share the same objectives. They don't!

FIVE FUNCTIONS OF PROJECT MANAGEMENT

The last feature of the project is the five functions of project management, five system objectives that need to be managed (Figure 1.2). These are the scope of work, the project organization (the people who will do the work) and the quality, cost and duration. Many books on project management focus only on the last three of these, many really describe only the management of the last two, and some only the last one. In Figure 1.2, I deliberately drew the

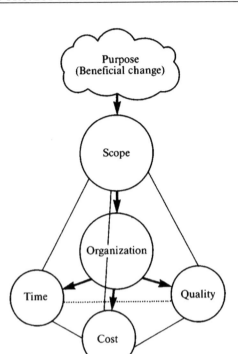

Figure 1.2 The five functions of project-based management

balls for scope and organization larger than the other three, as these two are the essential functions of project management: without work there would be no project, and without the people, the work would not get done. I have also shown the definition of the scope quite clearly driven by the purpose, or expected benefit. The other three functions, quality, cost and time, are just constraints. They are important constraints, but just constraints. Furthermore, the balance between them will differ from project to project. The so-called 'time/cost/quality triangle' (Figure 1.3) is used to illustrate this. Some project managers treat time as the only important function, and focus on that to the detriment of the others. Certainly there are projects for which time is of overriding importance, the Olympic Games for instance. The time the athletes will start parading up the stadium is known six years in advance, and if they are late, the whole world will be watching. The organizers cannot ring up the athletes two weeks before they are due to start, and tell them to come two weeks later. They must start on time. It is certainly the case that a tight time schedule focuses the mind, but on other projects cost is more important, and on yet others the quality is sacrosanct – but without the work and the functionality it produces there will be no benefit.

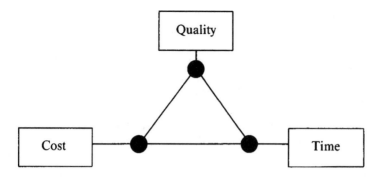

Figure 1.3 The time/cost/quality triangle

Figure 1.4 shows various tools and techniques used to manage the five functions. Table 1.7, in Section 1.5, summarizes these, and shows where in the book they are covered.

1. The scope is managed through product and work breakdown, as described above. We define a hierarchy of objectives from vision, mission, facility, team and individual objectives. This hierarchy is called the *product breakdown structure* (PBS).

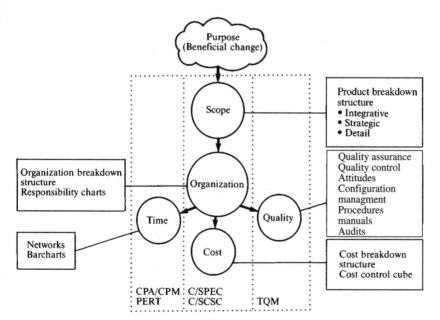

Figure 1.4 The tools and techniques of project-based management

2. Organisation is managed through an organization breakdown, by which we break down the skill sets of the people who will do the work. This is called the *organization breakdown structure* (OBS). At any level of breakdown, the products to be delivered and the skill sets involved define a two-dimensional matrix, called a *responsibility chart*, which indicates who will do what work to deliver the products. Conventionally products are put in the rows and skills in the columns. The cells then represent the work of the project. The hierarchy of responsibility charts defines a hierarchy of work to be done, called the *work breakdown structure* (WBS). Pedantically there is a difference between PBS and WBS. However, on many projects the difference is slight, each product is synonymous with the work to deliver it and so people sloppily refer to them as the same thing. Most of the time I will not draw a clear distinction between them, but occasionally I will, as when discussing *configuration management* in Chapter 7.

3. The cost is managed through a third breakdown structure of cost types, labour, materials, overhead, finance. This is called the *cost breakdown structure* (CBS). The three breakdown structures combined produce what is called the *cost control cube*, and are part of a methodology invented by the US military in the 1950s called the *cost and schedule control systems criteria* (C/SCSC).

4. Time is managed using networks and bar charts. Networks are a mathematical tool to help calculate the time scale, bar charts are a communication tool to communicate the schedule to the project team. Networks are part of a methodology variously called *critical path analysis* (CPA), *critical path method* (CPM) or *programme evaluation and review technique* (PERT).

5. Quality is managed using techniques of *total quality management* (TQM) including quality control, quality assurance, configuration management, procedures manuals and audits.

These five functions of project management are the first dimension of the structured approach. They are the five things that need to be managed throughout the project life cycle, together with the risk that pervades all five. They are the subject of Part Two of this book. We turn our attention now to the life cycle or management process.

The management process

The second dimension of the structured approach is the management process, the life cycle that takes us from the vision to reality, from the first idea that there is a potential for achieving benefit to delivering an operating facility that will enable us to achieve that benefit. We cannot go straight from a germ of an idea to doing work. Effectively we need to pull the project up

by its boot straps, gathering data and proving viability at one level in order to commit resources to the next. There are many versions of the life cycle, and we will discuss several here. However, there is growing agreement about a basic four step process as shown in Figure 1.5 and Table 1.2.

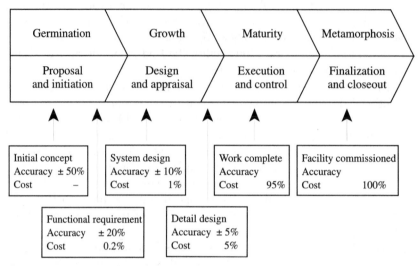

Germination	Growth	Maturity	Metamorphosis
Proposal and initiation	Design and appraisal	Execution and control	Finalization and closeout

Initial concept
Accuracy ± 50%
Cost   –

System design
Accuracy ± 10%
Cost   1%

Work complete
Accuracy
Cost   95%

Facility commissioned
Accuracy
Cost   100%

Functional requirement
Accuracy ± 20%
Cost   0.2%

Detail design
Accuracy ± 5%
Cost   5%

Figure 1.5   Basic four-stage life cycle

Table 1.2   The basic project management life cycle

Stage	Name	Process	Outputs
Germination	Proposal and initiation	Develop proposals Gather information Conduct feasibility Estimate design	Functional design Commitment of resources to design Estimates ±20%
Growth	Design and appraisal	Develop design Estimate costs and returns Assess viability Obtain funding	Systems design Money and resources for implementation Estimates ±10%
Maturity	Execution and control	Do detail design Baseline estimates Do work Control progress	Effective completion Facility ready for commissioning Estimates ±5%
Metamorphosis	Finalization and close-out	Finish work Commission facility Obtain benefit Disband Team Review achievement	Facility delivering benefit Satisfied team Data for future projects

1. We start with a proposal. We believe there is a problem to solve or opportunity to exploit which is of some value to us. For instance, we may think that if we spend £100, we can make £50 per year; two-year payback; that is good business. However, at this level of accuracy, the £100 might be as little as £50 and might be as much £150, and the £50 something between £25 and £75. To spend £50 to get £75 per year is wonderful, eight-month pay-back. To spend £150 to get £25 per year is awful, six-year pay-back. However, at the mid-range the project seems worth while so we initiate the project by conducting a feasibility study.

2. During the feasibility study, you gather more information, develop a functional design, and improve the estimates. In our example, say, you show the cost is more like £120, and the benefit £40, still three-year payback, probably good business. However, the £120 may range from £100 to £140, and the £40 from £30 to £50. Best and best is now two-year pay-back, still excellent. Worst and worst is almost five-year pay-back, marginal. However, the mid-range value is still worth while and so we commit resources to systems design, and initiate the project proper. On an engineering project, up to this point we have typically spent 0.2 per cent of the cost.

3. In design and appraisal, we develop a fuller systems design and compose a capital expenditure proposal. We prove the viability of our project, and find a sponsor to pay for it. In our example, say, we may confirm the £120 cost, now accurate to £10, and the £40 per year benefit, accurate to £5. We prepare a project manual and move into implementation. On an engineering project, up to this point we have typically spent 1 per cent of the project budget.

4. We can then move into detail design and execution. We now prepare working drawings and detail activity plans. In the process, we spend about 5 per cent of the project budget on an engineering project. We then do the work of the project.

5. We must then complete the project. This requires us to ensure all work is finished. We must commission the facility and transfer its ownership to the users. We must ensure it is being operated in a way that will deliver the benefit expected to justify the cost. We must disband the team in a way that looks after their development needs, and repays any commitments we made to them during the start-up stages of the project. Finally, we must review how we did. We cannot improve performance on this project, but we can improve performance on future projects.

There are many forms of the life cycle, ranging from two steps to ten or more. Several are given in Chapter 18, but I will describe a few here. Figure 1.6 and Table 1.3 show a ten-step problem solving cycle. This effectively

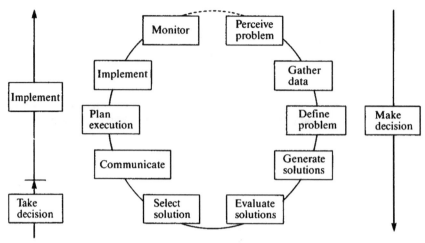

Figure 1.6   The ten-step problem-solving cycle

Table 1.3   Management process derived from the ten-step problem-solving cycle

Step	Management process
Perceive the problem	Identify an opportunity for providing benefit to the organization
Gather data	Collect information relating to the opportunity
Define the problem	Determine the value of the opportunity and its potential benefits
Generate solutions	Identify several ways of delivering the opportunity and associated benefits
Evaluate solutions	Identify the cost of each solution, the risk and expected benefit
Select a solution	Choose the solution that gives best value for money
Communicate the solution	Tell all parties involved of the chosen solution
Plan implementation	Complete a detail design of the solution and plan implementation
Implement the solution	Authorize work, assign tasks to people, undertake the work and control progress
Monitor performance	Monitor results to ensure the problem has been solved and the benefits obtained

treats the project as a problem to be solved and applies standard problem-solving techniques. Figure 1.7 is a four-step process due to Henri Fayol.[9] Fayol put the word 'command' in the central box. I did not like this; it is too reminiscent of command and control structures. First I changed the word to 'lead', but then decided that leadership and management are

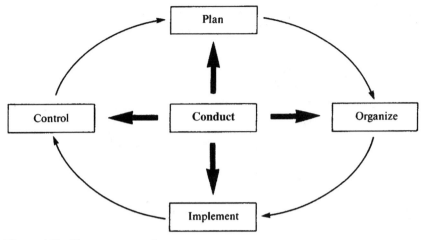

Figure 1.7   Five processes of management

different things.[2] So I put 'direct' in the box, but decided that, too, was reminiscent of command and control structures, and so have now settled on 'conduct'. That is what project managers do, they conduct the team through the project. Figure 1.8 shows that the three versions of the life cycle in Figures 1.5, 1.6 and 1.7 are the same thing, and Figure 1.9 that project management is fractal management. This means that each stage of the project is a little mini-project in its own right, and each part of each stage likewise. Hence the initiation stage has to be planned, organized, implemented, controlled and conducted, and the planning of that stage is undertaken by applying the ten-step problem-solving cycle.

PROPOSAL AND INITIATION	DESIGN AND APPRAISAL	EXECUTION AND CONTROL	FINALIZATION AND CLOSE-OUT
Perceive problem / Gather data	Define problem / Generate solutions / Evaluate solutions / Select solution	Communicate / Plan execution / Implement	Monitor
	Plan / Organize / Implement / Control		

Figure 1.8   Relating the three views of the life cycle

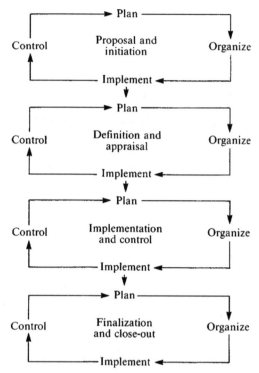

Figure 1.9   Project management is fractal management

What all three of these versions of the life cycle emphasize is that you cannot go from initial idea to doing work in one step. The base life cycle in Figure 1.5 shows that may result in you initiating a project for which you have not properly checked out its viability. You check viability at the current level of accuracy to commit resources to the design at the next level, and so gradually improve your understanding to the point at which you are able to commit significant amounts of money to project execution. The ten-step problem-solving cycle shows that if you go from idea to doing work, you will probably cover up the symptoms of the problem without curing the underlying malaise. Only by solving the problem, in a structured way can you identify and eliminate the root cause.

Two industry-specific versions of the life cycle are given in Tables 1.4 and 1.5. Table 1.4 is the life cycle used by the World Bank. This quite closely follows the 10-step problem-solving cycle, and shows that the banks' concern is in solving the true needs of economic development. Table 1.5 is a version proposed by the European Construction Institute for the engineering construction industry.

Table 1.4   Stages in the project life cycle used by the World Bank

Identification of project concepts
Preparation of data
Appraisal of data and selection of project solution
Negotiation and mobilization of project organization
Implementation including detail design and construction
Operation
Post-project review

Table 1.5   Stages in the life cycle proposed by the European Construction Institute

Concept
Feasibility
Front-end design
Project plan
Specification
Tender and evaluation
Manufacturing
Construction
Commission
Operation and maintenance
Decommission
Disposal

The levels

The third and final dimension of the structured approach is the levels over which the project is managed. There are three fundamental levels, the integrative, strategic and detail levels.

THE INTEGRATIVE LEVEL

The purpose is stated, and the facility required to deliver it is defined through quantitative and qualitative objectives. Areas of work and categories of resource required to undertake them are defined, and basic parameters or constraints determined for time scales, costs, benefits and performance. Any risks and assumptions are stated. The *Project Definition Report* (Chapters 5 and 11) is a tool used to record this information. A *functional design* of the facility is developed. This defines the basic features or processing steps of the facility required. For a chemical plant or computer program this will be a *flow chart* showing inputs and outputs from each major processing element. For a training programme it will be the definition of the major elements of the programme, and the learning objective of each.

THE STRATEGIC OR ADMINISTRATIVE LEVEL

Intermediate goals or milestones required to achieve the objectives are defined. Each milestone is the end result of a package of work. The responsibility of organizational units, functions and disciplines for work packages is defined. Work packages are scheduled in the project, and budgets developed. At this level the manager aims to create a stable plan which remains fixed throughout the project. This provides a framework for the management strategy, and allows changes to be contained within the third level. Responsibilities are assigned to organizational units. The *milestone plan* (Chapter 5) and *responsibility chart* (Chapter 6) are tools used for this purpose. A *systems design* of the facility is developed. This shows what each of the major processing elements does to deliver its outputs, and includes a design of the processing units within each element. For a chemical plant, the systems design is based on a *piping and instrumentation diagram*, and includes specifications of all the pieces of equipment. For a computer program, it describes what each subroutine within the program achieves, how each handles the data and the hardware architecture. For a training programme, it will break each element into sessions, and describe the format and learning objectives of each session.

THE TACTICAL OR OPERATIONAL LEVEL

The activities required to achieve each milestone are defined, together with the responsibilities of named people or resource types against the activities. Changes are made at this level within the framework provided at the strategic level. The *activity schedule* (Chapters 5 and 12) and *responsibility chart* are tools used for this purpose. A *detail design* of the facility is developed. This provides enough information to the project team to make parts of the facility, and assemble them into a working whole which meets the purpose of the project. For a chemical plant, this includes piping layout and individual equipment drawings. For a computer program, it includes the design of data formats, the definition of how each subroutine achieves its objectives, and the detail specification of the hardware. For a training programme, it will include the script and slides of lectures, structure of exercises and, perhaps, details of testing procedures.

Youker[10] gave a much wider view of the levels (Figure 1.10). This illustrates a cascade of objectives at different levels of management, from development objectives for the parent organization down to task objectives for individuals. At each level, the strategy for achieving the objectives at that level will imply the objectives at the next level down. I quite like this model because it gets away from hair-splitting arguments about visions, missions, aims, goals, etc (although I did use some of these words earlier in this chapter). We just have

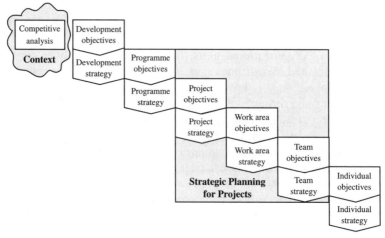

Figure 1.10   Cascade of objectives

objectives at different levels of management. Youker, who used to work for the World Bank, illustrated this by reference to a project to develop a palm-nut plantation in Malaysia (Example 1.2), a project he had helped finance while with the World Bank. I show in the example how this project illustrates an important point, that often our projects do not deliver their full potential until we have completed other projects in the programme of projects of which they are a part. Sometimes, as in the case of the palm-nut plantation, we will get no benefit at all. Table 1.6 shows the components in the PBS and the work elements in the WBS that result at different levels of Youker's cascade. This also acts as something of a vocabulary for the use of these words in this book. (Throughout the book I recognize that people may want to use different words to me. What I hope they will focus on is the concept, rather than the words being used.)

Table 1.6   Standard product and work breakdown structures, PBS and WBS

Level	Product	Example 1.2	Work	Duration
	Vision	Good life		
Development	Mission	Economic growth		5 years
Programme	Aim or purpose	Oil industry		2 years
Project	Facility	Plantation	Project	9–18 months
Work area	Subfacility	Cultivation	Work area	9–18 months
Team	Milestone	Orchards	Work pack	2 months
Individual	Deliverable	Planted trees	Activity	2 weeks
		Dig holes	Task	1 day

The project is a palm-nut plantation. The work areas are things like:

- the cutting down of the jungle and the planting of trees
- the development of an establishment to run the plantation
- the development of systems for gathering, storing and shipping nuts.

A team will be given objectives to plant areas of trees, and on a given day, an individual will be given a bag of trees, and told to plant them. (This illustrates quite nicely that the lower the level the more the product and the work are synonymous, and that the higher the level the more the objectives have many ways of being achieved, and thus are not so directly related to the work that will deliver them.) Working upwards, the programme of which the project is a part is the development of a palm-nut oil industry for Malaysia, and the development objectives are economic growth and employment in Malaysia. (This also illustrates that the higher up the hierarchy the less specific are the objectives.)

There is one final point. The project is part of a programme to develop a palm-nut oil industry. Other projects in the programme include:

- the creation of distribution systems to take nuts from plantations to factories
- the building of factories to process nuts into oil
- the creation of distribution systems to take oil from factories to customers.

Now, the palm-nut plantation project will not deliver any benefit until these other projects are completed. If all we do is develop a palm-nut plantation, all we will end up with is mountains of useless nuts. We can give those nuts a notional value, and work out the returns on the plantation, but we cannot realize those returns until we have completed all the projects in the programme. Many of our projects are like this, we can only get the full benefit from the project when we have completed other projects in the programme.

Example 1.2 Cascade of objectives for a project to develop a palm-nut plantation

1.4 The process approach

I said earlier that project management is the management of the unique, novel and transient, and functional hierarchical line management is the management of the routine. Then during the discussion of life cycle, I emphasized that the life cycle is a process that converts the project's inputs into desired outputs for the customer. Contained in this discussion are two perspectives on management:

- the management of the routine versus the management of the unique, novel and transient
- a discrete, internally focused approach versus a process-based, customer-focused approach.

Comparison of these two parameters together defines four types of management (Figure 1.11) (the first of many two-by-two matrices to be introduced). Traditional functional, hierarchical, line management is the discrete approach to the management of the routine. The work is artificially broken up to match the existing functional structure of the organization, to which it is assigned, and the product moves through the organization like a baton in a relay race, except that rather than being physically passed between successive steps, it is 'thrown over the wall'. Traditional project management, when it was first introduced in the 1950s, followed a similar approach. The project followed a life cycle, but each step in the life cycle became the responsibility of a function of the organization, design, procurement, construction, and the project passed between them also like a baton in a relay race, thrown over the wall. However, in the management of the non-routine, the problems associated with this discrete, internally focused approach became more apparent. It is almost impossible to divide the work up to be the responsibility of one function at a time, and it is almost impossible to define the interface between one function and the next to create a discrete handover. Indeed, companies trying to do this as they write their quality procedures according to ISO 9000 find that they cannot write procedures that cover all eventualities, and soon find themselves repeatedly being 'non-compliant'. Hence on projects, people tend to get driven towards adopting the process approach. The project becomes a process by which the inputs are converted into desired outputs. The Milestone Plan introduced in Chapter 5 is the process flow diagram for the project. The process approach requires four things:

1. Functions may need to work together at some steps of the process.
2. Functions definitely need to work together at the handover from one function to the next at each step in the process.
3. The way functions work together may vary project by project to meet the requirements of the particular customer.
4. As the project passes from one stage to the next, one function to the next, it needs to be approved against the end customer's requirements.

The process approach is that recommended by the PRINCE (PRojects IN a Controlled Environment) methodology developed by the CCTA[11] (the government's Central Computer and Telecommunications Agency), and by ISO 10006, the international procedure for quality in project management[12] (see Chapter 15). It is also the approach adopted in this book. Indeed, that is how I differentiate between project management and project-based management. The former is the discrete, functional approach to the management of the non-routine, and the latter is the process approach.

Figure 1.11 shows the process approach to the routine as the 'military

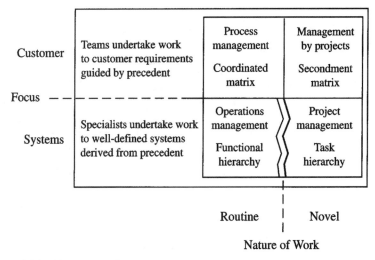

Figure 1.11   Four types of management

approach'. Some people would say that functional hierarchical line management is the military approach. It is not. The military approach is about defining process chains to support the soldier in the front line. During the battle, you cannot extend the time taken to supply him, by having functions work separately, waiting until one function is finished before the next begins. People must be empowered to support the customer within the constraints set by their orders. Functional, hierarchical, line management is used in private industry and parts of the civilian civil service. Finally, note that in the process approach, the customer for the people working on one stage is not just the end customer for the project's outputs, but also people working on later stages. Hence, at the transition from one stage to the next, the product must be checked not just against the requirements of the eventual customer, but the people working on later stages, and the procedures adopted at an earlier stage must be similarly adapted.

1.5 The strategic management of projects

Youker's model implies that at each level of management we need a strategy to achieve the objectives at that level. The project is part of the strategy by which the parent organization achieves its development objectives, but the project manager needs a strategy for undertaking his or her project. In Chapter 4, I give a detailed model of the strategy for undertaking a project. For now, suffice it to say that we should adopt a structured approach to the management of our project. Figure 1.12

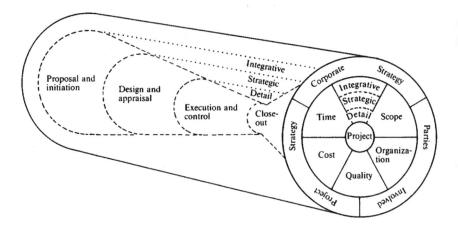

Figure 1.12   The structured approach to project management

combines the three dimensions into a single model for the management of projects. It shows that as we work through the first three stages of the management process, we improve our understanding of the five functions, scope, organization, quality, cost and time. It then shows that on completion of the work, in the close-out stage, we deliver first the completed work, then the commissioned facility and then the operating benefit. The figure also shows the project taking place within a context, which itself has three components: the strategy of the parent organization, which we have already met, the people involved, and the project strategy. Figure 1.13 is a more integrated model of the structured approach, and Figure 1.14 shows how the project plans for scope and organization form a contract between the parties involved in a project. We will meet this again in Chapter 6. Figure 1.2 shows some of the tools and techniques used in the process of managing the project, and these are shown in Table 1.7, which also lists where in the book they are covered.

Figure 1.12 is the basis of the structure of this book. In Part One, I describe the context of the project. Chapter 2 describes the relationship between the project and the strategy of the parent organization, Chapter 3 the views of the parties involved, and Chapter 4 how we judge projects to be successful, what the pitfalls to that success are and how we can develop a project strategy to avoid them. Part Two describes the management of the five project management functions and the risk inherent in them. Chapter 5 explains the management of the scope, Chapter 6 the project organization, and Chapters 7, 8 and 9 the quality, cost and time respectively. Chapter 10 describes the management of risk inherent in projects. Part 3 covers the

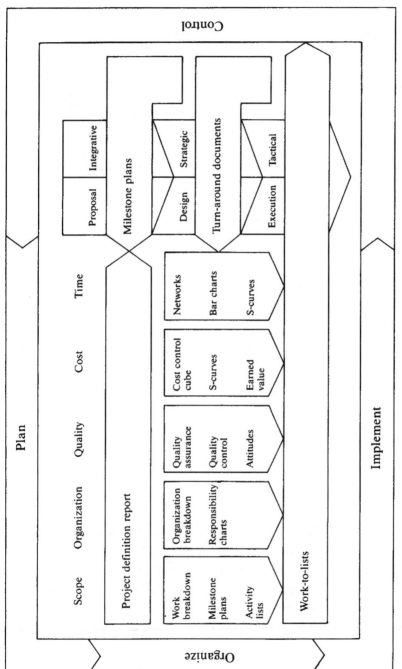

Figure 1.13   An integrated model of project management

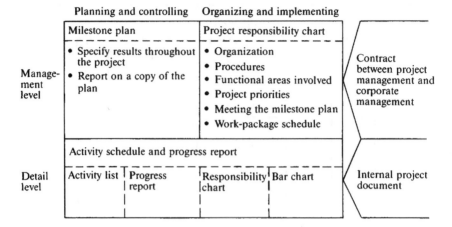

Figure 1.14   A contractual model for project management

Table 1.7   The tools and techniques of the approach

Method	Techniques	Tools	Chapter
Managing scope	Product breakdown	Milestone plans	5
	Work breakdown	Activity schedules	5
	Configuration management		7
	Data management	PMIS	15
Organization	Organization breakdown	Responsibility charts	6
	Organization development		3
Quality	Quality assurance/control	Quality plans	7
	Quality management	Procedures manuals/audits	15
	Analysis	TQM techniques	7
Cost	Cost control cube		8
	Estimating techniques		8
	Earned value		8
Time	PERT/CPA	Networks/bar charts	9
Risk	Risk management		10
Start-up	Start-up workshop	Definition report	11
Definition	Definition workshop	Definition report	11
Implementing	Baselining	Work-to lists	12
Control	Rolling-Waveplanning	Turn-around documents	12
		S-curves	
Close-out		Checklists	13

management process. In Chapter 11, the start-up processes, project definition and feasibility are described. Chapter 12 covers implementation and control, and Chapter 13 close-out. Part Four covers the systems and procedures of project management. In Chapter 14, I consider the management of programmes of projects, and the role of the project support office. In Chapter 15, I discuss the use of procedures, including PRINCE, and procedures manuals. I also consider the use of information systems to support project management. Chapter 16 describes the use of project health checks and audits. I explain two health checks, one which checks whether the working environment in the organization supports the project-based way of working, and the other which checks the health of an individual project. I then describe how to conduct more extensive audits of projects. In Chapter 17, I describe the role of the project manager in managing his or her project team. Part Five considers applications of project-based management. Chapter 18 describes applications of project-based management, with projects from different stages of the product development life cycle, and from different industries. It describes similarities and differences between these different types of project. Chapter 19 describes the management of international projects. Finally, in Chapter 20 I summarize some of the principles of good project management introduced in the book.

1.6 The goals and methods matrix

I want to end this chapter by discussing two further issues relating to project management in general. The first is a classification of projects which will influence some of the thinking throughout this book. The other is a view of management which challenges some of the traditional thinking.

It is possible to classify projects according to two dimensions, the first is how well defined are the goals of the projects, and the second is how well defined are the methods of achieving those goals.[13] This introduces another two-by-two matrix (Figure 1.15) defining four types of projects. (It is assumed you do not have a project until you have a purpose or business objective.)

– *Type 1 projects*: for which both the goals, and methods of achieving those goals, are well defined. These are typified by engineering projects. Because the goals and methods are both well defined, it is possible to move quickly into planning the work to be done, and so you will find on engineering projects an emphasis on activity-based planning.
– *Type 2 projects*: for which the goals are well defined, but the method of achieving them is poorly defined. These are typified by product development projects, where we know the functionality of the product,

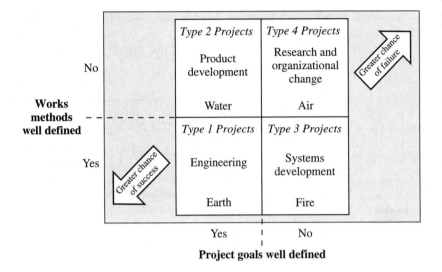

Figure 1.15   The goals and methods matrix

but not how it will be achieved. Indeed, the point of the project is to determine how to achieve the goals. Now it is not possible to plan activities, because the project will determine them. Hence we use milestone planning, where the milestones represent components of the product to be delivered.

– *Type 3 projects*: for which the goals are poorly defined, but the methods well defined. These are typified by information systems projects. When I started to work as a consultant and trainer in project management, it used to amuse me that when people from the information systems industry talked about project management, all they talked about was life cycles and phases. The goals and methods matrix explains why. On an information systems project, to get the users to say what they want is difficult enough, to get them to hold their ideas constant for any length of time is impossible. All people have to hold on to is the definition of the life cycle. Hence on information systems projects you tend to use milestone planning, where the milestones represent the completion of life-cycle stages.

– *Type 4 projects*: for which both the goals and methods of achieving them are poorly defined. These are typified by research or organizational change projects. The planning of these may use soft systems methodologies,[14] and the plan itself will again be milestone-based, but the milestones will represent gateways, go/no go decision points, through which the research project must pass or be aborted.

We see each of the four types of project require a different approach to their planning and management. In reality, a given project will involve more than one type of project. The example project used from Chapter 5 onwards has engineering work (type 1), product development work (type 2), information systems work (type 3), and organizational change work (type 4). There is a question that does the rounds about whether a non-information systems professional can manage an information systems project. Some say that information systems is a black art, and you need to know the black art to manage the project. If not, the project team may lie to you about progress, and you will not know the difference. How sad to think that the project team may deliberately try to mislead the project manager like that, but if you define the milestones well, it should not matter. On the other hand, there are those who say project management is a generic skill and you can apply it to any discipline. In reality, a young person at an early stage of their career will learn project management in one discipline, and must apply it there. As their skill and maturity grows, they will begin to work on projects with a wider scope, involving many disciplines, like the example project later. You will not have the choice of choosing someone from the one discipline, because the project will cover several. The reality of modern project-based management is that the project manager cannot be a technical expert in all the areas of the project, and perhaps it is best if he or she is not a technical expert, because they can then delegate the work of the project and concentrate on their role which is coordinating the work of others. (See Example 1.3.)

In September 1994 I was at a meeting of the Major Projects Association, and one of the speakers, a partner with Andersen Consulting, said you needed an information systems professional to manage an IS project, and best if it was an Andersen consultant. I was seated next to Don Heath, formerly programme director for the Electrification of the East Coast Main Line, and at the time programme director for Crossrail, a £2 billion project. Don is a civil engineer. I asked Don what proportion of his project was information systems, and he said 10 per cent, £200 million. What was more, 20 per cent was electronics (driverless trains and automatic signalling), 30 per cent was a mechanical engineering (new rolling stock), and only 40 per cent was from his discipline, civil engineering (tunnels and track). So from what the partner from Andersen Consulting is saying, has Don Heath to ignore 10 per cent of his project? Or is it that this experienced project manager is able to develop management systems that enable him to keep track of the entire project.

Example 1.3 Multi-functional project-based management

1.7 Project management as sailing a yacht

I have an analogy of project management, indeed all management, as being like sailing a yacht. This analogy works on two levels.

Microlevel

When yachts are sailing in a race, they sail around in a triangle, the longest leg of which is arranged to be sailing up wind. If while sailing that leg, the crew aims their boat directly at the next buoy, they will be blown backwards. What they have to do is sail across the wind, called tacking, and slowly make their way upwind by tacking back and forth. Hence they achieve the next objective, not by sailing directly towards it, but by sailing for something they can achieve, and then something else they can achieve, and eventually make the objective. There is a joke about asking someone the way to the station, and he says, 'I wouldn't start here, if I were you'. You should not start at this buoy to get to the next one upwind, but you have to, and you do it by taking it in steps you can achieve. All life is like that, all management is like that.

While tacking the current leg, you will choose a sail setting and a rudder setting, and plan to sail so far, say 100 yards, before tacking about. While sailing that leg, you do not say: 'This is my sail setting, this is my rudder setting, good project management is adhering to my plan come what may.' You continually adjust your sail and rudder setting as the wind fluctuates. You monitor the actual conditions and respond accordingly. And if the wind comes around far enough, it may be better to be tacking in the other direction and you will change course.

Macrolevel

Take the example of the 1997 Whitbread Round the World Yacht Race. The yachts sailing in the race will have spent months before the race pouring over weather charts, and will have chosen a strategy for the race based on the normal range of weather conditions. But while they are sailing, they must respond to the conditions they actually encounter. They will have a strategy for the race, but will determine their detail plans as they sail the race, responding to today's conditions and the forecast for tomorrow. In spite of not being able to plan the detail, there are three things they can do:

– they can predict the duration of the race to a very high degree of accuracy, a few days in nine months
– the boats that come first and second, after nine months, are only a few hours apart
– there is a large degree of luck involved.

The crew who win is not the crew with the best detail plan to which they adhere doggedly. The people who win are the ones with the best strategic plan, and who respond best to the actual conditions on the day. But in spite of having to change the plan as the race progresses, the competition are encountering the same conditions, and are very close behind. The most competent crew, with the best strategic plan, is the one that wins. (See Example 1.4.) Our projects are the same.

The crew first into Cape Town in October 1997 were generally regarded as the third best crew. The two best crews arrived a day later, a couple of hours apart, having repeatedly overtaken each other over the preceding few days. The team that won, took a more southerly, longer route, but picked up a stronger easterly wind. They had a better strategy, based on an assessment of the chance of achieving a stronger wind to compensate for the longer route, and their risk assessment paid off.

Example 1.4 The Whitbread Round the World Yacht Race

1.8 Summary

1. There are three dimensions to the management of projects:
   – the project
   – the management process
   – the levels.
2. The project is a unique endeavour, undertaken by people working together in novel ways, over a limited period of time. They work under a sense of urgency and uncertainty, and must integrate their working patterns. To coordinate their efforts they must have a plan which is robust but flexible, and that means it should be goal oriented and staged.
3. The essence of project management is managing the risk and uncertainty.
4. The project is an endeavour to deliver a facility, which will be owned and operated to deliver a benefit to repay the effort to build it.
5. There are six functions of project management, managing the scope, project organization, quality, cost, time and risk.
6. The project life cycle is the process by which the project is undertaken. There are several views of the life cycle, including:
   – the standard view
   – the problem-solving cycle
   – Henri Fayol's five management processes.
7. The standard view is that there are four basic stages:
   – proposal and initiation
   – design and appraisal

- execution and control
- finalization and close-out.

8. Projects can be categorized according to how well defined are the goals and the methods of achieving the goals. This give four types of project with four different approaches to planning:
  - type 1: well-defined goals, well-defined methods, activity-based planning
  - type 2: well-defined goals, poorly defined methods, component milestone-based planning
  - type 3: poorly defined goals, well-defined methods, life-cycle-based planning
  - type 4: poorly defined goals, poorly defined methods, gateway-based planning.

9. Project management is like sailing a yacht:
  - you cannot always achieve your objectives in one step
  - you must continually adapt your plan in response to changing circumstance
  - you cannot plan the detail, you can only plan the strategy
  - even so it is possible to achieve an accurate forecast of the cost and duration of the project
  - the winners are the most competent team, with the best strategic plan, who respond best to the conditions actually encountered.

References

1. Weber, M., *Wirtschaft und Gesellschaft*, Mohr, 1956.
2. Turner, J.R., Grude, K.V. and Thurloway, L., (eds), *The Project Manager as Change Agent*, McGraw-Hill, 1996.
3. Johansson, H.J., McHugh, P., Pendlebury, A.J. and Wheeler, W.A., *Business Process Reengineering*, Wiley, 1993.
4. McHugh, P., Merli, G. and Wheeler, W.A., *Beyond Business Process Reengineering*, Wiley, 1995.
5. Gareis, R., 'Application of the new management paradigm in the Project Oriented Company', in *Proceedings of IPMA '96, the 13th World Congress on Project Management, in Paris, France*, AFITEP, June 1996.
6. Gareis, R., *The Handbook of Management by Projects*, Mohr, 1990.
7. Management Charter Initiative, private communication, 1996.
8. Jain, A., at the Global Project Management Forum in St Petersburg, September, 1995.
9. Fayol, H., *General and Industrial Management*, Pitman, 1949.
10. Youker, R., 'Defining the hierarchy of project objectives', in *Proceedings of the PMI 24th Annual Symposium, Smooth Sailing with Project Management, San Diego*, Project Management Institute, October 1993.
11. CCTA, *PRINCE 2: Project Management for Business*, The Stationery Office, 1996.

12. A complete list of all ISO procedures relating to quality are given in Table 7.6.
13. Turner, J.R. and Cochrane, R.A., 'The goals and methods matrix: coping with projects for which the goals and/or methods of achieving them are ill-defined', *International Journal of Project Management*, **11**(2), 1993.
14. Checkland, P.B. and Scholes, J., *Soft Systems Methodology in Action*, Wiley, 1990.

PART ONE

THE CONTEXT OF PROJECTS

2
Projects for implementing corporate strategy

2.1 Introduction

We saw in Chapter 1 that projects involve considerable uncertainty and risk. Why then do organizations undertake them? The answer addresses the first element of the project's context; the purpose of projects. Organizations undertake projects when they can achieve their business objectives more effectively than by doing routine things; when the potential benefits outweigh the risks. Projects may be the most effective medium, and sometimes the only medium, for managing change in an organization.[1] Managers might then say, if their company is successful now, could it not remain successful by maintaining the status quo. The short answer is it cannot, if it is to maintain competitive advantage. Porter[2,3] shows how organizations cannot remain static in the modern environment. The competition are changing the way they do their business, so if an organization fails to adapt, it will lose its markets. All projects should therefore arise from a need to fulfil specific strategic objectives to achieve competitive advantage. This is true whether they are business projects, government infrastructure or defence projects, humanitarian projects, or private and social projects.

The role of the manager is to identify and select projects within his or her area of responsibility which:

- are aimed at achieving the organization's mission
- are aimed at achieving corporate objectives and strategy
- deliver timely benefits which justify the expense.

Unfortunately, this is often not the case. Projects are initiated at junior levels of management for what seem compelling reasons, which perhaps match the previous direction of the company, but now are contrary to the development of the business (see Example 2.1).

In this chapter, I shall describe the role of projects in corporate strategy, review the business planning process, and consider how that can lead to continuing routine operations and new projects. The chapter concludes with a review of methods of selecting projects. How the manager defines a project required to achieve specific objectives is covered in Chapter 5.

I worked with a company in the computer industry running a series of project launch workshops in the research and development department. One project was to develop an accountancy package, which a salesman had suggested as a result of several requests. However, this was at a time when the senior management of the company were trying to focus on software more oriented towards the requirements of managers (such as estates management and manufacturing planning), rather than functionally oriented packages. When we came to assign resources, the only person available was the project manager, and the project quickly died.

Example 2.1   A project not aligned with corporate strategy

2.2 The business planning process

There are four essential steps in the business planning process (Figure 2.1).

– define the mission of the business
– set long-term objectives for achieving the mission
– develop strategies for achieving the objectives
– develop tactical plans for achieving each element of strategy.

Define the mission of the business
The mission is the axiom which initiates the business planning process. It is a statement of the reason for the organization's existence; its purpose for being in business. It may be a statement as simple as to make profit for the shareholders. However, it is more common to include statements on:

– the type of products
– the positioning of the products in the marketplace
– the relationship with the employees
– other hygiene factors
– relationships with other stakeholders, especially local communities.

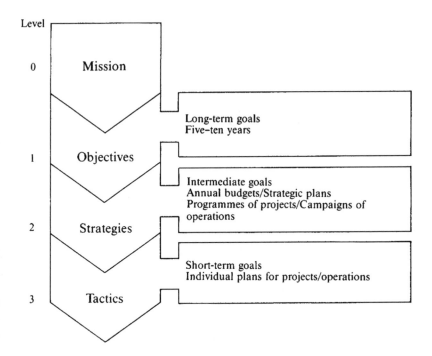

Figure 2.1   The hierarchy of the business planning process

A 'mission statement' is given in Example 2.2.

TRIMAGI COMMUNICATIONS BV
MISSION STATEMENT

TriMagi Communications is in business to supply visual, voice and data communication networks based on its leading edge in glass fibre and laser technology. It will supply two-way cable television services to domestic and educational customers, data communication networks to these and commercial, customers, and telecommunication services through its cable and data networks. It will be the first choice provider in the European countries within which it operates.

The company will provide secure, competitve employment for its staff. All its services will be provided in a way which has no impact on the environment. Above all, TriMagi Communications will supply its shareholders with a secure investment which increases in value annually.

Example 2.2 Mission statement

Set long-term objectives for achieving the mission

Having defined the mission, the company sets objectives for the next five to ten years to deliver it. These are statements of the position the organization will reach in the relevant time scale, covering:

- the types and ranges of products, and turnover from each
- return on sales and assets, and growth of dividends
- type, number, skills and remuneration of employees
- environmental impact
- social and community activities.

A set of objectives is given in Example 2.3.

TRIMAGI COMMUNICATIONS BV
OBJECTIVES

From its current domination of the market in the Benelux countries, TriMagi Communications will establish operating subsidiaries in the following regions:

Year 1: France
Year 3: Germany, British Isles
Year 5: Iberian Peninsula, Italy, Austria and Switzerland
Year 7: Scandinavia, Baltic States.

Each new subsidiary will break even within two years, with a turnover of at least 100 million Euro, and from there will achieve a growth of 50 per cent per annum for the next three years. By the fifth year it will have achieved a return on assets of 20 per cent, and will contribute 10 per cent of turnover to the parent company to fund further product development.

Each subsidiary will employ operating personnel, and sufficient technical staff to install and maintain the networks. They may maintain a small marketing effort to develop local opportunities for using the network. These local opportunities will contribute at least 15 per cent of turnover.

The parent company will employ technical staff to maintain the company's leading technical edge, and to develop new products and opportunities for using the networks. New products and opportunities will enable established subsidiaries to maintain a growth of at least 20 per cent over and above that available from increased market, or increased market share, beyond their initial five years.

Example 2.3 Example of a corporate objectives statement

Develop strategies for achieving the objectives

Having set objectives, the organization can then develop strategic plans for achieving the objectives. These can take several forms.

ANNUAL BUDGETS

These show, year by year, how the business will develop towards the position envisaged in the long-term objectives. The budgets for the current and immediately following year are the plans to which the business is presently working. Budgets for future years will become increasingly more speculative, and will be revised annually. For example, each of TriMagi's subsidiaries would have annual budgets for capital expenditure, income and revenue costs.

SUBSIDIARY GOALS AND MILESTONES AGAINST EACH OBJECTIVE
The annual budgets show where the business is expected to be at each year-end against the objectives. These can be summarized into a plan against each objective, showing intermediate milestones for achieving each one. These are sometimes called the goals of the business, and may be drawn as one or more milestone plans[1,4] for the development of the objectives (see also Chapter 5).

CAMPAIGNS OR PROGRAMMES FOR FUNCTIONS, OPERATIONS OR PROJECTS
The annual budgets will set, or be based on, campaigns or programmes for individual departments or functions within the organization, several of which are described below. These may be campaigns for continuing operations, or programmes for new projects. The business planning process is iterative, and so these programmes are developed in parallel with the annual budgets, by a process of negotiation and compromise. Furthermore, there may be several iterations between levels before the plan is agreed. However, all but the first of the programmes below tend to be set within constraints of the annual budgets. The first sets the basis from which the budgets and goals are derived. There are several types of campaign or programme including:

1. *Programmes of corporate planning or marketing*, which describe evolution of technologies, products or markets of the business. The corporate planning programme tends to deal with the time scale of the objectives. The term *strategies* is sometimes reserved for the corporate planning programme, because that sets the basis for deriving the goals and annual budgets. The marketing campaign is shorter term, and deals more with the balance between products, pricing, distribution channels and promotional campaigns to achieve annual budgets. There are several tools for deriving these programmes. The Ansoff Matrix[5] (Figure 2.2) proposes that an organization has four basic strategies for growth:
   – grow existing products and markets
   – penetrate new markets with existing products
   – develop new products for existing markets
   – diversify into totally new territory, by developing new products for new markets.

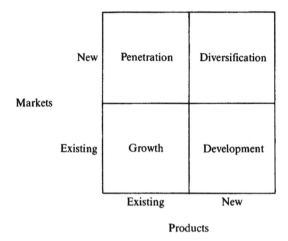

Figure 2.2   Ansoff matrix

The Boston Consulting matrix[6] (Figure 2.3) views products in terms of their market size and growth, and identifies products at four stages of development: cash cows, rising stars, dogs, and problem children. Cash cows are cash positive, but will eventually become dogs. Rising stars are cash neutral, but if nurtured will become cash cows. Dogs are cash neutral, but will become cash negative. Problem children are cash negative, but will either become rising stars or should be shed. The aim is to use cash cows to fund development of new ones from rising stars and problem children, and to shed dogs at the best time. The choice of

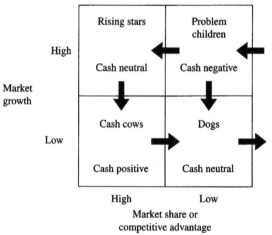

Figure 2.3   Boston Consulting matrix

whether to maintain existing products or markets, or to develop new ones, and the choice of which problem children and rising stars to support, and which dogs to shed, may be based on SWOT analysis – a review of the organization's Strengths, Weaknesses, Opportunities and Threats. Porter[2,3] describes several, more sophisticated, corporate planning techniques.

2. *Campaigns for existing operations*, which are undertaken when a business decides to maintain its existing products, markets or cash cows. This may be for production, or sales, or services.

3. *Programmes for new projects*, which are undertaken when the analysis suggests the business should adopt new products, markets or technologies, or undertake some other improvement to its existing operations. The projects will deliver new facilities, in the form of product designs, factories or technologies to produce them, computer systems to manage their production, or new organization structures with trained staff and managers to undertake the production.

Example 2.4 describes the options facing TriMagi.

The objectives which TriMagi has set indicate that it will maintain its existing operation, in the Benelux countries. It will fund further growth by using the income from those operations to expand into new markets, then achieve further growth as each new market becomes established. Initially, it will sell existing products into the new markets, but, as they become established, develop new products for them. It will also try to use those new products in its old markets, where possible, to achieve further growth. The objectives also imply that the operation in the Benelux countries will split into an operating company, and a parent company undertaking new product development.

Example 2.4 The strategic options facing TriMagi

Develop tactical plans for achieving each element of strategy

Plans for individual campaigns or programmes, or for functions, operations or projects are the tactical level plans. They describe how the organization will achieve each element of its strategic plans. These tactical plans may be marketing plans, production plans, or milestone plans for projects.

2.3 The role of projects and operations

I have just shown how the business planning process can identify a need for routine operations and projects. These are the vehicles through which organizations achieve competitive advantage. Either they do more of the same, though always striving to improve efficiency through habitual increment improvement (HII), or they do new things with novel organizations, that is projects. Until the 1980s, the former dominated. However, with the development of more sophisticated corporate planning techniques,[2,3] and with the explosion of technical innovation and communication, the second is beginning to dominate. Thus management by projects is becoming the way in which organizations fulfil their business plans.[1] Just like the business as a whole, each operation and project has three levels of planning (Figure 2.4): the integrative level, the strategic level and the tactical level. There may be lower, more detailed levels of planning. For particularly large projects, there can be up to seven levels of work breakdown, and we shall return to this concept in Chapter 5.

The integrative level defines the purpose of the campaign or programme, as defined by the corporate objectives, and the objectives it must achieve in order to satisfy the annual budgets.

1. For *sales and marketing* this will be objectives for turnover expected from each product, and budgets for distribution, promotion and overheads for the sales department.
2. For *operations* this will be production targets and budgets for cost of sales.
3. For *projects* this will be a definition of what the project is to produce, the specification and constraints of time and cost.

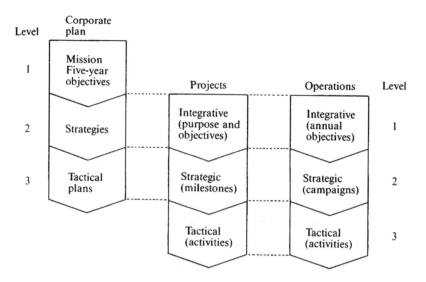

Figure 2.4   The project and operations hierarchy (product breakdown structure)

The strategic level defines subsidiary objectives each function must achieve to satisfy its overall objectives.

1. For *sales and marketing*: this may be individual campaigns for selected products, product launches, advertising campaigns, or testing of new outlets (each of which may result in a project).
2. For *production*: this will be targets for each product, or for efficiency improvements.
3. For *projects*: this will be a milestone plan or work package plan for the project.

The tactical level defines the detail of how the work to achieve each of the subsidiary objectives is to be achieved.

2.4 Selecting projects

The business planning process will identify several possible projects. Usually, there will be insufficient resources (money, people and materials) to fund them all, and so the organization must assign priorities to select projects which are most beneficial. There are several quantitative and qualitative techniques for making this selection. It is not my intention to give a detailed description of them here; that is more appropriate for a book on project finance.[6] However, it is worth while to give a brief introduction to some of the concepts which will be met later. I want to focus on four issues:

1. Prioritizing projects.
2. Investment appraisal and the planning gap.
3. Accounting for risk in quantitative methods.
4. Managerial judgement.

Prioritizing projects
The selection of projects should be driven 'top-down' from the business plans, and (almost always) should only be adopted if they deliver the organization's objectives. Further, projects should only be adopted if there are adequate resources to allow them to be delivered in a timely and efficient manner. Projects must compete for resources with operations and other projects, existing and new. Because the business planning process is iterative, it should be confirmed in the annual budgets that there are adequate resources to undertake all the new projects envisaged. (There may be a level of contingency for projects arising during the year which prove imperative.) Unfortunately, this is often not the case:

1. Projects arise at a low level in the organization, and, although they may

be 'good' projects, they are not aimed at achieving corporate objectives, and so are starved of resources. Example 2.1 describes one such case. One of the R&D staff in the company asked me: 'What if the project is right?' Even if it is right, it will be starved of resources, unless a champion can be found to make it central to the organization's business plan.

2. Projects, even some arising at a high level, are not adopted as part of a structured business planning process, so are not given priority alongside other projects or existing operations. The result, again, is that they are not given sufficient resources to undertake them (see Example 2.5).

Both of these conditions lead to ineffective use of resources. People waste time, which could be better spent elsewhere, working on projects which are never completed. Techniques for managing projects in this multi-project environment, and for assigning priorities are described in Chapter 14. (To prove that there are no absolutes in management, see Example 2.6.)

I worked in a company in the food industry, where no projects were given priority. In one factory, the three largest projects were consuming 30 per cent of the factory managers' time. If individuals are working Monday to Friday on their operational duties, they are working Saturday and Sunday morning on their project work. We were able to identify a hundred projects in total. Because no priorities had been set, individuals were assigning their own priority, with the result that no projects were being achieved.

Example 2.5 Assigning priority to projects

There is the story of the man, who worked for the multinational company, 3M, who invented glue that did not stick. The story goes that the company tried to stop the research project because selling glue that did not stick was not part of their development objectives. Undeterred the man pressed on, and found a use for the glue. He sang in his local church choir and wanted to mark the hymns in his hymnal. Bits of paper often fell out, but if he pasted them with his glue, he could securely mark his place, and remove them at the end of the service. He went back to his organization and said he had found a use for his glue. His organization said that not many people sang in choirs. Still undeterred the man made some sample pads of the paper that did not stick (in blocks of yellow paper), and gave it to the secretaries to try out. Soon, the pads were in use everywhere. The organization decided that perhaps there was a market for this product after all, and the rest, as they say, is history.

Example 2.6 The man who invented the glue that wouldn't stick

Investment appraisal and the planning gap

An organization undertakes projects because the planning process identifies a difference between what it would like future revenues to be, and what it predicts they will be if the status quo is maintained. This difference is called the planning gap (Figure 2.5). Projects are expected to fill this gap. They do not ideally for two reasons. First, almost all projects have negative cash

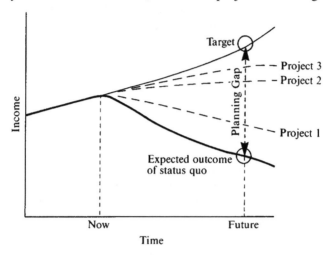

(a) The planning gap

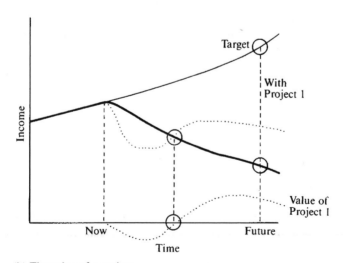

(b) The value of a project

Figure 2.5   Differential cash flows

flow initially, while the facility delivered by the project is being constructed. Secondly, after the facility is commissioned, the income usually reaches a maximum and then tails off, Figure 2.5.

Most techniques for appraising projects assess whether the predicted cash outflow during the life of the project are justified by the predicted inflow after the facility is commissioned. The cash flows appraised should be the difference between those which would be obtained with the project, and those which would be obtained if the status quo were maintained. This may not necessarily be the same as the direct cost of the project and the income generated. The project may reduce income from existing products, or enhance them, or save maintenance or other costs which would otherwise be incurred.

When appraising projects it is common to apply a discount factor to the cash flows. This is a nominal interest rate, or return on investment, which is deducted from future cash flows. The affect is to give greater weight to money in early years than in later years. Income must overall be greater than expenditure, and quick early returns are of greater value than increasing cash flow into the future.

The approach is to assess cash flows against certain quantitative criteria, using given norms for the business. There are several investment criteria which are used for judging the value of the cash flows, all of which give different weightings to different projects:

1. The *net present value* (NPV) is the total of all the cash flows, out and in, over the expected life project and its product.
2. The *internal rate return* (IRR) is the discount rate which gives zero NPV over the life of the project and its product.
3. The *pay-back period* is the time the product takes to pay for the project: the time to give zero NPV at the chosen discount rate.

Accounting for risk in quantitative methods
In quantitative approaches such as this, there are two common methods of accounting for perceived risk, and its predicted impact:

– making some allowance in the figures calculated
– calculating a range of possible outcomes, and the chance of each.

An allowance for risk can be made in one of three ways: by reducing the predicted income, by increasing the expected cost, or by increasing the discount factor, or required IRR. The allowances which are made will depend on the impact of the risk, its chance of occurring, and the strategic importance of the project.

A range of possible outcomes for the project: can be calculated if we can estimate the impact of elements of risk, the factors which may adversely effect the project. If there is only a single element, we try to determine the worst case, the best case, and the most likely outcome, and the chance of each of these occurring. The investment criteria can be assessed for each outcome. With a few elements of risk, this can be repeated for each element. A simple model is built up, in which the project has several, but a small number, of possible outcomes, each of which is assessed as before. Where there are multiple elements of risk, a Monte Carlo analysis is performed. A comprehensive model is made of the project, with ranges put on each element of risk. The criteria are then calculated many times; 100, 500 or 1000 is common. Each time they are calculated, a random value is chosen for each element of risk, within the range of possible values, to give a range of possible outcomes for the project, together with the likelihood of each occurring. In this way, the chance of the project's meeting its investment criteria is determined. The project can then be accepted or rejected as before, depending on its strategic importance.

A word of caution is necessary. The more elements of risk incorporated into the model, the more difficult it is to determine which are primarily contributing to the variability of the output. It is then more difficult to determine where to put management effort to reduce the risk, should the project be adopted. A simple model, based on a work breakdown structure, provides more management information for assessing and controlling risk.[7,8] (Risk Management is described in Chapter 10.)

Managerial judgement
We have discussed quantitative models for selecting projects. Often, however, the final selection rests not on the outcome of these models, but on 'gut feel' of the managers making the judgement. The reason is there are many qualitative or heuristic elements to the decision, which it is impossible to quantify. The quantitative model is only part of the overall decision. These heuristic elements include:

– moral considerations
– the reputation of the organization
– the impact on existing businesses
– the view of the shareholders
– the impact on the hygiene factors in the mission statement
– the impact on the environment
– public opinion.

When shown, through quantitative data alone, that his pet project would not work, the chairman of one of the UK's top 100 companies is reputed to have said:

Don't confuse me with the facts, tell me how it can be made to work!

2.5 Summary

1. Projects should only be undertaken which:
   - deliver the parent organization's mission
   - are aimed at achieving corporate objectives
   - deliver timely benefits which justify the expense.
2. There are four levels to the business planning process:
   - the mission
   - the strategic objectives
   - the strategic plans
   - the tactical plans.
3. The strategic plans will suggest an organization should:
   - continue with existing operations, gradually improving efficiency
   - undertake projects, either to introduce new operations, or to deliver bespoke products.
4. In selecting projects:
   - priorities must be assigned to projects so that there are adequate resources to undertake those selected
   - they must meet agreed investment criteria
   - allowance must be made for risk
   - final selection is based on managerial judgement, taking account of both quantitative and qualitative criteria.

References

1. Turner, J.R., Grude, K.V. and Thurloway, L., *The Project Manager as Change Agent*, McGraw-Hill, 1996.
2. Porter, M.E., *Competitive Strategy*, Free Press, 1980.
3. Porter, M.E., *Competitive Advantage*, Free Press, 1985.
4. Andersen, E.S., Grude, K.V. Haug, T. and Turner, J.R., *Goal Directed Project Management*, 2nd edn, Kogan Page, 1995.
5. Ansoff, H.I., 'Strategies for diversification', *Harvard Business Review*, 113–124, May 1957.
6. Turner, J.R. (ed.), *The Commercial Project Manager*, McGraw-Hill, 1995.
7. Chapman, C.B. and Ward, S.C., *Project Risk Management*, Wiley, 1996.
8. Simon, P., Hillson, D. and Newland, K., *Project Risk Analysis and Management Guide*, Association for Project Management, 1997.

3
Projects and the parent organization

3.1 Introduction

The management of a project requires the integration of various parties into a novel project organization. The primary party is the parent organization, the one funding the project as part of its strategic development. Others are internal and external to the owner organization. Not all parties share the owner's stated, or overt, objectives for the project; they have their own covert objectives. Although the project is subsidiary to the parent organization, it always has an impact on it, and in two ways. First, the project is undertaken to introduce change, because the organization recognizes it cannot achieve its objectives by doing routine things. This change may be technical change, to produce physical facilities, or cultural change, to change the structure of the organization, its people and systems. It is these cultural changes which are the source of many of the covert objectives mentioned above, and the manager must recognize and manage them. Secondly, the processes required to manage through projects may be foreign to an organization used to doing routine things, and so the mere act of undertaking a project can have an impact.

In this chapter, I consider the parties involved in a project, and the impact of projects and project management on the parent organization. I also describe how to implement management by projects where it does not already exist.

3.2 The parties involved

The owner/contractor model

It is common to talk about the project team, as a single group of people, all with the same objectives. This is not the case. Figure 1.1 proposed at least two groups involved with each project, the owner and the contractor. Figure 3.1 extends this model.

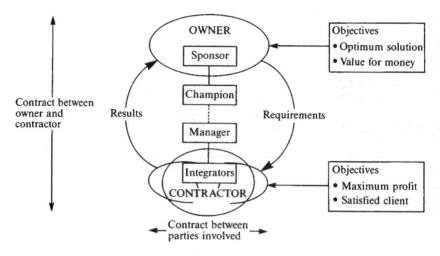

Figure 3.1   The owner/contractor model

1. The *owner* is the person, or group, who will own and operate the facility. They define the requirements, provide the resources (money, people and materials) to undertake the project and deliver the facility, and will benefit from its products. Their objectives are to achieve the optimum product at the best price.
2. The *contractor* is the person or group who consume resources to deliver the facility. They define the work required to achieve the objectives, do the work, and deliver the results to the owner. They achieve their reward from doing the work, and, unless they are also eventual users, cease to be involved once the project is finished. Their objectives are to maximize their profit, while satisfying the client.

Even with this simple model, the two groups involved have conflicting objectives: the owner wants best price, the contractor maximum profit. On a project like the Channel Tunnel, where owner and contractor are different organizations (see Table 3.1), these conflicting objectives are clear; that is the basis of the contract between them. When a project takes place within a single organization, the people involved often still adopt these two positions, although in this case 'maximum profit' is usually from non-financial sources. This can cause a conflict of interest, especially where users have both an owner and contractor role.

FOUR KEY ROLES

Figure 3.1 shows four further roles associated with the model:

1. The *sponsor* is the person or group who makes the resources available to buy the project's products. They have the owner's objectives in Figure 3.1.
2. The *champion* is a senior user representative, who convinces the sponsor that this project should have priority for their support ahead of others. The champion usually wants the best product, but is only concerned about price in that this project must gain priority ahead of others.
3. The *manager* is the person (or group) who is responsible for planning, organizing, implementing and controlling the work so that the facility is delivered to specification, under budget and on time. They have the contractor's objectives.
4. The *integrators* are responsible for ensuring the transient teams of people are able to work together effectively for the duration of the project. They usually have the contractor's objectives, but often view the project manager as an owner's representative.

The champion, project manager and senior user representatives often form a *steering committee*. The project manager, integrators, and often the champion, may form a *project management team*. On engineering projects the integrators are often called *project engineers*. Other terms include *project leader*, *assistant project manager*, *work package manager*, and *milestone manager.*

OTHER GROUPS INVOLVED

Figure 3.1 provides a simple view of the parties involved. In reality there are many other groups, including:

- *users*: the group who will operate the facility on behalf of the owner. They may or may not include the owner. Their objective is usually to obtain the best (not optimum), product, at any price. They will only be concerned about price if they include the owner, or if they, like the champion, need to get priority for their project ahead of others.
- *supporters*: groups who provide goods or services to the owner and contractor. They include: subcontractors, suppliers, financiers, insurers, government and users as resource providers. Their objectives are usually those of the contractor, except, being one step removed, they will be more concerned about satisfying the manager than the owner.
- *stakeholders*: all the people or groups whose lives or environment are affected by the project, but who receive no direct benefit from it. These can include: the project team's families, people made redundant by the changes introduced, people who buy the product produced by the facility and the local community (sometimes called NIMBYs – not in my back yard).

Table 3.1 The parties involved in the Channel Tunnel project

Role	Position	Group
Owner		Eurotunnel and its shareholders
Users	Operator	Eurotunnel
	Provider of services	Eurostar, Le Shuttle
Manager		Trans Manche Link
Supporters	Financiers	Banks, shareholders
	Subcontractors	Partners in TML consortium
	Suppliers	Railtrack and SNCF
	Auditors	W.S. Atkins
Stakeholders	Buyers	Travelling public, hauliers
	Competitors	Cross-channel ferries
	Communities	London, Kent, Pas de Calais

Overt vs covert objectives

A theme running through this discussion is that the parties involved have different objectives. A standard mnemonic on how to judge project success is that it is completed on time, to cost, and to specification, but who judges: the owner, champion, users, manager, stakeholders? (I return to the question of success in the next chapter.) Individuals will judge a project to be successful if it meets their personal objectives. These may not be the same as the stated, overt, objectives, and the time, cost and quality constraints imposed. Individual's personal objectives are their hidden agenda, or covert objectives. Typically they may be:

– project managers aim to enhance their careers
– operations managers want to maintain the status quo
– managers hope to widen their sphere of influence
– managers plan to reduce head count
– people want to protect their jobs
– people are generally resistant to change.

Sometimes these covert objectives support the overt objectives. Often the two sets are in conflict. That will cloud an individual's judgement about the success of the project, and, more importantly, reduce their motivation towards successful completion. This is especially true for users or stakeholders who stand to loose (see Example 3.1). The manager must attempt to identify the covert objectives, to reinforce those which are in unison with the overt objectives, and reduce those which are in conflict. This is part of the skill of managing the change within the parent organization.

I was involved with a project where the user representative on the project team stood to be made redundant if the project was successful. He had been appointed by the 'champion', the general manager of the department, because the project was likely to make a large proportion of his department redundant, reducing his empire. The project was not successful; and in fact came to an abrupt halt when we held a Project Definition Workshop (see Chapter 11). It was impossible to maintain the pretence. However, two years later it was overtaken by a larger project which merged several subsidiary companies into a larger unit. The general manager lost his job.

Example 3.1 Covert objectives

3.3 Changing the parent organization[a]

Technical vs cultural change

The change introduced by a project will be of two types:

1. *Technical change*, i.e. change to the technology or physical environment of the organization. This may be as a result of:
   – engineering work: civil, mechanical, electrical, chemical, etc.
   – IT work: hardware, software, networks, etc.
2. *Cultural change*, i.e. change to the culture of the organization itself. This may involve changes to:
   – the people of the organization: their skills, attitudes, values and knowledge
   – the management processes and systems: the ways of working
   – the structure of the organization itself.

Some projects result in purely technical change, others in purely cultural change. However, the vast majority result in a mixture (Figure 3.2). The term *PSO-projects* (people, systems and organization), was coined to describe these projects.[1] In Figure 3.2, I describe building a road as a purely technical project. However, the people of Dorset, Manchester or Kent may not agree that building the A30 link road, a second runway at Manchester Airport, or the rail link from the Channel Tunnel to the centre of London, respectively, are purely technical projects. Even projects which at first sight appear purely technical often involve a mixture of technical and cultural work. In those three cases it is the cultural work which caused the greatest delay, and this is common on all projects (Figure 3.3). The cultural changes are more difficult and time consuming than technical changes. The latter can be described in concrete terms, and is quantifiable. It is therefore easy to plan and implement. The cultural work can only be described in abstract terms. It also requires people to change, and they may resist that. Because

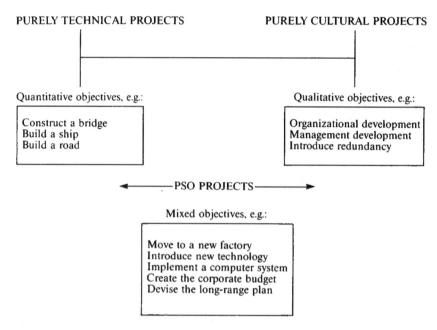

Figure 3.2　The spectrum of PSO projects

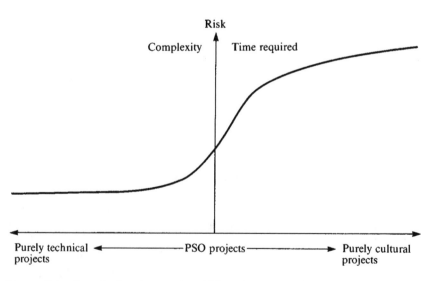

Figure 3.3　Complexity of managing PSO projects

technical work is quantifiable, our attention tends to run down the curve in Figure 3.3 to the technical end of the spectrum. However, we ignore the cultural work at our peril (see Example 3.2).

I used to doubt Figure 3.3. The Channel Tunnel is a purely technical project which took 200 years. I wondered whether what was plotted was a quantum of change, and with major projects the complexity was magnified. However, when you compare the Channel Tunnel to the recently constructed CERN nuclear accelerator near Geneva a different picture emerges. The former is three 20-mile holes through chalk, which weaves to avoid flaws in the rock and involves road and rail technology. The latter is a 60-mile hole through granite, a perfect circle and a perfect plane and involves technology at the boundary of particle physics. The former has taken 200 years; the latter was completed on time and to budget in about four years. The nuclear accelerator is clearly the technically more difficult project; the Channel Tunnel the culturally more difficult, involving English–French cooperation, a scar on the Kent landscape, parliamentary bills, creating Eurotunnel plc, and collaboration of different cultures.

Example 3.2 A purely technical project

Organizational development: managing the cultural change
Managers of projects therefore need both technical and people management skills. It is the people affected by the change, the users and stakeholders, who ultimately determine its success or failure, and it is the cultural change which has the greatest impact on them. It is often said people resist change; it is more true to say they resist having change imposed on them. If they are involved in the change process, they may accept it more readily. Increasingly, project managers are finding they can benefit from the practical application of the principles of organizational development. This involves the planning and managing of change in a manner which emphasizes the involvement of people in all aspect of the change process. The project manager, as change agent, achieves this by:

- planning the change effectively
- recognizing the causes of conflict and resistance to change
- overcoming the resistance by building motivation and commitment to the planned change.

Planning the change
Once it has been decided to make a change, the project manager needs to plan its integration into daily operations. This means designing the technical change, and defining strategies to enable people in the organization to accept the proposed changes and internalize the cultural

element. To plan adequately, the change manager must set clear goals and expectations, both to give the project implementation some form or structure, and to give guidelines of events to the people in the organization. The use of a plan which is developed at a detailed level only will not help this process. If there are no milestones, it will be hard to carry through implementation, and difficult to get people to accept the project and its objectives. It is therefore essential to develop the plan through a breakdown structure, which balances the technical and cultural elements, and shows how they deliver the overall purpose of the project (see Chapter 5).

Planning from a people perspective means reviewing the present systems, and overlaying options likely to achieve the project objectives. This will highlight the gap between present practices and future needs, and it is this gap which the project manager needs to close. As part of this process, the manager should consider possible reactions from all groups. Ideally representatives from each party should be involved in discussions at the planning stage. It is important that the manager remembers that, although plans should always be made, unknown variables or changes in circumstances may require revisions to the plans, and hence allowances to enable flexibility should be incorporated.

Conflict and resistance to change

These can come from the people affected by the change, or from the culture of the organization itself. The people affected, and their fear of planned changes underly much of the resistance. We see below how much of this can be avoided by communicating with people, and involving them in the change process. To do this we need to be able to identify the fears and concerns, which may include:

– fear that working relationships may change, upsetting both formal and informal relationships
– fear that the nature of work may change, requiring the learning of new, very different skills
– fear of job loss
– fear of loss of control or autonomy over one's own or others' work.

Conflict is also likely when people:

– are not consulted or told what is going on
– do not understand or agree with the changes made, or understand the benefits they may bring
– have different perceptions of what changes are needed, or whether they are needed at all

– have not internalized previous changes fully or such changes have not been implemented properly
– are fed up with constant change or are just set in their ways.

The organizational culture itself can create a resistance to change, by creating an inertia to its introduction.[2,3] When I worked as a management consultant, I often found this was the cause of the greatest resistance to proposed changes. Culture influences every facet of the organization including management styles, attitudes, goals, standards, dress and adaptability to change. This can be true not only for the organization as a whole, but also for subcultures which exist at department or group level. The effect of culture must be considered throughout the project.

Overcoming the resistance
There are many ways to help overcome the conflict and resistance to change. Effective communication is central to the successful management of change. This means talking to, and persuading, the right people to take action or accept the proposed changes. However, it is important to remember that communication also means listening and using information received. Project managers should use both the formal and informal communication systems (especially face to face). They should constantly walk the patch, to break down barriers and mistrust caused by remoteness, build up working relationships with people at all levels, and attempt to instil confidence in those affected by the change. Machiavelli, in Chapter 3 of his book *The Prince*,[4] describes the importance of walking the patch, to discover and cure problems early, before they cause real trouble. Organizational structure can also affect communication systems and the change process. Many large companies have tall, stratified hierarchies, with complex communication channels. This may lead to information being filtered out, distorted or lost. Formal, centralized structures tend to be less flexible, particularly to change, than flatter organizations. However, even in the latter communication flows can be distorted or broken. This is most likely to occur when people who are used to working on their own feel they may lose personal autonomy and control through proposed changes.

PARTICIPATION
Implicit within the notion of organizational development is the need for people to participate fully in the change process. For this to be effective, the manager should ensure the need for change is fully explained and understood, and the objectives and benefit of the project to both specific groups and the organization as a whole are understood by all. The benefit of allowing people to participate is that it helps them to feel they have some

control over their work and the change process. If they understand the project's objectives, and see that they may be of benefit to them, they are more likely to contribute positively to its success. This is part of the process of negotiation (see Figure 1.14).

TRAINING AND DEVELOPMENT

Training aims to provide people with specific skills to do a job. Development is a continuous process, which aims to identify and fulfil the long-term potential of individuals and to focus this potential on to the organization's objectives, thereby enhancing the performance of both. While training (especially when new technology or different systems are introduced) is a natural response to change, many companies ignore the long-term development of their employees. However, there are advantages from implementing programmes which address this need. Development of employees, especially managers, contributes to overall commitment to common goals and processes. Development programmes can also help motivate staff and gain their acceptance of both change and specific training needs implicit in the change process. Employee development further improves internal communication and participation, which underpins the success of many projects. (A training programme and the initiation of a development programme are themselves projects.)

TEAM DEVELOPMENT

The project manager should encourage people to work together in teams, and to interact with others in the organization. This is not just confined to the project team, but should cover all departments and groups involved in the change. The project manager needs to be aware that subcultures and different goals may exist in each group, and that these may open up the opportunity for potential conflict, as each tries to protect their position. If this occurs, it is to the detriment of the project and the organization as a whole. One of the most effective ways to stimulate team development and intergroup cooperation is to encourage them to communicate frankly with each other. This can help them understand each other's perspective, and may help develop mutual goals which override individual interests, contributing to the project's overall success.

LEADERSHIP

It may seem that by allowing people to participate in planning and managing the change, the project manager relinquishes responsibility and leadership. The opposite is true. Managing projects in this style requires clear leadership, direction and vision from the manager, so people understand what is expected of them. Leadership means knowing when to delegate downwards and across functions, and when not to. It may also be necessary for the project manager to act as arbiter to resolve conflict. I return to the project manager as leader in Chapter 17.

COMMITMENT FROM THE TOP

For the application of organizational development practices to the management of projects to be effective, the project manager needs to have the backing and commitment of top management. This is because using this approach needs long-term planning and dedication at all levels of the organization, and because the project manager needs to have, and be seen to have, the authority and autonomy to design and implement development programmes. However, top management must feel confident in the project manager. They must also feel able to delegate authority for the process to the project manager. Hence the project manager needs to involve them fully in all aspects of the project, and keep them informed by regular progress reports.

3.4 Introducing project-based management

I have described how organizations undertake projects to implement change, and shown how the techniques of organizational development can be used to facilitate this process. However, the very act of undertaking projects introduces change. An organization which has traditionally done routine work needs to adapt considerably to accept the different culture of projects. This can occur in one of two ways: in a hybrid environment, in which projects and operations sit alongside each other; or in a project environment, in which all the organization's work is managed through projects. In the hybrid environment, the organization undertakes a few isolated projects to introduce specific changes into the operations environment. This creates an interface between operations and projects, which requires careful management. This was the situation in the food factory mentioned in Example 2.5, and will be the situation in TriMagi's operating companies in Example 2.3. The project environment has traditionally been used by engineering contractors and consultancies, but is now being adopted, at least in part, by organizations such as British Telecom, which has recognized that 75 per cent of its operations are project based. It will also be the approach used in TriMagi's head office for product development.

In this section and the next, I discuss these two environments, starting with the project-based organization. The reason is that by understanding the developments associated with the adoption of management by projects in that environment, the cultural difference across the project/operations interface in the hybrid environment can be easily explained.

Developments associated with project-based management

When an organization changes from a functional line structure to a project-based structure, it needs to change its management structure, its management systems and procedures for running the business, and its working lives of the people employed. Many people (managers and workers) are uncomfortable with the impact these developments have on the working environment, creating further resistance to change.

ORGANIZATION

Most organizations doing routine work have management structures based on functional hierarchies. This is the case in the process industries, production manufacturing, and most of the public sector. This structure can be very efficient for repetitive tasks. It is also possible to manage projects through a functional hierarchy, but it tends to be inflexible, so it is common to adopt more flexible structures for the management of projects. These include matrix structures, in which individuals have dual lines of reporting to functional and (transient) task managers, or approaches based on core/peripheral workers, or even structures based entirely on transient teams, which form and reform for each new task.

SYSTEMS

With task teams, companies may adopt flatter management hierarchies, with communication bypassing the centre (see Figure 6.6). Decisions can be made within teams, or by communication directly between teams, without involving senior management. We have called this the 'versatile organization'.

PEOPLE

With rapidly changing technology, and the use of transient teams, there has been a shift from the employment of clerical and manual workers, to entrepreneurial, knowledge workers. These knowledge workers no longer need to be permanent employees, but can be employed on a freelance basis, directly into the transient teams as they form and reform. They may also use modern technology to work from home.[5,6]

The impact of project-based management

The impact of these developments on the organization, its systems and people is not always welcome (Table 3.2).

ORGANIZATION

A purely task-based structure can also be inflexible. Without a functional hierarchy, it is difficult to share resources between projects to reflect

Table 3.2 Impact of developments associated with project-based management

New developments	Impact areas		
	Organization	*Systems*	*People*
Organization Matrix structure Task hierarchy	Inefficient and ineffective use of resources	No permanent expertise or new systems	Dual reporting and lack of career structure
Systems Flat hierarchies and devolved decisions	Lack of overall coordination	Managers lack formal controls	Lack of career opportunity
People Freelance and knowledge workers	Lack of strong culture and identity	Difficult to track and motivate	Unfulfilled development and career needs

changing demands. In addition, organizations employing freelance workers may lose corporate culture and identity.

SYSTEMS

Companies with a purely task-based structure cannot develop expertise without a functional hierarchy in which to store experience as teams form and reform. Task groups are usually not interested in developing new management systems, being unwilling to carry the additional overhead. With the distributed decision making, managers may feel they lack control. They may need to make greater use of informal networks and information systems to monitor and control the projects.

PEOPLE

Many people are uncomfortable with the uncertainty created by dual reporting and diffused decision making. They try to impose structures which suit them, but which are at odds with corporate strategy. People in a matrix organization are subject to divided loyalty between two superiors. Usually the functional manager receives the subordinate's loyalty, as they conduct the annual appraisal. People may not have a conventional career structure within this environment – freelance workers because they do not belong to the company and permanent staff because flatter hierarchies creates less promotion opportunities, and because without a functional hierarchy there is no defined route. Maslow[7] suggests people work for social and developmental reasons. These needs are unlikely to be satisfied for freelance workers working from home, or for transient teams members. (We return to this in Chapter 17.)

Historical lessons
There are historical lessons which indicate how this impact can be resolved, and turned to the organizations benefit. An early statement on matrix management appears in Exodus 20.3:

> Thou shalt have no other gods before me.

Clearly it was believed that people could not cope with the uncertainty of dual reporting; but at that time the priests were also the rulers. That was not the case by the time of the Roman empire, when church and state in Israel were separate. When he and his followers were accused of challenging the imperial authority (Matthew 21.22), Christ said:

> Render unto Caesar the things which are Caesar's; and unto God the things which are God's.

However, early Christians gave their primary allegiance to God. It was not until church and state were later merged under the Emperor Constantine that people were able to give their loyalty to both without conflict. Throughout most of European history the most stable government has been achieved where church and state are merged. Machiavelli[4] devotes a chapter to this. In the Holy Roman Empire this was achieved by the kaiser being crowned by the pope, in the Vatican by the pope himself being head of state, and in England by the king declaring himself head of the church. Since Henry VIII did that, only three kings have lost their crown, Charles I, James II and Edward VIII. All three lost their position as head of the church, the last two by their own making.

Historically, matrix management has worked best when a person's two managers, priest (functional head) and governor (project head) are seen to be ultimately responsible to the same authority, and to be working to the same common goals. An individual can then fulfil his or her needs by satisfying both managers together. This historical review probably contains few surprising messages for managers of projects:

- the management style preferred by most people is a line hierarchy
- some endeavours may have both secular and non-secular requirements, and matrix management may then be the most effective style
- functional (permanent), and task (temporary), managers must then be seen to be working to the same corporate goals.

Successfully implementing management by projects

This approach may resolve some of the issues identified above.

ORGANIZATION

The optimum style for management by projects may be process management.[2] This may overcome the inflexibility associated with both functional and task hierarchies. The task hierarchy focuses on achieving goals, while the functional hierarchy allows sharing of resources between tasks, and focuses on developing expertise and management systems and provides people with a career structure. However, senior management must ensure that task and functional managers are seen to be working to the same corporate objectives, to resolve the uncertainty created by dual reporting. This can be achieved, by cascading the corporate strategy to lower management levels through a clearly defined structure of objectives, a product breakdown structure (Chapter 5).

SYSTEMS

By clearly defining the corporate strategy through a cascade of subsidiary objectives, senior management can delegate decision-making processes to task teams. They monitor achievement of the objectives, and pay close attention to decision making where results deviate from requirements. People can also identify their career opportunities through the corporate strategy, rather than a top-heavy functional hierarchy.

PEOPLE

The corporate strategy, and retained functional hierarchy may also provide the focus for developing corporate culture and identity. It remains only for senior management to satisfy the developmental needs of freelance knowledge workers.

3.5 Creating a culture for project management

The transition from functional organization to project organization just described is a PSO project involving a single transition. The cultural problems arising can be overcome by adopting a matrix organization in which functional and task managers are seen to be committed to the same corporate mission. In a hybrid organization, the interface between projects and operations exists permanently. Operations managers replace functional managers, but the same message applies; they and the project managers must be seen to be working to the same strategic objectives. Both have a

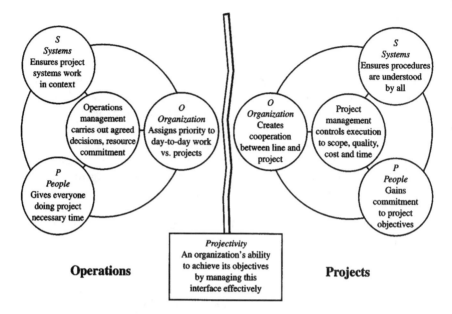

Operations

Projectivity
An organization's ability
to achieve its objectives
by managing this
interface effectively

Projects

Figure 3.4   The projectivity model

responsibility to ensure that project staff know what is required of them to deliver the organization's development objectives, and that the staff do not suffer a conflict of loyalty due to unclear priorities. This dual relationship is illustrated in the *Projectivity Model*[8] (Figure 3.4). (The word 'projectivity' is used to represent an organization's ability to achieve its development objectives through projects.)

Responsibilities of the operations managers

The responsibility of the operations manager is to ensure the organization delivers adequate resources to enable selected projects to take place. Once priorities have been assigned, the operations manager must ensure they are adhered to. This primarily means a commitment to taking professional decisions for which they are responsible, and supplying the resources required by the project, at the time agreed in advance. They must support projects by ensuring:

– staff are given time to meet their project goals
– project systems are understood in the operations environment
– the project has priority alongside the daily operations.

Operations managers must be aware of their commitments to enable the project to take place, and achieve its objectives. Symptoms of a lack of commitment are that agreements are forgotten, meetings are not attended, there is a lack of interest in the project by the management team, or failure becomes a self-fulfilling prophecy because the line managers give the project inadequate support. Operations managers make their commitment by agreeing a contract with the project (Figure 1.14). The project contracts to deliver development objectives of benefit to the operations manager, and in return they promise to provide resources and support. The benefit may merely be to enable them to fulfil their role more effectively, but that is consistent with what was said above.

Responsibilities of project managers
The responsibility of the project manager is to manage the achievement of results. This means planning the scope of work required, organizing by assigning roles and responsibilities to the parties involved, implementing by assigning tasks to resources, and controlling by monitoring progress and taking timely, corrective action to achieve the development objectives. In particular, to manage the interface with operations effectively, the project manager must:

– ensure all participants understand and are committed to the project's goals
– ensure that the projects systems and documents are understood by all
– create cooperation between project and operations by communicating project plans in a form in which they and their consequences are understood and accepted.

Symptoms of inadequate project management are described in Section 4.3. To fulfil their responsibility project managers must play their part in the negotiations leading to the contract between project and organization. In particular, the requests for resources must be based on sound data, so commitments made by the other side are realistic. Further, the manager would do well to follow the principles of organizational development (Section 3.3). Undertaking an education programme to ensure that all staff understand the consequences of the project, and ensuring that project reports concentrate on the achievement of future results, and do not dwell on past mistakes, are particularly valuable.

3.6 Implementing project-based management

Implementing the management of change through projects, whether within a project-based or hybrid environment, is a PSO project, with a heavy cultural element, and should be implemented as a project as part of the corporate development programme.[9] The managing director or other senior manager should manage this project. There are six steps:

1. *Assign priority to development work*: the first requirement is to assign priority to the organization's development programme, and the projects in it (Sections 2.4. and 3.5).
2. *Make a contract between operations and project managers*: the second requirement is for operations managers to commit resources to projects. This is achieved by negotiating a contract at the strategic level of the project hierarchy (Figure 1.14).
3. *Formalize the resource requirements*: the resource requirements are formalized at the next level, where work is allocated to specified resources. Plans are made to release personnel to the project on the due date, against the contract made at the higher level.
4. *Give visibility to the plans*: for the setting of priorities, making of the contract and allocation of resources to be effective, it is vital that plans and progress reports are clearly visible. People can then see clearly what is required of them, and make alternative arrangements in response to changing circumstance. Visibility is achieved by:
   – adopting single page reporting at each level of the project or work breakdown structure
   – expressing documents in a language understood by all involved, and avoiding the use of jargon.
5. *Adopt a company wide approach to project management*: cooperation is further enhanced if the organization uses a company wide approach to project management, at least at the integrative and strategic levels. All people then understand the project plans, and projects are compared on a common basis when assigning priorities. This is especially true where projects cross international or other cultural boundaries.
6. *Educate all personnel in its use*: training is an important element of the organizational development approach, and this applies to the implementation of project management. Educating people means not only training them in project management techniques, but also making them aware of the strategic importance of project management in the organization's development programme. This should be repeated periodically to continue to raise the organization's efficacy at achieving its development objectives through projects, that is its projectivity.

However, people must be allowed to continue to use their own approaches to project management at a detail or tactical level, both to ensure that their projects are managed in a way appropriate to their projects, and to avoid conflict and resistance (Chapter 14).

3.7 Summary

1. The parties involved in a project include:
   - *the owner*: the organization whose strategic plan creates the need for the project
   - *the sponsor*: the person or group who authorize expenditure on the project
   - *the users*: the people who will operate the facility on behalf of the owner
   - *the champion*: a senior user who campaigns for the project
   - *the contractor*: the group which designs and builds the facility for the owner
   - *the project manager*: the person or group who plans, organizes, implements and controls the work of the contractor to deliver the facility within constraints of time, cost and quality
   - *the supporters*: parties who provide goods and services to the work of the project
   - *the integrators*: people who coordinate the work of the supporters for the manager.
2. The parties involved have two sets of objectives:
   - overt objectives are the stated objectives derived from the owner's strategic plan
   - covert objectives are personal objectives which may conflict with the overt ones.
3. The work of the project is of two types:
   - technical work
   - cultural work.
4. Cultural work is easily ignored, yet is more difficult to manage. It can be managed using the techniques of organizational development. The following can help in overcoming resistance:
   - communication
   - participation
   - training and development
   - management by objectives
   - team development and leadership
   - commitment from senior management.
5. The change to a project-based organization has associated cultural changes. The most effective management structure may be a matrix organization, but this requires both functional and task managers to be seen to be working to the same corporate mission.

6. In a hybrid environment operations managers must ensure:
   - staff are given time to meet project goals
   - project systems are understood in the operations environment
   - projects are given priority alongside daily operations;
   and project managers must ensure:
   - all participants are committed to project goals
   - project management systems are understood by all
   - cooperation exists between projects and operations.
7. Implementing management by projects is a PSO project with six steps:
   - assign priority to the organization's development work
   - make a contract between project and operations managers
   - formalize the resource requirements
   - adopt clear and simple documentation
   - adopt a company wide approach to project management
   - educate all personnel involved in projects in its use.

References

1. Anderson, E.S., Grude, K.V., Haug, T. and Turner, J.R., *Goal Directed Project Management*, 2nd edn, Kogan Page, 1995.
2. Turner, J.R., Grude K.V. and Thurloway, L., *The Project Manager as Change Agent*, McGraw-Hill, 1996.
3. Elmes, M. and Wileman, D., 'Organizational culture and project leader effectiveness', *Project Management Journal*, **19** (4), 55–63, 1988.
4. Machiavelli, N., *The Prince*, 1514, reprinted, Penguin, 1961.
5. Handy, C., *The Future of Work: A guide to changing society*, Blackwell, 1988.
6. Drucker, P., *The New Realities*, Heinemann, 1989.
7. Maslow, A.H., *Motivation and Personality*, Harper & Row, 1954.
8. Haug, T. and Turner, J.R., 'Projectivity: creating an environment for increasing productivity and effectiveness in project work', in *Proceedings of the 13th INTERNET International Expert Seminar*, R. Gareis (ed.), INTERNET, 1989.
9. Payne, J.H. and Turner, J.R., 'Company-wide programme management: the planning and control of projects of different type' in *International Journal of Project Management*, **16** (4), October 1998.

Note

a. Section 3.3 contains some material based on a contribution originally made by Lynn Thurloway of Henley Management College.

4
The strategic management of projects

4.1 Introduction

I now turn to the third element of the project's context, the development of a strategy for the management of the project. The way one approaches a project determines how successful it will be. In Section 1.3, I indicated that time spent planning a project is time well spent, yet people consistently spend too little time in the early stages of a project, failing to consider adequately the range of issues which will subsequently cause problems. Managers of projects need to think at an early stage about what will influence the success of their projects, and to manage all the internal, external and strategic factors that will deliver that success. Figure 4.1 shows a model for the strategic management of projects developed from that originally proposed by Morris.[1,2] Projects are subjected to seven forces:

External context: Two forces are imposed by the external context, as described in the previous two chapters:

– sponsorship and schedule: the finance provided by the owner, the benefit expected in return, and the time scale which makes that benefit worth while, and will repay the finance
– external influences: the political, economic, social, technical, legal and environmental influences of and on the parties involved.

Project strategy: Two forces arise from within the parent organization, from the strategic importance given to the project, and the strategy for undertaking it:

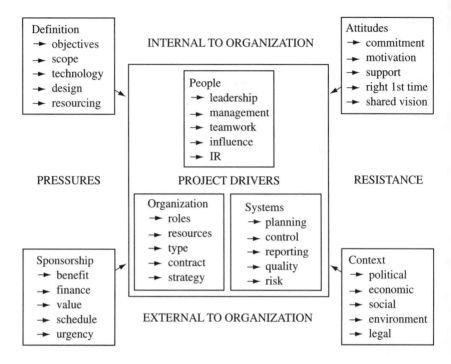

Figure 4.1 The seven forces model of project-based management

- attitudes: representing the importance attached to the project and the support given from all strata of management, from the leaders to the followers
- definition: what the project is required to do, the approach to its design and technology expected to deliver it.

Internal implementation: Three driving forces come from within the project:

- people: their management, leadership, teamwork and industrial relations
- systems: of planning, reporting and control, by which progress will be measured and managed
- organization: the roles, responsibilities and contractual relationships between the parties involved.

This model is expanded in Section 4.4. In the next two sections, I discuss how we judge projects to be successful, and the pitfalls to achieving that success. It is important to know how a project will be judged successful before choosing a strategy for its implementation. I close this chapter by describing five principles of good project management on which the approach described in this book is based.

4.2 Judging project success

Research has shown that if a project manager, his or her team and other stakeholders agree before they start how they are going to judge the project's success, then they maximize their chance of success.[3,4] If they do not, then they maximize the chance that the people involved will use the project to achieve their own covert objectives. There is the standard mantra of many traditional project managers that projects are about achieving time, cost and quality (Section 1.3). At best this is far too simplistic, and at worst it is positively detrimental to good project management. There is an apocryphal story about research conducted in Australia into how projects were perceived five years after completion. All the projects completed to time, cost and specification were five years later perceived to be failures. The implication is that in the drive for time, cost and specification, the project team sacrificed functionality and the product of the project had proved less than useful. When you challenge traditional project managers about their mantra, they will often extend the definition of quality to mean almost anything, but that misses the point, as it does not provide adequate guidance to project teams. Example 4.1 describes a project I worked on where completing early left us feeling dissatisfied, whereas finishing late, but having had the chance to prove our great management skill would have been more satisfying.

In the early 1980s, I worked as a maintenance engineer on four ammonia plants in the north-east of England. Every six months we closed a plant for biennial refit. Over a period of four weeks we did 100 000 man-hours of work. We planned the overhauls to within four hours, but we were usually two days late. But we were *only* two days late. We pulled out all the stops, and managed our way through all the problems to deliver the project within two days of target. Once we coasted in four hours early, and felt we had failed. If we had been given a tighter target, we could have really proved ourselves and achieved a shorter duration! That overhaul did not fulfil our need to prove ourselves as managers.

Example 4.1 Completing projects on time

A project is undertaken to deliver a facility, which in turn produces a product. The owner is primarily interested in the benefit the product brings, although to be of value it has to be available within a certain time and for a certain price, and meet certain quality standards. Time, cost and quality are constraints which affect the owner's judgement, but are not their primary concern. The contractor, on the other hand, wants to complete the project on time in order to be paid, within budget in order to make a profit, and to specification so that the owner will accept the facility and pay the contractor. The actual people involved in the project may also have a host of covert objectives which will cloud their judgement, regardless of the outcomes above (Section 3.2). Morris and Hough[2] reviewed performance on eight major projects from the 1960s, 1970s and 1980s, and derived four criteria for success: the project delivers its functionality; it is on time, to cost, to quality; it is profitable for the contractor; and if necessary, it is terminated early. They judged their eight case studies against these, and found again that subjective perceptions can cloud the judgement. In particular:

- the Fulmar Oil Field in the North Sea was late, but extremely profitable for the owner, so was judged to be successful
- the Thames Barrier was late and overspent, and was quite poorly managed in its early stages, but it works, is a tourist attraction and made a profit for most of the contractors, so is judged a success
- Concorde was late and overspent, but was a technical success, gave France an aerospace industry, and contributed to Britain's entry to the EU, so is judged to be successful
- Heysham II Nuclear Power Station was well managed, and nearly on time and budget, but the judgement is clouded by the rest of Britain's nuclear power programme, and the public's perception of the nuclear industry, so it is judged to be unsuccessful.

These projects were major infrastructure projects. The benefits were social good, not financial return. Morris and Hough therefore only say that a project should achieve its functionality, not that it should provide a profit. For all projects, I would propose a more extensive list for judging success:

- it achieves its stated business purpose
- it provides satisfactory benefit to the owner
- it satisfies the needs of the owner, users and stakeholders
- it meets its prestated objectives to produce the facility
- the facility is produced to specification, within budget and on time
- the project satisfies the needs of the project team and supporters
- it makes a profit for them.

There are several interesting points. First, most of the criteria are subjective; only time and cost are objective. Secondly, the judgement is affected by the assessor's covert objectives. Thirdly, the measures are not necessarily compatible, so the judgement depends on a complex balance. However, they are not mutually exclusive, so it is possible to satisfy them together, but you must start with that objective, and through the strategy for implementation negotiate the balance. You cannot force them to be compatible at the end of the project. Finally, the measures are not judged simultaneously. The first two can only be judged after the facility has been commissioned, and the product obtained. Sometimes that is many years after completion of the project. The Thames Barrier is awaiting the first major flood, and the public image of Concorde has improved with time. The next three are judged on completion of the project, as the facility is commissioned, and the last occurs throughout the project.

Wateridge[3] distributed a questionnaire to people working on IS projects asking them their role on projects (sponsor, user, analyst or project manager) and asked them to think of two projects they had worked on, to say whether those projects were successful or not, and against what criteria they judged that. He found that on successful projects, all four groups could agree the success criteria, that it should provide value for the sponsor. On unsuccessful projects:

- the sponsor wanted to make a profit
- the users wanted the functionality they first thought of
- the analysts wanted to design a clever solution
- and the managers wanted to finish on cost and time.

It is amazing that on successful projects people are working to the same end, and on unsuccessful projects they are tearing themselves apart. It is sad that on unsuccessful projects what people are focusing on is important, to make a profit: to have good functionality, to have a well-designed solution, and to finish on cost and time. However, there seems to be a way of working together, each achieving what is important to you, but oriented towards the common good, and another way of working (I will not say together), where you achieve what is important to you, but undermine the other project participants. Optimizing the common objectives does not necessarily optimize the individual objectives, and vice versa. I have had project managers say to me that in their annual appraisal they are judged on how many of their projects finished on cost and time, not on how many made a profit for the owner. They therefore ask me whether I am saying that the appraisal system works against successful project management, and I have to say that unfortunately it seems to.

Hartman[4] suggests that during the start-up process you ask the project team the three questions:

Q1: What will the project team deliver on the last day of the project?
Q2: How will the successful achievement of that be judged?
Q3: Who gets to vote on questions 1 and 2?

Hartman describes running start-up workshops with each of two companies, where the project teams gave contrary answers to his three questions.

The first project was the construction of a petrochemical complex in Alberta. There were two project managers, one for the design stage of the project and the other for construction. In response to question 1, one said the project was over at mechanical and electrical completion, and the other when the plant delivered 100 per cent nameplate capacity, two dates 15 months apart, and yet both gave the same completion date.

The other team were implementing replacement accounting software for their organization. About 30 people attended the workshop, and in response to the first question answers ranged from:

- beta test successfully completed
- the system has run for twelve months without fault
- 30 people have been made redundant.

The first two of these are again at least 15 months apart. The third was unfortunate because some of the people in the room were those to be made redundant and this was the first they had heard of it.

The teams probably blamed the failure of their projects on circumstances beyond their control, saying 'We were unlucky'.

Example 4.2   Failure to agree completion criteria

Hartman describes examples of the failure to reach agreement on these (Example 4.2). In Chapter 11, I describe how to build these questions into the start-up process, and in Chapter 16 I give a Project Health Check, which asks whether or not this agreement has been reached, and suggests to the people completing the questionnaire possible measures of success to reach this agreement.

4.3 Pitfalls of project management

This view of success is the basis for the implementation strategy (Section 4.4). First I describe pitfalls which threaten successful implementation. Pitfalls are not risks in the work itself (Chapter 10), but are management mistakes made by project managers. They occur in the way the project is established, or the way it is planned, organized, implemented or controlled. The following pitfalls were observed by Grude,[5] from his experience as managing director of a firm of software engineers.

Pitfalls in establishing the project
The pitfalls in the way the project is set up within the parent organization include:

PROJECT PLANS ARE NOT ALIGNED WITH BUSINESSS PLANS

Project plans must be derived from the business plans (see Example 2.1). This pitfall often arises by starting with detail planning, and is the one pitfall which will usually cause a project to fail.

PROCEDURES FOR MANAGING PROJECTS ARE NOT DEFINED

Projects use transient teams to undertake novel assignments. The teams form quickly in order to undertake the task successfully. A properly structured start-up process is therefore important (Chapter 11). A consistent, company-wide approach to project management can also help. However, it is necessary to obtain a balance between the need for such an approach and the need to respect the individuality of project types (Chapters 14 and 15).

PRIORITIES ARE NOT COMMUNICATED TO PARTIES INVOLVED

Example 2.5 describes what can happen when priorities are not communicated. People assign their own, usually different, priorities, with the result that there is no coordination and no work is done.

THERE IS NO SHARED VISION

Shared vision can be a powerful motivator and a way of building commitment to the project and its objectives. We saw in Section 3.4 how it is essential to stable government, and to effective project management.

Pitfalls in planning

The pitfalls in the way the work is defined, the time and cost schedules calculated, and communicated to the project team include:

PROJECT PLANS DEVELOPED ON A SINGLE LEVEL

The use of breakdown structure is how we ensure the work delivers the required benefit. The usual pitfall is to plan at a detailed level only; computer software unfortunately encourages this. Sometimes work is planned only at a very high level, and there is no coordination. The following Chinese proverb illustrates that in almost every area of human endeavour work is planned on many levels. Projects should be no different:

A journey of a thousand miles begins with a single step. (Mao Tse-Tung)

On a journey there are at least two levels of planning between the end objective and the steps: the milestones (towns and villages) and the route map (roads). The former is the strategic plan, comprising intermediate goals or products, and the latter the tactical plan. At the milestone level, we make our plan robust but flexible, providing key, fixed points for measuring progress towards our objective, but able to incorporate changes at a lower level without changing the milestone definition. The road map we also try to keep fixed. However, there are two ways we can build in flexibility. If we find the route blocked, we can make a detour, but still aim to reach the next milestone. Sometimes the detour is better than our original route, but changes are contained at a low level. We can also adopt *rolling-wave planning*: we do not need to define the route between the last two towns until we reach the penultimate town. Sometimes we cannot get that information until we get there. All we need to estimate is the distance between the towns to plan the time and cost of the journey. The single steps are planned as we progress.

USING CUMBERSOME TOOLS

The complexity of project planning tools has grown over the last 30 years, due to the increasing power of software. However, at best, complex plans achieve nothing, at worst, they confuse the situation (see Example 4.3). The plans and progress reports should be cascaded through WBS (Figure 1.10). This can help build the vision for the project.

A delegate on a project management course at Henley Management College said that he had three people on his project team of 20 who spent all day every day developing plans on a well-known PC-based package, and he got no useful information out. Thus 15 per cent of his team were contributing nothing!

Example 4.3 Cumbersome, unfriendly tools

One reason why detail planning tools have developed is they were used so successfully on the Polaris Project in the USA in the 1950s. There is no doubt that PERT (the programme evaluation and review technique), which was first developed on the project, was a powerful analytical tool which helped identify and eliminate risk, and so remove two years from an eight-year schedule. The project manager was also very charismatic and used the technique to help build the vision for the project.[6] However, the following quotation illustrates a covert use of the technique:

> These procedures were valuable in selling the importance of the mission. More importantly, the PERT charts and the rest of the gibberish let us build a fence to keep the rest of the Navy out and get across the message that we were the top managers.[6]

Complex plans were deliberately used to confuse outsiders getting too closely involved in the project, and thereby protecting the project team from interference. This is a valid use of complex plans, but you also need to maintain the simple plans, or you will also confuse yourself.

CREATIVITY DISCOURAGED

It is the reality of modern projects that the project manager cannot be an expert in all areas of a project. Yet it is not uncommon to see project managers dictating to people more expert than themselves through the plan, telling them how to do their jobs. This can demotivate the experts, and isolate them from the project. What the project manager should do is delegate elements of the strategic plan to the experts, telling them which milestones they are responsible for, by when and at what cost, but allowing them to determine the best method of achieving that. In this way, they can retain their integrity, while meeting the project's goals.

UNREALISTIC ESTIMATES

There are several causes of unrealistic estimates. It is common when preparing an estimate, to believe that the owner may not accept them and reduce them. Inevitably the work turns out as originally estimated, resulting in perceived failure. Secondly, there may be inadequate historical data to estimate the work accurately. In that case, the risk must be identified, and an appropriate contingency added. Thirdly, people have different abilities. You must plan for the people you have, not some unobtainable ideal. Finally, it is sometimes assumed that project personnel are able to work 260 days (2080 man-hours), a year. A person working full time on a project is available much less than that. Lost time is caused by holidays, bank holidays, sickness, training, group meetings, etc. When planning, this lost time must be accounted for (Chapters 6 and 9).

Pitfalls in organizing and implementing
The pitfalls in building the project organization and assigning work to people include:

LACK OF COOPERATION

It is not uncommon on projects to wonder if you all work for the same organization, as covert objectives get in the way of the overt objectives. Cooperation is achieved in two ways: by building a clear vision for the project and by negotiating agreement to the plans (Chapter 3).

RESOURCE PROVIDERS NOT COMMITTED

Project managers often use resources on secondment from other managers. They will not willingly release their resources if they are not committed to the project.

RESOURCES NOT AVAILABLE WHEN REQUIRED

It is not adequate just to send the resource providers a plan and expect their people to be available at some point. Even if they are committed, you must ensure they understand the requirements. This is helped by using simple plans, by discussing the requirements of the plan with the resource provider, and by negotiating their release. They must also plan to release their resources at the required time.

MANAGEMENT RESPONSIBILITY NOT DEFINED

When defining roles on projects, it is common to consider only those people who do work, cutting metal or writing code. However, people have other roles which consume time or can delay the project. These tend to be management roles, especially those which cause delay. These roles include taking decisions, managing information, and managing progress.

POOR COMMUNICATION

Surprisingly, poor communication on projects is often caused by too much rather than too little. Communication out of a project is often achieved by sending every piece of information to everyone involved. People soon learn that only a few documents are relevant to them, so all go straight in the bin. The project manager must define those who need the information, so that when people receive something they know they ought to read it. If some other person wishes to be included in the circulation, that can be negotiated. Similarly, committees are often used for communication into a project. Once invited people tend to stay on the committee, even if they are no longer required. Committees grow organically. Worse still, it is those people who have least to contribute who do most of the talking at meetings, as they talk to justify their presence. Channels of communication into a project must be clearly defined and limited, and any additions discussed and negotiated.

TECHNICAL VS PROJECT MANAGEMENT

One reason why construction of the Thames Barrier was poorly managed in the early stages was that there was no integrative project management.[2] The 'project managers' were primarily technical managers, with responsibility for managing the design. There was little integration of the work in the modern sense of project management. It is still common to hear design managers refer to themselves as project managers, especially on IS projects. Often, these 'project managers' are not good at delegating work. They believe, quite rightly, they can do the work better than anyone else, and so surround themselves with idle people while they work themselves into an early grave. It is my view that an industry has truly matured in the management of projects when they stop calling design managers 'project managers', and stop using design engineers as such.

Pitfalls in Control

Finally, pitfalls in monitoring and control are illustrated by Example 4.4 and include:

I once audited a project where the manager felt he had lost control, but was unsure why. The project was to put on a trade exhibition to be held in Birmingham in December of one year. There were 15 syndicates of four companies collaborating in this exhibition. Work started in June. Each syndicate prepared their own material, bringing it to a test site in September, moving it to Birmingham in late November. The project manager was a contractor. In June he had a meeting with the representative of each syndicate, showed them his plan, and said if the syndicate had any problems with the plan to let him know. That was his first and second mistakes: he dictated to the experts by telling them his plan, not developing a plan with them, and no comment was interpreted as agreement. The project manager then held weekly meetings attended by the representatives at which they gave verbal progress reports. Each person spoke for about 15 minutes, resulting in a four-hour meeting; but the project had been set up in such a way that they were not interested in what each other was saying. The whole point of dividing the project into 15 syndicates was each syndicate could work on its own in the early stages. Each meeting therefore consumed 64 man-hours to no effect. At each meeting the representatives usually reported that everything was going to plan. I was called in mid-September because, in spite of that, materials were not arriving at the test site at the due time. The manager wondered what was going on. What had happened was that after the first meeting most of the syndicates had ignored the project manager's plan and worked to their own. When they said things were going according to plan, they meant their own, but the project manager assumed they meant his, and the two bore no relation.

Example 4.4 Pitfalls in control

THE PURPOSE OF CONTROL IS NOT UNDERSTOOD

The purpose of control is not to hold meetings or talk about progress. The purpose is to monitor progress, to compare progress to the plan and to take necessary action to achieve the project's goals. This may mean continuing to follow the existing plan, revising the plan, or revising the goals.

PROGRESS IS NOT MONITORED AGAINST THE PLAN

Control will only be effective if there is a common basis for control, which means a common plan. This is achieved most effectively by reporting progress on a copy of the plan.

INEFFECTIVE REVIEW MEETINGS

In order to be effective formal review meetings must be held, with controlled attendance; fixed criteria for reporting; and at fixed intervals.

Discussing progress at the coffee machine may be part of good leadership and team building, but not of good control. At the other extreme, large meetings where most people are not interested in what others are saying waste time. People must only be invited if they have something to contribute. Holding review meetings at two or more levels of the planning hierarchy can aid this. (The manager in Example 4.4 should have had weekly meetings with the representatives individually, and less frequent meetings with the whole group to discuss common issues.) The meetings must have a fixed agenda, which means reporting against fixed criteria, including the plan. Without a structure people will report progress in a way which puts them in the best light. Finally, people sometimes hold meetings only when they have something to discuss. By then control is reduced to damage limitation. Meetings must be held at fixed intervals, although the frequency may vary depending on the risk, and the point in the project life cycle.

RESPONSIBILITY WITHOUT AUTHORITY

This is an impossible position for any manager. The manager in Example 4.4 had no direct authority over the syndicates, and was not able to use other sources, including that obtained by negotiating agreements. Without authority for control, the manager cannot take action to achieve the project's goals.

4.4 The strategic management model[a]

Youker's model (Figure 1.10) implied that to achieve objectives at any level requires a strategy, and the project objectives are no different. In Section 4.1, I introduced the model for the strategic management of projects adapted from that developed by Morris.[1,2] A project is subjected to seven forces or pressures, each of which must be managed.

The external context and strategy of the parent organization

The strategy of the parent organizations and for the external context imposes two forces.

SPONSORSHIP AND SCHEDULE

The project cannot begin without finance, and that will only be forthcoming if the owner expects adequate benefit from the project (Chapter 2). Finance is the largest item of project expenditure,[7] and influences all other areas of project strategy. Much of the project definition will be driven by the available sources of finance, the financiers wishing to minimize risk, especially in the choice of technology. Where significant amounts of money are raised externally, a certain amount of boot strapping may be required, where some tasks cannot be completed until some money is raised, but must be completed before more money is raised. This was implied by the base version of the life cycle (Figure 1.5).

A key parameter in a project's viability can be the completion date, with even a small slippage leading to a significant loss of revenue as well as increased financing charges. Determining the overall timing of the endeavour is crucial to calculating the risks and dynamics of its management. How much time is available for each stage, together with the amount and difficulty of the work to be accomplished, influences the nature of the task to be managed. Therefore, in specifying the project, the manager should ensure that the right amount of time is spent within the overall duration. Milestone scheduling is crucial at the earliest stage. It is important that the development stage is not rushed or glossed over (a fault that has caused many project catastrophes in the past).

A degree of urgency should be built into a project, but too much can create instability. The manager should avoid beginning implementation before technology development and testing are complete. This situation is known as *concurrency*. (Concurrency is sometimes employed quite deliberately to get a project completed under exceptionally urgent conditions, but it often brings major problems in redesign and reworking.) Concurrency is now increasingly synonymous with *fast track*: that is, building before design is complete. If faced with this, be under no illusion as to the risk. Analyse the risk rigorously, work element by work element, milestone by milestone. The term *fast build* is now being used to distinguish a different form of design and construction overlap: that where the concept, or scheme, design is completed, but the work packages are priced, programmed and built sequentially, within the overall design parameters, with strict change (configuration) control being exercised throughout. With the use of fast build, the design is secure and the risks are much less.

EXTERNAL INFLUENCES

External influences are a primary cause of many project overruns.[2] The analysis of these factors is often called *PESTLE Analysis*, the factors being political, economic, social, technical, legal and environmental in nature. It may be asked how much management can influence these factors. Often some influence can be exerted, if only to provide some protective action or contingency.

Most projects raise political issues and, hence, require political support. These issues must be considered from the outset. People working on a project must be attuned to political issues and be ready to manage them. To be successful, project managers must manage upwards and outwards, as well as downwards and inwards.[8] The project manager should court the politicians and influential managers, helping allies by providing information needed to champion their programme. Adversaries should be coopted, not ignored.

Stakeholders, especially the local community, are an important external influence. The management of change must take account of this influence, and so techniques such as the environmental impact analysis (EIA) procedure have now been adopted.[7] This process shows how dialogue can help reduce potential opposition. The value of the EIA process is that it allows consultation between developers, the community, regulators and others, and yet forces time to be spent at the 'front end' in examining options and ensuring that the project appears viable. Thus, the likelihood of community opposition and of unforeseen external shocks arising is diminished. Furthermore, in forcing project developers to spend time planning, the EIA process emphasizes precisely that project stage which traditionally was rushed, in spite of the obvious dangers.

The parent organization

Two influences arise from within the parent organization, and the strategy of the programme of which the project is a part.

PROJECT DEFINITION

The development of the project's definition is vital to its success. A comprehensive definition should be developed from the start, stating its purpose, ownership, technology, cost, schedule, duration, financing, sales and marketing, and resource requirements. If this is not done, key issues essential to the viability of the project may be omitted or given inadequate attention, resulting in poor performance later on. Through the project definition, the vision for the project is created, the purpose of the project is defined, the project plans are aligned with the business plans and the basis of cooperation agreed. Project definition is described in Chapter 11, and is achieved by:

– setting the project's objectives
– defining the scope through a strategic, or milestone, plan
– setting the functional strategies and assessing technical risk
– carefully managing the design process
– managing resources and the context.

Setting objectives: Little can be done until clear, unambiguous objectives have been set for the project. I have shown how a project's success can be compromised by objectives that are unclear, do not mesh with longer term strategies and are not clearly communicated and agreed.

Defining the scope: Scope definition, and cost, time and performance criteria are intimately related. If they are unrealistic, expectations for the project will not be met and it will be said to 'fail'. The strategic plan for attaining the project's objectives must also be developed in a comprehensive manner from the start. If the project objectives change, the scope definition and investment criteria must be reconsidered.

Setting functional strategies: The setting of a project's functional strategies must be handled with great care, and requires the determination of the design, the technology to be used, the method of its implementation and eventual operation best suited to achieving the objectives. The design standards selected will affect the difficulty of construction and eventual operation of the plant. Technical risk in particular needs to be assessed. Technical problems can have a huge impact on the likelihood of project overrun.[2]

Managing the design process: No design is ever complete; technology is always improving. A key challenge is to achieve a balance between meeting the schedule and making the design that bit better. Central to modern project management is the orderly progression of the design and its technical basis through a sequence of review stages. At each stage, the level of detail is refined, with strict control of technical interfaces and changes (through 'Configuration Management', Chapter 7). Changes can result in extensive rework, as people on other parts of the project may have based their assumptions on the agreed design. You should therefore aim to achieve a progressive design freeze as soon as possible. This is usually feasible in traditional engineering projects, but an early design freeze may conflict with meeting the customer's requirements (see Chapter 7), especially in organizational development, high technology and information systems projects. In setting up projects, care should be taken to appraise technical risk, prove new technologies, and validate the project design, before freezing the design and moving into implementation. The management of the design process is described in Chapter 11 and its application in concurrent engineering and information technology projects in Chapter 18.

Resources: It is no good defining what you want to achieve if you do not have the right number of good, committed people, sufficient money, adequate infrastructure, etc. In fact, getting adequate resources, managing them well and ensuring that the context is supportive are at the heart of successful strategic management, yet are rarely addressed by the literature on strategy. I cover resources under both the project's internal organization and its external context, in Chapters 6 and 3 respectively.

ATTITUDES

This is probably the most important force. The chances of success are substantially diminished unless:

– there is a major commitment to making the project a success
– the motivation of everyone working on the project is high
– attitudes are supportive and positive.

To achieve positive attitudes it is vital to develop a clear vision or mission by linking project's plans to business plans and by functional and task managers being seen to cooperate to achieve the same objectives. It is particularly important that the project receive visible commitment and support from the top; without which it is probably doomed. (The study of the Advanced Passenger Train[2] illustrated this clearly.) However, while commitment is important, it must be towards viable ends. Great leaders can become great dictators. If sensible projects are to be initiated, they must not be insulated from criticism. Critique the project at the specification stage, and ensure that it continues to receive frank reviews as it develops.

Internal implementation

The third set of forces or drivers arise from the internal implementation:

PEOPLE ISSUES

Projects usually demand extraordinary effort from the people working on them (often for modest reward, and with the prospect of working oneself out of a job). In Chapter 3, we saw how significant institutional resistance must be overcome in order for the factors listed here to be achieved. This puts enormous demands on the qualities of those working on the project, from senior management through the professional teams to artisans. The initial stages of a project may require considerable leadership and championing to get started. Beware though of unchecked champions and leaders: of the hype and optimism which too often surrounds projects in their early stages. The sponsor must be responsible for providing the objective check on the feasibility. The sponsor might be considered as the person providing the business case and the resources. Evidently they ought to be convinced of the merits of the project on as objective a basis as possible. The project champion, however, is by definition someone who is promoting the project: pushing it, and hence being less objective than the sponsor.

We should recognize the importance of team working, of handling the conflicts which arise on projects positively and of good communications. Consideration should be given to formal start-up sessions at the beginning of a team's work, mixing planning with team building (Chapter 11). The composition of the team should be looked at from a social angle as well as from the technical one: people play social roles on teams, and these will be required to vary as the project evolves (Chapter 17).

PLANNING AND CONTROL SYSTEMS

Appropriate systems must be used to plan and control all the significant functions, including scope, quality, cost, time, risk and other elements identified as appropriate. Table 1.7 lists many of the tools and techniques used, and Figures 15.1 and 15.2 show how many of the systems interrelate. Plans should be prepared by those technically responsible for their work, and integrated by the Project Support Office (Chapter 14). Initial planning should be at a broad, systems level with detail only being provided where essential, and in general on a rolling-wave basis (Chapter 5). Similarly, cost estimates should be prepared by work breakdown element, detail being provided as appropriate (Chapter 8). Cost control should be in terms of physical progress, and not in terms of invoiced value. Cost should be related to finance, and be assembled into forecast out-turn cost, related both to the forecast actual construction price and to the actual product sales price. All changes to the proposed project baseline, proposed as well as actual, should be monitored extremely carefully. Implementation of systems and procedures should be planned carefully, so that all those working on the project understand them properly. Start-up meetings should develop the systems procedures in outline, and begin substantive planning while simultaneously 'building' the project team (Chapters 11 and 17).

PROJECT ORGANIZATION

There are three organization issues which must be considered at the earliest stages:

– the relevant management structure – project-matrix-functional
– the extent of owner involvement
– the expected use of contractors and contract strategy.

Management structure: A project structure is expensive on resources (Section 3.4.) Many projects begin and end with a functional line structure, but change to a matrix during implementation. In addition, implementing a matrix takes time, and effort must be put into developing the appropriate organizational climate. Assistance from organization behaviour may be considered in adopting a matrix organization. (The issues in selecting a structure are described in Section 6.3.)

Owner involvement: The issue is the extent to which the owner continues to be involved, even after hiring contractors to undertake the work. They may feel they have a legal or moral responsibility to ensure it is done to a certain standard, or may just want to ensure it is for their own comfort. The dilemma is between not being involved at all, versus constantly tinkering with the design, both frustrating the contractor and adding expense. The balance will depend on the nature of the project. A solution is to schedule milestone review points and limit owner involvement to those reviews.

Use of contractors: Virtually no organization has the skills or resources to undertake all its project work for itself and must therefore buy in goods and services. At a very early stage of project definition it will be necessary to determine the contract and procurement strategy. Indeed, financiers may not lend money without knowing who the suppliers will be, so that they can judge their reliability. So, to an extent that takes us full circle, and completes the discussion on project strategy. The selection of contractors, and contract strategy are beyond the scope of this book.[7]

4.5 Principles of good project management

The remainder of this book focuses on three forces within the strategic model, the definition of the project, the planning and control systems and the organization of the project. I do also consider attitudes and people issues, although they are more widely addressed elsewhere.[8] The external issues are beyond the scope of this book.[7] The book describes a process-based approach to the management of projects, as outlined in Chapter 1, first describing the project management functions, the management of scope, organization, quality, cost, time and risk, and then describing the project management process through the life cycle, covering definition, implementation, control and close-out. In order to successfully address the seven forces and avoid the pitfalls, the approach described in this book is based on five principles of good project management:

– manage through a structured breakdown, with single point responsibility
– focus on results: what to achieve not how to do it
– balance results through the breakdown structure
– organize the project by negotiating a contract with the parties involved
– adopt a clear and simple management reporting structure.

Structured breakdown
Almost everything we do in life, we plan over several levels, breaking our understanding down in a structured way. Projects are no different. Using a breakdown structure lets us:

– define and control the scope
– isolate changes
– isolate risk.

By breaking the facility down in a structured way, we can determine the essential components required to achieve our project and business objectives. We then do the work because we know it is going to deliver a result we need, not because it seems like a good idea. By dividing the project up in this way we can ring-fence elements of the work and help to do the same to the changes and risk, as with changes to the journey described in Section 4.3. The breakdown structure is the core of project management and almost all the planning and control systems are based on it.

Hence the project organization is very closely linked to the breakdown structure, and it is common to identify one person or team as being responsible for the successful delivery of each element of work at a given level. A person or team is given *single-point responsibility* for each element of work.

Focus on results
The primary breakdown structure is the *product breakdown structure* (PBS) by which we break the facility up into its components. We plan the project in terms of the results, or *deliverables*, we want to achieve rather than the work to be done. The reason for this is it makes the plan robust but flexible, and because it gives better control of the scope:

1. The plan should be robust or stable, because the definition of the expected results should be stable. If the definition of the results changes substantially, then the project changes. Even where the configuration or specification of the results may be poorly defined (Figure 1.15 and Section 7.4), we can still plan in terms of deliverables, the precise specification of which is yet to be determined. On the other hand, if we plan in terms of the work, the plan can be constantly changing, especially if the goals or methods are poorly understood, in which case the early stages of the project will define the work to be done in the later stages.
2. It gives better control of the scope because we only do work which delivers results we know we need to achieve. Planning in terms of the work, it is possible to define work that seems like a good idea, but which in fact does not deliver useful results.

Balance results through the breakdown structure
The plan at the strategic level can be used to ensure that proper emphasis is given to all areas of work, to balance the levels of ambition for different areas of technical work, and for changes to people, systems and

organization, and to ensure they are appropriate to the project's purpose. I showed in Chapter 3 how the team's attention can focus on the technical work. A balance must be achieved through the strategic plan.

Organize the project by negotiating a contract
Nobody is altruistic; nobody does something for nothing. People will only work on your project because they expect some benefit in return. The expected benefit can take several forms, positive returns or absence of negative returns:

- the project may contribute to the success of the organization for which you all work
- working on the project may be the person's job, and if they do not they will not get their annual bonus
- they may like and respect you, and expect that if they contribute to your project, you will contribute to theirs.

Whatever the expected benefit, in asking for someone's contribution to your project you must negotiate their contribution, which means:

- you must trade their inputs against expected benefits, as just discussed
- the agreement must be reached through open discussion
- the agreements must be represented through clear, simple, open, visible plans which represent the expected contribution and the promised returns.

It is not uncommon for project managers to plan their projects on their own and then to tell the project team what they are expected to do. However, a contract is not agreed by one party telling the other party the answer; it is agreed through discussion and trading of positions. It must be the same with the project plan. This also allows the project team to contribute their ideas, and the experts to retain their integrity by determining how they will achieve the milestones for which they are responsible. I describe group planning in Chapters 5, 6 and 11.

Clear and simple reporting structure
The plans must also be clear and simple so that the project team members can see precisely what their contribution is and how that contributes to the objectives of the parent organization. Complex plans confuse (see the quote in Section 4.3), and confuse the project team as much as they confuse the outside world. You need to adopt a simple reporting process, with single page reporting at each level of breakdown:

- you try to represent the project objectives and the business purpose on a single page

– you develop a single page strategic, or milestone plan, representing the overall approach to the project through one to two dozen milestones
– for each milestone you develop a list of activities, showing how that milestone is going to be achieved.

4.6 Summary

1. There are seven forces defining the strategy for the successful management of projects:
   – the sponsorship, benefit and schedule expected by the owner
   – external issues, including political, economic, social, technical, legal and environmental issues
   – the attitudes within the parent organization
   – the definition of the project
   – the people working on the project
   – the management systems used to manage the project
   – the project organization.
2. The criteria for judging success of a project are:
   – it achieves its stated business purpose
   – it provides satisfactory benefit to the owner
   – it satisfies the needs of the owner, users and stakeholders
   – it meets its prestated objectives to produce the facility
   – the facility is produced to quality, cost and time
   – the project satisfies the project team and supporters
   – it makes a profit for the contractor.
3. Pitfalls in establishing the project include:
   – project plans are not aligned with the business plans
   – procedures for managing the project are not defined
   – project priorities are not communicated
   – there is no shared vision.
4. Pitfalls in planning the project include:
   – using cumbersome, unfriendly tools
   – discouraging creativity
   – estimating unrealistically.
5. Pitfalls in organizing the project include:
   – lack of cooperation
   – resource providers uncommitted
   – resources unavailable when required
   – unclear management responsibility
   – poor communication
   – technical management rather than project management.

6. Pitfalls in controlling the project include:
   - the project members do not understand the purpose of control
   - the plans and progress reports are not integrated
   - the review process is not formalized
   - the project manager has responsibility but no authority.
7. The approach to project management followed in this book is based on five principles:
   - manage through a structured breakdown
   - focus on results
   - balance results
   - organize a contract between parties involved
   - keep it simple.

References

1. Morris, P.W.G., *The Management of Projects*, 2nd edn, Thomas Telford, 1997.
2. Morris, P.W.G. and Hough, G.H., *The Anatomy of Major Projects: A study of the reality of project management*, Wiley, 1987.
3. Wateridge, J.H., 'IT Projects: a basis for success', *International Journal of Project Management*, **13** (3), June 1995.
4. Hartman, F., 'Absolute Performance: a project management maturity model', in *Proceedings of Vienna IV Research Workshop within the Project Management Research Network*, R. Gareis and B. Gratzenberger (eds), Department of Project Management, Wirtschaft Universitet Wien, November 1997.
5. Andersen, E.S., Grude, K.V., Haug, T. and Turner, J.R., *Goal Directed Project Management*, 2nd edn, Kogan Page, 1995.
6. Deal, T.E. and Kennedy, A.A., *Corporate Cultures: The rites and rituals of corporate life*, Addison-Wesley, 1986.
7. Turner, J.R. (ed.), *The Commercial Project Manager*, McGraw-Hill, 1995.
8. Turner, J.R., Grude, K.V. and Thurloway, L., *The Project Manager as Change Agent*, McGraw-Hill, 1996.

Note

a. Section 4.4 incorporates material from the first edition based on a contribution originally made by Professor Peter Morris of UMIST.

PART TWO
THE PROJECT MANAGEMENT FUNCTIONS

5
Managing scope

5.1 Introduction

In this part, I describe methods, tools and techniques for managing the five project management functions: scope; organization; quality; cost; and time. I start with scope. The next four chapters deal with the other four functions. I shall then describe the management of the risk inherent in them all.

Scope management can be defined as the function of *ensuring that enough, but only enough, work is undertaken to deliver the project's purpose successfully*. There are three key elements to this definition:

– an adequate, or sufficient, amount of work is done
– unnecessary work is not done
– the work which is done delivers the stated business purpose.

There are four essential steps to scope management:

1. Developing the concept through the project's objectives and product breakdown structure.
2. Defining the scope of work through the work breakdown structure.
3. Authorizing and executing the work, and monitoring and controlling progress.
4. Commissioning the facility to produce the product and obtain the benefit.

It is through the process of managing the scope that the owner's requirements are converted first into the definition of a facility to produce the expected benefit and then into a statement of the work required to construct and commission that facility, and that the work identified is brought to a successful conclusion. This is the *raison d'être* of project management, and so scope management is the principal project management function. The other four are enabling functions or constraints.

In this chapter, I describe the methods, tools and techniques used to manage scope. I shall start by revisiting the principles of good project management introduced in Section 4.5, and show how these are achieved by the use of product and work breakdown structure. In the next three sections, I shall explain how the products and work of the project are defined at the three fundamental levels of breakdown: how to define the facility required to achieve the owner's purpose and the broad areas of work required to construct that facility; how to break the facility into intermediate products, or milestones, in each of the areas of work; and how to specify the work, as activities or tasks, required to produce the intermediate products. I close the chapter by illustrating the concepts with several case studies.

5.2 The principles of scope management

Four of the principles introduced in Section 4.5 relate to scope management:

- manage through a breakdown structure
- focus on results
- balance objectives and levels of ambition
- keep it simple.

All four of these principles can be met by the use of a breakdown structure. The second will be achieved if the primary breakdown is via a *product breakdown structure* (PBS). The third is achieved by ensuring that results are delivered in all the areas of the project, and by balancing the work through the work breakdown structure (WBS). The fourth is achieved if we use single page reporting at all levels of the structures. In this section I consider the principles of product and work breakdown.

Breakdown
Breakdown is a technique by which *the project is divided and subdivided for management and control purposes.* Rather than breaking the work of the project into a low level of detail in a single step, it is devolved through increasing levels of detail. Focusing on results means we start with a PBS. The PBS is developed by breaking the facility into intermediate or sub-products. The work required to produce each subproduct and the work required to assemble and commission the facility from the subproducts is then identified. I previously described three fundamental levels of breakdown: integrative, strategic and detail levels. However, a WBS can be developed to many more levels and I have seen seven used on large engineering projects. Table 5.1 shows a typical structure, with several levels of deliverables, associated work elements, and possible relative durations for a project lasting about a year. This structure shows the project as part of a much larger programme of work, required to deliver the company's 5- or 10-year objectives.

Table 5.1   Typical products and work breakdown structures

Deliverable/product	Work element	Duration
Corporate development objectives	Programme	5–10 years
Specified change	Project	9–18 months
Individual project objective	Areas of work	6–18 months
Milestone	Work package	1–3 months
Component	Activity	1–3 weeks
	Task	days
	Step	hours

There is no universal agreement on the terms to be used for the work elements and their deliverables. There is one supplier of project management software which uses the sequence project-phase-activity-task in one of its products and project-phase-task-activity in another.

Advantages of using a breakdown structure
There are several reasons for using breakdown:

– it provides better control of work definition
– it allows work to be delegated in coherent packages
– it allows work to be defined at an appropriate level for estimating and control for the current stage
– it allows containment of risk.

BETTER CONTROL

The use of a breakdown structure satisfies the first three principles of good management listed in Section 4.5. One of the pitfalls in planning is to develop the work definition at a single, detailed level. Developing the work definition in a structured way ensures better results. Further, by defining work through its deliverables ensures that, as the project progresses, only work which is necessary to produce the facility is done, not work which was envisaged some months previously, but is no longer required. Hence, the plan also becomes more stable. The work required can change in changing circumstances, but only certain results build towards the required end objective. This is clearly the case in research and development projects, where the process of doing the project defines the work to be done. However, it can also be true of engineering, construction, information technology and organizational development projects. For example, the construction of an aeroplane and a submarine involve similar activities:

- the fabrication of metal into a cylindrical pressure vessel
- internal outfitting to support life in a hostile environment
- the fitting of propulsion equipment.

On a detail level the work appears the same. However, one set of inter-mediate products leads to an Airbus, and another set to a submarine. The high levels of the structure can also be used to balance areas of work on a project. By developing the definition at a detail level only there is a risk that we give undue emphasis to one area only. This may be technical work over cultural work (Section 3.3), or it may be our own area of expertise at the expense of another. On Heysham 2 Nuclear Power Station, the computer systems required to operate the plant were not given sufficient emphasis in the plan, swamped by the amount of engineering work, and would have delayed the commissioning of the station several months, if it were not for another technical problem. A small amount of work could have kept a multi-billion pound investment lying idle.[1]

COHERENT DELEGATION

The parcelling of work in a breakdown structure is natural, because it is aimed at achieving a product. Responsibility can be assigned to individual parties for each product. In fact, they can be left to identify the actual work required, and in this way experts retain their integrity, while being set measurable targets. Sometimes this can be the only way to control progress on a research project, as the work itself is unknown, only the measurable, intermediate results can be measured. If work is defined at a detail level and amalgamated into packages, then they may not actually be natural packages of work, and the project manager can appear to be telling people more technically skilled than themselves how to do the work.

LEVELS OF ESTIMATING AND CONTROL

The lowest level of work breakdown appropriate for estimating and control depends on several factors:

- the size, type and duration of the project
- the purpose for which the estimates will be used
- the current stage in the project management life cycle
- the requirement for effective control.

I find on projects of a year's duration that activities of two weeks' duration are the lowest appropriate level for planning and control. There is a law of diminishing returns which makes it inefficient to plan and estimate at lower levels, except in areas of high risk.

Lowest level of work breakdown: If the activity level is the lowest level of estimating and control, it is also the lowest level for central planning. However, team leaders may assign work to people at the task level, and individuals may plan their own time at the item level. The lowest level does depend on the size of the project. On the four-week overhaul of ammonia plants, the lowest level of planning was activities of two to four hours. On the other hand, I worked briefly on a project of seven years' duration, on which people were planning steps of four hours' duration six months in advance. The plans were meaningless.

Lowest level of estimating: Because of inherent uncertainties, there is only a certain level of accuracy you can expect. It is pointless to plan in greater detail. The people on the seven-year project thought that planning at lower levels improved the overall accuracy. Unfortunately, that is not the case. Probability theory tells us that the percentage error of the part as a ratio of the percentage error of the whole is inversely proportional to the square root of the size:

$$\frac{\pm e\%}{\pm E\%} = \sqrt{\frac{S}{s}}$$

We might expect to finish a year-long project, $S = 52$ weeks, to within a month, $E = \pm 10$ per cent. Therefore on an activity of two weeks' duration, we need to be accurate to within one week, $e = \pm 50$ per cent. On a task of two days' duration, we need to be accurate to within two days, $e = \pm 100$ per cent. The accuracy on steps is even more meaningless.

Planning in greater detail also requires more effort in estimating. The formula above implies that to double the accuracy of the estimate requires four times as much planning effort, and this has been measured in the petrochemical industry.[2] Therefore, at early stages of the project, you want very course estimates, obtained by planning at high levels of work break-down, with lower levels developed only as the project is shown to be viable at the high levels. You also reach a point at about $E = \pm 5$ per cent accuracy, at which it costs more to estimate than the value of the data you are getting. This sets a limit on the lowest worthwhile level of work breakdown for estimating purposes. I return to this concept in Chapter 8.

Lowest level of control: Similar arguments apply to the level at which the project is controlled. Controlling at a lower level can mean more time is spent in control than doing work; controlling at a higher level means slippages can get out of hand before they are recognized. The appropriate size of activity for control is the same as the frequency of control meetings.

If meetings are once a fortnight, activities should, on average, be a fortnight long. Then, at each review an activity is either not started, finished, or half finished – three simple states. If activities are very much shorter, it will be difficult to determine what is critical for completion. If they are very much longer, the percentage completion will be reported as the elapsed time divided by the original duration while that is less than one, and 99 per cent while it is greater until the activity is actually finished.

CONTAINMENT OF RISK

I qualified remarks above by saying it did not apply in areas of high risk. In fact there is no need to take the WBS down to a consistent level. The lowest level of WBS may vary according to the level of risk: in areas of low risk you may stop as high as the work-package level; in areas of high risk you may continue to a very low level of WBS. The lowest level of WBS may depend on:

– the uncertainty introduced by the risk
– the need to contain the risk.

Figure 5.1 illustrates a project in which all risk is thought to be in work-package A, activity A3 within that, and task A3A within that. At the task level, the uncertainty introduced by the risk, ±100 per cent, is less than the estimating error, ±150 per cent, and since the task is only of two days' duration, the maximum impact it can have on the project's duration is two days.

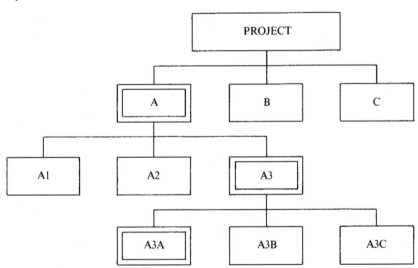

Figure 5.1   Containment of risk in the work breakdown structure

5.3 Project definition

Project definition initiates the project and therefore relates the work of the project to the owner's business objectives. To achieve this, it is necessary to identify the owner's requirements, including the facility expected to satisfy them, and then to identify the broad areas of work required to construct the facility. The following three should be defined:

– the purpose
– the scope
– the outputs.

THE PURPOSE

This is a statement of the business need to be achieved by the project. It may be a problem to be solved, an opportunity to be exploited, a benefit to be obtained, or the elimination of an inefficiency, but will derive from the strategic objectives of the parent organization (Chapter 2). The statement of the purpose should be clear and precise, and should contain both quantitative and qualitative measures. Once the project is underway, it will become the 'mission' of all those involved in the project, both as project team members and as resource providers. It can be a powerful motivating force if it is seen to be worth while and beneficial to the business, and can help to build cooperation. Of course it can be a powerful demotivator if it is seen to conflict with individuals' self-interest (Example 3.1).

THE SCOPE

This is an initial, high-level description of the way in which the purpose will be satisfied. If the purpose is viewed as a problem to be solved, the scope will identify possible solutions, and the one selected for further work; the fourth, fifth and sixth steps in Figure 1.6. The statement of scope includes three things:

– the work within the remit of the project, required to solve the problem and achieve the benefits
– the work which falls outside the remit of the project
– interfaces with other projects in the programme.

The inclusions will later be made redundant by the initial stages of work breakdown. However, it is important to include them in the statement of project definition. They are a key step in the problem-solving process, which indicates the thought processes of the people drawing up the definition. The exclusions can arise either because the work is not required to achieve the benefits (although it would be nice to have) or because it is being handled elsewhere. The owner does not have a limitless pot of gold, and so a boundary must be set on the work to be done. Sometimes the potential benefit must be reduced to match the available funds. Also, when a project is taking place as part of a larger programme, it may share work with other projects. It can then be more efficient to have one project handle all the joint work. This is especially true when projects create a need for redeployment or redundancy. One project may then delegate the work to the other. For whatever reason, the exclusions must be clearly stated, so that they are understood by people joining the project later, and so that interfaces with other projects are identified and managed (Chapter 14). These exclusions will include the definition of interfaces with other projects in the programme.

THE OUTPUTS

These are quantitative and qualitative measures by which completion of the project will be judged. In effect they identify the facility to be produced by the project. If the facility is an engineering construction (factory, dam or chemical plant, say), then the outputs may be something like:

> when the facility has been constructed, the supporting establishment is in place, the facility has been commissioned, and is operating to a certain percentage of capacity.

A similar statement can apply to a computer system, management development programme or organizational change. You will notice that the statement implies that the facility has been shown to be able to achieve some of the benefits. People are usually quite happy with this for a factory, less so for a computer system or organizational change process. In the latter cases, the project is over once the system is commissioned, and the project team have no responsibility for ensuring that it works properly! In Section 4.2, I said that it is not always possible to set the project's benefits as the objectives, as they may not be achieved until some time after the end of the project, and the facility has been commissioned. However, it is important that the outputs are likely to deliver the benefits, and the project team address the question of how they are to be attained. Further the outputs should:

– address all the work within the scope of the project
– not address work outside the scope of the project
– begin to set parameters for managing quality, cost and time.

You will see now why it is important to record the scope of the project.

Initiating work breakdown

The statement of the outputs completes the project definition. It is now possible to define *areas of work*, which begins the process of work breakdown. Each area of work delivers one of the project's objectives, linking the integrative level (level 1), to the strategic level (level 2). The areas of work may form subprojects, as in Table 5.1. In Chapter 11, I describe the Project Definition Report. The statement of purpose, scope and objectives appears in an earlier section, and sets the scene for the project. The areas of work appear in the section on work breakdown. Again it is important that the areas of work cover all the objectives, but no more.

Standard documentation

Some companies use standard forms for defining purpose, scope, objectives and areas of work. They can serve a useful purpose in enforcing discipline in project proposal. However, I prefer a standard document, produced on a word processor. That gives greater flexibility, and can be built into the Project Definition Report later. Whichever is chosen, the document should be no more than two or three pages long.

Case study

The concepts can be illustrated by a case study. This is based on a real example, but is adapted to illustrate the points. A project brief is given in Example 5.1, followed by a statement of purpose, scope, outputs and areas of work. These would be Sections 1, 2 and part of 3 of the contents of a Project Definition Report (Chapter 11), and are written as such. The model is developed as new concepts are introduced.

The definition of the project contains a statement of the expected time scale: five months to the commissioning of the first offices and nine months to completion of the project. At this stage these are targets. People familiar with the technology should be able to say whether they are realistic, but the precise time scale would only be determined as the project plan is developed to lower levels. However, I am a great believer in being *goal directed*, aiming to achieve this target and scheduling the work appropriately, rather than allowing rather theoretical mathematics in the form of a network to impose a longer duration. Often tight time scales can be achieved with management effort. Similarly, there is already enough information for experts to begin to develop initial estimates of capital cost and revenue for the project.

TRIMAGI COMMUNICATIONS BV - PROJECT DEFINITION REPORT
Rationalization of the Customer Repair and Maintenance Offices

1 Background

With its expansion in Europe, TriMagi Communications intends to rationalize its Customer Repair and Maintenance Offices, CRMOs, in the Benelux countries, starting in its home base in Holland.

There are currently 18 CRMOs in the region. Each office is dedicated to an area within the region. An area office receives all calls from customers within the area reporting faults. The fault is diagnosed either electronically from within the office, or by sending an engineer to the customer's premises. Once diagnosed the fault is logged with the field staff within the office, and repaired in rotation. Each area office must cope with its own peaks and troughs in demand. This means that the incoming telephone lines may be engaged when a customer first calls, and it can take up to two days to diagnose the fault.

To improve customer services the company plans to rationalize the CRMO organization within the region, with three objectives:

- never have engaged call receipt lines within office hours
- achieve an average time of two hours from call receipt to arrival of the engineer at the customer's premises
- create a more flexible structure able to cope with future growth both in the region and throughout Europe, and the move to 'Enquiry Desks', dealing with all customer contacts.

This improvement can be achieved by changing the CRMO structure using new technology recently developed by the company's R&D department. In the new structure, there will be three call receipt offices, two diagnostic offices and four field offices servicing the entire region. It would be possible to have just one office for each of call receipt and diagnosis, but that would expose the service to technical failure.

Incoming calls would be switched to a free line in one of the call receipt offices. It will be logged automatically, and passed on to a diagnostic office. The diagnostic office will try to diagnose the fault electronically, which should be possible in 90 per cent of cases. The diagnostic offices are also able to discover faults before the customer notices them. The diagnostic offices will pass the faults to the field offices to repair the faults, and diagnose the remaining 10 per cent. The field offices will be nominally assigned to an area within the region, but will share cases to balance their workload.

2 Project definition

PURPOSE: The purpose of the project is to rationalize the CRMO organization:

(a) to improve customer service so that:
   - all customers calling the receipt offices obtain a free line

– all calls are answered within 10 seconds
– the average time from call receipt to arrival of an engineer on site is two hours.
(b) to improve productivity and flexibility so that:
– the costs are justified through productivity improvements
– the call receipt offices can be made part of a unified 'enquiry desk'
– but there are no redundancies so that all productivity improvements are achieved through natural wastage, redeployment or growth.

SCOPE: The work of the project includes:

(a) changing from the existing structure of 18 area offices to three call receipt offices, two diagnostic offices and four field offices
(b) investigating which of two new CRMO networking technologies is appropriate for the new structure, and to implement that chosen
(c) refurbishing the nine new offices to current standards
(d) training and redeploying staff to meet the needs of the operation of the new CRMOs
(e) installing hardware to connect the CRMOs to the new Customer Information System, and to implement a statistical package to analyse fault data.

The work of the project excludes the retrenchment of any staff who are surplus to requirements within the CRMO structure; they will be passed to central personnel for redeployment on other expansion projects; with the implementation of the new Customer Information System, the call receipt offices may within the next two years be incorporated into unified 'enquiry desks' dealing with all customer contacts. However, it will not be the project team's responsibility to achieve that integration.

OUTPUTS: The outputs of the CRMO Rationalization Project are:

(a) when the CRMO facilities have been installed in nine offices (three call receipt offices, two diagnostic offices and four field offices), within nine months
(b) when appropriate networking technology has been selected and implemented, together with statistical MIS to achieve the required customer service levels
(c) when appropriate operating systems have been designed and implemented, together with procedures to achieve the required customer service levels and productivity improvements
(d) when staff have been trained and redeployed to fill new positions, and vacate old positions
(e) with the objective that the first offices should be operational within five months and the work complete within nine.

3 Work structure

AREAS OF WORK: To achieve the project's objectives, the following areas of work are required:

A   *Accommodation*: Refurbish new offices, install hardware and furniture. (There is only one floor area available in the region large enough to take the first call receipt and fault diagnosis offices. The remaining eight offices must be housed in existing CRMO space.)

T   *Technology*: Decide on networking technology to be used, implement statistical MIS, implement networking technology in new offices.

O   *Organization*: Communicate all changes to the staff involved, define the operation of the new CRMOs, train and redeploy staff to fill new positions.

T   *Project*: Plan the project, organize the resources, obtain financial approval.

MILESTONE PLAN: The Milestone Plan for the project follows:

....

....

Example 5.1   Project definition for the case study project

5.4 Planning at a strategic level: milestone plans

Having defined the project, we are in a position to develop the work break-down structure to the second level, the strategic level. In this section, I shall describe the requirements for planning at this level, and then introduce a tool, the *milestone plan*,[3] which satisfies these requirements.

Requirements for planning at the strategic level

At the second level of breakdown, the manager sets the strategy for his or her project. The plan at this level:

– shows how the intermediate products, or deliverables, build towards the final outputs

– sets a stable framework, fixed goal-posts, for the team, and thereby provides a common vision

– controls devolution of the management of the scope to other parties.

I described above how similar activities are involved in the manufacture of an Airbus or submarine, yet one set of intermediate products delivers an aircraft, another a submarine. It is at the second level of the work break-down that we set the strategy, showing how the intermediate products build towards the facility to be delivered by this project. Because only one set of intermediate products delivers the required final objective of this project, the plan at this level can be made stable. This can be a powerful motivating tool, giving the project team a common vision.

To build a common vision, the plan should be represented on one page. It then presents a clear picture of the strategy for the project. It is through this single page, the milestone plan, that the project manager communicates the overall strategy of the project upwards to the project sponsor and champion, and downwards to the project team. This was the fifth principle of good project management introduced in Section 4.5. It is also at this level that focusing on the deliverables can help delegate work to subproject teams. A team accepts responsibility for the delivery on an intermediate product, and plans its own work to deliver that milestone independently of other project members. They know that they must achieve their milestone by a certain date to enable the project to proceed, but they are able to work without interference. We have seen how this can allow professional people to retain their integrity when working for a project manager from a different discipline.

Milestone planning

It is common, when developing the plan at the second level to define the packages of work first, and then define the deliverable which results from each work package. However, for the reasons above, I suggest that you define the deliverables, or milestones first, in the form of a milestone plan.[3] The packages of work which result in each milestone are derived later. The milestone plan is a strategic plan, or framework, for a project, defined in terms of intermediate products, or results, to be achieved. It shows the logical sequence of the conditions or states a project must pass through to achieve the final objectives, describing what is to be achieved at each state, not how the state is to be achieved.

Figure 5.2 illustrates the milestone plan, with the circles representing the milestones, the lines joining them representing the logical dependency between them. Hence, the milestone plan represents a logical network for the project.

We return to networks in Chapter 9 where two types are described; *Precedence* and *Activity-on-Arrow Networks*. In precedence networks, work is represented by the nodes of the network. These are joined by arrows representing the logical dependency of the work. In an activity-on-arrow network work is represented by the arrows. The nodes are events in time, and the logic is represented by the way the arrows join at the nodes. The milestone plan is a precedence network. The circles in Figure 5.2 represent packages of work, defined by the results they deliver. The arrows show how one work package follows another, and are known as *end-to-end dependencies*: the end of one package (milestone), is dependent on the end of the previous one. They say nothing about the start of the work: one package can start before the previous one has finished. This allows greater flexibility in scheduling the work.

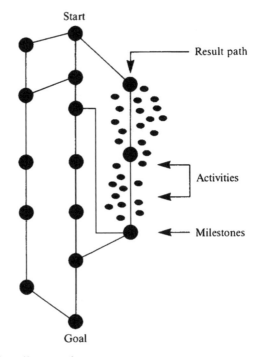

Figure 5.2   The milestone plan

Result paths or areas of work
In Figure 5.2, the milestones are grouped into vertical columns representing the areas of work. These vertical columns have been called result paths. One of the principles of project management (Section 4.5), was to balance the changes and level of ambition. I suggested that the WBS should be used to ensure that equal emphasis is given to work in different areas. The result paths give visual representation to this. By inspecting the result paths, you can ask yourself one of two questions, as illustrated in Example 5.2:

– Have all the areas of work been covered, or has something been left out? In particular, have the cultural changes been addressed?
– Is equal emphasis given to all areas of work?

I did some work with a research establishment where they were installing a larger computer to store the empirical data from a particularly large experiment they were conducting. I helped them plan the project to make the change. The plan had three result paths:

- hardware and software
- the database
- the establishment.

Down the first path there were a large number of milestones:

- hardware and software selected
- hardware installed
- operating system loaded
- database software loaded
- system tested.

There were a similar number of milestones in the third path:

- computer room ready to receive machine
- furniture obtained
- operating procedures written
- operators recruited
- operators trained.

There were only two milestones in the central path:

- data transferred
- system commissioned.

Without prompting from me, the two people working with me on the development plan said, 'Hold on! The purpose of this project is not to obtain new hardware and software, and not to create a new establishment. It is because the data has got too large for the old machine. We ought to be giving greater emphasis to the database.' They therefore inserted two more milestones in the centre column. One dealt with data cleanse, removing incorrect, incomplete or redundant data. The other dealt with restructuring the database to meet future, rather than historical, requirements. Some people say that these two milestones may have made the rest redundant!

Example 5.2 Balancing objectives through the result paths

Selecting milestones

A good milestone plan:

- is understandable to everyone
- is controllable, both quantitatively and qualitatively
- focuses on necessary decisions
- is logical, with decisions and work packages in the right order
- gives an overview at the right level.

UNDERSTANDABLE

The milestone plan is a tool to build cooperation and commitment to a common vision. It must therefore be understood by all those involved in the project. This requires the milestone descriptions to be written in English, not in technical jargon, only understandable to a few.

CONTROLLABLE

The plan is also a tool for control, and so the descriptions must be precise, so that you can determine when they have been achieved. Technical milestones can be given a quantitative measure, e.g. 'when the new machine tool is operating at design capacity'. Other milestones must be given a qualitative description, with some measure of quality written in. For example, it is not adequate to say: 'when a report is written'. Two lines on the back of an envelope satisfy that. The report must:

– meet certain requirements
– satisfy a steering committee
– allow a decision to be made.

DECISIONS

Milestones represent states en route to the final objective. Often the interesting state is not the production of a design or report. That is not the purpose of the work. It is the taking of a decision, based on the design or report, to allow more work to proceed. That is the required deliverable, and is controllable. The responsibility chart (Chapter 6), defines who is to take the decision.

LOGICAL

The milestone plan is a logical plan. It contains a network, which shows the strategy for building through the intermediate products to achieve the final objective.

SINGLE-PAGE OVERVIEW

The objective is to produce a plan on a single page, which clearly communicates the project strategy. This is only achieved if the number of milestones and areas of work are limited. I find the ideal number of milestones is somewhere between one and two dozen. With fewer the plan does not give a useful structure, and with more it becomes confusing. Similarly, I recommend three or four result paths. Setting limits on the number of milestones determines the size of the work packages, rather than allowing the size of work packages to determine the number of milestones. On small projects this will be the only level of planning. On large projects it will be the first of several.

Standard form for the milestone plan

In Figure 5.2, the milestone plan is drawn down the page, whereas it is common to draw a network across the page. The reason is simple. I suggest a form for the milestone plan[3] (Figure 5.3), with three columns:

- the central one is for drawing the network
- the right-hand one is for writing the description of the milestones (which in themselves describe the packages of work)
- the left-hand column is for the milestone dates, once the work has been scheduled (Chapter 9).

The right-hand column gives adequate room to write a full description of the milestone, whereas if you draw the network across the page, you have to write small to fit the description of the work package into the box or on to the arrow. It may seem heretical to draw the network down the page, but it does allow the network and a full description of the work to be portrayed on a single page. It also represents the milestone plan as a process flow diagram for the project, emphasizing the process nature. Figure 5.4 is a milestone plan for the CRMO Rationalization Project, showing the use of the form.

MILESTONE PLAN		Company:	
		Project description:	
Planned date:		Milestone:	

Figure 5.3   Blank milestone plan form

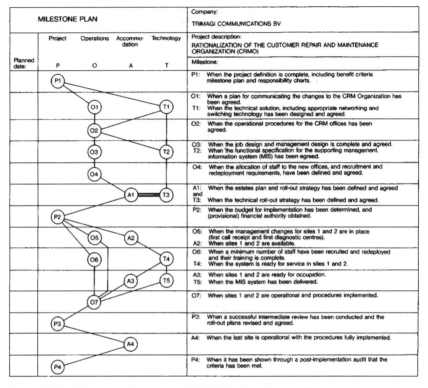

Figure 5.4 Milestone plan for the CRMO Rationalization Project

Developing the milestone plan

Ideally, the milestone plan should be developed in a launch workshop (Chapter 11) with selected key managers and project personnel present. Developing the plan in a group session builds greater commitment than the project manager developing it on their own and trying to impose it on the team. However, to be effective the workshop should not have more than about six people present. The process I recommend for developing the plan has six steps:

1. Start by agreeing the final milestone, the end of the project. The Project Definition Report should help this.
2. Generate ideas for milestones. Brainstorm them on to flip charts.
3. Review the milestones. Some will be part of another milestone. Some will be activities, but will generate ideas for new milestones. As you rationalize the list record your decisions, especially where you have decided that a milestone is part of a larger one.

4. Experiment with result paths. Draw them on a flip chart or white board. Write the milestones on 'Post-It' notes and stick them on the paths, in the order they occur down the path. Experiment with different paths, and review them as suggested above. Note this may change the definition of the areas of work.
5. Draw the logical dependencies, starting with the final objective and working back. This may cause you to review the definition of milestones, add new milestones, merge milestones, or change the definition of the result paths.
6. Make a final drawing of the plan.

Work breakdown structure
The milestone plan, as shown in Figure 5.4 is a communication tool to communicate the project strategy to the parties involved. It represents both the work and its logical relationship. However, we should not lose sight of the fact that we are developing level 2 of the WBS. Figure 5.5 shows the WBS tree, to that level for the CRMO Rationalization Project. It is this representation of the work, coupled with the logic in the milestone plan, which may be used to derive the more formal precedence network (Figure 5.6) when scheduling the project.

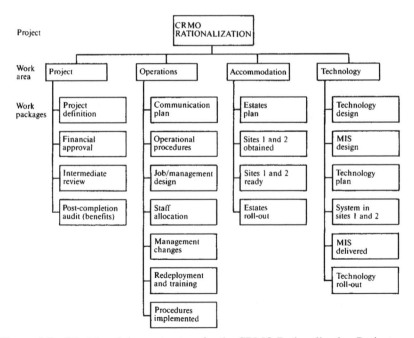

Figure 5.5   Work breakdown structure for the CRMO Rationalization Project

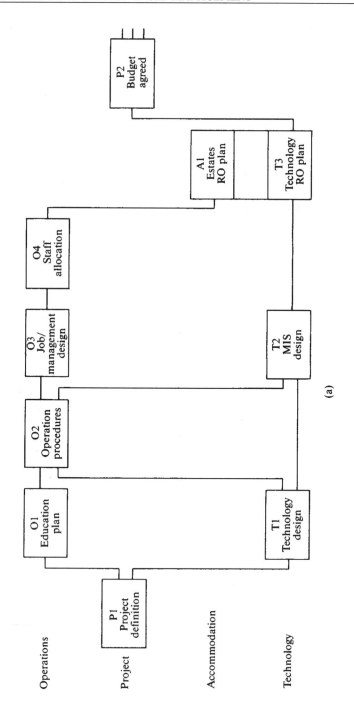

(a)

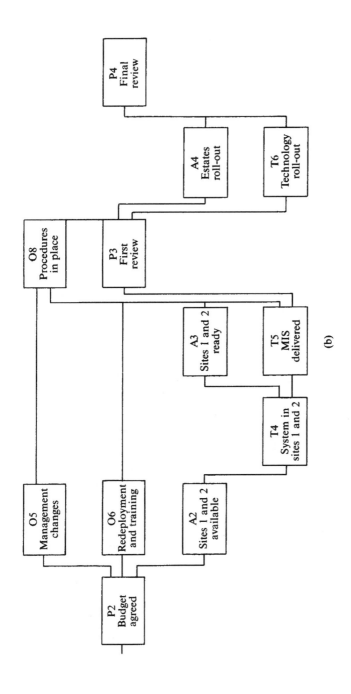

Figure 5.6 Precedence network for the CRMO Rationalization Project

5.5 Planning at lower levels

The plan at level 2, the milestone plan, is part of the WBS and will therefore be supported by plans at lower levels. These will include:

– activity plans
– work-package scope statements
– subsidiary milestone plans.

Activity plans

These detail the work packages which lead to the milestones. They describe the work at the next level of work breakdown, level 3. Following the principle of single-page reporting, the number of activities making up a work package should be limited to 15. I usually find 6 to 10 is about right. This again determines the size of activities. Figure 5.7 is an activity plan for milestone P1 in the CRMO Rationalization Project.

There are some project management methodologies which recommend that a full definition of all the activities required by the project be derived before any work is done. Those people who misuse networking systems, creating the activity definition without the supporting WBS, are forced into this. However, most modern approaches to project management recommend what is called a *rolling-wave* approach to activity planning.[4] Fully detailed activity plans are only derived and maintained for those work-packages which are current, or about to start. The detailing of later work packages is left until necessary, so that as much current information as possible is used to derive the activities. Some computer-based networking packages will support this approach by allowing the nesting of networks. There are several reasons for this approach:

1. You wait until you know you are likely to do the work before expending effort on detail planning. I spoke above of increasing the accuracy of the estimates during subsequent stages of the life cycle by spending increasing time on planning and design. To prepare estimates at project initiation stage you should estimate at the work-package level, and not prepare the activity definition. Some people find this uncomfortable, but I have worked in organizations which have prepared quite detailed designs and estimates for projects, only to find the project uneconomic.

2. You prepare detail activity plans when you have maximum information. If you prepare a detail plan for a year-long project at the start, the only thing you can guarantee is that you will be wrong. You will have left out things which should be included, and included things which should be left out. It is better to prepare the detail activity definition when you have gathered information about the best way to achieve the milestone. This is

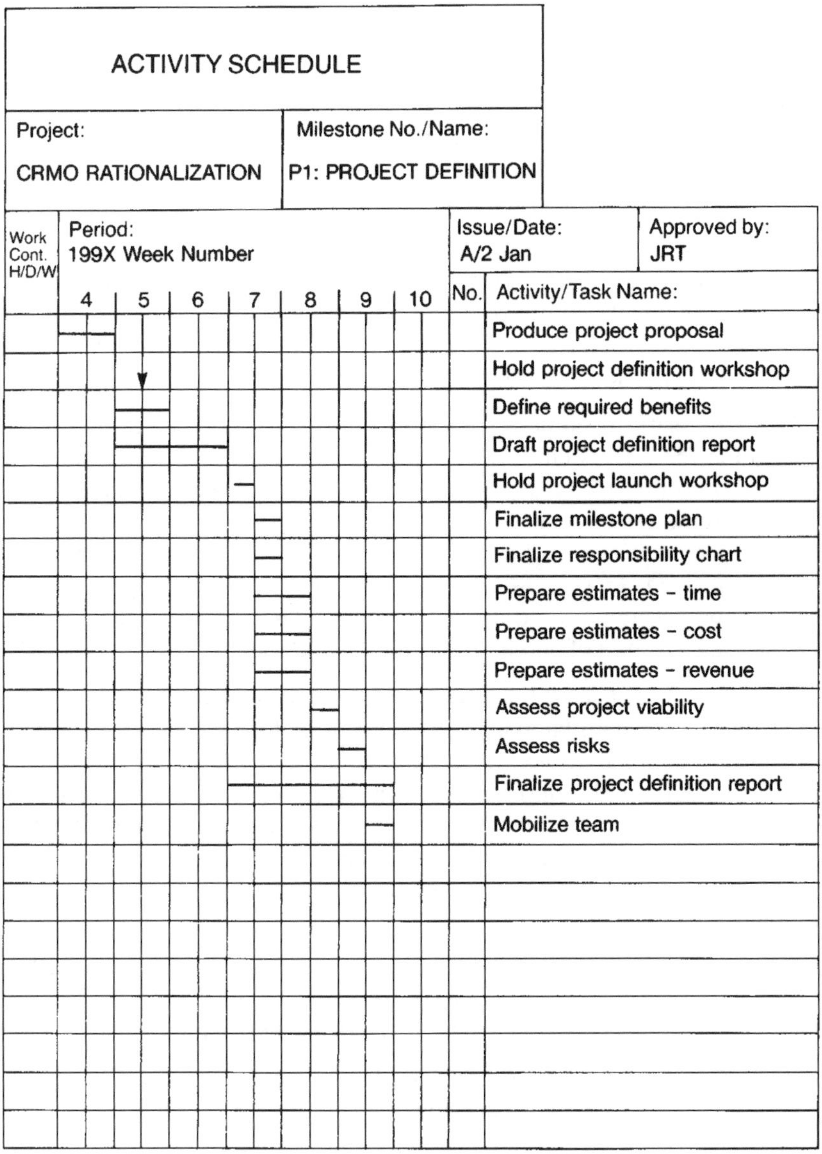

ACTIVITY SCHEDULE

Project:	Milestone No./Name:
CRMO RATIONALIZATION	P1: PROJECT DEFINITION

Work Cont. H/D/W	Period: 199X Week Number							Issue/Date: A/2 Jan	Approved by: JRT
	4	5	6	7	8	9	10	No.	Activity/Task Name:
									Produce project proposal
									Hold project definition workshop
									Define required benefits
									Draft project definition report
									Hold project launch workshop
									Finalize milestone plan
									Finalize responsibility chart
									Prepare estimates – time
									Prepare estimates – cost
									Prepare estimates – revenue
									Assess project viability
									Assess risks
									Finalize project definition report
									Mobilize team

Figure 5.7　Activity plan for milestone P1 in the CRMO Rationalization Project

especially true on development projects, where work in the early stages will determine work in the latter stages. You will know what the later milestones are, if you are to reach your final objective, but you will not know how they are to be achieved. Furthermore, there is no point in trying to guess, because it serves no purpose, and wastes time.

3. You can delegate the definition of activities to reach a milestone to the teams who will be undertaking the work, as described before.

Work-package scope statements

Although the detail activity planning is done on a rolling-wave basis, it is necessary to prepare some definition of the scope of each work package at an earlier stage. There are several reasons for this:

1. It is necessary to prepare some form of estimate of work content and duration for early, high-level estimating and scheduling. This should be based on some substance, even if it is only an approximate statement of the most likely outcome.
2. Work packages may include activities with a long lead time. These must be recognized and started in time.
3. While preparing the milestone plan you may not include one milestone, assuming it is part of another. This must be recorded.

These requirements can be satisfied by preparing work-package scope statements. These will be akin to the definition of scope and areas of work for the project as a whole, but on a smaller scale. The milestone name, remember, defines the purpose and objectives of the work package. The work-package scope statement can also include a measure of completion for configuration management purposes (Chapter 7). Example 5.4 contains a sample work-package scope statement for milestone P1 in the CRMO Rationalization Project.

TRIMAGI COMMUNICATIONS BV
WORK-PACKAGE SCOPE STATEMENTS

MILESTONE: P1 – when the project plans have been prepared and resources assigned to the project.

SCOPE: The work package requires the preparation of high-level plans and estimates, to enable resource budgets to be prepared and their availability agreed.

POSSIBLE WORK: Identify key managers
                   Hold launch workshop

Finalize milestone plan and project responsibility chart
Estimate resource requirements and durations
Schedule resource requirements
Discuss requirements with managers
Plan and agree their availability.

Measure of completion	Project plans approved by the steering committee Resource managers sign agreements to resource availability.

Example 5.4 Work-package scope statement

Subsidiary milestone plan

Sometimes there is a milestone which requires a particularly large amount of work. You may want to define intermediate milestones as control points through that work, but there may be no natural milestone to use on the level of the milestones plan. It is not sufficient to define milestones such as:

SM1: when the work is 25 per cent complete

because that will not be measurable. In these circumstances it may be worth while to derive a subsidiary milestone plan for that package of work. In effect the work package is treated as a mini-project. Figure 5.8 is the

MILESTONE PLAN					Company: NORTHERN ELECTRONICS
Planned date:	Quality T	Computer Development C	External E	Documentation D	Project description: EVE COMPILER DESIGN
					Milestone:
06 Jun	T1				T1: When the team has agreed the plan and the procedures to be used to check the quality of the product. Milestone includes the order of intermediate builds.
20 Jun		C0			C0: Project start. Assume there is a rebuilt subset front end with most of the subset functionality. This is assumed stable enough as a basis for design.
27 Jun			E1		E1: When the requirement document and product-definition has been approved by the technical planning committee.
18 Jul	T2				T2: When the build procedures operate.
29 Aug	T3				T3: When test procedures operate, and have been used to check the grammar in the compiler against the ACVC tests.
29 Aug				D1	D1: When the user interfaces are defined and agreed. This includes only the language independent parts.
07 Nov		C1			C1: When the team agrees that the data structure definitions are adequate for further work (i.e. 'complete').
28 Nov		C2			C2: When the design of the modules is 'complete', i.e. adequate to write the case. Agreement is reached by reviews.
12 Dec	T4				T4: When the specification for all external modifications have been accepted by the relevant teams to do the job (debugger, linker and scheduler teams).
12 Dec				D2	D2: When the manual craft for the user interface has been written and reviewed.
31 Dec		C3			C3: End of Phase One.
01 Jan		C4			C4: Phase Two.

Figure 5.8   Milestone plan for developing a compiler language

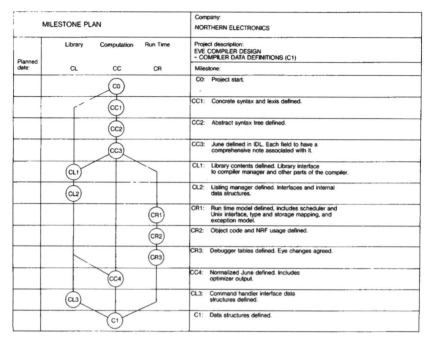

Figure 5.9   Subsidiary milestone plan for milestone C1

milestone plan for developing a compiler for a computer language. Milestone C1 is of the type described, requiring five months of work to achieve it. However, there are no natural milestones on the level of this plan to define control points through the work. The team therefore derived a subsidiary plan (Figure 5.9) for that milestone alone.

5.6 Applications

I close this chapter by describing two applications of milestone planning:

– milestone planning at different stages of the life cycle
– milestone planning of subprojects on large, multi-disciplinary projects.

Different stages of the project management life cycle
Milestone plans can be prepared for work at all stages of the project management life cycle. For instance, you can prepare plans for:

– the feasibility study in proposal and initiation
– the design study in design and appraisal

– project implementation in implementation and control
– commissioning in finalization and closure.

The management emphasis changes throughout each of these stages:

1. At the early stages, the emphasis is on encouraging creativity. The milestone descriptions should enable this by allowing maximum flexibility in the way the milestones are achieved, and the results delivered, while still providing a framework for control.
2. At the later stages, the emphasis will be on completing the work. Money is being spent, and so the benefits must be obtained as quickly as possible. Therefore the milestone names will be more prescriptive, providing more rigid control.

Large, multi-disciplinary projects
I have worked on several large multi-disciplinary projects which, for management purposes, we divided into several subprojects almost independent of each other, and each the responsibility of a separate discipline. The project team derived a milestone plan for each subproject, and each discipline was then able to work virtually independently of the others, corresponding only at key milestones. I have applied this approach to construction projects, development projects and IT projects.

NORTH SEA OIL FIELD DEVELOPMENT
This development consisted of two phases each of £3.0 billion. In the first phase, the project used ARTEMIS and planned at a fairly low level of detail. Management reports were 150 pages of computer output, and the management team had no visible control. In the second phase, it was recommended that they adopt a work breakdown structure. The development was divided into several contracts, and each contract into several stages, such as:

– feasibility
– design
– procurement
– construction
– link-up
– commissioning.

Figure 5.10 illustrates this work breakdown. A milestone plan was prepared for each contract stage. Figure 5.11 is an example of a typical plan. The management team monitored progress against the milestone plans. The project teams supported these with lower level plans.

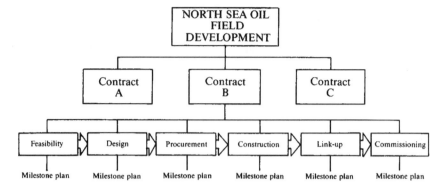

Figure 5.10 Work breakdown structure for the development of a North Sea oil field

REGIONAL HEALTH AUTHORITY, REGIONAL DISTRIBUTION

The Health Authority was changing from distributing supplies through each of the 15 districts, to regionally coordinated distribution. The project was divided into 22 subprojects, each with its own milestone plan, and each the responsibility of a separate discipline. There were a few, easily monitored links between each plan. The projects were:

– construction of the regional warehouse
– creation of the warehouse establishment
– implementation of computer systems
– recruitment, redeployment and training
– switching from district buying to regional buying
– switching from district revenue to regional revenue
– district implementation (15 districts)
– commissioning the warehouse.

Each discipline met once a fortnight to monitor progress against their plan. The team leaders then met every six weeks to monitor progress of the project overall, by comparing progress on each plan.

COMPUTERIZATION OF THE NORWEGIAN SECURITIES SERVICE

This project consisted of four subprojects:

– design and implementation of the computer system
– creation of a company to operate it
– registration of dealers and holders of stock
– legal basis.

An overall milestone plan was developed for the project as a whole.

MILESTONE PLAN

| | | | Company: NORTHERN ENERGY AND CHEMICAL INDUSTRIES PLC | | Project manager: | Contractor: | Contract no: |

| Engineering | Vendor selection | Procurement | | Project description: NORTH SEA OIL FIELD DEVELOPMENT – STANDARD PROCUREMENT CHAIN | | Plan issue: | Approved by: | Date: |
| E | V | P | | | | | | |

| | | | | Lead text: | Definition: | Project procedures: | | Contractor's procedure: |

Milestone	Lead text	Definition	Plan issue	Approved by
P1	Preliminary requirement raised	Transmittal of short package description with ref. to req. no. and pck. no. from engineering discipline to procurement.		
	Preliminary enquiry issued	Preliminary enquiry comprising short package description issued to approved vendors (by telex).		
V1	Bidders list approved	List of all approved bidders for package.	PS-CB30	PS-CA13
	Requirements for enquiry approved	Transmittal of provisional package with all necessary documentation attached.		PS-CA13
P2	Enquiry issued	A complete invitation to tender issued to approved bidders.	PS-CB31	
	Bid closure date	Deadline for bidders to submit tenders as stated in the ITT covering letter.	PS-CB32	
P3	Preliminary bid evaluation	Preliminary evaluation of bids by Engineering and Procurement. Joint recommendation compiled by Procurement.	PS-CB32	
V3	Bidders' short-list approved	Bidders short-listed from evaluation.	PS-CB32	PS-CA13
P4	Bid evaluation	Evaluation of bids by Engineering and Procurement. More information may be obtained from vendors. Joint recommendations compiled by Procurement.	PS-CB32	
V4	Recommended vendor approved	Vendor selected and approved.	PS-CB32	PS-CA13
	Purchase order requirements approved	Issue of revised requisition for purchase.		PS-CA13
P5	Purchase order issued to vendor	Issue of signed purchase order to selected vendor.	PS-CB33	PS-CA13
P6	Purchase order acknowledgement approved	Acknowledgement of purchase order received from selected vendor and approved.	PS-CB33	
P7	'Dear John' letters issued	Unsuccessful bidders informed of decision.		

Planned date:

Figure 5.11   Sample milestone plan for the development of a North Sea oil field

Subsidiary milestone plans were also prepared for the first two subprojects. This project involved one million people, and yet was managed to a successful conclusion using manual planning methods only by taking this structured approach. At one point the Norwegian government tried to delay passing the enabling legislation by twelve months. Using the top-level plan, the project team was able to demonstrate to the minister that that would delay the project by twelve months, and effectively kill it. The argument won the day and the bill was passed.

CUSTOMER SERVICE SYSTEM IN A REGIONAL SUPPLY COMPANY OF A LARGE
PUBLIC UTILITY
Implementation of the CSS required several projects:

- implementation of hardware and software
- transfer of data
- networking of buildings
- estates refurbishment
- writing operating procedures
- training
- commissioning.

Again, an overall milestone plan was developed, supported by milestone plans for each subproject.

You may notice that the last three of these projects involve a mixture of:

- construction or building work
- IT
- organizational change
- recruitment, redevelopment and training.

They each also had a duration of about 15 to 24 months, and each was finished on time and to cost.

5.7 Summary

1. The purpose of scope management is to ensure:
   - adequate work is done
   - unnecessary work is not done
   - to achieve the project's purpose.
2. Work breakdown is a process by which the work of the project is subdivided for management and control purposes.
3. The project is defined at the strategic level, through:
   - the *purpose*: the problem to be solved, or the opportunity to be exploited, or the benefit to be obtained

- the *scope*: the solutions to the problem, and covering the inclusions (work within the remit of the project) and the exclusions (work outside the remit, because it is deemed unnecessary, or because it is shared with other projects)
- the *outputs*: the facility to be measured, quantitative and qualitative measures of when the project is complete.
4. At the strategic level, the milestone plan:
   - shows how the intermediate products, or deliverables, build towards the final objectives of the project
   - sets a stable framework, fixed goal-posts, for the project team, and thereby provides a common vision
   - controls devolution of the management of the scope.
5. A good milestone plan:
   - is understandable to everyone
   - is controllable
   - focuses on necessary decisions
   - is logical
   - gives an overview to build cooperation and commitment of all the parties involved.
6. The are six steps in milestone planning:
   - agree the final milestone
   - brainstorm milestones
   - review the list
   - experiment with result paths (areas of work)
   - draw the logical dependencies
   - make the final plan.
7. Plans at lower levels of work breakdown include:
   - subsidiary milestone plans
   - work-package scope statements
   - activity plans developed on a rolling-wave basis.

References

1. Morris, P.W.G. and Hough, G.H., *The Anatomy of Major Projects: The reality of project management*, Wiley, 1987
2. George, D.J. (ed.), *A Guide to Capital Cost Estimating*, Institution of Chemical Engineers, 1988.
3. Andersen, E.S., Grude, K.V., Haug, T. and Turner, J.R., *Goal Directed Project Management*, 2nd edn, Kogan Page, 1995.
4. CCTA, *PRINCE 2: Project Management for Business*, The Stationery Office, 1996.

6
Managing project organization

6.1 Introduction

I now turn to the second mandatory project management function – managing organization. Without an organization there are no resources to undertake the project. Through the organization, the manager defines the type and level of resource input and how they are to be managed to achieve the project's objective. Once the organization has been defined, the project team can determine how much the project will cost and how long it will take, thus providing a baseline for managing quality, cost and time. The definition of scope and organization together make a contract between the project and the parent organization, that is between the contractor and owner in Figure 3.1. It is through the contract that project managers negotiate their authority.

6.2 Principles of project organization

The purpose of project organization is *to marshal adequate resources (human, material and financial), of an appropriate type to undertake the work of the project, so as to deliver its objectives successfully.* The use of the word 'adequate' implies that the resources should be of sufficient number, but only just sufficient: too few, and the organization will be ineffective and the project will flounder; too many, and the organization will be inefficient. This chapter focuses primarily on human resources, although material resources are considered at the end. Negotiating financial resources is beyond the scope of this book.[1]

In the next section, I recall the principles of managing the project organization, and the processes of negotiating a contract between project and business. I describe types of project organization available, including a range of line, matrix and versatile approaches. I shall introduce the *responsibility chart* as the primary tool for defining the project organization and negotiating the contract, and show that this satisfies the principle of single-page reporting. In order to agree the contract, the responsibility chart requires the manager to identify both the type of resource input and the level of effort, the *work content*. I shall describe how to incorporate estimates of work content and close the chapter by explaining the use of equipment and drawing registers to manage non-human resources.

Three of the five principles of good project management, introduced in Section 4.5, relate to managing the project organization:

– negotiate a contract between parties involved
– assign roles and responsibilities at all levels of work breakdown
– adopt a clear and simple reporting structure.

Organizing a contract

The organization breakdown structure (OBS) runs in parallel to the PBS. Table 6.1 shows the parties involved at the three fundamental levels. The project manager must organize a contract between the parties involved at all levels (Figures 1.14 and 3.1), that is:

– between the owner and contractor at the project level: the contract
– between the parties making up the contractor at the strategic level
– between the members of the project team at the tactical level.

It is also in the project manager's interest to ensure there is cooperation between the parties which make up the owner. This is usually beyond their responsibility, but not beyond their influence. The project manager negotiates the contract by building a clear mission or vision for the project, and cascading that mission down to objectives at each level of the OBS. Cooperation can then be gained by building a commitment to the objectives. The negotiation should go something like this:

– Do you believe that the purpose of the project is worth while?
– Do you believe that to achieve that purpose we need to achieve the identified end and intermediate objectives?
– Do you believe that it is the responsibility of your group to deliver some or all of those objectives?

Table 6.1   Three fundamental levels of organization breakdown

No.	Level	Resource type
1	Integrative	Company, department or group
2	Strategic	Function, discipline or section
3	Tactical	Named person, group of people or skill type

If the answer to the first question is 'no', the project manager needs to find some way of making the project of value to the people concerned. If the answer to the second question is 'no', you can involve the group of people in the planning process to gain their views. If the answer to the third question is 'no' then you can gain their opinion on whose responsibility it might be. If you cannot gain agreement on the second and third question, then you must doubt the groups answer to the first, and work further on making the project beneficial to them.

Defining roles and responsibilities

The contract is defined by defining roles and responsibilities of the parties involved for the work elements at each level of breakdown. Many project management systems focus on just one role: Who is to do the work? There are several roles and responsibilities on a project as listed in Table 6.2.

Table 6.2 Roles and responsibilities

Responsibility	Role
For work	Who is to undertake the project's tasks?
For management	Who is to take decisions? Who is to manage progress? Who is to guide and coach new resources?
For communication	Who must provide information and opinions? Who may provide information and knowledge? Who must be informed of outcomes?

Keep it simple

Below, I introduce the responsibility chart as a single-page document to define resources and their input. It defines the contract at all levels of breakdown (Figure 1.14), and is the document against which it is negotiated and agreed. The responsibility chart can be used to build cooperation and to ensure the novel organization of a project is brought into operation quickly and effectively. However, before describing the responsibility chart more fully, I describe the types of organization which can be used for managing a project.

6.3 Types of project organization

Selecting the type of project organization is the first step in its management, and is the step by which we develop the concept (Section 5.1). I consider first the overlapping of a project organization on a functional line management organization (Sections 3.4 and 3.5). There are two key issues when selecting a project organization in this environment:

– isolated vs integrated resources
– line vs matrix structure.

I shall then describe the trend towards versatile project organizational models. The Project Definition Report (Chapter 11), is used to define the type of project organization to be adopted, and to detail the organization breakdown structure.

Isolated vs integrated resources
The first issue is where to locate the project resources. There are two extremes (Figure 6.1), each of which have their advantages and disadvantages. Resources can be:

– isolated from operations by being placed in a task force
– integrated with operations by working on the project from their normal place of work.

Isolated: The advantages are that the project team member can work without distraction and on secret work. The disadvantages are that users seconded to the team lose contact with normal operations, users not seconded mistrust the project, operational managers are reluctant to release their best people, and it is inflexible (Example 6.1).

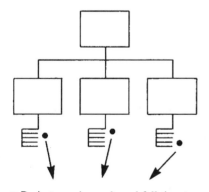

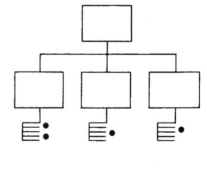

● Project members released full time to a separate project room

● Project members work in their normal environment

(a) Isolated

(b) Integrated

Figure 6.1   Locating resources

Integrated: The advantages and disadvantages above are reversed. To be successful this requires the manager to give his subordinate space to work on project tasks, the individual to focus on the task at hand without distraction, and the environment not to impose on the individual while working on project tasks.

Intermediate positions are possible, giving advantages of both models. Individuals seconded part time to a project can be given a quiet room, close to their normal place of work, to use while working on the project.

A public utility adopted this approach for the design and development of their integrated customer database system. People were seconded from the districts into a central design team. The development process took two years, at the end of which time the design was two years out of date. Furthermore, many users seconded to the development team were given temporary promotions. When they returned to operations they expected their promotions to be made substantive, but were often less use to their districts than before they left as their experience was now also two years out of date. However, the alternative, the integrated team, is extremely unlikely to have delivered the design in anything like two years, so the isolated approach was the only option.

When I described this story to a group of Russian managers on a course at Henley Management College, they said the people should have taken greater responsibility for managing their own careers! When I described it to a group of managers from the utility, one of them said he had been a member of the task force, and he had tried to manage his career, but still his earlier boss did not want to know. He changed districts.

Example 6.1 Isolated project teams

Line vs matrix structure

There are two extremes for creating an OBS. At one extreme an existing functional hierarchy within the parent organization is used, and the PBS is massaged so that responsibility for delivering products falls wholly within the realm of resource units within the line management structure. This gives a project organization in which the OBS, PBS and WBS are aligned with the functional hierarchy (Figure 6.2(a)). At the other extreme a natural WBS is developed, independent of the organization with dedicated multi-discipline resources assigned to the delivery process – production in the PBS. This gives a project organization in which the OBS and WBS are both aligned with a project hierarchy (Figure 6.2(b)). Both of these structures are inflexible.

Overlapping the two structures gives a matrix structure in which people have both project and functional responsibility (Figure 6.3). It is now common to consider five types of project organization,[2] with three types of

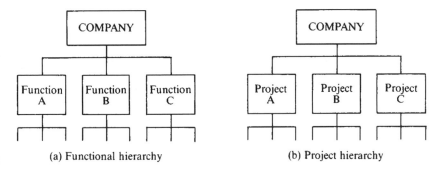

(a) Functional hierarchy   (b) Project hierarchy

Figure 6.2   Line organizations

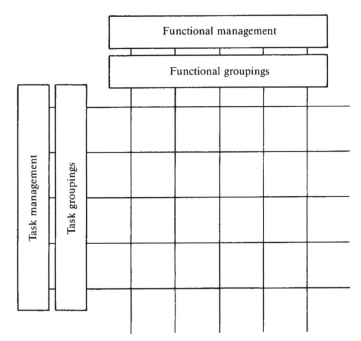

Figure 6.3   Matrix structures

matrix structure between the two extremes (Figure 6.4):

– functional hierarchy
– functional matrix
– balanced matrix
– secondment matrix
– project hierarchy.

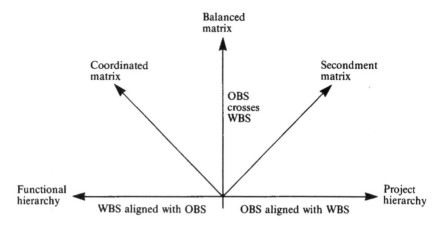

Figure 6.4　Range of matrix structures

Functional hierarchy: Project tasks are assigned to relevant operational areas, whose managers take responsibility for achieving tasks in their area. Unfortunately, different managers may have different views on the priority of the project, and so one area may be delayed by lack of support from another.

Coordinated matrix: Functional managers assign work to people day by day. A project controller is appointed with responsibility for coordinating tasks between functions, but with limited authority for ensuring priority is given for resources. Having responsibility but no authority is an impossible position.

Balanced matrix: A project manager is appointed to oversee the project and they share responsibility with the operational managers. The project manager is responsible for time and cost, the operational manager for scope and quality. The balanced matrix is probably difficult to maintain, depending on the relative strengths of the project and operational manager. By default it may become either a functional or a secondment matrix.

Secondment matrix: The project manager has primary responsibility for resources, and assigns their work day by day. The operational managers second personnel, full- or part-time to the project as required, and oversee the quality of the work done. The project manager now has more effective control, but the users begin to lose influence over the project's outcome.

Project hierarchy: The project manager manages a dedicated project team, and the operational managers have no involvement. The project manager now has total control, but the users have lost all influence, and this structure is inflexible.

You may have an idea about which of these five structures gives the most successful outcome of projects in your industry. The balanced matrix is probably the ideal, giving the project manager control, while maintaining user involvement. However, it depends on the relative strengths of the project and operational managers. Gobeli and Larson[2] surveyed a large number of projects, and, subject to the discussion of Chapter 4, judged whether or not they were successful. Their results are illustrated diagrammatically in Figure 6.5. They split projects into two types: development projects and implementation projects.

DEVELOPMENT PROJECTS

The three project structures are almost equally successful, with the secondment matrix slightly ahead. The purpose of development projects is to define the products of future projects and of the organization as a whole. Therefore, user involvement is also important to gain their acceptance of the end product. It is also difficult to predict the resource requirements and so flexibility is important. The secondment matrix allows greater user involvement than the project team, and provides some flexibility while still maintaining control.

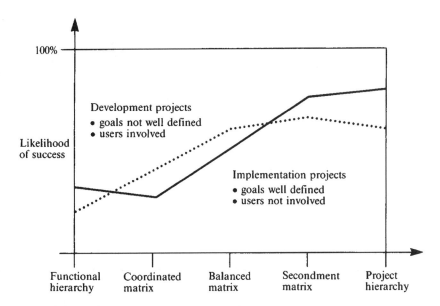

Figure 6.5   Project success rates

IMPLEMENTATION PROJECTS

The project hierarchy is very successful, with the secondment matrix close behind. On implementation projects the size of the team can be accurately forecast, so inflexibility does not matter, and the product is defined so user involvement is reduced. Furthermore, the project team can build a commitment to a common goal. This commitment may also explain the rise in effectiveness of the functional hierarchy. I also think that the straight line from the functional matrix to the secondment matrix shows that the balanced matrix will become one or other depending on the relative strengths of the project and operational managers.

In spite of this, Example 6.1 is a case where the project approach was used for development stage and the functional approach for implementation. However, that was appropriate in those particular circumstances.

The versatile organization

The foregoing discussion has described how to overlay a project organization on to an existing functional, hierarchical, line-management structure. Up until the early 1990s, this represented the vast majority of organizations. It may still represent a simple majority of them, but many are now project based, and some have adopted flexible, versatile approaches.[3,4,5] Indeed, Gareis[5] has argued that matrix organization structures will not work for reasons outlined in Sections 3.4 and 17.5.

In the pure project-based organization, the firm does away with the functional hierarchy, and people belong to project teams only. This was a popular approach in the late 1980s, and many people presenting papers at the IPMA World Congress in Vienna described how their organizations had adopted this approach and reported great success. However, I wondered at the time how many would still be reporting success one or two years later. For reasons outlined below, it is not possible to do away completely with the functional hierarchy, as many of the speakers claimed to have done. There is a syndrome, called the 'Hawthorne effect', that says if you make a change, efficiency will improve because people will be learning the new ways of working, and taking an interest.[3] You can only judge the true impact of a change after a new equilibrium has been reached, which may take several months.

Peymai and I suggested[3] the adoption of a versatile organization (Figure 6.6) based on Peymai's experience implementing total quality management in a medium-sized construction company, and IBM's experience changing their organization structure at their European headquarters in La Defense, Paris. In the versatile organization, most people belong either to process teams or project teams. Both types of team are the primary medium by

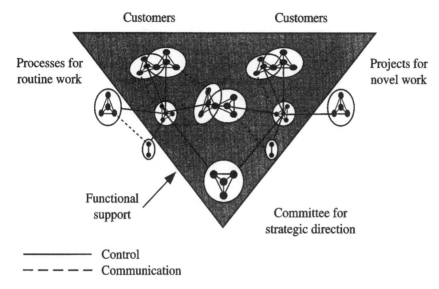

Customers   Customers

Processes for   Projects for
routine work   novel work

Functional
support   Committee for
                                     strategic direction

————————— Control
— — — — — — Communication

Figure 6.6   The versatile organization

which work is done for and products delivered to customers. Process teams
do fundamentally routine work, whereas project teams do fundamentally
novel work. However, the size and composition of both types of team is
constantly changing. The project teams are unique, novel and transient. But
even the process teams need to change as customers' requirements, though
fundamentally repetitive, can still vary. The idea of some quality advisers
that an organization's procedures can be unchanging is quite absurd
(Chapter 7). Different customers have different requirements and hence
processes and procedures need to constantly adapt, and, indeed, since
quality is about continuous improvement, they must be constantly
enhanced. As the size and composition of teams change, people move
between them. In the versatile organization, the process teams effectively
operate as a coordinated matrix and the project teams as a secondment
matrix. However, essentially in the versatile organization people have only
one boss; they either belong to a team, in which case they take their
instructions from the team leader, or they are in the functional organization,
in which case they take their instructions from the functional manager. The
advantages of the versatile approach are:

– the size and composition of the teams can be changed in response to
  changing customer requirements, enabling the organization to re-engineer
  its capabilities quickly
– it provides a process focus; the organization's procedures are written to

describe how it processes products to satisfy customers' requirements, not how functions perform, again enabling responsiveness to changing customer requirements
- people have one boss, avoiding the problems of split loyalties outlined in Sections 3.4 and 17.5
- it retains the functional organization, avoiding the problems outlined below which arise with the pure project-based approach.

It is essential to retain the functional organization. IBM at their European headquarters reduced the size of the functional organization by 90 per cent, not by making people redundant, but by assigning them to teams. IBM at their South African headquarters in Johannesburg tried to do away with the functional organization completely and suffered for it. British Telecom, as the result of an organizational change they called Project Sovereign, adopted a project-based organization structure.[3] However, in their new structure 70 per cent of the work is project based, and 30 per cent functionally based. (When you investigate what they mean by project based it includes process teams (Example 1.1).)

The reasons for retaining the functional organization are:

- it provides a career structure; transient teams cannot provide a career, just learning experiences as part of one's development
- it retains the knowledge of the organization
- it develops new systems and procedures; systems and procedures are an overhead, and each project manager will try to minimize the cost of his or her project and so not develop new systems
- it can share people between projects when they are only partly utilized
- it can provide a resting place between projects; the chance of one project starting as another ends is slight, and so between projects people can spend time capturing their knowledge.

Without a functional organization structure, in time the organization loses its knowledge and culture, and withers and dies.

6.4 Responsibility charts

The use of responsibility charts to define the project organization is now widespread.[6,7] Typically a chart is a matrix with deliverables shown as rows and organizational units as columns (Figure 6.7). Symbols are placed in the body of the matrix to represent the involvement of each resource type in the work element required to produce the deliverable. The matrix can be used at any level of breakdown. This provides a one-to-one correspondence between the levels in the PBS and the OBS (as one might expect). Even

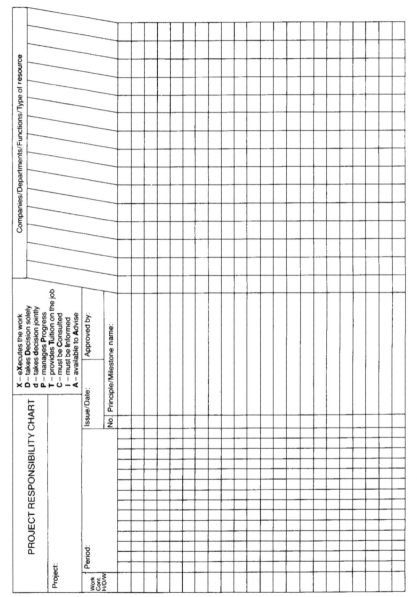

Figure 6.7 Blank responsibility chart

though the responsibility chart is a matrix, it can be used to describe any one of the five organization types, or any mixture of them or it can be used with the versatile organization. The use of a responsibility matrix does not imply a matrix organization. I have often encountered mixed organization types, but particularly a project line surrounded by a coordinated matrix.

Use of symbols to describe types of involvement
Cleland and King[7] give examples of the use of numbers, letters or geometric shapes to represent the type of involvement. When Grude and Haug[6] first developed their chart they used geometric shapes, but found eventually that the use of letters was more natural. When facilitating project launch and definition workshops (Chapter 11), I find the use of letters which suggest the role or responsibility helps aid communication. I would therefore recommend the use of the eight letters developed by Grude and Haug[6] to represent eight types of roles and responsibilities (Table 6.3). I find that these cover most requirements.

Table 6.3   Types of role and responsibility

Letter	Role or responsibility
X	eXecutes the work
D	takes Decision solely or ultimately
d	takes decision jointly or partly
P	controls Progress
T	provides Tuition on the job
C	must be Consulted
I	must be Informed
A	available to Advise

The symbols are used as follows:

1. *Responsibility for work*
   X: eXecutes the work: this is self explanatory.

2. *Management roles*
   D: takes Decision solely or ultimately
   d: takes decision jointly or partly

There are various modes of decision making (Table 6.4). An example of D2 might be the selection of a financial management system. The financial manager agrees it meets the company's financial requirements. The IT manager agrees it meets the company's systems strategy. If they fail to agree, the decision is referred to the financial director, their joint

Table 6.4 Four modes of decision taking

Decision mode	Person			Description
	A	B	C	
D1	D	–	–	A takes the decision alone.
D2	–	d	d	B and C share the decision. If they agree, the decision stands. If not, it is referred up the usual management channels.
D3	D	d	d	B and C close options and recommend. A has the ultimate authority.
D4	D	d	C	C's opinion must be sought (but can be ignored). B closes options and A has the ultimate authority.

boss. In decision D3, there can be a fine line between being consulted, C (as shown in decision D4), and truly closing options, d. This may be the case with the trade union representatives with no authority but significant disruptive power. You have to use the symbols to represent the way you want to manage your project.

P: controls **P**rogress: this is the person responsible for ensuring that the work is planned, organized, implemented and controlled. The project manager is ultimately responsible, but uses the symbol to delegate responsibility at lower levels of the WBS.

T: provides **T**uition on the job: this assumes that the people doing the work do not have sufficient skill, so they are coached on the job. As their skill grows the 'T' may change to a 'P'.

3. *Communication channels*
C: must be **C**onsulted. These people must be consulted in the course of the work. They have information or opinions which the project must take account of in doing the work and taking decisions. However, they do not have decision-taking responsibility: their opinions can be ignored.

I: must be **I**nformed. These people must be provided with information about the outcome on one part of the project to enable them to do work or take a decision on another part.

A: available to **A**dvise. These people may have information or opinions which the project team may want to use, but cannot know until they reach that part of the project. In effect, the symbol represents 'may be consulted'.

'C', 'I' and 'A' control the flow of information. If people feel they should be consulted or informed that is negotiable as part of the contract.

The symbols must be used flexibly and imaginatively. Nothing is served by being pedantic. The project team paint the picture they want, and use the chart as a communication tool. For instance, in a training course is the trainer 'T' and the tutee 'X', or is the trainer 'X' and the tutee 'I'? It does not matter as long as everybody understands.

Use of the responsibility chart

The responsibility chart can be used at all levels of the breakdown. In particular it can be used at the three fundamental levels as follows:

PROJECT LEVEL: PROCEDURAL RESPONSIBILITY CHART

At this level the chart is used to define procedures, principles or policies for managing the project. For example that may be:

– procedures for monitoring and control
– change control procedures
– quality control procedures
– configuration management procedures.

Figure 6.8 is a procedure for monitoring and control. A time chart is used to define a regular cycle throughout the project. The resources at this level are companies, organizational units (departments, groups, sections), or management functions (finance director, IT manager, project manager). It is important that people are described by their roles. If the R&D manager is also project manager, and has responsibilities as both, they should appear as both. If they leave part way through the project, they may be replaced by one person as R & D manager, and another as project manager. Procedural responsibility charts may be included in the Project Definition Report and Manual (Chapter 11).

STRATEGIC LEVEL: MILESTONE RESPONSIBILITY CHART

At this level the chart is used to define roles and responsibilities for achieving milestones. Figure 6.9 is a chart for the CRMO Rationalization Project. The resources at this level are the same as above. This leads us to using the same version of the form for both, and calling it a project responsibility chart. Sometimes both milestones and procedures are included on the same page. This is why these two levels were merged into a single, management level in Figure 1.14. Figure 6.9 also includes a time schedule. I discuss scheduling in Chapter 9.

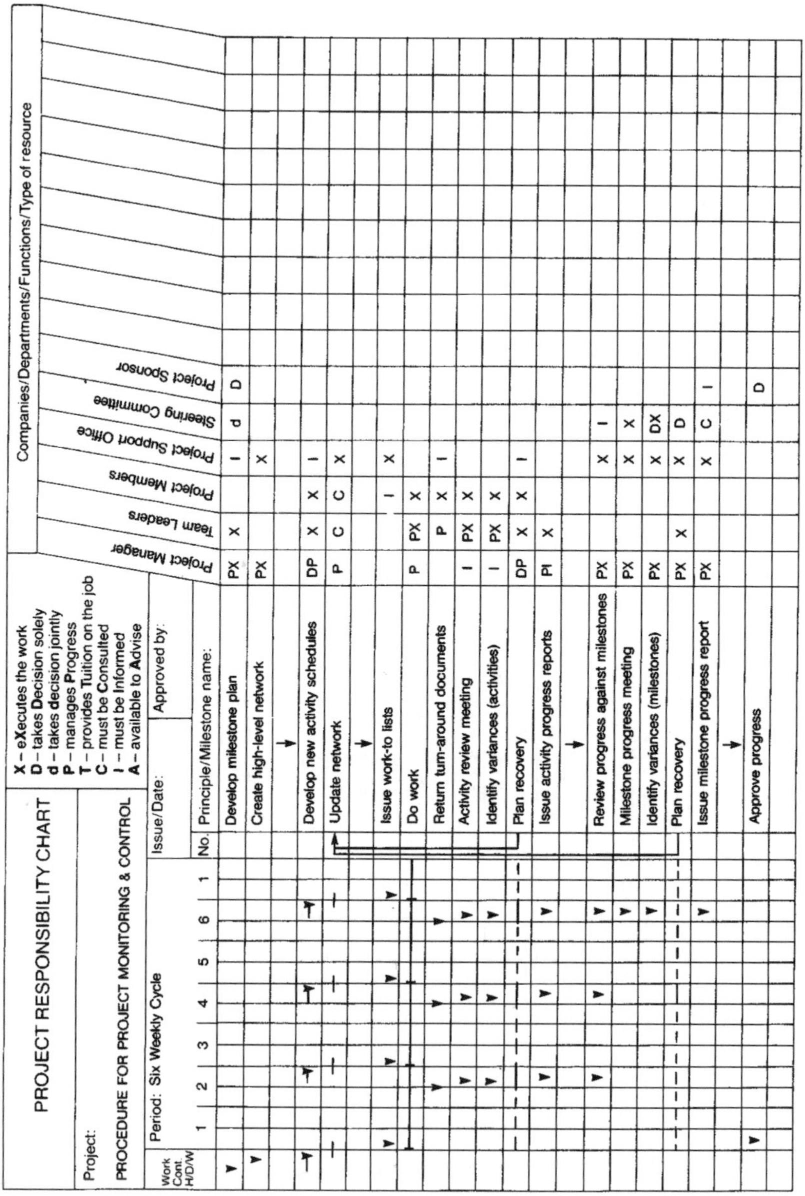

PROJECT RESPONSIBILITY CHART

Project: _____

PROCEDURE FOR PROJECT MONITORING & CONTROL

Issue/Date: _____   Approved by: _____

Period: Six Weekly Cycle — 1 2 3 4 5 6 1

Work Cont. H/D/W

X – eXecutes the work
D – takes Decision solely
d – takes decision jointly
P – manages Progress
T – provides Tuition on the job
C – must be Consulted
I – must be Informed
A – available to Advise

Companies/Departments/Functions/Type of resource

No.	Principle/Milestone name	Project Manager	Team Leaders	Project Members	Project Support Office	Steering Committee	Project Sponsor
	Develop milestone plan	PX	X		I	d	D
	Create high-level network	PX			X		
	Develop new activity schedules	DP	X		I		
	Update network	P	C	C	X		
	Issue work-to lists		PX	I			
	Do work	P	P	X			
	Return turn-around documents		PX	X	X		
	Activity review meeting	I	X	I			
	Identify variances (activities)	I	PX	X	I		
	Plan recovery	DP	X	X			
	Issue activity progress reports	PI	X	X			
	Review progress against milestones	PX			X	I	
	Milestone progress meeting	PX			X	X	
	Identify variances (milestones)	PX			X	DX	
	Plan recovery	PX			X	D	
	Issue milestone progress report	PX			X	C	
	Approve progress				I		D

Figure 6.8   Procedural responsibility chart for monitoring and control

PROJECT RESPONSIBILITY CHART

Legend:
- X – eXecutes the work
- D – takes Decision solely
- d – takes decision jointly
- P – manages Progress
- T – provides Tuition on the job
- C – must be Consulted
- I – must be Informed
- A – available to Advise

Project: CRMO RATIONALIZATION
Issue/Date: Approved by:
Period: 199X — 199Y

Companies/Departments/Functions/Type of resource

No.	Principle/Milestone name	Regional Board	Operations Director	CRMO Managers	CRMO Team Leader	CRMO Staff	Project Manager	Project Support Office	Estates Manager	Estates	Network Manager	Networks	IT	Operations	Personnel	Suppliers
P1	Project Definition	D	d	dX	dX	I	PX	X	X	I	X	I	C	C	C	A
O1	Communication plan	I	D	d	PX						PX	X	C	C	TX	
T1	Technology design	I	D								X	X	X			
O2	Operational procedures	I	D	d	PX	C		X				X	C	C	TX	
O3	Job/Management design	I	D	d	PX	X					PX		X			
T2	MIS Functional spec.	I	D	d	dX	C		X					X			
O4	Staff Allocation	D	d	d	PX	C	C	X	XP	X	C			—	—	C
A1	Estates roll-out plan	D	d	C	X		C	X	C	X	C	—	—	—	A	C
T3	Technology roll-out plan	D	d	X			PX	X	C		PX	X	C	A	—	C
P2	Financial approval	I	d					X			C					
O5	Management changes		DX	X	C		P		PX		—				TX	
A2	Sites 1 and 2 available		I	—	PX	I					PX	X				X
O6	Redeployment/Training		I	I	—	X					P	X				
T4	Systems in sites 1 and 2		I	—	X	X				X		A	X	—		
A3	Sites 1 and 2 ready		D	—	X		P		A	X	A	X	X	A	X	X
T5	MIS delivered		D	I	X				—		—		A	—	—	
O7	Procedures implemented	D	d	PX	X		PX	X	A		PX	X	A	A	X	X
P3	Intermediate review	D	d	C	C	X	PX	X	—		PX	X	A	A	A	X
A4	Roll-out implemented	I	D	dX	dX	X	PX	X		X	P	A	X	A	X	X
P4	Post completion audit (benefits)	D	d	C	C		PX	X			PX	X		C		

Figure 6.9   Project responsibility chart for CRMO Rationalization Project

At this level the chart defines the roles and responsibilities of named people to do work to achieve a milestone. Because Activity Schedules are prepared on a rolling-wave basis during implementation planning, the people involved can now be named. They are unlikely to change on the time scale of a work package, and if they do the work should be replanned. Furthermore, because the activities are now more certain, more effort can be put into ensuring that the chart is correct. Figure 6.10 is an activity schedule for milestone P1 in the CRMO Rationalization Project.

Developing the responsibility chart

I described in Section 5.5 how the milestone plan is best developed in a group working session, specifically at a project launch or definition workshop, Chapter 11. The same applies to the responsibility chart. It is very effective to copy the blank form on to an acetate, project it on to a white board, and then complete it with the team participating. Entering the symbols directly on to a paper form can isolate members of the group, with the result that they may not accept the end product. However, I find that if everyone is involved, then when they allow a symbol to remain under their name, they internalize the result, and accept that as their responsibility. Estimates and schedules can be entered on the projected form in the same way.

6.5 Incorporating work content

In negotiating the contract between project and business, it is necessary to include estimates of the resource requirements. Functional managers cannot commit to releasing resources without knowing what the requirement is. I explain here what consumes resource, describe how to communicate the estimates as part of the contract, and end with a cautionary remark about accounting for lost time. Estimating work content, and using that to calculate duration, is covered in Chapters 8 and 9.

Consumption of resources

Two of the eight roles and responsibilities primarily consume resource:

X: eXecutes the work
C: must be Consulted.

Many project management methodologies only include estimates of the former. However, the latter can consume as much if not more resource and must therefore be included in the estimate. The four management responsibilities are overhead resources and are considered to be part of the

ACTIVITY SCHEDULE

Project: CRMO RATIONALIZATION   Milestone No./Name: P1: PROJECT DEFINITION

Period: 199X   Issue/Date: A/2 Jan   Approved by: JRT

Key:
X – eXecutes the work
D – takes Decision solely
d – takes decision jointly
P – manages Progress
T – provides Tuition on the job
C – must be Consulted
I – must be Informed
A – available to Advise

Companies/Departments/Functions/Type of resource

No.	Activity/Task name	Regional Board	Operations Director	CRMO Managers (2)	CRMO Team Leader	CRMO Staff	Project Manager	Project Support Office	Estates Manager	Estates	Network Manager	Networks	IT	Operations	Personnel
1	Produce project proposal	C	D	d	dX		PX	A	A		A		A	A	A
2	Hold project definition workshop	C	DX		X		PX	X							
3	Define required benefits	C	D	d	dX		PX	X	I		I		I	I	I
4	Draft project definition report	C	D	d	dX		PX	X							
5	Hold project launch workshop		D	X	d	X	PX	X	X		X		X	A	C
6	Finalize milestone plan		D	d	d		PX	X	C		C		C	A	A
7	Finalize responsibility chart		D	d	d		PX	X	C		C		C		A
8	Prepare estimates – time				A		P	X	A		A		C	A	A
9	Prepare estimates – cost			A	A		P	X	A		A		A	A	A
10	Prepare estimates – revenue		A	A	A		P	X	A		A		A	A	A
11	Assess project viability		D	d	d		PX	X	C		C		C	C	C
12	Assess risks		D	d	d		PX	X	C		C		C	C	C
13	Finalize project definition report	D	D	d	dX	I	PX	X	X	I	X	I	IX		I
14	Mobilize team														

Work Cont. H/D/W — Week Number 199X: 4 5 6 7 8 9 10

Figure 6.10   Activity schedule for milestone P1

holders' day-to-day duties. Therefore, estimates will usually not be included. The main exceptions to this will be where T refers to the involvement of a trainer, or an external consultant whose bill will be charged to the project. D and d should consume little time if they are limited to decision taking as opposed to decision making. Unfortunately, I often come across decision takers who want to repeat the decision-making process. With the other two communication roles, it should consume little time until the person starts work, especially if the reports are well constructed, and A is not certain to consume resource. An allowance may be made.

Communicating the estimate

There are several ways of communicating resource estimate, using:

– the responsibility chart
– estimating sheets
– resource histograms.

The responsibility chart: This can be used in one of two ways. There is a column at the extreme left-hand end of the chart, and this has been used in Figures 6.9 and 6.10. This will refer to the X and C resource. Alternatively, the estimates can be written in the body of the matrix (Figure 6.11).

Estimating sheets: These are commonly used for preparing the resource estimates. Figure 6.12 is an estimating sheet for the work package P1: Project Definition from the CRMO Rationalization Project, prepared on a PC using a spreadsheet. These can also be used to communicate the estimates. The use of estimating sheets is described further in Chapter 8.

Resource histograms: These provide a visual picture of the estimates (Figure 6.13). However, they require a schedule for the work elements, and so are discussed further in Chapter 9 where examples are given.

Accounting for lost time

When agreeing resource availability, the project managers and resource providers must have the same understanding of how much time is actually required. It is quite clear that one man-day means a day's work by one person. But how much work is a man-year, 260 days or something less? Figures quoted in man-weeks, man-months and man-years are usually interpreted as a statement of both resource requirement and duration; that is how many people are needed for how long. They therefore should include an allowance for the fact that somebody working on a project full time is not available 5 days per week for 52 weeks per year. Time is lost through sickness, holidays, training, group meetings, etc. This lost time is said, on average, to be 30 per cent of the

PROJECT RESPONSIBILITY CHART

X – eXecutes the work
D – takes Decision solely
d – takes decision jointly
P – manages Progress
T – provides Tuition on the job
C – must be Consulted
I – must be Informed
A – available to Advise

Project: HARPENDEN FACTORY - CENTRE DEVELOPMENT

Issue/Date: A 14 Dec 87   Approved by:

Period: FY 9X | FY 9Y | FY 9Z

Companies/Departments/Functions/Type of resource — *Resources in Man Days*

No.	Principle/Milestone name	H/den - Quality	H/den - Accounts	H/den - CIB	H/den - Personnel	H/den - Engineering	H/den - Production	H/den - Factory Manager	H/den - Centre Mgt	Engineering	Finance	Quality	MIS	Contractors	Consultants	R & D
ST1	Define structure	1	1	1	1	1	1	1								
PE1	Determine message	1	1	1	1	1	1	1	1							
PE2	Change attitudes	5	3	4	12	25	26	1	20							
PE3	Select managers	1	1	1	1	1	1	1	15							
SY1	Write job outlines	3	2	2	6	13	13	1	15							
SY2	Determine crewing	5	5	5	5	5	5	5	10							
PE4	Determine redeployment/recruitment	1	1	1	1	1	1	2	6		2	2	3	25	2	
ST2	Define factory facilities	5	5	5	5	5	5	1	20		10		10	25	2	
PE5	Define training programme	2	2	4	20	4	2	5	15		10		40	5		
SY3	Decide cost control information	2	20	20	1	2	1	20	25							
SY4	Specify computer systems	4	2	10	2	5	1	5	15	1113				large		
ST3	Build facilities	20	10	10	15	20	2	15	60							
SY5	Implement revised cont sys.	1	1	1	50	20	1	2	200			3		25		
ST4	Share rev. cost cont. resp.	2	2	2	15	2	2	2	45					25		
PE6	Recruitment	25	15	20	50	50	10	5	3					5		
PE7	Training	15	15	15	15	15	2	1	3							
PE8	Achieve minimum staffing	1	1	1	1	1	1	1	3							
ST5	Transfer personnel resp.	1	1	1	1	1	1	1								3
ST6	Transfer engineering resp.															
ST7	Transfer quality resp.															
ST8	Achieve centre management															

Figure 6.11 Responsibility chart showing resource usage

ESTIMATING SHEET		TRIMAGI COMMUNICATIONS BV				02-Jan-9X

PROJECT:	CRMO Rationalization	CODE:	C1	ISSUE:	A
WORK AREA:	Project	CODE:	C1P	AUTHOR:	LJN
WORK PACKAGE:	Project Definition	CODE:	C1P1	APPRVD:	JRT
ACTIVITY:	....	CODE:	....	DATE:	02-Jan-9X

ACTIVITY/TASK		WORK CONTENT			RESOURCES				9 People	
		No of steps	Effort/ step	Total effort	Prjct Mgr	Prjct Offc	CRMO TL	CRMO Mgrs	Ops Direct	Other Mgrs
Number	Description	(days)	(days)		1	1	1	2	1	3
1	Produce project proposal	1	4	4	1	2	1			
2	Hold project definition workshop	1	4	4	1	1	1		1	
3	Define required benefits	1	2	2	1		1			
4	Draft Project Definition Report	1	8	8	2	6				
5	Hold project launch workshop, 1.5 day duration	1	12	12	1.5	1.5	1.5	3		4.5
6	Finalize milestone plan	1	2	2	1	1				
7	Finalize project responsibility chart	1	2	2	1	1				
8	Prepare estimates – time	20	0.1	2		2				
9	Prepare estimates – cost	20	0.1	2		2				
10	Prepare estimates – revenue	1	1	1		1				
11	Assess project viability	1	1	1	1					
12	Assess risks	1	3	3	1	1	1			
13	Finalize Project Definition Report	1	5	5	2	3				
14	Mobilize team	1	3	3	0.5	0.5	0.5			1.5

		SUB-TOTAL:	51	13	22	6	3	1	6
TOTAL EFFORT:	56 DAYS								
TOTAL COST: £K	22.22	ALLOWANCE %	10	10	10	10	10	10	10
DURATION:	DAYS								
TARGET START:		TOTAL EFFORT:	56	14	24	7	3	1	7
TARGET FINISH:									
		UNIT RATE: £K/day	0.5	0.3	0.3	0.5	0.8	0.5	
		COST: £K	7.15	7.26	1.98	1.65	0.88	3.30	

Figure 6.12   Estimating sheet for milestone P1: *Project Definition* from the CRMO Rationalization Project

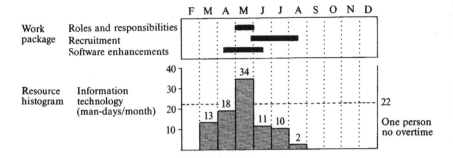

Figure 6.13   Resource histogram

working year. When converting from man-days to man-weeks, man-months or man-years I would suggest you use the following ratios:

- 5 × 0.7 =   3.5 man-days/man-week
- 22 × 0.7 = 15.5 man-days/man-month
- 52 × 3.5 = 180 man-days/man-year.

If you are employing a labourer from a contractor, you can clearly expect a person on every day you want one. If the person you had one day is not available the next, a replacement can be sent. The contractor accounts for lost time in the rates charged. The same is not true for professional people. It is very inefficient for an engineer or software programmer, or training professional to hand over part way through the design of a programme.

You must also not double account. Having used these ratios, an individual is available 260 days per year. For instance, if you have a resource calendar which allows you to account for individual holidays, you should use a ratio of 0.8, which gives 4.0 man-days/man-week, 16.5 man-days/man-month, and 210 man-days/man-year. (A resource calendar is a calendar which identifies working days and rest days during the life of a project. It can also identify the number of hours worked per day. There can be resource calendars for the project as a whole, for individual resources within it, and for different geographical locations.)

6.6 Equipment and drawing registers

Up to this point I have focused on human resources. Other types of resources include:

- drawings representing the designs of material, plant and equipment
- materials to be consumed in the delivery of the facility

- plant and equipment to be used, but not consumed, doing the work of the project
- finance to pay for the project.

Finance is beyond the scope of this book.[1] Drawings, materials, plant and equipment are often managed using lists or registers. These are lists of the resources against each activity in the project. Maintaining these in an electronic database, enables the project manager to monitor the delivery of the resources against the start date of the activity. Often, the resources go through several stages of development before final delivery. For instance, drawings go through:

- functional, systems and detail design
- various iterations and stages of sign-off of the drawings

and materials go through:

- production of drawings
- procurement
- manufacture
- assembly
- delivery
- kit marshalling.

On a small project, these steps may be included as activities in the project plan. However, on larger projects this can be cumbersome. The stages of development are then monitored in the registers, effectively as separate packages of work. Standard or known lead times are used to work out the due date for completion of each step, from the start date of the activity in which the resource is used.

Shortly before the start of an activity, the material register becomes a kit-marshalling list. This is used to check that all the materials required for the activity have been delivered, and to collect them together, so that they are ready for use when the activity starts.

6.7 Summary

1. The purpose of project organization is:
   - to marshal adequate and appropriate resources
   - to undertake the work of the project
   - to successfully deliver its objectives.
2. The principal tools and techniques of organization management are:
   - the contract between the parties involved
   - organization breakdown structure, matching work breakdown

– responsibility charts.

3. There are two issues in choosing a project organization for a functional parent organization:
   – location of resources
   – type of organization structure.

4. The versatile organization provide a more flexible approach to creating project organizations.

5. There are five types of organization structure:
   – functional hierarchy
   – functional matrix
   – balanced matrix
   – secondment matrix
   – project hierarchy.

6. Eight types of role or responsibility are suggested for use in the responsibility chart:
   – **X**   e**X**ecutes the work
   – **D**   takes **D**ecision solely or ultimately
   – **d**   takes **d**ecision jointly or partly
   – **P**   controls **P**rogress
   – **T**   provides **T**uition on the job
   – **C**   must be **C**onsulted
   – **I**   must be **I**nformed
   – **A**   available to **A**dvise.

7. The contract requires recording of estimates of work content, so that resource providers can commit to release of their people.

8. Drawings, materials, plant and equipment are managed using registers, lists against the activities in which they are required.

References

1. Turner, J.R. (ed.), *The Commercial Project Manager*, McGraw-Hill, 1995.
2. Gobeli, D.H. and Larson, E.W., 'Project structures versus project performance', in *Proceedings of the 11th INTERNET International Expert Seminar*, H. Schelle (ed.), INTERNET, 1987.
3. Turner, J.R., Grude, K.V. and Thurloway, L. (eds), *The Project Manager as Change Agent*, McGraw-Hill, 1996.
4. Turner, J.R., 'The versatile organization: achieving centuries of sustainable growth', *The European Management Journal*, October 1997.
5. Gareis, R. (ed.), *The Handbook of Management by Projects,* Mohr, 1990.
6. Andersen, E.S., Grude, K.V., Haug, T. and Turner, J.R., *Goal Directed Project Management*, 2nd edn, Kogan Page, 1995.
7. Cleland, D.I. and King, W.I. 'Linear responsibility charts in project management', *The Project Management Handbook*, D.I. Cleland and W.I. King (eds) Van Nostrand Reinhold, 1988.

7
Managing quality

7.1 Introduction

The last two chapters described two mandatory project management functions: managing scope and project organization. Let us now turn to three secondary functions or constraints: managing quality, cost and time. Contrary to common practice, they will be addressed in that order, which is the order I believe they should be addressed in first project definition (Figure 1.13).

This chapter addresses quality. I start by considering what we understand by good quality in the context of projects. I then introduce a five element model for achieving good quality, and describe each element of the model. I consider whether quality is free on a project, and then describe configuration management, which I believe is the key tool of project management for delivering the quality and functionality of the project's outputs. I end the chapter by describing other tools used in the management of quality.

7.2 Quality in the context of projects

It is frequently said that a project is successful if it is finished on time, to cost and to quality. We all understand how we measure cost and time, but very few people understand what they mean by good quality in the context of a project. Indeed, in spite of it being stated as one of the major three criteria of project success, surprisingly little is written about it.

There are several possible definitions of good quality on a project. The project is said to be good quality if the facility or project's output:

– meets the specification
– is fit for purpose
– meets the customer's requirements
– satisfies the customer.

Meets the specification: The facility is produced in accordance with the written requirements laid down for it. The requirements can be specified on several levels, mapping on to levels of the PBS: customer, functional, system and detail requirements. The requirements may specify engineering or technical design standards applied within the organization. (The word specification tends to be used for something which is project specific and provides standards for something which applies to all projects undertaken by the organization.) The specification may also set requirements for the time and cost of the project, needed to make it viable, and also set specific parameters for the service levels required to be met by the facility. Finally there are the various 'abilities of the facility: availability, reliability, maintainability, adaptability, etc. . . .

Is fit for purpose: The facility, when commissioned, produces a product which solves the problem, or exploits the opportunity intended, or better. It works for the purpose for which it was intended.

Meets the customer's requirements: The facility meets the requirements the customer had of it. Here we mean what the customer thinks they require, the thoughts they had, not the way they interpreted their thoughts as words, and not the way those words got written down as a customer requirements specification.

Satisfy the customer: The facility and the product it produces actually makes the customer feel satisfied. Now there is also a difference between satisfying the customer, 'That's all right then', and delighting the customer, 'That's wonderful'. If you can delight the customer at very little extra cost, then obviously you should try to do that. However, if that is going to make your project significantly unprofitable, then clearly you should aim only to satisfy the customer. If you still cannot make a profit, you need to massage the customer's expectations to make them more realistic.

Questions
These four definitions of quality raise several questions.

DO THEY MEAN THE SAME THING?
The answer to this is quite clearly 'no'. I implied above that the concept the customer had, and what was written as the 'customer requirements' specification are almost certainly not the same thing. Human fallibility being what it is, the chances of the customer being able to vocalize their actual requirements is vanishingly small, and the chances of the project team writing down what the customer says, let alone capturing the customer's unvocalized concepts, is also vanishingly small. Thus delivering

the specification does not necessarily mean you meet the customer's requirements. The chances of the customer being able to solve their problem initially is also small, as is the chance of the project team doing that. Hence, what the customer thinks they require and what is written into the specification at the first attempt are unlikely to coincide, and it is very likely that the specification will not be fit for purpose. Finally, even if it works, and even if it meets the specification, and even if it is what the customer actually required, they may still have had some totally different concept, and so may be left feeling dissatisfied.

WHAT THEN IS THE CORRECT DEFINITION OF QUALITY?
The widely accepted definition of good quality is now taken as delivering project objectives that are fit for purpose, that is that they achieve the desired result. It is not slavishly delivering the specification, if what is specified will not work, and it is certainly not following predefined business processes, if those processes deliver a product that will not work.

DOES THIS MEAN WE HAVE TO CHANGE THE SPECIFICATION?
'Yes', is the simple answer. This is one of the two great dilemmas of project management. There are traditional project managers who say good project management is freezing the specification on day one of the project and then delivering it come what may. In my view, it is not good project management if the end product does not deliver the desired result. On the other hand, if you change the specification frequently, you will never finish the project, and that is most definitely not good project management. Hence, you must be willing to change the specification as you become aware that your original proposal is less than perfect, but changing it is something you must do sparingly and with great ceremony. Later in this chapter I describe *configuration management*, a technique by which the specification can be refined in a controlled manner as the project progresses to ensure that, by the end of the project, its products produce the desired results.

WHO IS THE CUSTOMER?
The customer may be:

– the sponsor, or owner of the facility
– the operators of the facility, or users of the services it provides
– the consumers of the eventual product it produces
– the media, or local community, or politicians.

The answer is that they are all the customer, and all their requirements must be satisfied. They will usually have different requirements and to satisfy them all will be a difficult juggling act. The owners must be willing to pay for it. The operators must believe it will work; they can make failure a self-fulfilling prophecy. The consumers must want to buy the product. Configuration management can also be used to try to gain agreement from the various parties (warring factions) as the project progresses.

DO YOU GIVE THE CUSTOMERS WHAT THEY WANT OR WHAT THEY NEED?

This is another dilemma, but less significant. The attitude in the 1970s of British engineers was to give customers what they needed, not what they wanted, that they knew better than their customers what the latters' requirements were. This arrogant attitude led to the demise of many British industries. It is arrogant to think you know better than your customers, it is arrogant to think you are unfailingly correct. By the late 1980s, this attitude had changed. It now did not matter what trivial whim the customers had, the 'customer was king', give them what they ask for. On the one hand, you give customers what you think they need. They look at the product and say, 'That's not what we asked for', and refuse to use it. On the other hand, you give them what they say they want. When it does not work, you say, 'The customer is king', and they say, 'But it was your duty to advise us it would not work'. The way out of this dilemma is that you must use configuration management so that by the end of the project what the multi-headed customers now think they want, what they actually need and what you think they need are the same thing.

WHAT IS THE DIFFERENCE BETWEEN GOOD QUALITY AND HIGH QUALITY?

To consider the difference between good quality and high quality, ask your self the question:

Is a Rolls-Royce a good quality motor car?

A Rolls-Royce is a high-quality, well-engineered car. However, if you want a car that is economical to run, easy to manoeuvre in tight city streets, and easy to park, is a Rolls-Royce a good-quality car? If you want a car that can drive off the road, across farmland, and survive a collision with a kangaroo, is a Rolls-Royce a good-quality car? If you want a car that represents your status as a successful manager, is a Rolls-Royce a good-quality car? The answers are probably no, no and no. It is important not to over-engineer the product, but to produce something that satisfies, even delights the customer, but is good value for money to achieve the project's goals. Often something which is over-engineered will not delight the customer because it will not work.

7.3 Achieving quality on projects

Figure 7.1 is a five element model for managing quality on projects:

– two elements represent what we must manage the quality of: the product and the management processes
– two represent how we manage their quality: through quality assurance and quality control
– the fifth represents the attitudes of the people involved.

Quality of the product is the ultimate goal. It is the product which satisfies all the criteria in the previous section, and which influences attitudes for years to come, long after the project is finished.

Quality of the management processes is also a significant contributor to the quality of the project's product. Following well-defined, previously proven, successful ways of doing things increases the chance of success; designing new project management processes at the start of every project increases the chance of failure. We shall see below, that this means developing procedures for the organization to be used as flexible guidelines, not rigid rule.

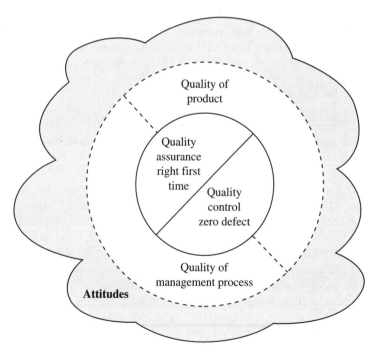

Figure 7.1   Total quality management of projects

Quality assurance is preventive medicine, steps taken to increase the likelihood of obtaining a good-quality product and management processes. It is about trying to get it *right first time.*

Quality control is curative medicine, which recognizes human fallibility and takes steps to ensure that any (hopefully small) variations from standard which do occur are eliminated. This is about trying to get it *right every time*, with *zero defects.*

Good attitudes is essential to successful project management. We saw this under strategy in Section 4.5. I used to tell Example 7.1 as a joke or apocryphal story, but somebody on one of my courses said it once happened to him. The commitment to quality must be at all levels of the organization, it cannot be delegated downwards, or pushed upwards. In the days when quality circles were popular, people implementing them had top-down teams and bottom-up teams to emphasize this point.

An organization ordered a batch of capacitors from a Japanese company, and specified that there should not be more than 0.5 per cent faulty capacitors in the batch. The consignment arrived in a big box and a small box. They started testing the capacitors in the big box and found they were all perfect. They then tested the capacitors in the small box and found them all to be faulty. At that point they realized that the small box was 0.5 per cent of the consignment!

Example 7.1 Eliminating the culture of expecting failure

Assuring the quality of the product
In order to assure the quality of the product it is beneficial to have:

CLEAR SPECIFICATION
Without a clear idea of what is to be achieved, the team has no direction. It is possible to specify both the end product of the project, and the intermediate products: milestones resulting from work packages; and deliverables of the activities at lower levels. The lower the level at which the deliverables are specified the tighter the control. However, there are risks associated with a highly detailed specification: it may be inconsistent; it may confuse rather than clarify; and the lower level products may become an end in their own right, rather than a means of achieving the facility. It is possible that if the client overspecifies, the contractor can meet the specification, but not satisfy the client's purpose.[1] *Cardinal points procurement*[2] attempts to overcome this.

The next three are about trying to maximize the use of previous experience.

USE OF DEFINED STANDARDS

These are standard designs and packages of work which, from previous experience, are known to be able to deliver results of the required specification. One of the great differences between the project environment and a routine manufacturing facility is that, in the latter, each day's production becomes a standard against which to improve the next day's production. In a project environment it may be some years before you repeat a process, and then the environmental conditions may be different. However, the use of standards will be beneficial in the long run.

HISTORICAL EXPERIENCE

Hence, the greater the historical experience, the better will be the standards and specification. For this reason, it is not always possible to create a clear specification of R&D, high technology and organizational development projects. However, the more historical data that are used the better. In the next chapter it will be shown that there is a clear learning curve in industries with time, with it taking perhaps 50 years to build up a credible body of data.

QUALIFIED RESOURCES

If the people used on the project have access to that body of data, either through their own experience or training, then that makes them better able to apply standards and achieve the specification. This applies equally to professional staff (engineers, IT staff, researchers, trainers, managers) and artisans (electricians, mechanics, programmers). It is common in the engineering industry to put artisans through strict testing procedures before allowing them to do critical work. The use of qualified resources also applies to material and financial resources, but these can be tested against the standards.

IMPARTIAL DESIGN REVIEWS

The use of auditors to check the design can help to assure that the customer's requirements are properly met. You may think that this is insulting to the design team, but there is ample evidence that people find it very difficult to discover their own mistakes (Example 7.2), and hence the use of auditors, sometimes called the red, pink or blue teams, to check that the design is satisfactory. However, you need to check that you do not overdo it. There are apocryphal stories about auditors outnumbering the project team, and since they are there to find fault, they tend to find it where none exists: the design may be adequate but not perfect.

Psychologists have done experiments in which they have shown people pictures that get progressively out of focus, and ask the people to identify them. In this way, they establish how far out of focus the picture has to be before people will identify it wrongly more often than not. They then show people pictures that are well out of focus, and ask them to identify them, and then slowly bring them back into focus. The picture has to be brought into focus well beyond the point at which a person would normally make a correct identification before an incorrect identification will be changed.

This happened during the incident at Three Mile Island in the 1980s. In the plant there was one instrument which should have been indicating a fault, but was not working because it was faulty. A second alarm started and the operators made what would have been a correct diagnosis of the fault based on that one, and not on the first, and reacted accordingly. A third alarm started which should have told them that their diagnosis was wrong, but they continued to react according to their original one. It was some time before they changed their diagnosis, after several alarms were indicating something different. (They reacted in time to avert a major accident. Nobody was hurt. This is interesting, because Three Mile Island was a nuclear station the incident remains seared on our brains, whereas the Piper Alpha disaster, which killed about 250 people when an oil platform exploded, is slipping into distant memory. We will return to the irrationality of risk assessment in Chapter 10.)

Example 7.2 Discovering ones own mistakes

CHANGE CONTROL
This is vital to achieve the specification where change is necessary. It does not mean that changes are eliminated, because that can result in a product that does not meet requirements. The purpose of each change must be carefully defined, the impact on the design assessed, and the cost compared to the benefit, so only those changes that are absolutely necessary and cost-effective are adopted.

Controlling the quality of the product

Quality control is a process of diagnosis and cure. As the facility is erected and commissioned it is checked against the specification to ensure that it is of the required standard, and any variances are eliminated. There are four steps in the control process (Figure 7.2):

– plan the work required, and do work to deliver results
– monitor the results achieved
– compare the results to the plan, to calculate variances
– take action to eliminate variances.

The quality plan for the project's product means understanding how every deliverable at all levels of the PBS will be judged to have been achieved. The work-package scope statement introduced in Section 5.5 had space for entering the criteria for judging achievement of the milestone. I usually say that the specification for the overall facility (the client requirements and functional specifications) should run to several pages, that for each milestone (in the systems specification) should be half a page, and that for the deliverable of each activity (the detail specification) should be a couple of lines. I was challenged on this on one course. The delegates said it should be the exact opposite. The specification for each activity should be a couple of pages, and for the facility a couple of lines. The point they were trying to make is that if you get the detail right, there is no need to check the overall facility. This is right, but it seems a recipe for a bureaucratic nightmare to me.

Monitoring results and calculating variance means checking the specification of each deliverable as it is achieved. It is important to do this from the start, from the earliest activity for the earliest milestone. It is no good waiting until the end of the project, and then finding a mistake was made on the first day. Mistakes must be identified as they occur, hence the comments from the delegates above.

Taking action from the start will build up a momentum for success that will be carried through the project.

There is a major difference here between project and operations. In an operation where you are doing something repetitively, once the process is

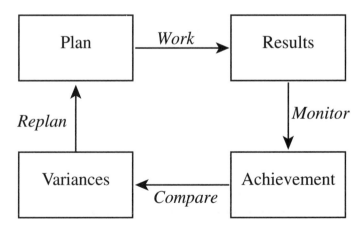

Figure 7.2   Four-stage control cycle

set up correctly, it will usually not go wrong suddenly. The process will drift. Hence you tend to monitor sparingly, using processes such as *statistical process control*. This may involve the destructive testing of, say, every 100th product. Once the process is working, the emphasis is on quality control. On a project you cannot destructively test every 100th product, you only do it once, so wrong once is wrong every time. This shifts the emphasis much more on to quality assurance, and quality control at early stages of the project as described.

Assuring the quality of the management process
To assure the quality of the management processes, a similar list as that for the product applies, which means having a set of defined procedures for managing projects. Procedures clearly specify how projects are to be managed by qualified resources, and are derived from standards based on historical experience. They may be derived from the company's own experience, or based on standard procedures.[1,3] Many client organizations have their own procedures which they require their suppliers to use, and regularly audit contractors against them.

It is essential that the procedures are used, and this requires three things: they should not be bureaucratic; they must be sensible; and they must have management commitment. Experience shows[4] that the procedures should describe how the organization processes product, not what the functions of the organization do (Example 7.3). The procedures should also be flexible guidelines, not rigid rules. This means that if the customer requires something different, then the procedures should be changed to meet their requirements, not the requirements changed to meet the procedures. This can be achieved in a controlled way by having a procedure for changing the procedures, and by project teams regularly developing a quality plan as part of start-up. Finally, at the end of every project the procedures should be reviewed to see how well they served the project, and the organization's procedures updated if necessary. Quality is about continuous improvement, not compliance to 20th century ways of working.

The procedures are often based on the ISO quality standards, a complete list of which are in Table 7.1 at the end of the chapter. The use of procedures manuals is described in Chapter 15.

Peymai was quality manager for a medium-sized construction company during implementation of BS5750. At first they wrote their procedures to describe how each function of the organization worked, design, procurement, site construction. Quality fell as the departments argued between themselves about what was and was not their respective responsibilities. Nothing is perfect, but departments would not cover gaps in the procedures, particularly where the product was handed over between them, because that would make them 'non-compliant'. Further, where a customer required the design department, say, to do something unusual, they would refuse saying it would make them 'non-compliant'. The company reimplemented BS5750, writing their procedures to describe how they processed an order, and importantly making departments responsible for working together at hand-over, and insisting that the project specific procedures should be derived from the generic procedures, but taking account of the particular requirements of the project. Quality went up.

Example 7.3 Procedures for process versus function

Controlling the quality of the management processes
The method of monitoring the management processes is through project audits. An audit is a detailed check of the operation of the management processes against standards of good practice, such as the organization's procedures manual or that of an external agency. (Audits are described in Chapter 16.)

The quality plan
At the start of the project, the manager should draw up a quality plan to define how quality will be achieved, how the company's procedures will work on this project, and how the manager intends to assure and control quality. In qualifying the procedures, it may contain new ones where items are either not covered or inadequately covered for this project in the overall procedures, and may include such things as: disputes, documentation, reporting mechanisms, customer liaison, etc. For the quality control process, it may contain a detailed activity and resource plan. The quality plan may form a section of the Project Definition Report (Chapter 11).

7.4 Configuration management[a]

Configuration management is a technique used to manage the refinement of the specification and work methods on development projects. The technique was first developed in the US defence industry during the early 1950s to track the versions of components as they were configured in the facility, and to control changes as they occurred. In particular, where several prototypes are being developed, configuration management tracks the design, or configuration, of each prototype. It has now become a desirable, if not essential, tool to control the functionality and quality of components in the product breakdown, and work methods in the work breakdown, to be used on software, technology, engineering or organizational change projects.

So what is configuration management, and how can the control of configuration be of use in a development project? Configuration management controls the specification of the product breakdown structure, it expresses the facility delivered by a project, as a configuration of component parts. The configuration can take various forms: a car, space shuttle, design, plan, software system, training programme, organizational structure. Each component may then be regarded as a configuration in its own right, made up of other components. This process, of course develops the bill of materials, or product breakdown, of the project. Figure 7.3 illustrates the concept using a book as the configuration. The components are chapters: the subcomponents sections; etc.

Configuration management is not a radical discovery that revolutionizes the way the facility is developed and maintained. It is a set of good working practices for coping with uncertainty and change and gaining commitment of the projects participants as the design evolves. Many projects use elements of configuration management, especially in the application of change control. However, to be effective, it must be a systematic, consistent approach to managing change on complex projects. From the outset, structures must be put in place to support it. These include specified individuals with responsibility for configuration management, and procedures supported by senior management. It also involves all project participants. There may be one or more project review boards, with responsibility for approving the specification of the facility, and to approve changes to the specification. Depending on the size and complexity of the project, there may be a group of people dedicated to the function of configuration management.

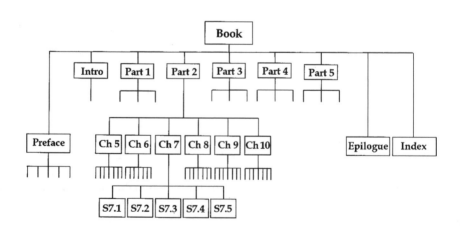

Figure 7.3   Configuration of a book

Basic approach

Figure 7.4 illustrates the basic approach to configuration management. In line with the goals and methods matrix (Figure 1.15), we accept that there may, at the outset of the project, be some uncertainty about the specification of the project's deliverables, and some uncertainty about the methods of delivering them. Rather than trying to pretend that this uncertainty does not exist, that these things are precisely prescribed, it is better to accept the lack of clarity, and manage the refinement of our understanding.

So at the start of the project we write the specification of the deliverables and the work methods as best as we are able, and then agree that specification with the multi-headed client: sponsors; owners; operators; users, marketing representing the consumers. We agree that the eventual solution lies somewhere within the large rectangle, but we do not know where. We then start work on the project, and refine our understanding. At a predetermined review meeting, we sit down with the multi-headed client and agree the current status. We repeat the process and hopefully get agreement as we home in on the eventual solution. Perhaps at a review meeting one or more of the participants disagrees with the current status. In that case, one of two things has happened: either the previous specification was not correct, or the work to go from the previous position to the current

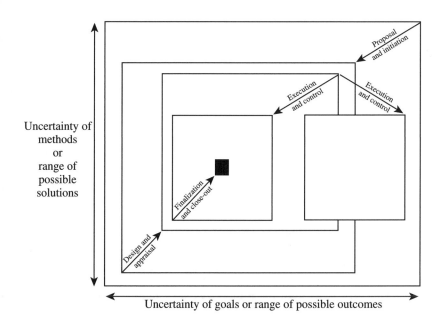

Figure 7.4 The basic approach to configuration management

one was wrong. In the former case, we need, through change control, to change the specification. With luck, if the problem is found early enough, the change can be made at little or no extra cost. If the change is made very late in the day, it can be inordinately expensive. If the latter is the case, we need to go back and repeat the work. Both of these are anathema to traditional project managers: changing the specification, or doing extra work at additional cost and time. However, at the end of the day, you have to ask yourself whether it is better to finish according to arbitrary time and cost targets, or produce something that works. On some projects (the Olympic Games, Project Giotto) the time is imposed by external constraints and so must be achieved. But on many projects it is better to take a bit longer and pay a bit more to deliver something that works.

Implementing configuration management

Implementing configuration management requires the definition of tasks to be performed and procedures to be adopted. The tasks must be allocated, which requires the organization to be established, responsibilities assigned, and appropriate recourses (people, money, equipment, accommodation) deployed. The appropriate procedures depend on the specific project, its size and complexity, but typically configuration management comprises four processes:

- configuration identification
- configuration reviews
- configuration control
- status accounting.

CONFIGURATION IDENTIFICATION

Configuration identification is the process of breaking a system into its component parts, or *configuration items*, each of which can be individually documented and placed under change control. Ideally, each configuration item will have maximum cohesion; that is, it would not be useful to subdivide it further for the purpose of documenting it or controlling changes to it. Also, the configuration items will have minimal coupling; that is, it would not be useful to merge two or more items to form a single item for documentation and change control (Example 7.4).

In its simplest form, configuration identification involves locating all the configuration items required to deliver the facility so that nothing is overlooked, and then establishing the information to keep track of those items throughout the life of the project. Most systems can be broken down using a hierarchical product breakdown structure (PBS). When the system has been broken down to its lowest level, the resultant configuration items form the project inventory, or bill of material. All deliveries and revisions are tracked and controlled against two forms of configuration item recording: the planned set of items and the produced/approved set. The identification of the sets of items should cover the entire development cycle for both the facility and the supporting documentation. The definition and recording provided will support the activities of configuration control and status accounting. A complete list of all configuration items will be derived from the design specification. The configuration is complete when all items have been delivered. If extra configuration items are delivered, or some are not delivered, then this will only be acceptable if the design specification, and therefore the list of items, has been amended accordingly.

When I was writing this book, my list of configuration items was the list of section headings, as recorded in the table of contents (Figure 7.3). However, I must admit that the sections did not conform precisely to the principles of cohesion and decoupling. In this chapter, the definition of the section headings was quite stable. In others, Chapter 5 and 6 for instance, the definition changed as I wrote the chapter. The chapter was perhaps therefore the configuration item. Some chapters were not configuration items on their own. Chapters 14, 15 and 16 were reconfigured as I wrote the book.

Example 7.4   Configuration identification

CONFIGURATION REVIEWS

Configuration control procedures manage the movement of configuration items from one stage of the life cycle to the next, through formal review processes conducted at the end of each stage. At the end of the initiation stage, the first configuration review audits that the specifications are:

– *up to date*: they accurately reflect the concept of the product
– *complete*: all the configuration management documentation that should exist at this point in the life cycle actually does exist
– *agreed*: they have the support of all the project's participants.

At the conclusion of this stage, a requirements definition is produced, as part of the Project Definition Report (Chapter 11) and reviewed, approved, baselined and handed over to configuration management before it moves on to the design and appraisal stage. Similarly, at the end of design, the design specifications are produced, as part of the project requirements definition or project manual, which are again reviewed, approved, baselined and handed over. Once the configuration identification moves into execution, it evolves from documentation into actual deliverables, whether physical or abstract. These are again reviewed at the end of this stage, to draw up the list of outstanding items for finalization and close-out, and yet again at the end of this last stage, before the documentation is archived as the *as-built design*. Configuration management is the central distribution point for each stage of the life cycle of the project, but it becomes more critical during the last stage, finalization and close-out, as the facility is tested and commissioned.

CONFIGURATION CONTROL

Controlling the baselined configuration items through each stage of the life cycle is the basis of configuration management. The project depends on the baselined items and the record of any changes. Periodically during the life of an item, the baseline may need to be revised. It should be revised whenever it becomes difficult to work with the baseline documentation and authorized changes to it. All authorized changes to the documentation should be consolidated, as should those relating to any authorized repairs and emergency modifications. When the documentation has been completed, reviewed and approved, the baseline becomes revised. All subsequent change proposals should be made to the revised baseline.

Changes may arise internally or externally. External ones come from changes to business requirements; internal ones from forgotten requirements or problems found during the project. A procedure is required to report problems with baselined configuration items. Change control is the process of proposing, reviewing, approving and, where necessary, implementing change to the approved and maintained items within the PBS. Through the process of change control, the impact of all changes is properly assessed, prior to deciding whether to authorize the change. Impact assessment will determine the changes in scope the change will bring about, not just in the immediate area of the change, but on the whole project. Often the change can have a far-reaching impact. The consequences for organization, quality, costs and benefit, and schedule are also assessed. It can help to have a standard form such as that shown as Figure 12.12, to guide this assessment. It is important not to place items under change control too early, as unnecessary inflexibility and delay may occur. The steps of change control are listed in Section 12.6.

Review boards may differ for changes at different stages of the life cycle. Prior to the change review, the team determines what impact changes to configuration items has on resource requirements, and prioritize change against requirements for all projects in the organization. The impact is documented for the board. Once a change has been approved, the person responsible for the item makes the change, and passes the rebaselined documentation to configuration management. Information on revisions to the item is recorded. The revised specification for the item is passed to all interested parties, and then secured by configuration management.

For major changes, it is sometimes desirable to adopt a top-down approach in which changes to the requirements specification are agreed prior to any work being done to define consequential changes to the specification. This, in turn, is agreed prior to changes being made to the product and component specifications. Configuration management can handle this by defining the major enhancement as a separate configuration with its own baseline. When a major enhancement becomes operational, it supersedes the current system. Until then, the current operational system continues to have its own baseline changes as necessary. This can be taken one step further, where several prototypes have their separate baselined configurations operational in parallel, each subject to separate change control. When a change is made to one, it may or may not be made to some or all of the others.

STATUS ACCOUNTING

Status accounting is the fourth function of configuration management. It supplies information on request about baselines, configuration items, their versions and specification, change proposal, problem reports, repairs and modifications. For example, status accounting may identify authorized repairs and modifications awaiting the completion of amended documentation. Unless documentation is amended to be consistent with the facility, it is not accepted as being valid. Status accounting also keeps track of the complexities caused by superseding (major enhancement) configurations.

Status accounting enables people on large, volatile projects to avoid using outdated versions of documents and components. This is important for contracting companies responsible for components that need to interface with each other. It is also important for people responsible for user acceptance tests. They need the most current version of the requirements specification and the agreed functional and physical characteristic of the configuration, so they can determine whether or not the specification (quality) requirements of the contract have been met. That is, the facility functions as envisaged within its environment to produce the required product and benefit.

Configuration management and the life cycle

A common mistake, thankfully now made less frequently, is to confuse design management and project management. In the early days of project management it was common to make the chief designer the project manager:

– in the software industry systems analysts were called project managers
– in civil engineering, design contractors were labelled 'the engineer', and fulfilled an advisory role which included project manager, and put them

into a conflict of interest with their main role as design manager – in the building industry the architect worked also as project manager with similar consequences.

Design management and project management are different, and often at odds with each other, as the designer tries to perfect the design and the project manager tries to deliver an adequate design on time and cost. However, two techniques have as common elements life cycle and configuration management. In the software industry, SSADM (the structured systems analysis and design methodology), is a design methodology, although it does include sections on project and configuration management. On the other hand, PRINCE 2[3], is a project management methodology also with a section on configuration management.

Figure 7.5 illustrates the evolution of configuration management through the life cycle. It shows a rule of thumb from most industries, that for every £1 it costs you to right a mistake during feasibility, it costs you £n in design, £n^2 in execution and £n^3 in close-out. For the ship-building industry, n is said to be 3, and the ratios are $1:3:9:27$, and for the software industry n is said to be 10 and the ratios are $1:10:100:1000$. Hence it is a very good idea to try to agree the specification by the end of design, and move forward to execution with the design frozen. Thus the emphasis of configuration management changes as you move from design to execution. In feasibility and design the emphasis is on gaining the commitment of the project participants to the design, and the key processes are identification, review and change control.

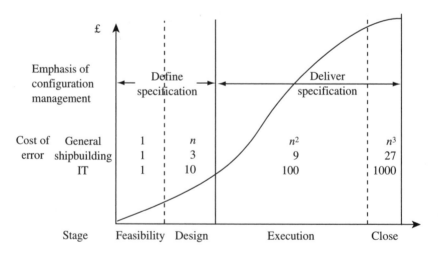

Figure 7.5   Configuration management and the life cycle

In execution and close-out the emphasis is on delivering the agreed design, and the key process is status accounting. That is not to say that if a show-stopper is discovered during close-out, a change will not be made. But the change is made in the full knowledge of how much it will cost, and the benefit of the change must also be significant to justify it.

7.5 The cost of quality

Applying the above techniques costs money, and so you may wonder whether the cost justifies the benefit. What is the cost of achieving quality? You will often hear people say that the cost of quality is free.[5] This is based on measured results of implementing total quality management in manufacturing companies, producing savings something like those shown in Figure 7.6. This views the cost of quality as being made up of three elements, as proposed by Crosby:[5]

– the cost of failure
– the cost of appraisal and control
– the cost of prevention and assurance.

Applying the above techniques certainly increases the cost of prevention, but it reduces the number of failures. That has an effect on the cost of failures, and as the number of failures falls the need for appraisal and control falls, reducing that cost as well. Eventually, the total cost of quality is less than it was at the start, even though the cost of prevention has risen. That, too, may begin to fall as the attitudes to quality become ingrained.

However, we now encounter a feature of project management: *projects are transient*. In a manufacturing company, the time to show any

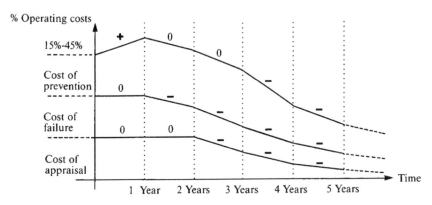

Figure 7.6   The cost of quality

improvement is typically about 18 months (the duration of many projects), and the time to the point where prevention costs begin to fall is typically four years. This means that if the technique is applied to a project, no return will be seen within that project's lifetime. The solution is for the prevention costs to be borne by the parent organization as an overhead, with the whole organization benefiting as savings feed back into more effective projects. That will be effective where the project team is drawn wholly from within the organization, which is the case on organizational development projects and in project-based organizations such as an engineering design consultancy, construction contractor or software house. However, it may still be difficult to get contractors to adopt the prevention techniques if they have no long-term commitment to the client and the client's future projects. The solution is to develop integrated supply chains and to adopt partnering arrangements whereby the contractor has the necessary commitment. This is the approach adopted by Marks and Spencer for the supply of their clothes and food, and it is being adopted by the oil majors in the United States. However, further description of these arrangements is beyond the scope of this book.[6]

7.6 Summary

1. There are four possible definitions of good quality on a project:
   - meets the specification
   - is fit for purpose
   - meets the customer's requirements
   - satisfies the customer.
2. The four are not the same thing, and like in many areas of project management, overall optimum may not optimize any one of them. An overall compromise must be sought.
3. However, being fit for purpose is thought by many to be the primary criterion.
4. There are five elements of achieving quality of a project:
   - quality of the product vs the management process
   - quality assurance vs quality control
   - good attitudes.
5. Assuring the quality of the product requires the use of:
   - a clear specification
   - use of defined standards
   - historical experience
   - qualified resources
   - impartial design reviews
   - change control.

Table 7.1   List of ISO and IEC quality procedures

Number	Title
ISO 9000-1:1994	Quality management and quality assurance standards – Part 1: Guidelines for selection and use
ISO 9000-4:1993	Quality management and quality assurance standards – Part 4: Guide to dependability programme management
ISO 9001:1994	Quality systems – Model for quality assurance in design, development, production, installation and servicing
ISO 9004-2:1991	Quality management and quality system elements – Part 2: Guidelines for services
ISO 9004-4:1993	Quality management and quality system elements – Part 4: Guidelines for quality improvement
ISO 10005:1995	Quality management – Guidelines for quality plans
ISO 10006:1998	Quality management – Guidelines to quality in project management
ISO 10007:1995	Guidelines for configuration management
ISO 10011:1991	Guidelines for auditing quality systems
ISO 10013:1995	Guidelines for developing quality manuals
ISO 10014:-1	Guidelines for managing the economics of quality
ISO/IEC 12207:1995	Information technology – Software life cycle processes
ISO/IEC Guide 2:1996	Standardization and related activities – General vocabulary
IEC 300-3-3:1995	Dependability management – Part 3: Application guide – Section 3: Life cycle costing
IEC 300-3-9:1995	Dependability management – Part 3: Application guide – Section 9: Risk analysis of technological systems

6. Controlling the quality of the product requires a clear understanding of the specification of each deliverable (at the time it is completed), and achievement of this specification must be measured, and action taken to eliminate variance.
7. Assuring the quality of the management process requires the use of procedures, which should
   – be used as flexible guidelines, not rigid rules
   – reflect how the product is processed not what functions in the organization do
   – should be continuously improved, project by project.
8. Controlling the quality of the management processes requires them to be audited.

9. Configuration management is a technique to manage the quality and functionality of the project's deliverables, and obtaining agreement of the project's participants. It has four steps:
   - configuration identification
   - configuration review
   - configuration control
   - status accounting.
10. Quality is free, but not in the lifetime of a single project.

References

1. Kiely, D.G., *Defence Procurement, the Equipment Buying Process*, Tri-Service Press, 1990.
2. ISO 10006, *Quality Management – Guidelines to Quality in Project Management*, International Standards Organization, 1997.
3. CCTA, *PRINCE 2: Project Management for Business*, The Stationery Office, 1996.
4. Turner, J.R. and Peymai, R., 'Organizing for change: a versatile approach', in *The Project Manager as Change Agent*, J.R. Turner, K.V. Grude and L. Thurloway (eds), McGraw-Hill, 1996.
5. Crosby, P.B., *Quality is Free*, McGraw-Hill, 1979.
6. Turner, J.R. (ed), *The Commercial Project Manager*, McGraw-Hill, 1995.

Note

a. Section 7.4 incorporates material from the first edition based on a contribution originally made by Richard Morreale.

8
Managing cost

8.1 Introduction

Let us now consider the fourth project objective, managing cost, by which the project manager ensures the project's product is financially viable and worth while. The next section considers the purpose of estimating costs, and shows how this leads to several types of estimate, of different accuracy prepared at different stages of the project management life cycle. Later sections explain how the estimate is structured through the cost control cube, and describe several methods for preparing the estimate. Finally, we shall discuss how costs are controlled by comparing actual expenditure against the value of work done, and show how S-curves can provide a pictorial representation of this.

8.2 Estimating costs

There are several reasons why we estimate costs. The most obvious is to provide a measure against which to control costs. Other reasons are given below.

AS A BASIS FOR CONTROL

The estimate is prepared as a measure against which to control expenditure on the project. This measure is known as the *baseline*. The classic control process has four steps (Section 7.3):

– estimate future performance
– monitor actual performance
– calculate the difference, called the *variance*
– take action according to the size of the variance.

There are three basic actions:

– if the variance is zero or negligible: continue without change

– if the variance is significant but recoverable: plan recovery
– if the variance is large: revise the estimates.

As a basis for control the estimate may need to be quite detailed, prepared at a low level of the WBS.

ASSESS PROJECT VIABILITY

Before getting to a position where you need to prepare a control estimate, you need to determine whether the project is worth undertaking. You therefore prepare an estimate of the costs to compare with the estimates of returns. (Methods of assessing project viability are beyond the scope of this book, except as they were covered in Chapter 2.[1]) Furthermore, the appraisal estimate goes through various stages of increasing accuracy, at the start of proposal and initiation, at the transition from that stage to design and appraisal, and at the transition from that stage to execution and control.

OBTAIN FUNDING

After approval has been obtained, the project must be financed. Funding will also be awarded on the basis of a comparison between estimates of costs and future returns. The accuracy will usually be similar to that for project approval. (Obtaining finance is also beyond the scope of this book.[1])

MANAGE CASH FLOW

Once funding has been obtained, and work starts, the project must be managed so that work takes place and consumes cash no faster than the rate agreed with the financiers (bankers). There are apocryphal stories about zealous project managers finishing their projects early and underspent, (Figure 8.1), and wanting a pat on the back. However, the company has gone into liquidation because the bankers called in the overdraft half-way through the project.

ALLOCATE RESOURCES

Human resources are a special form of project funding. The business plans their allocation in advance against an estimate of the accuracy of the project approval estimate. They will be assigned to the project week by week against the control estimate.

ESTIMATE DURATIONS

The duration of a work element is calculated by comparing the estimate of work content to resource availability, and so the cost estimates form an input to time estimating. Time estimating is performed for similar reasons to cost estimating, and so similar types of estimate are required.

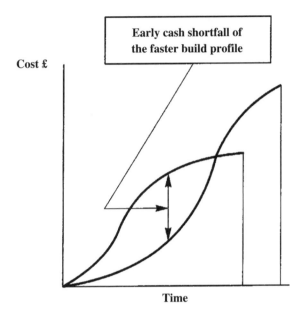

Figure 8.1   Different build profiles for a project

PREPARE TENDERS

Contracting firms tendering for bespoke contracts need to prepare estimates for the tender. They may use the cost estimate in several ways including:

– to forecast the profit by subtracting the estimated cost from the market price
– to calculate the price by adding a fixed percentage to the cost
– for passing on to the client. Clients in the public sector often demand a cost breakdown.

8.3 Types of estimate

The same estimate cannot satisfy all six purposes above. Five types of estimate, of varying accuracy, are required (Table 8.1). There is another purpose for each type, namely to prepare the equivalent estimate of duration. The levels of accuracy in Table 8.1 are those obtainable on engineering projects. Those for IS projects are said to be half this level (double the figure). Table 8.2 summarizes an idea first introduced in Section 5.3: you obtain increasing accuracy of estimate by estimating at lower and lower levels of WBS. If the estimates are truly mean values, errors cancel out. Table 8.2 implies that to obtain an estimate to the correct accuracy at

Table 8.1   Types of estimate: purpose and accuracy

Type of estimate	Range of accuracy (%)	Purpose
Proposal	±50	Appraisal viability to start, feasibility study
Budget	±20	Appraisal viability to start, systems design
Sanction	±10	Appraisal viability to approve project, obtain funding, allocate resources
Control	±5	Measure progress, assign resources
Tender	±2	Prepare tender

Table 8.2   Types of estimate: level in work breakdown structure

Type of estimate	Lowest level of estimate in WBS	Accuracy of estimate (%)			
		Project	Work area	Work pack	Activity
Proposal	Areas of work	±50	±100	–	–
Budget	Work packages	±20	±40	±100	–
Sanction	Work-package scope statements	±10	±20	±50	±150
Control	Activities	±5	±10	±25	±75
Tender	Tasks	±2	±4	±10	±30
Assumed number per project		1	4	25	200

the project level, you need only estimate to the order of magnitude at the currently lowest level of the WBS. There are two provisos to this:

1. A consistent error will reinforce: for instance if all activities are under-estimated by 20%, the project will be under-estimated by 20%.
2. The absolute error at the project level is worse than at the lower levels.

Table 8.2 can be taken to lower levels of WBS for larger projects. On one large engineering project worth several hundred million pounds, I prepared a WBS which had approximately 100 areas of work and a ratio of 1:10 for each subsequent level of work breakdown, down to the task level. On the same project, estimators were estimating costs accurate to the nearest pound at all levels of WBS, and yet including contingencies of several hundreds of thousands of pounds at the work-package level. This is clearly absurd. It is the right level of contingency, but the wrong level of accuracy. Table 8.3 shows appropriate levels of accuracy and contingency at different levels of the WBS for a project worth £100 million. The table is based on three simple ratios:

1. The average cost of an element of work is inversely proportional to the number in the project.
2. The accuracy as a percentage is proportional to the square root of the number in the project, or inversely proportional to the square root of the size, (see Section 5.3).
3. The accuracy as an absolute value is the accuracy as a percentage multiplied by the average cost.

At any level of breakdown, there is no point calculating and quoting estimates to a greater degree of accuracy than the figure in the right-hand column. Any contingency added at that level of breakdown must be at least this amount as a level of contingency is already included through the accuracy to which figures are calculated.

Table 8.3   Levels of estimating in a large engineering project

Level of breakdown	Number in project (N)	Average cost (£) (C)	Accuracy as ratio (%)	Accuracy as value (±£)
Project	1	100 000 000	± 1	±1 000 000
Area of work	100	1 000 000	± 10	± 100 000
Work package	1000	100 000	± 30	± 30 000
Activity	10 000	10 000	±100	± 10 000
Task	100 000	1 000	±300	± 3 000

8.4 When to estimate costs

It follows from Table 8.2 that to prepare estimates of increasing accuracy requires increasing effort as you estimate at lower levels of breakdown. Ratio 2 above implies that to double the accuracy at the project level requires you to estimate at a level of breakdown with four times as many work elements, requiring four times the effort. This has been measured in the engineering industry[2] (Table 8.4). When plotted (Figure 8.1), this is a learning curve, with greater effort giving greater accuracy, but with diminishing returns. In addition, there is a point, at 5 per cent accuracy with effort 5 per cent of project cost, where the effort does not justify the return. This has three consequences:

1. On projects internal to an organization, it is not worth while producing an estimate more accurate than the control estimate, because it costs more to produce than the value of the data. This is a consequence of the uniqueness of projects (Chapter 1). On a production line, costs may be estimated to a low level of detail, because the saving is made many

Table 8.4 Level of effort and stage of production of project estimates

Type of estimate	Accuracy (%)	Level of effort as % of project cost	Stage of production
Proposal	±30–±50	0.02–0.1	Preproposal and initiation
Budget	±20–±35	0.1–0.3	Proposal and initiation
Sanction	±10–±25	0.4–0.8	Design and appraisal
Control	± 5–±15	1–3	Implementation planning
Tender	± 2–± 5	5–10	Tender preparation

times over. On projects, the saving is made once only. It is not worth while producing plans in great detail, because the effort is not rewarded. It is better to put management effort into eliminating risk, not quantify it. The problem arises for contracting companies who, when tendering, must prepare estimates which will allow them to make a profit (Example 8.1).

2. The way to improve accuracy of estimates is not to put more effort into estimating, but to improve the estimating data, effectively to move the curve in Figure 8.2 to the left using historical data. However, this too

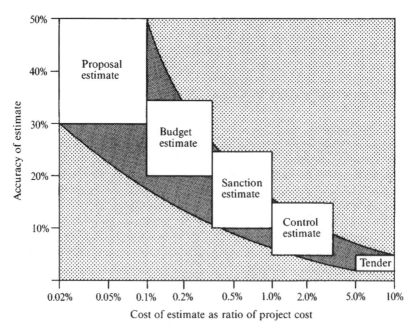

Figure 8.2 Accuracy of estimate vs cost of estimate (a learning curve following an inverse square law)

suffers from the law of diminishing returns. On engineering projects, 80 years of effort has gone into preparing data.[2] The IS industry has only 20 years of experience, which is why the accuracy of estimates for each type is only half as great (double the figure) – four times the effort doubles the accuracy.

3. The estimate at one level should not be prepared before the estimate at the previous level. Each estimate is therefore prepared at a given stage of the life cycle (Table 8.4), and these stages should be followed rigorously. Effectively, the comparison of costs and returns at the end of one stage of the life cycle justifies the commitment of resources to planning, design and estimating at the next stage. If the project is not viable at these high levels of estimate, work should not proceed to the next stage (Example 8.2).

I facilitated a bid management workshop run by a major IS vendor at Henley Management College. They spend 3 per cent of contract value preparing estimates, are successful at winning one contract in five, and have traditionally made profit margins in excess of 50 per cent. The contract they win pays the estimating costs of the four they do not, but the net margin was still in excess of 35 per cent. However, margins are being squeezed, and they are now lucky if they make a gross margin of 15 per cent. That means they must increase the number of contracts won, reduce the estimating costs, or make a loss. A bid manager from one of the major engineering contracting firms in the petrochemical industry spoke at the workshop. He said they had reduced the bidding costs to 0.75 per cent of contract cost. They also win one contract in five, but need to make a margin of only 4 per cent on that contract to cover the bidding costs on the five. The way they reduced bidding costs is to have a department of bid managers, who are the centre of expertise for tendering. That department can make maximum use of historical data. Effectively:

– they accelerate the learning curve
– they reduce the unique elements of projects, and so turn the bidding process into a repetitive operation
– they achieve quality through using historical data (Chapter 7).

Example 8.1 Recovering the cost of estimating on contracts

I worked in one company where the IS Department prepared control estimates at project initiation, only to find projects were not viable. If you expect an internal rate of return of 20 per cent on projects, you can only make that mistake three times per year until you cannot afford projects at all.

Example 8.2 Tailoring the estimate to the current stage of the project

8.5 Structuring the estimate

Cost components

The cost of a project may consist of several components, some of which are detailed below.

LABOUR

This includes the cost of people employed by the parent company involved in executing project tasks, including people designing and delivering the facility. I have worked in some manufacturing companies that do not attribute design labour to contracts. It is absorbed into company overheads and shared between all contracts. The result is the company only wins contracts with a high design element, and they have no control over design costs. Some other labour costs are included under other headings. The labour cost may be measured in monetary terms, or in man-hours. The latter is also called the *work content* (Section 6.5), and is a measure of the total effort required, independent of the duration and number of people performing the task. Clearly, effort can be converted into monetary terms by applying known costs per man-hour for each resource.

MATERIALS

This includes the cost of materials bought via the parent company and consumed in delivering the facility. This may be materials contained in the final product or consumables used on project tasks. On engineering projects materials include machinery, vessels, piping, structures, and instrumentation, but also include things like welding rods and coffer dams. On information systems projects, materials include main and peripheral hardware, proprietary software and coding sheets. On organizational development projects, materials may be more peripheral to the project, but include materials used on training programmes, furniture for new offices and stationery for new management procedures.

PLANT AND EQUIPMENT

These are materials used in delivering the facility, but which are not consumed, and so are available for re-use on subsequent projects. They may be either bought or hired, but either way each project only pays a part of their price new. This cost component should only include the cost of plant and equipment borne by the parent company. On engineering projects, plant and equipment includes welding machines and earth moving machinery. On information systems projects it includes hardware used by programmers. On organizational development projects it may include equipment used in the preparation and delivery of training programmes, temporary accommodation used during office moves and printing equipment if hired especially for the project.

SUBCONTRACT

This includes the cost of labour and materials as above provided by outside contractors. Costs will be included in this heading where their control is not within the scope of the parent organization.

MANAGEMENT

This should include the cost of people and materials involved in managing the project. These costs are directly attributable to the project, but not specific tasks, and include the cost of the manager and team leaders (integrators); the project support office; a project management information system if required; and temporary site services. The cost of management gets smaller as a proportion of the total cost as the size grows. Typically it is about 5 per cent on a project of £10 million, and 1 per cent on a project of £1 billion.[2] For projects of less than £10 million, many of the routine project management tasks must be undertaken by the manager if this is not to become a burdensome overhead, and on very small projects it may not be treated as a direct cost at all, but borne by the parent organization as an overhead. (The risk of this, of course, is the same as treating design as an overhead.)

OVERHEADS AND ADMINISTRATION

This should include the cost of administering items included in labour, materials and subcontract. These will include: costs directly attributable to some items such as transport, but included under this heading for convenience; costs shared between items such as procurement and storage; and absorption of some parent company overheads.

FEES AND TAXATION

Fees may include insurance, finance; licence agreements; and taxation may be regarded as a special type of fee.

INFLATION

This may or may not be ignored in the estimates.

1. Two cases when it is ignored are on publicly funded projects, and projects where project costs, raw material costs and revenues are expected to inflate at the same rate. In the former case it is assumed tax revenues will rise as fast as costs, and so the project will not become a larger burden on the public purse. For many public projects there are no

direct revenues; the benefit is to the economy and is expected to grow in real terms. The Thames Barrier for instance was 400 per cent overspent on the original budget, but it is claimed that 80 per cent of that was due to inflation.[3] Only 20 per cent of the overspend was due to unforeseen costs. In the latter case, accounting for inflation will make the returns from the project appear better than they actually are, and so it is often ignored. In fact its main impact will be to decrease financing costs as a percentage of the total cost, but to increase taxation as the project will appear to be more profitable than it actually is.

2. Two cases where it is not ignored are where there is expected to be differential inflation between project costs, raw material costs and revenues, and by contractors preparing fixed-price tenders. In the former case it is necessary to account for it to calculate the true return of the project (Example 8.3). In the latter case, the contractor must either include inflation in the price, or agree with the client to increase the price against an agreed index, called escalation.

When preparing the case for the construction of an Ammonia plant for ICI in the mid-1980s, I had to account for inflation. The price of the plant was expected to rise with the construction index (CI), which was running ahead of the retail price index (RPI), the price of the gas feedstock was expected to rise faster than the CI, the price of electricity with the RPI, while it was expected that the price of the product, ammonia, would remain static.

Example 8.3 Allowing for inflation in the estimates

CONTINGENCY

Contingency may be added as blanket figures or calculated according to risk. In the copy of the estimate shown to the owner, contingency is usually distributed among the other headings. In the copy shown to the team, the manager should keep contingency back, and show them just the raw estimates. Given that 'work done expands to fill the time available', if contingency is included in the subbudgets given to work package managers and subcontractors, then they will spend up to that amount. In fact it is common for project managers to maintain three or four estimates:

1. The *baseline* or *estimated prime cost*: the raw estimate without contingency. This is the sum of the most likely out-turn for each activity (Chapter 10). There is typically no chance of achieving an out-turn less than this, but it is given to the project team to provide them with a tight target.
2. The project manager consumes contingency to give a *current estimate*

when there is significant variation. Then baseline is impossible to achieve, and to hold the team to it would be demotivating. Contingency is consumed to update the baseline, but this must be done through strict change control. If the baseline is updated lightly, the project is always on budget and control is lost. On the National Gallery Extension, the project manager would allow no contingency to be apportioned to any of the work packages as he wanted to maintain strict control of costs.

3. The *most likely out-turn* is the estimate the project manager thinks is most likely, with contingency apportioned appropriately. This is the sum of the average out-turn in each activity (Chapter 10). There is typically a 55 per cent chance of achieving an out-turn less than this.

4. The *budget* is the amount the owner is willing to spend. This is what the project manager is measured against by the owner, and is justified by the expected returns from the project. There should typically be an 80 per cent chance of achieving an out-turn less than this.

On a typical engineering project the budget will be 10 to 20 per cent greater than the baseline, and the most likely out-turn half way between. On IS and R&D projects the contingency may be much higher.

FINANCE

Finance is the most significant cost on a project,[1] being greater than any other single cost and yet is ignored by most project managers. To them it is almost a phantom cost. It is the one area still remaining to make significant cost savings on projects.

Structuring the estimate

These components constitute a third breakdown structure, the *cost breakdown structure* (CBS). The CBS is usually simpler than the other two, although one more level of breakdown can be derived under most headings. The three structures, PBS, OBS and CBS, form the *cost control cube* (Figure 8.3), developed by the United States Defense Department, in the 1950s, as the basis of their C/SCSC methodology for controlling project costs. All costs can be assigned to a cell of the cube, and through the cube all costs have a position in each of the three breakdown structures. A project aggregate can then be prepared by summing along any of the three directions. Of course a large number, often the majority, of cells in the cube will contain no costs. For instance:

– a work element may be assigned to one subcontractor, a single entity in both the OBS and CBS
– a work element may consume labour only and of one type only
– a work element may be created to assign management costs.

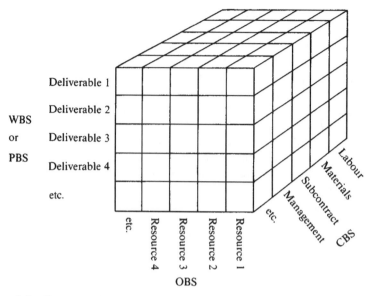

Figure 8.3   Cost control cube

Any two of the breakdown structures taken together form a matrix:

– the matrix formed by the PBS and OBS forms the responsibility chart, (Chapter 6)
– the matrix formed by the OBS and CBS is called a 'code of accounts'; it is used to apportion the costs in the parent company's accounts
– the third matrix is seldom encountered.

The cost control cube provides a structure for the estimate, is used to create it and is used in the subsequent control of costs. The PBS and OBS are evolved to the current lowest level according to the stage of production (Table 8.4), and costs assigned to each element in the PBS/OBS matrix against each costs element. The estimate is then aggregated to the project level. In this way, the cost control cube is amalgamated through a series of pages (Figure 8.4). Figure 8.5 shows a typical OBS for a chemical plant, and is adapted from an estimate I prepared for ICI. A page like this would be prepared for the facility as a whole. That is aggregated from similar pages for each part (intermediate product) of the facility, and those in turn for each subassembly of the part. Figure 8.6 is the plant in Figure 8.5 at a lower level of work breakdown.

Estimates can be similarly structured for IS, organizational change, training and other projects. Figure 6.12 contains a simpler estimating sheet for a smaller project, the CRMO Rationalization Project. This sheet has

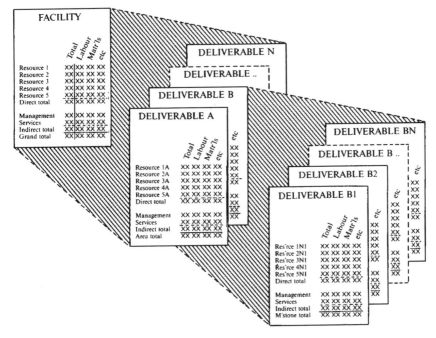

Figure 8.4   Cascade of estimates through the PBS, OBS and CBS

only two dimensions of the cost control cube, work and organization. It relates to only one component of the CBS, labour. If estimates were required for other components, such as materials or plant and equipment, then similar sheets could be developed, or more columns added to this sheet, especially if it is held in a spreadsheet package on a personal computer.

8.6 Estimating techniques

There are several ways of preparing estimates for the various cost components. The most direct is to break the work down to a lower level of detail, estimate the cost at that level and sum back up. However, the arguments of Section 8.4 imply that level of detail cannot always be justified, especially at earlier stages of the project life cycle. It is therefore necessary to use other methods which enable estimates to be produced at higher levels of work breakdown. The engineering and civil construction industries have well advanced methods of estimating at all levels of work breakdown.[2,4] These rely heavily on historical data and include step

PROJECT ESTIMATE	NORTHERN ENERGY AND CHEMICAL INDUSTRIES PLC	02-Jan-9X

PROJECT:	Petrochemical Plant	CODE:	THNS	ISSUE:	A
WORK AREA:	....	CODE:	....	AUTHOR:	JRT
WORK PACKAGE:	....	CODE:	....	APPRVD:	CME
ACTIVITY:	....	CODE:	....	DATE:	02-Jan-9X

	1000 tonne per day plant				SCALE	COST	1500 tonne per day plant			
	Material £,000	Erection £,000	Function £,000	Plant £,000	EXPONENT n	FACTOR 1.5^n	Material £,000	Erection £,000	Function £,000	Plant £,000
Main plant items										
- Vessels	13.33	0.63	13.96		0.65	1.30	17.35	0.82	18.17	
- Furnace and boiler	2.89	0.14	3.03		0.70	1.33	3.84	0.18	4.02	
- Machines and drives	9.73	0.46	10.19		0.75	1.36	13.19	0.62	13.81	
- Vendor packages	6.77	0.32	7.09		0.75	1.36	9.18	0.43	9.61	
- Other	0.00	0.13	0.13		0.70	1.33	0.00	0.17	0.17	
MPI total: Materials	32.72	—	32.72				43.55	—	43.55	
MPI total: Erection	—	1.67	1.67				—	2.22	2.22	
Bulk Items										
- Piping	1.22	1.88	3.10		0.70	1.33	1.62	2.50	4.12	
- Instruments	0.64	1.10	0.74		0.60	1.28	0.82	0.13	0.94	
- Computer control system	1.56	0.88	2.44		0.70	1.33	2.07	1.17	3.24	
- Electrical	1.82	0.53	2.35		0.70	1.33	2.42	0.70	3.12	
- Structural		0.26	0.26		0.65	1.30	0.00	0.34	0.34	
- Civil		2.11	2.11		0.65	1.30	0.00	2.75	2.75	
- Painting		0.10	0.10		0.65	1.30	0.00	0.13	0.13	
- Insulation		1.50	1.50		0.65	1.30	0.00	1.95	1.95	
- Buildings		0.12	0.12		0.65	1.30	0.00	0.16	0.16	
- Plant modification		0.70	0.70		0.70	1.33	0.00	0.93	0.93	
Bulk items total	5.24	8.18	13.42				6.93	10.75	17.68	
TOTAL DIRECT COSTS				47.81						63.45
Engineering - Design			8.40		0.50	1.22			10.29	
- Software			0.53		1.20	1.63			0.86	
Construction - Management			3.22		0.65	1.30			4.19	
- Services			1.50		0.65	1.30			1.95	
Works - Start-up			6.70		0.65	1.30			8.72	
- Working capital			9.56		1.00	1.50			12.69	
Contingency			4.78						6.34	
TOTAL INDIRECT COSTS				34.69						45.05
CAPITAL COST OF ERECTED PLANT				82.50						108.50
Inflation			4.13						5.42	
Licence fees and royalties			0.41						0.54	
Insurance			0.83						1.08	
TOTAL OVERHEADS				5.36						7.05
TOTAL CAPITAL COST				87.86						115.55

Figure 8.5   Sample OBS for a chemical plant (plant level)

PROJECT ESTIMATE		NORTHERN ENERGY AND CHEMICAL INDUSTRIES PLC					02-Jan-9X

PROJECT	Petrochemical Plant	CODE:	THNS	ISSUE:	A
WORK AREA:	Synthesis	CODE:	THNS5	AUTHOR:	JRT
WORK PACKAGE:	....	CODE:	....	APPRVD:	CME
ACTIVITY:	....	CODE:	....	DATE:	02-Jan-9X

					Parametric ratio	
	Material	Erection	Function	Plant	Function	Plant
	£,000	£,000	£,000	£,000	%MPI	%MPI
Main plant items						
- Vessels	4.85	0.23	5.08			
- Furnace and boiler	0.00	0.00	0.00			
- Machines and drives	3.67	0.17	3.84			
- Vendor packages	1.55	0.07	1.62			
- Other	0.00	0.00	0.00			
MPI Total: Materials	10.07	—	10.07		100.0%	
MPI Total: Erection	—	0.47	0.47		4.7%	
Bulk items						
- Piping			1.21		12.0%	
- Instruments			0.23		2.3%	
- Computer control system			0.82		8.1%	
- Electrical			0.81		8.0%	
- Structural			0.09		0.9%	
- Civil			0.76		7.5%	
- Painting			0.03		0.3%	
- Insulation			0.50		5.0%	
- Buildings			0.06		0.6%	
- Plant modification			0.24		2.4%	
Bulk items total			4.74		0.47	
TOTAL DIRECT COSTS				15.29		1.52
Engineering - Design			1.72		17.1%	
- Software			0.09		0.9%	
Construction - Management			0.80		7.9%	
- Services			0.33		3.3%	
Works - Start-up			1.43		14.2%	
- Working capital			3.06		30.4%	
Contingency			1.53		15.2%	
TOTAL INDIRECT COSTS				8.96		0.89
CAPITAL COST OF ERECTED PLANT				24.24		2.41
Inflation						
Licence fees and royalties						
Insurance						
TOTAL OVERHEADS				0.00		
TOTAL CAPITAL COST				24.24		

Figure 8.6   Sample OBS for a chemical plant (plant area level)

counting, exponential, parametric, and detailed and computerized methods. The IS industry is now developing similar techniques, and it is possible to postulate similar approaches for organizational development projects. I describe the methods from these three industries, engineering construction, building and IS. I hope that from these you may be able to develop techniques appropriate to your industry.

Methods in the engineering construction industry
The engineering construction industry has well-advanced methods of estimating at all levels of work breakdown[2] (Table 8.5). These rely heavily on historical data and include:

STEP COUNTING METHODS
These assume cost is a function of the number of functions and plant throughput. In the engineering construction industry standard formulae and tables have been derived from empirical data. Some of these formulae are still valid after 20 years, because of the stability of the technology. The formulae exist at several levels of breakdown, the plant level, plant area level or main plant item (MPI) level.

EXPONENTIAL METHODS
These assume cost is proportional to the size of the facility, to some power. In the engineering construction industry, this is called the 'two-thirds power law' because the exponent is usually between 0.6 and 0.75. If you know the cost of a plant of standard size, the cost of a larger or smaller one can be derived. The law can be applied at several levels of breakdown; the lower the level, the more accurate the estimate at the plant level. Figure 8.5 contains exponents from George[2] for a chemical plant, applied at the first level of OBS, showing how they can be used to convert from a 1000 tonne/day plant to a 1500 tonne/day plant.

Table 8.5   Estimating methods used to prepare types of estimate

Type of estimate	Accuracy (%)	Estimating methods
Proposal	±50	Step counting Exponential (plant level)
Budget	±20	Exponential (MPI level) Parametric (plant level)
Sanction	±10	Parametric (MPI level, vendor quotes)
Control	± 5	Parametric (MPI level, firm prices)
Tender	± 2	Detailed estimating

PARAMETRIC METHODS

These assume costs are proportional to some core cost. On chemical plants this is the MPI. Tables of ratios exist giving the cost of other items as ratios of the MPI, dependent on its value, its type and the severity of duty. These tables exist at several levels of WBS. Figure 8.6 contains data at the plant area level, from George.[2] The techniques are so advanced in the engineering construction industry, that estimates based on prices of a placed order and derived at the equipment levels are sufficiently accurate for the control estimate. It is in this way that the cost of estimating is being reduced.

DETAILED ESTIMATES

They are prepared by contracting companies tendering for work, where the level of accuracy is of the same order of magnitude as the expected profit margin. At the lowest levels the costs are derived from standard cost books or from parametric data.

COMPUTER AIDED ESTIMATING

This has been derived to support parametric estimating and detailed estimating. These are often based on a bill of materials (BOM) or a bill of quantities (BOQ) for standard components.

Possible sources of data for preparing estimates are:

– suppliers' quotations (typical, budget, detailed)
– trade literature, technical literature, textbooks, government literature
– company historical data, standard costs, personal records
– computer systems.

Estimating methods in the building industry

Table 8.6 shows when by whom and how estimates are made in the building industry. Methods of estimating include:

APPROXIMATE METHODS

The cost is assumed to be proportional to the lettable floor area for a building of appropriate type, use and quality. Tables of figures are given, for instance, in Spon.[4,5] The figures given include costs not only for the whole building, but also for individual services within the building (all related back to the area of the whole building). The cost, given in £/million^2, can range by a factor of three for a given type of building, and so it is important to be aware of the use and quality. The user must also be aware of what services are and are not included in the costs calculated. However, the figures give estimates accurate enough for proposal estimates. The figures given are also only valid in Outer London at a certain time. Tables are given to update the estimates for other locations and other times (see below).

Table 8.6   Method of estimating vs stage of use

Level	WBS unit	Estimate	User	Method	Design stage
1	Unit	Preproposal	QS	Functional	Brief
2	Space	Proposal	QS	Approximate	Sketch
3	Element	Budget	QS	Elemental	Sketch/detail
4	Feature	Sanction	QS	Empirical	Detail
5	Item	Control	QS	BOQ	Detail/working
6	Operations	Tender	Contractor	Network	Working
7	Resources	Work	Contractor	SOR	Working

FUNCTIONAL METHODS

A coarser method of approximate estimating is to estimate in terms of the functional requirements, that is cost per bed in a hospital, the cost per pupil in a school, the cost per seat in an office building. These estimates have the same validity in terms of location and time as the approximate methods, and will be prepared at an earlier stage of the project than the approximate methods.

ELEMENTAL ESTIMATING

The building is broken down into major elements, and the cost estimated as a ratio of the assumed duty or floor area of that element. The difference between this and the previous method is that the cost of each service is calculated from the size of that service, not the floor area of the whole building. This method can produce an estimate accurate enough for budget, or even sanction, purposes. Once this estimate has been accepted, it can be used to generate a complete bill of quantities.

EMPIRICAL ESTIMATING

Costs are extrapolated from the cost of schemes of similar size, scope and type. Historical data is used to establish overall parameters and indicators which influence cost. These can be derived by regression analysis or curve fitting, from established data or industry standard formulae.[4]

SCHEDULE OF RATES

This is not so much an estimating method, as a detailed breakdown of the cost of doing individual tasks on a building or construction site. A schedule of rates can be used for building up a detailed estimate. Or they can be used for building up costs associated with small projects, or even individual, isolated tasks, such as maintenance projects and maintenance jobs respectively. A schedule of rates will often be used on cost plus contracts.

BILL OF QUANTITIES

This is equivalent to the computerized estimate described above. It will often be built up from a CAD drawing of the building, using standard bills of quantities for repeated elements.

Estimating methods in the IT industry

The IT industry has developed a set of estimating techniques to meet its own particular needs. There are major differences between estimating on software projects vs construction projects, for the following reasons:

1. Software projects are not mechanistic, (though neither is engineering design). The activities are indeterminate and cannot be measured by simple means. Task size and complexity can be assessed by experts, but this is not normally reliable. The more complex the project, the less reliable the estimate.
2. Because of the rapid change of technology, there is not a wealth of historical data. The COCOMO model described later was based on information from 63 projects. While it gives a good base estimate for software projects, it is only applicable to programming using 3GLs.

Techniques for estimating on software projects are described by many authors,[6] and include:

ANALOGY

Estimates are made by comparison to previous, similar projects. This is probably the most valid technique for many organizations, but does rely on historical records. The technique relies on the use of a consistent software development life cycle. Using the technique to extrapolate between projects of different size can also be fraught with danger, given the non-linear relationship between size, effort and time scale.

TOP-DOWN ESTIMATING

The estimate is made against stages of a standard life cycle, and activities within the life cycle, often applying fixed percentage allocations to each stage. This approach has several advantages:

– a detailed design of the final system is not required, so the approach can be used at an early stage
– the technique is comparatively inexpensive
– it does not constrain the use of other techniques.

BOTTOM-UP ESTIMATING

This is the detailed estimate built up from a knowledge of the design of the system. It is most effectively used to provide an estimate of the next stage of a project prepared on completion of the current stage. The technique is expensive, and has several disadvantages which means it must almost always be used in conjunction with other techniques:

- errors tend to compound, usually resulting in underestimation of the total cost of a system
- it takes no account of the shortened project time scales – two people do not take half the time of one person to do a job.[7]

MATHEMATICAL MODELS

These relate effort and time to lines of code, similar to step counting and exponential methods. They rely on historical data, and must be tailored to an organization's needs. The models only apply to the development stage of a project. In many of the models, the equations take the following form:

$$\text{effort} = A * (\text{size})^b$$
$$\text{time} = C * (\text{effort})^d$$

where size is measured in thousands of lines of code, effort is measured in man-months, and time in months. Table 8.7 contains coefficients for several models.[8] In most cases, the exponent b is greater than one, giving relatively larger cost for bigger systems. These models take no account of the effects of time compression. The constraint models provide correction factors. Table 8.7 also shows the effort and time predicted by the different methods for a system of 40 000 lines of code, and software development costs of £4 000 per man-month. The figures vary quite wildly. Each model was all developed within one organization, and therefore represent its own characteristics. This means organizations should develop their own models. It also means they should question their software development environment if their estimates are uncompetitive.

Table 8.7 Mathematical estimating models

Model	A	b	C	d	Effort (m-mths)	Duration (months)	Cost (£'000s)
Watson Felix (IBM)	5.2	0.91	2.47	0.35	149	14.2	592
Nelson, SDC	4.9	0.98	3.04	0.36	192	19.8	728
COCOMO, organic	2.4	1.05	2.5	0.38	115	15.2	462
COCOMO, semi-d	3.0	1.12	2.5	0.35	187	15.6	747
Frederic	2.4	1.18	–	–	186	–	746
COCOMO, embedded	3.6	1.20	2.5	0.32	301	15.5	1205
Phister	1.0	1.275	–	–	110	–	441
Jones	1.0	1.4	–	–	175	–	700
Halstead	0.7	1.5	–	–	177	–	708

FUNCTION POINT ANALYSIS

The mathematical models apply only to the development stage of the project (cutting code), which typically accounts for only 50 per cent of the cost. Function point analysis count the function points, which represent the total functionality of the system.[8] Function points include:

- inputs: forms and screens
- outputs: reports and screens
- end-user enquiries
- logical data files
- interfaces to other systems.

Function points are converted to an estimate by:

- comparison with previous systems – applicable to the whole life cycle
- converting to lines of code – applicable to the development stage only.

CONSTRAINT MODELS

The models above take no account of the reducing efficiency caused by decreasing duration.[7] Reducing duration increase costs. Constraint models have been developed in an attempt to calculate the effects of time-scale compression. They are still relatively new.

The methods compared

Table 8.8 compares the methods from the three industries. The equivalence is not exact, but hopefully the comparison will help you to derive similar approaches for your industry.

Table 8.8   Comparison of the estimating methods for three industries

ECI	Building	IS
Step counting: plant level	Functional Approximate	Mathematical
Step counting: area level	Elemental	Function point analysis
Exponential	Empirical	Analogy
Factorial	–	(Function point analysis)
Detail	Schedule of rates	Bottom-up
Computer based	Bill of quantities	Top-down

Updating estimates

Estimating data is only valid at a certain time, in a certain place and in a given currency. It will often be necessary to allow for inflation, and may be necessary to convert from one country to another and one currency to another. Tables of ratios exist for these conversions.[2] Without any other guidance you can use the retail price index (RPI). However, tables exist for many industries giving inflation rates different to RPI. Tables are published for most countries of the world. They also exist for ratios of exchange rates for years past, and for differences in labour and material costs between different countries. Therefore, given the price of a project in one country in its local currency in a year past you can calculate the cost of the same project in another country in its local currency in another year past.

8.7 Controlling costs: obtaining value for money

Up to this point of the chapter, I have talked about estimating costs. I close by discussing the control of costs. This was stated as the first purpose of preparing the estimate, and so the structure has been derived to facilitate this process. In Section 8.2, I said that the estimate is prepared as a measure against which to compare actual performance. In this section I consider:

- the appropriate measure for cost control
- when to make the comparisons
- using the comparison to forecast cost to completion
- the use of S-curves to provide a visual representation.

We shall not discuss how to overcome variances (differences) identified for now, but leave that to Chapter 12, where we shall discuss execution and control. The techniques described below are known as *earned value analysis.*[9]

The measure for cost control

The commonest mistake of cost control is to use as the measure, or baseline, for control the predicted rate of expenditure with time, and to compare the actual rate of expenditure with this. A cost estimate is prepared against the work breakdown structure. This is then scheduled in time by scheduling the work elements to produce an expenditure profile. (How to schedule the work will be discussed in Chapter 9.) This predicted rate of expenditure is variously called:

- scheduled cost
- predicted cash flow
- baseline cost of work scheduled (BCWS)
- planned cost of work scheduled (PCWS).

The last two are the most descriptive. As work is done, actual expenditure is recorded. This actual rate of expenditure is variously called:

- the accrual
- the actual cash flow
- the actual cost of work complete (ACWC).

To determine whether the project is over- or underspent, actual expenditure is compared to the scheduled cost, and if less all is assumed to be well. However, this assumption may be false because no measure is made of what work has been done for the expenditure. In the most extreme case, no work may have been done, and yet expenditure accrued. I conducted a post-completion audit on a project where the company's finance director realized something was wrong when all the project's budget had been spent and yet only 50 per cent of the work done. To control costs you must compare the actual expenditure not to the schedule of expenditure, but to some measure of the value of work done. The PBS or WBS provides the means to do this. As an element of product is delivered, or work is completed, (the former is better), you can compare how much it actually cost against what it was estimated to cost. This estimated cost of the actual work done is variously called:

– earned value
– baseline cost of work complete (BCWC)
– planned cost of work complete (PCWC).

The *earned value* for a work package or the whole project is the sum of the estimate of the completed activities which constitute it. Cost is controlled by comparing the earned value to the actual expenditure, and calculating a *cost variance*:

$$\text{Cost variance} = \text{Accrual} - \text{Earned value}$$
$$\% \text{ Variance} = (\text{Variance/Earned value}).$$

If this variance is positive the project is overspent, and if it is negative it is underspent. Action is taken if this variance is non-zero (positive) (Section 8.2).

If we used the strict definition of earned value given above, based only on work complete, a bias would be introduced, because no allowance is made for work in progress. At the work package or project level some allowance must be made for activities started but not finished. A subjective estimate of percentage completion of activities can be made, but this is usually an over estimate (always 99 per cent!). It is more accurate to assume that on average activities in progress are half finished. We therefore have:

– for activities:
$$\% \text{ Completion} = 0\%, 50\% \text{ or } 100\%$$
– for the project and work packages:
$$\% \text{ Completion} = (\text{earned value/original estimate})$$
– where:
$$\text{Earned value} = \text{Sum of } (\% \text{ completion} \times \text{original estimate})$$
with the sum taken over the constituent activities.

It was implied above that the comparison between the scheduled cost and actual cost is meaningless. If the actual cost is less than the scheduled cost it does not tell us whether the project is underspent or late. It was shown that it is the comparison between earned value and actual cost that indicates whether the project is over- or underspent. The comparison between the earned value and the scheduled cost does however, tell us whether the project is early or late; if the earned value is greater than the scheduled cost, the project is on average early, and if it is less, it is on average late. I say on average, because it gives us no information about progress on the critical path. Critical work can have been delayed, but a larger, non-critical job brought forward, and the project appears to be early. We can calculate a second variance, the volume variance:

Volume variance = Earned value − Scheduled cost
% Variance = (Variance/Scheduled cost).

Example 8.4 presents a simple example of an earned value calculation, for a project to make a hundred pairs of shoes. Accountants talk about variances being favourable or unfavourable, rather than positive or negative, since the latter can be misleading. In this simple production model, it would be more common to talk about the cost variance as being £2 per pair (or 20 per cent) on the standard cost of £10 per pair; and the volume variance as being 20 pairs (or 20 per cent) on a production target of 100 pairs. Because projects are unique, it is not possible to talk of 'standard costs', and because they usually comprise quite a variety of work, the only standard for comparison is in expenditure, either of money or man-hours, and so everything must be translated to this standard for control purposes. Example 8.4 shows that earned value analysis is just standard management cost accounting, but applied to an endeavour which is unique, novel and transient, rather than repetitive.

Consider a very simple example of a 'project' to make 100 pairs of shoes at £10 per pair. At the end of the period, only 80 pairs have been made at £12 per pair. In this simple case we have:

Scheduled cost   =   100 pairs @ £10 per pair = £1000
Actual cost   =   80 pairs @ £12 per pair = £ 960
Earned value   =   80 pairs @ £10 per pair = £ 800

Cost variance   = £960 – £800   = £160 unfavourable
                                          = 20% unfavourable

Volume variance = £800 – £1000   = £200 unfavourable
                                          = 20% unfavourable

Example 8.4 Earned value calculation

When to make the comparisons

A second mistake in cost control is to record accrual and earned value only as invoices are paid. Although this provides a valid comparison, it is too late to overcome problems. You must therefore record accrual and earned value at an earlier time. This is usually as the cost is committed, when effective action can be taken. The cost may be committed either when the order is placed, or when the work is done:

1. The cost is committed when the order is placed for:
   – large material items
   – fixed price contracts.
2. The cost is committed when the work is done for:
   – labour
   – cost plus contracts
   – bulk materials.

For cost control purposes, it does not matter what is assumed for individual cost elements, as long as the same assumption is made throughout for each element; that is, the cost is accrued and the value earned together, and at the same time as the planned expenditure. However, the above gives the most effective means of control.

Forecasting completion

The variance calculation can be used to forecast the likely cost to complete the project. There are two simplifying assumptions:

1. The absolute variance at completion equals the variance to date:
   – Cost at completion = original estimate + variance to date.
2. The percentage variance at completion equals the percentage variance to date:
   – Cost at completion = original estimate × (1+% variance to date).

The latter is more realistic, but it is common to use the former because:

– some cost overspends are unlikely to be repeated
– those likely to be repeated may be reduced using experience to date
– some cost savings will be made to balance further overspend.

In fact the most accurate forecasts are obtained by applying the second formula above at lower levels of the WBS, using as the percentage variance to date, than on similar work elements modified in the light of experience.

Figure 8.7 shows a cost report prepared during the CRMO Rationalization Project, showing estimates percentage of completion and expenditure to date against both labour and materials, and comparing these to the scheduled percentage of completion, planned cost of work scheduled

PROJECT COST REPORT

PROJECT: CRMO RATIONALIZATION
WORK AREA: —
WORK PACKAGE: —

TRIMAGI COMMUNICATIONS BV

31-Aug-9X

WORK PACKAGE NO	DESCRIPTION	ORG DUR (D)	REM DUR (D)	BASE COMPL (%)	PERCT COMPL (%)	BASELINE LABOUR (£,000)	BASELINE MATL (£,000)	BASELINE TOTAL (£,000)	CURRENT ESTIMATE LABOUR (£,000)	CURRENT ESTIMATE MATL (£,000)	CURRENT ESTIMATE TOTAL (£,000)	SCHEDULED COST LABOUR (£,000)	SCHEDULED COST MATL (£,000)	SCHEDULED COST TOTAL (£,000)	EARNED VALUE LABOUR (£,000)	EARNED VALUE MATL (£,000)	EARNED VALUE TOTAL (£,000)	ACTUAL COMMITMENT LABOUR (£,000)	ACTUAL COMMITMENT MATL (£,000)	ACTUAL COMMITMENT TOTAL (£,000)
P1	Project definition	30.0		100.0%	100.0%	11.2	6.4	17.6	11.2	6.4	17.6	11.2	6.4	17.6	11.2	6.4	17.6	11.0	6.3	17.3
T1	Technology design	40.0		100.0%	100.0%	12.8		12.8	12.8	0.0	12.8	12.8	0.0	12.8	12.8	0.0	12.8	12.1	0.0	12.1
O1	Communication plan	5.0		100.0%	100.0%	1.2	2.5	3.7	1.2	2.5	3.7	1.2	2.5	3.7	1.2	2.5	3.7	1.2	2.4	3.6
O2	Operational proc.	15.0		100.0%	100.0%	9.6		9.6	9.6	0.0	9.6	9.6	0.0	9.6	9.6	0.0	9.6	9.8	0.0	9.8
O3	Job/Management desc.	20.0		100.0%	100.0%	12.8		12.8	12.8	0.0	12.8	12.8	0.0	12.8	12.8	0.0	12.8	12.5	0.0	12.5
T2	MIS function spec.	15.0		100.0%	100.0%	4.8		4.8	4.8	0.0	4.8	4.8	0.0	4.8	4.8	0.0	4.8	4.5	0.0	4.5
O4	Staff allocation	15.0		100.0%	100.0%	3.6		3.6	3.6	0.0	3.6	3.6	0.0	3.6	3.6	0.0	3.6	3.7	0.0	3.7
A1	Estates plan	10.0		100.0%	100.0%	1.6		1.6	1.6	0.0	1.6	1.6	0.0	1.6	1.6	0.0	1.6	1.6	0.0	1.6
T3	Technical plan	10.0		100.0%	100.0%	0.8		0.8	0.8	0.0	0.8	0.8	0.0	0.8	0.8	0.0	0.8	0.8	0.0	0.8
P2	Financial approval	15.0		100.0%	100.0%	3.6	1.5	5.1	3.6	1.5	5.1	3.6	1.5	5.1	3.6	1.5	5.1	3.6	1.5	5.1
A2	Sites 1&2 available	15.0		100.0%	100.0%	8.4	6.6	15.0	8.4	6.6	15.0	8.4	6.6	15.0	8.4	6.6	15.0	7.5	6.9	14.4
O5	Management changes	10.0		100.0%	100.0%	2.4		2.4	2.4	0.0	2.4	2.4	0.0	2.4	2.4	0.0	2.4	2.4	0.0	2.4
O6	Redeployment/train	40.0	10.0	100.0%	75.0%	25.6	55.2	80.8	24.4	52.6	77.0	24.4	52.6	77.0	18.3	52.6	70.9	17.9	52.2	70.1
T4	System in sites 1&2	30.0	20.0	100.0%	33.3%	19.2	44.0	63.2	19.2	44.0	63.2	19.2	44.0	63.2	6.4	44.0	50.4	4.5	42.4	46.9
A3	Sites 1&2 ready	15.0	15.0	50.0%	0.0%	8.4	60.0	68.4	9.2	66.0	75.2	4.6	66.0	70.6	0.0	0.0	0.0			
T5	MIS delivered	15.0	9.0	50.0%	40.0%	4.8	38.0	42.8	4.8	38.0	42.8	2.4	38.0	40.4	1.9	38.0	39.9	1.6	40.2	41.8
O7	Procedures implem.	10.0	10.0	0.0%	0.0%	4.0	10.8	14.8	4.0	10.8	14.8	0.0	0.0	0.0	0.0	0.0	0.0			
P3	Intermediate rev.	40.0	40.0	0.0%	0.0%	1.6		1.6	1.6	0.0	1.6	0.0	0.0	0.0	0.0	0.0	0.0			
A4	Roll-out implem.	80.0	80.0	0.0%	0.0%	64.0	240.0	304.0	70.4	264.0	334.4	0.0	0.0	0.0	0.0	0.0	0.0			
P4	Benefits obtained	60.0	60.0	0.0%	0.0%	2.4		2.4	2.4	0.0	2.4	0.0	0.0	0.0	0.0	0.0	0.0			
						202.8	465.0	667.8	208.8	492.4	701.2	123.4	217.6	341.0	99.4	151.6	251.0	94.7	151.9	246.6

Figure 8.7 Cost report for the CRMO Rationalization Project

(SCHEDULED COST), and planned cost of work complete (EARNED VALUE). Table 8.9 contains an explanation of abbreviations used. At the time of the report, the project is behind schedule, marginally underspent on labour and overspent on materials.

Table 8.9   Explanation of abbreviations in Figure 8.7

Abbreviation	Meaning
ORG DUR	The originally planned duration of each work package
REM DUR	The remaining duration with some work done
BASE COMPL	The expected (baseline), percentage completion at the time of reporting
PERCT COMPL	The actual percentage completion, calculated as: (ORG DUR – REM DUR)/ORG DUR
BASELINE	The original estimates of labour and material
CURRENT ESTIMATE	Are updated estimates after the project manager has consumed contingency
SCHEDULED COST	Is the planned cost of work scheduled for completion by this date
EARNED VALUE	Is the actual cost of work complete
ACTUAL COMMITMENT	Is the expenditure to date against each cost item

S-Curves

It is common to plot earned value and accrual on a time chart at each reporting period. As the project progresses they form the customarily shaped curve, called an 'S-curve'. The shape is caused by the work of the project taking some time to accelerate at the start, and slowing down towards the end. It provides a visual representation of whether the project is under- or overspent as it progresses. If the originally planned expenditure profile also happens to be plotted on the curve, the comparison of earned value to planned expenditure tells you whether the project is ahead or behind schedule (on average) and so provides an element of time control. Figure 8.8 shows S-curves for the four cases of projects over- and underspent and ahead and behind schedule.

8.8 Summary

1. A cost estimate is prepared as:
   – a basis for control
   – to assess the projects viability
   – to obtain funding

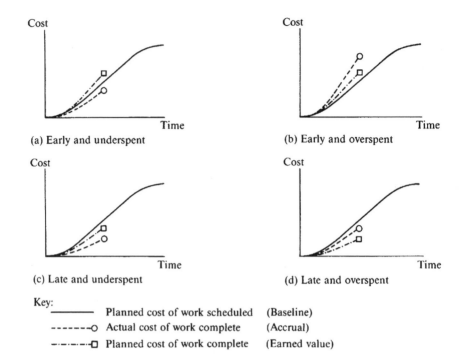

Key:

———— Planned cost of work scheduled   (Baseline)

------○ Actual cost of work complete   (Accrual)

—·—·—·□ Planned cost of work complete   (Earned value)

Figure 8.8   Monitoring costs using S-curves

- to allocate resources
- to estimate durations
- to prepare tenders for bespoke contracts.
2. There are five types of estimate of increasing accuracy requiring proportionately more work to prepare:
- proposal estimate
- budget estimate
- sanction estimate
- control estimate
- tender estimate.
3. The proposal estimate is prepared at proposal and initiation to commit resources to the first stage of the project. The budget estimate is prepared during proposal and initiation to initiate the project, and commit resources to design and appraisal. The sanction estimate is prepared during design and appraisal to gain funding for the project, or approval from the project sponsor. The control estimate is prepared during implementation planning. A tender estimate is prepared as part of the process of bidding for a contract.

4. There are over ten types of cost to be estimated, including:
   – labour
   – materials, plant and equipment
   – sub-contract
   – management, overhead and administration
   – fees, and taxation, inflation, and other contingency.
5. The cost control cube, a three-dimensional matrix of the PBS×
   OBS×CBS provides a structure for estimating and controlling costs. The
   estimate is prepared by breaking the work down to an appropriate level
   of WBS, and then estimating the cost of each element in the cost control
   cube.
6. Methods of estimating from the engineering construction industry
   include:
   – step counting methods
   – exponential methods
   – parametric methods
   – detailed and computerized methods.
7. Estimating methods in the building industry include:
   – approximate methods
   – functional methods
   – elemental prices
   – empirical studies
   – schedule of rates
   – priced bill of quantities.
8. Estimating methods in the IT industry include:
   – analogy methods
   – top-down and bottom-up estimating
   – mathematical models and Function point analysis.
9. Cost is controlled by comparing the earned value, a measure of the
   amount of work performed to date, to the actual expenditure to date. A
   comparison of earned value to the originally planned spend helps to
   control elapsed time. S-curves provide a visual representation.

References

1. Turner, J.R. (ed.), *The Commercial Project Manager*, McGraw-Hill, 1995.
2. George, D.J. (ed.), *A Guide to Capital Cost Estimating*, Institution of Chemical Engineers, 1988.
3. Morris, P.W.G. and Hough, G.H., *The Anatomy of Major Projects: A study of the reality of project management*, Wiley, 1987.
4. Spon, E. & F.N., *Budget Estimating Handbook*, 1st edn, E. & F.N. Spon, 1990.
5. Spon, E. & F.N., *Mechanical and Electrical Services Price Book*, 22nd edn, E. & F.N. Spon 1991.

6. For instance, see: Boehm, B.W., *Software Engineering Economics*, Prentice-Hall, 1981; DeMarco, T., *Controlling Software Projects: Management, measurement and estimation,* Yourdon Monograph, Prentice-Hall, 1982; Londeix, B., *Cost Estimation for Software Development*, Addison-Wesley, 1987; Pressman, R.S., *Software Engineering*, McGraw-Hill, 1987.
7. Brooks, F.P., *The Mythical Man-Month*, Addison-Wesley, 1982.
8. Albrecht, A., 'Software function, source lines of code, and development effort prediction', *IEEE Transactions on Software Engineering*, November 1983.
9. Flemming, Q.W. and Koppelman, J.M., *Earned Value Project Management*, Project Management Institute, 1996.

9
Managing time

9.1 Introduction

Let us now discuss the last of the five functions, managing time, by which the project manager coordinates the efforts of those involved, delivers the facility to meet market opportunities, and so ensures revenues are derived at a time which gives a satisfactory return on investment. All three of these purposes for managing time imply it is a soft constraint on most projects. Being late reduces the benefit; it does not cause the project to fail absolutely. There are only a few projects for which there is an absolute deadline. Project Giotto, the spacecraft which intercepted Halley's comet in 1986 was one: there was a very small time window in which to make the rendezvous, and if missed it would not reoccur for 76 years.[1] Another is the preparation for the Olympic Games. The start date is known six years in advance, to the nearest minute, and to miss the date would be very embarassing. Such projects are rare. Unfortunately many project managers treat time management as being synonymous with project management, and much of the project management software is written on this assumption.

In the next section, I consider the purpose of managing time, define the concepts and terminology of the time schedule, and introduce tools for communicating the schedule, including activity listings and bar charts. I describe how to calculate the duration of work elements, and how to use networks to calculate the overall project duration. I then show how to adjust the schedule by balancing resource requirements and resource availability, and end by describing the use of the schedule in controlling the duration of a project.

9.2 The time schedule

The time schedule is a series of dates against the work elements in the work breakdown structure, which record:

– when we forecast the work will occur
– when the work actually does occur.

Purpose of the schedule

The purpose of recording these dates and times is:

- to ensure the benefits are obtained at a time scale that justifies the expenditure
- to coordinate the effort of resources
- to enable the resources to be made available when required
- to predict the levels of money and resources required at different times so that priorities can be assigned between projects
- to meet a rigid end date.

The first of these is the most important. It addresses the *raison d'être* of project management, achieving the overall purpose and mission. The second is the next most important as it enables the project to happen. The third and fourth are variations of this. It is the fifth item that gets most attention from project managers. They set a rigid end date, sometimes unnecessarily, and focus on this to the detriment of cost and quality. Indeed, part of the aims of managing the time is to optimize the cost and returns from the project. Figure 9.1 shows that the cost is made up of two elements:

- a work-dependent element; 100 man-days is the same whether 5 people take 20 days or 2 people take 50 days
- a time-dependent element; the project manager's salary for instance.

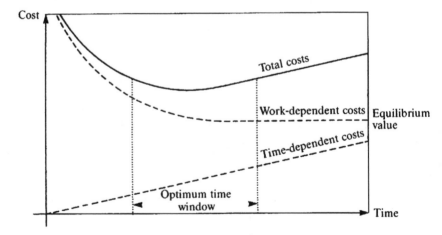

Figure 9.1   Timing of minimum cost of a project

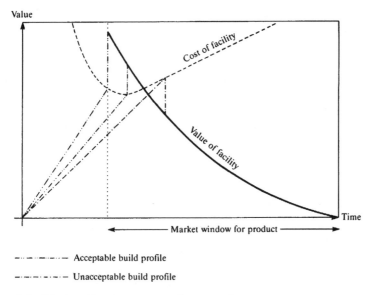

- ·· — ·· — ··· — Acceptable build profile

— · — ·· — · — · — Unacceptable build profile

Figure 9.2   Timing of optimum return from a project

However, the work-dependent element does actually increase as you try to shorten the project, and people interfere with each other, 10 people taking 12 days, and 20 people 8, perhaps. Adding the two together gives an optimum time window for the project in which cost is minimized. Figure 9.2 shows that maximum returns may not correspond to minimum cost. The value of the facility may decay with time, because of limited market window, and so on and hence highest profit may be made at a time earlier than minimum cost. Through the time schedule we must optimize cost and benefit.

The schedule

On a simple level, the schedule records the planned and actual start date, finish date and duration of each work element. We may also record whether there is any flexibility in when each element may start without delaying the completion of the project. This is called the *float*. Sophisticated schedules record up to five versions of each of the start date, finish date, duration, and float; the early, late, baseline, scheduled and actual dates.

THE DURATION

This is the time to do the work. It is common to treat a work element's duration as an immutable figure. For some, it is dependent on external factors beyond the control of the team. For others, it is a variable, which can be changed by varying the number of people working on the activity.

Methods of estimating durations are described in the next section and of balancing durations and resource levels in Section 9.5. For now we will assume they are fixed. Therefore, before work starts we have for each activity an estimated duration. Once work starts, but before it finishes, we can estimate a remaining duration. This may be equal to the planned duration less the time since the activity started, or we may re-estimate remaining duration based on the knowledge gained from doing the work so far. Once work is complete we can record an actual duration. It is useful to record actuals because a comparison of planned and actual figures may indicate trends which may be useful in the control process.

EARLY AND LATE DATES

These can be forecast from estimated duration of all the activities. In Chapter 5, it was stated that the start or finish of an activity may be dependent on finishing other work. Therefore there is an earliest date by which a work element may start. This is known as the *early start date*. The early start date plus the estimated duration is the *early finish date*, the earliest date by which the work can finish. Similarly, other work may be dependent on the element's being finished, so there is a latest date by which it can finish and not delay completion of the project. This is known as the *late finish date*, and correspondingly the late start date is this less the estimated duration. If the late start date is different to the early start date, there is flexibility about when the element can start, the *float*:

Float = Late start date − Early start date.

If the duration is immutable, the difference between early and late start and early and late finish is the same, (and indeed this is the assumption made in most scheduling systems). However, it is not too difficult to imagine situations in which the duration is dependent on the time of year the work is done.

A work element with zero float is said to be critical, its duration determines the project's duration. If a project is scheduled with minimum duration, then running through it will be a series of work elements with zero float. This series is known as the *critical path*. Work elements with a large float are known as *bulk work*. They are used to smooth forecast resource usage, by filling gaps in the demands made by the critical path. There are also work elements with a very small float. These are *near critical*, and should receive as much attention as the critical path. In Section 9.4, CPM (critical path method) networks are described, which are mathematical tools for calculating early and late start and finish and float.

PLANNED, BASELINED AND SCHEDULE DATES

These are dates between the early and late dates when we choose to do the work. These are *planned dates*. However, the date we planned to do a work element at the start of the project may be different to our current plan. It is important to record the original plan, because that is the measure against which we control time. This original measure is commonly known as the *baseline date*, and the current plan as the *scheduled date*. If the baseline start is later than the early start, then the planned or baseline float will be less than the available float. Likewise, as a project progresses, if the start or finish of a work element is further delayed, then the remaining float will be less than the original float.

THE TOTAL SCHEDULE

Hence in a full scheduling system, there are up to 15 dates and times associated with a work element (Example 9.1). The process of scheduling the project is the assignment of values to these dates and times. The first step is to estimate the duration and the second is to assign start and finish dates. This is usually done by calculating the early start and late finish dates and then assigning baseline dates somewhere between these, after taking account of other factors such as resource smoothing. It is sometimes necessary to assign a finish date after the late finish and thereby delay the project. If the logic is correct it will be impossible to schedule the start before the early start.

Early start	Duration	Early finish
Late start	Float	Late finish
Baseline start	Baseline float	Baseline finish
Schedule start	Remaining float	Schedule finish
Actual start	Remaining duration	Actual finish

where:

Planned duration = Planned finish − Planned start;
Planned float   = Late finish − Planned finish.

Example 9.1 Scheduled dates associated with a work element

For some projects with a well-constructed WBS, it is possible to schedule the project manually, by nesting the schedule at lower levels within that at higher levels. To be able to do this it must be possible to break the project into discrete work areas and work packages, with few logical links between them and little sharing of resources. The four large multi-disciplinary projects described in Section 5.7 were four such projects. In the Regional Health Authority warehouse and the Norwegian Security Centre projects, the project managers positively resisted computer systems because they felt they retained greater visibility without them. Where there are complex interdependencies and multiple shared resources, it may be necessary to use computer-aided support tools.

The processes of estimating durations and calculating and assigning dates, including the use of computer-aided network planning systems will be described in the next sections. However, first it is appropriate to describe tools by which the schedule is communicated.

Communicating the schedule

There are two accepted ways of communicating a project's schedule:

ACTIVITY LISTING WITH DATES

This is a list of some of the work elements at a given level of the WBS, with some or all of the dates and times above listed beside them. This method of communicating the schedule can give a comprehensive checklist, but is not very visible. Figure 9.3 is an activity listing for a simple project to erect a statue by early start/early finish. Although this list shows the float, I believe it should not be shown as it tends to be consumed.

BAR CHARTS

The schedule can be more visibly represented by the use of bar charts (sometimes called Gantt charts, after Henry Gantt who pioneered their use). Figure 9.4(a) is a simple bar chart for the project in Figure 9.3. Figure 9.4(b) is the same bar chart with the float shown. It is also possible to show the logic in a bar chart (Figure 9.4(c)).

LANDSCAPE LTD
ACTIVITY LISTING

PROJECT NAME: ERECT STATUE

Activity No Name		Duration (days)	Early start (day)	Early finish (day)	Float (days)
A	Grade site	3	0	3	0
B	Cast plinth	2	3	5	0
C	Plant grass	3	3	6	1
D	Set concrete	2	5	7	0
E	Place statue	1	7	8	0

Figure 9.3 Activity listing

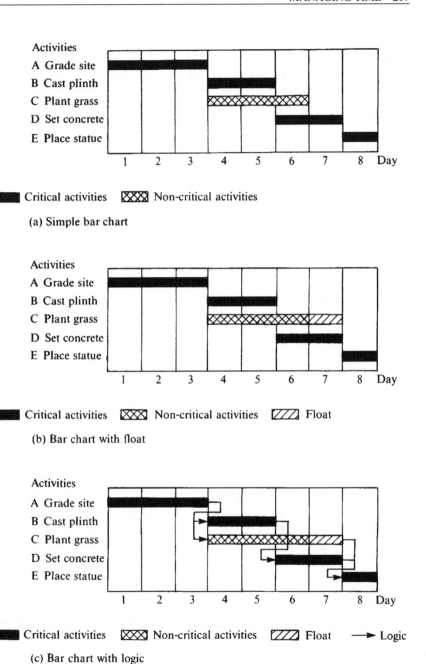

Figure 9.4   Bar charts for the activity listing in Figure 9.3

9.3 Estimating durations

The duration of work elements is central to the scheduling process, not only in relating the start and finish of a given work element, but in calculating its earliest start from the cumulative duration of the preceding activities, and the latest finish from the cumulative duration of the succeeding activities. The duration of a work element is dependent on one of three things:

- the amount of time it physically takes to do the work involved, which in turn is dependent on the number of people available to do it
- the lead time, or waiting time, for the delivery of some item, which is independent of the number of people doing the work
- some mixture of the two.

Duration dependent on work content
It is often assumed the duration of a work element depends on the amount of work to do and the number of people available to do it. Nominally:

$$\text{Duration (days)} = \frac{\text{Work content (man-days)}}{\text{Number of people available}}$$

I described the role of work content in negotiating the contract between project manager and resource providers in Chapter 6 and how to estimate it as a labour cost in Chapter 8. It is always necessary to add allowances to this raw estimate of duration, to calculate the actual duration. These allowances are to account for various factors, which include:

LOST TIME
Somebody nominally working full time on a project is not available 5 days per week, 52 weeks per year. They lose time through holidays, public holidays, sickness, training, group meetings, etc. It was suggested in Section 6.5 that for the average project worker these consume 80 days per year; somebody assigned full time to a project does on average 180 days of project work a year, equivalent to 70 per cent availability. To allow for this 40 per cent is added to the nominal duration ($1.4 = 1.0/0.7$). A smaller ratio will be added if the project's resource calendar allows for some lost time.

PART-TIME WORKING
Individuals may be assigned to a project part time. Therefore the number of people should be based on the number of full-time equivalents (FTE). However, you must be careful not to double account. If somebody is assigned two days per week to a project (40 per cent), you must be clear whether those two days include or exclude a proportion of the lost time above before adding the 40 per cent allowance.

INTERFERENCE

Doubling the number of workers does not always halve the duration, because people doing work can restrict each other's access to the work face, and so reduce their effectiveness. For instance, if the task requires access to a limited space with room for just one person, adding a second person will not double the rate of working. Two will work faster than one, because they can step each other off, but only one can work at a time. Adding a third person will not increase the rate of working, and may even reduce it by distracting the other two. A third person would be most effectively used to extend the working day through a shift system.

COMMUNICATION

Where more than one person works on a job, they need to communicate details of the work to each other to make progress. This is especially true of engineering design and writing software. With two people there is just one communication channel, so they may work almost twice as fast as one. With three people there are three channels, with four people six, and as the number of people grow, the channels grow exponentially. Hence, you reach a point where adding another person in fact reduces the amount of effective work (Example 9.2). The way to overcome this is to find ways of reducing the channels of communication, by using a central administrator or Project Support Office (Chapter 14). In the office in Example 9.2, the pool was split into four pools of three secretaries. It is commonly believed that in a professional office, three is the optimum team size, balancing the additional motivation from working in a team, with the added levels of communication.

In an office in which I worked, there were three managers each with a secretary. As the office grew, and new managers joined, the numbers of secretaries grew, until there were about twelve working in the same pool. We reached a point where adding a new secretary seemed to make no difference to the amount of work done in the pool. If we assume a new secretary spends a quarter of an hour each day talking to each of the others, (not an unreasonable amount of time for social interaction), then each conversation consumes half an hour's work, and since she has twelve conversations, six hours are lost, equal to the effective working day.

Example 9.2 Communication consumes time

ESTIMATING DURATIONS

Hence the estimate of duration for a work element is based on the formula above, but adjusted taking account of all the factors discussed, which may indeed dominate. This reinforces the fact that project management is not a mathematical exercise, but much more of a social science one.

Duration dependent on lead time

For some work elements the duration depends on the lead time or waiting time to obtain some item of material or information or to wait for some change to take place. This may include:

- delivery time for materials in procurement activities
- preparation of reports
- negotiations with clients or contractors
- obtaining planning permission or financial approval
- setting of concrete or watching the grass grow.

In these cases the likely duration will be known from historical data or the known cycle of events.

The work package, *05: Redeployment and Training*, from the CRMO Rationalization Project, may consist of the following activities:

- identify training needs of staff
- develop training material
- conduct courses
- transfer staff to new posts.

The first two of these are work-content dependent. The number of trainers assigned will depend on the number of people requiring training and the amount of material to be developed. However, two people will not work twice as fast as one because they will need to keep each other informed of progress. The duration of the third activity depends on the availability of the training facilities, and the fourth on how quickly people can be assimilated into new work environments.

Example 9.3 A work package from the CRMO Rationalization Project containing activities of mixed type

Duration dependent on work content and lead time

In some instances a work element contains lower level activities, some of which are work-content dependent and some lead-time dependent (Example 9.3). The duration of the work package must be calculated from the duration of each of the activities and their logical dependence, perhaps using the networking techniques described in the next section in more complex cases. (If you are adopting a rolling-wave approach to planning, at the start of the project you will estimate the duration of the work package as a whole working from a work-package scope statement and making use of previous experience, and only do the more detailed analysis when you are about to start the work.)

Estimating sheets
The estimating sheet (Figure 6.12) was introduced as a tool for estimating work content. The same sheet can be used for estimating durations (Figure 9.5). Example 9.4 provides a rationale.

---

1. The person with the most work to do is the project control officer, with 24 man-days.
2. Therefore the duration of the work package will be determined by their availability.
3. It is assumed that during Project Definition control officer will not take holiday. Therefore his or her availability will be greater than the average 70 per cent. A figure of 80 per cent is assumed.
4. The duration is therefore 30 (24/0.8) days.

Example 9.4   Rationale for the duration of the work package *P1: Project Definition*

9.4 Calculating the schedule with networks

Having estimated duration, we assign dates to work elements. In the distant past, that was done manually using bar charts (Section 9.2). With the increasing size and complexity of projects this became more difficult, until computer-aided tools were introduced in the 1950s. Since then, these have grown in power. The mathematical technique on which they are based is the critical path method (CPM), sometimes called critical path analysis (CPA), or the programme evaluation and review technique (PERT). The initials CPM, CPA and PERT are used interchangeably by many people, although they do mean something slightly different. Networks are a mathematical technique used to calculate the schedule. They are seldom useful for communicating the schedule. Bar charts or activity listings (Section 9.2) are best used for that. Networks will only be used where the project is too complex to be scheduled manually through the WBS and so will only be used in conjunction with computer-aided systems. In this section I describe the mathematical technique of networking. Computer-aided project management information systems (PMIS) are described in Chapter 15.

Types of network
There are three types of network:

PRECEDENCE NETWORKS
In precedence networks, work elements are represented by boxes, linked by logical dependencies, which show that one element follows another. Figure

ESTIMATING SHEET			TRIMAGI COMMUNICATIONS BV					02-Jan-9X	
PROJECT:	CRMO Rationalization	CODE:	C1		ISSUE:	A			
WORK AREA:	Project	CODE:	C1P		AUTHOR:	LJN			
WORK PACKAGE:	Project Definition	CODE:	C1P1		APPRVD:	JRT			
ACTIVITY:	....	CODE:	....		DATE:	02-Jan-9X			

ACTIVITY/TASK	WORK CONTENT			RESOURCES				9 People	
	No of steps	Effort/ step	Total effort	Prjct Mgr	Prjct Offc	CRMO TL	CRMO Mgrs	Ops Direct	Other Mgrs
Number Description	(days)	(days)		1	1	1	2	1	3
1 Produce project proposal	1	4	4	1	2	1			
2 Hold project definition workshop	1	4	4	1	1	1		1	
3 Define required benefits	1	2	2	1		1			
4 Draft Project Definition Report	1	8	8	2	6				
5 Hold project launch workshop, 1.5 day duration	1	12	12	1.5	1.5	1.5	3		4.5
6 Finalize milestone plan	1	2	2	1	1				
7 Finalize project responsibility chart	1	2	2	1	1				
8 Prepare estimates - time	20	0.1	2		2				
9 Prepare estimates - cost	20	0.1	2		2				
10 Prepare estimates - revenue	1	1	1		1				
11 Assess project viability	1	1	1	1					
12 Assess risks	1	3	3	1	1	1			
13 Finalize Project Definition Report	1	5	5	2	3				
14 Mobilize team	1	3	3	0.5	0.5	0.5			1.5
SUB-TOTAL:		51		13	22	6	3	1	6
ALLOWANCE % 10				10	10	10	10	10	10
TOTAL EFFORT: 56				14	24	7	3	1	7
UNIT RATE: £K/day				0.5	0.3	0.3	0.5	0.8	0.5
COST: £K				7.15	7.26	1.98	1.65	0.88	3.30

TOTAL EFFORT: 56 DAYS
TOTAL COST: £K 22.22
DURATION: 30 DAYS
TARGET START: 01-Feb-9X
TARGET FINISH: 15-Mar-9X

Figure 9.5 Estimating sheet with durations entered for the milestone *P1: Project Definition* from the CRMO Rationalization Project

9.6 is a simple precedence network with four activities A, B, C and D. B and C follow A and D follows B and C. Four types of logical dependency are allowed (Figure 9.7):

– *end-to-start*: B cannot start until A is finished
– *end-to-end*:   D cannot finish until C is finished
– *start to-start*: D cannot start until C has started
– *start-to-end*: F cannot end until E has started.

End-to-start dependency is usually used (a hangover from IJ networks). End-to-end and start-to-start dependencies are the most natural and allow overlap of succeeding work elements in time. It is not uncommon to build ladders of activities like C and D. It is the use of end-to-end and start-to-start dependencies which allows fast track or fast build construction (Section 4.4). Start-to-end are only defined for mathematical completeness. I have never come across a case where it might be used. I will introduce later leads and lags on dependencies. It is now increasingly common to use only end-to-start dependencies, and use leads to overlap

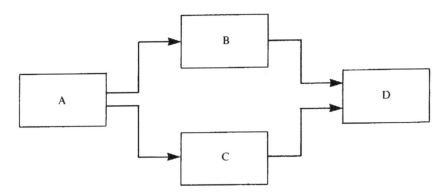

Figure 9.6   A simple precedence network

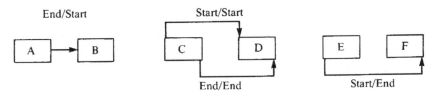

Figure 9.7   Four types of logical dependency

activities. This greatly simplifies the network, and is to be recommended for that reason.

The milestone plan (Section 5.5) is a precedence network. The circles, (nodes), represent the work. The lines are end-to-end dependencies, linking the milestones.

ACTIVITY-ON-ARROW NETWORKS

These are often called IJ networks, because each activity is defined by an IJ (start/finish) number. In this type of network a work element is represented by an arrow between two nodes. The activity is known by the number of the two nodes it links. Figure 9.8 is Figure 9.6 drawn as an IJ network. Activity A becomes 1–2, etc. Because activities must be uniquely defined two cannot link the same two nodes. Therefore B and C finish in nodes 3 and 4 respectively and these nodes are linked by a dummy activity. Because activities are linked through nodes, end-to-start logic is imposed. However, it is possible to introduce dummy activities to represent the other three logical links.

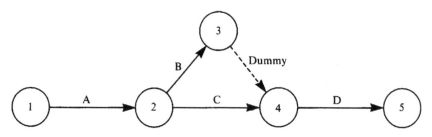

Figure 9.8   Activity-on-arrow network

HYBRID NETWORKS

These mix the two previous types. Work is represented by either a box (node) or a line (arrow). Furthermore there may be boxes and lines which do not represent work, just events in time and logical dependency. A line need not join a box at its start or finish, but at any time before, during or after its duration. In advanced hybrid networks, even the distinction between nodes and lines disappears. The mathematics of hybrid networks is fairly new so they will not be discussed further.

PRECEDENCE VS ACTIVITY-ON-ARROW NETWORKS

You will find some people fervently committed to one or the other. The early work in the 1950s was done with arrow networks, whereas precedence networks were not introduced until the 1960s. Therefore arrow networks tend to be the more widely used. However, precedence networks are gaining wider preference with practising project managers. There are several reasons for this:

1. It is more natural to associate work with a box.
2. It is more flexible for drawing networks. All the boxes can be drawn on a page and the logical dependencies put in later. In Section 6.5, I described how to develop a precedence network (milestone plan) by moving Post-It notes around a flip chart or white board. The same is not possible with an activity network because the activities are only defined by two nodes and that imposes logic.
3. It is easier to write network software for precedence networks. Most modern software is precedence only or both. That which is both has an algorithm to convert from precedence to IJ.
4. It is easier to draw a bar chart showing precedence logic with the bars representing the activity boxes and vertical lines showing the logical dependencies (Figure 9.4(c)). With an arrow network either more than one activity must be drawn on a line or dummies must be used to show logic, which virtually gives a precedence network. (This last statement reintroduces hybrid networks, and shows that the distinction between precedence and IJ networks really is slight.)
5. The work exists independently of the logic, and so you can draw a work breakdown structure and overlay the logic later. If you use the C/SCSC methodology and the approach described in this book, where you define the work of the project first, then you are almost forced to use precedence networks. (People who use IJ networks have to draw the network before developing the work breakdown structure.) For this reason precedence networks are treated more fully here.

Networking technique
All networks do is to calculate the early start and finish, the late start and finish and the float of work elements in a project given their duration and logical dependency. The reason this is so powerful is it allows you to explore many different options, called conducting a *what-if* analysis, assuming different durations and logical dependencies of the work elements. As I introduce networking technique, I will illustrate it by scheduling a simple project, represented by the network in Figure 9.6. An activity listing for the network is given in Figure 9.9. This is modified Figure 9.3 and you will see shortly that the activity, 'set concrete' has been replaced by a lag on the logical dependency from B to D.

In a precedence network, each work element is represented by a box with seven segments (Figure 9.10). The top three segments contain the early start, duration and early finish respectively. The bottom three contain the late start, float and late finish. The central one contains a description of the activity. Figure 9.11 is Figure 9.6 with durations entered. In an arrow network the node has four segments, the identifier, the early and late time and the float. The time is the start of the succeeding activity and the finish

LANDSCAPE LTD ACTIVITY LISTING			
PROJECT NAME: ERECT STATUE			
Activity No Description	Duration (days)	Preceding activities	Lead/Lag (days)
A Grade site	3	—	0
B Cast plinth	2	A	−2
C Plant grass	3	A	0
D Place statue on plinth	1	B, C	+2,0

Figure 9.9   Activity listing for a project to erect a statue

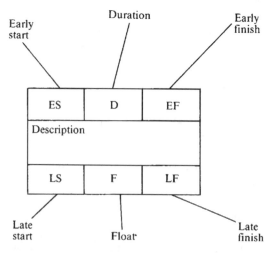

Figure 9.10   Activity in a precedence network

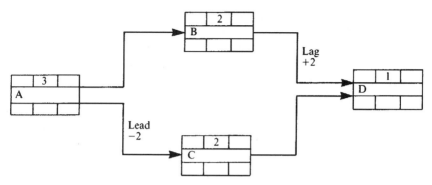

Figure 9.11   Precedence network: durations entered

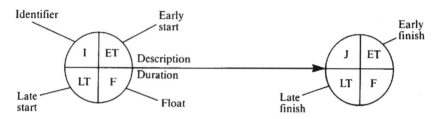

Figure 9.12   Activity in an IJ network

of the preceding activity. The duration is still associated with the activity (Figure 9.12).

LEADS AND LAGS

The dependencies connecting the activities in a precedence network usually have zero duration. However, they can be given positive or negative duration, and this is called *lag* or *lead* respectively. In Figure 9.9 the concrete must be left for two days to dry before erecting the statue. These two days can either be added to the duration of B (taking it to 4 days) or shown as a lag on the dependency. Similarly it might be possible to start planting grass on the second day after the first third of the site has been graded. This can be shown as a start-to-start dependency with a lag of 1 or a finish-to-start with a lead of −2. The latter is chosen. The leads and lags are also shown in Figure 9.11.

FORWARD PASS

Early start and finish are calculated by conducting a *forward pass* through the network. The early start of the first activity is zero and the early finish is calculated by adding the duration. The early finish is transferred to subsequent activities as the early start, adding or subtracting any lead or lag, assuming a finish-to-start dependency. For a start-to-start dependency it is the start time which is transferred to the start, for a finish-to-finish dependency the finish time is transferred to the finish, and for a start-to-finish the start time is transferred to the finish. Where an activity has two or more preceding activities the largest number is transferred. The process is repeated throughout the network. Figure 9.13 shows the example network after a forward pass.

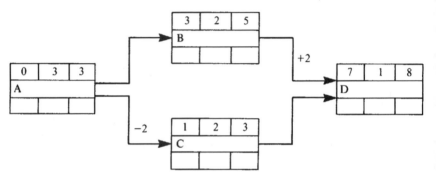

Figure 9.13   Network after forward pass

BACK PASS

The late start and finish and float are calculated by conducting a *back pass*. The early finish of the last activity becomes its late finish. The duration is subtracted to calculate the late start. The late start is transferred back to the late finish of preceding activities. Again it is the start or finish time which is transferred to become the start or finish time depending on the type of dependency. Where an activity has two or more succeeding activities it is the smallest number which is transferred, (after adding lags or subtracting leads). The process is repeated throughout the network. The float of each activity is calculated (Section 9.2). (This should be the same for both start and finish.) The float of the first and last activities should be zero. Figure 9.14 shows the network after the back pass.

IDENTIFYING THE CRITICAL PATH

This is the series of activities with zero float, here A–B–D. Some text books suggest you find the critical path, not by conducting a forward and back pass, but by identifying every possible path and finding that with the longest duration. This works with small networks, but it does not take many activities before this becomes an impossible task. The method of forward and back

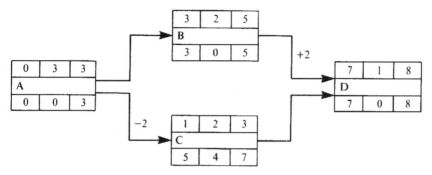

Figure 9.14   Network after back pass

pass is designed to cope with networks of limitless size. Since you only need to use networking on large projects, it is the approach recommended.

ARROW NETWORKS
Figure 9.15 shows figure 9.14 drawn as an arrow network after forward and back pass.

CASE STUDY PROJECT
Figure 9.16 is the precedence network (at work-package level) for the CRMO Rationalization Project.

SOFTWARE PACKAGES
Some software packages assume that if an activity has a start date of day 6

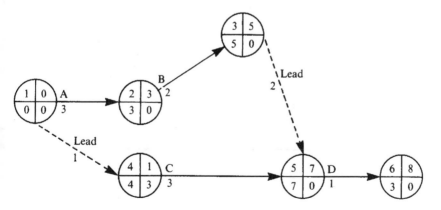

Figure 9.15   Arrow network after forward and back pass

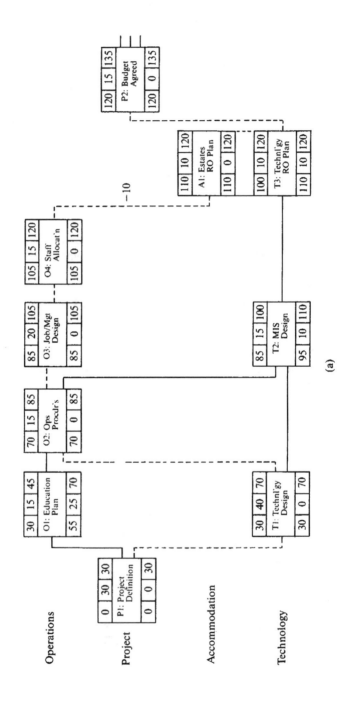

(a)

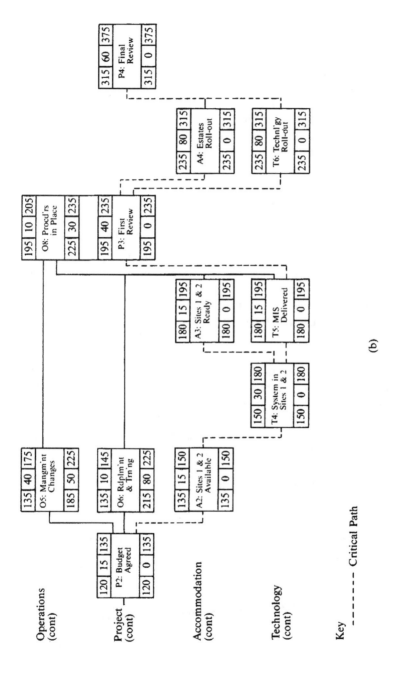

Operations
(cont)

135	40	175
O5: Mangm'nt Changes		
185	50	225

195	10	205
O8: Procd'rs in Place		
225	30	235

Project
(cont)

120	15	135
P2: Budget Agreed		
120	0	135

135	10	145
O6: Rdplm'nt & Trn'ng		
215	80	225

195	40	235
P3: First Review		
195	0	235

235	80	315
A4: Estates Roll-out		
235	0	315

315	60	375
P4: Final Review		
315	0	375

Accommodation
(cont)

135	15	150
A2: Sites 1 & 2 Available		
135	0	150

180	15	195
A3: Sites 1 & 2 Ready		
180	0	195

Technology
(cont)

150	30	180
T4: System in Sites 1 & 2		
150	0	180

180	15	195
T5: MIS Delivered		
180	0	195

235	80	315
T6: Technl'gy Roll-out		
235	0	315

Key

------ Critical Path

(b)

Figure 9.16   Precedence network at work-package level for CRMO Rationalization Project

(Monday, say) and duration 3, then it will finish on Wednesday evening, day 8. Therefore the finish is:

$$\text{Finish date} = \text{Start date} + \text{Duration} - 1.$$

However, if there is no delay to the start of the next activity, it starts on Thursday morning, day 9. Therefore a day is added as the finish date is transferred to the start of the next activity. The start date of the first activity is taken as day 1, Monday morning, rather than zero as used above. The overall effect is just to add one to all the start dates you would obtain using the method proposed above.

Scheduling the project

The network only calculates early and late dates. The baseline or scheduled dates must be chosen taking account of other factors. Hopefully they will be between the early and late dates. There are three options:

- *schedule by early start, (hard-left)*: used to motivate the workforce
- *schedule by late finish, (hard-right)*: used to present progress in the best light to the customer
- *schedule in between*: done either to smooth resource usage (Section 9.5) or to show management the most likely outcome.

Using networks

Networks are a mathematical tool to be used as appropriate. This does not depend on the size of the project. In Section 5.6, I gave examples of multi-million pound projects where they were not used. It depends on the complexity of the interdependencies and resource sharing and the manager's ability to analyse these without computer support. As a mathematical tool, they help the manager calculate the schedule and analyse the impact of changes (what-if analysis). However, except as a milestone plan, networks should not be used to communicate the plan or schedule: bar charts should be used for that purpose.

9.5 Resource histograms and resource smoothing

Using a network, you can calculate the early and late start and finish for work elements. However, in order to set the baseline or scheduled dates, it is necessary to take account of other constraints. Resource constraints are the most common. If the resource requirements for all activities are known, once the project has been scheduled you can calculate a resource profile for the project as a whole. This is known as the resource schedule and is either listed as a table of resource levels with time or is drawn as a resource histogram. This resource schedule can be compared to the known availability of each type of resource, and if the requirement exceeds availability it may be necessary to adjust the schedule to reduce the requirement. It may be possible to do this by consuming some of the float on non-critical activities. Alternatively, it may be necessary to extend the duration of the project.

The method of calculating the duration of an activity was given in Section 9.3. Although no mention was made at the time, this calculation assumed either a constant or stepped resource usage during the activity. Figure 9.17 illustrates four possible resource profiles for an activity: constant, stepped, triangular and normal. Constant or stepped profiles are almost always used at the activity level, and indeed the errors introduced by these simplifying assumptions cancel out at the work package or project level. Using triangular or normal profiles is something which is quite easy with modern computer systems.

Figure 9.18 is an activity listing for a small project which I will use to illustrate the concept of resource scheduling. There are two resource types: analysts and programmers. Figure 9.19(a) shows the bar chart and resource histogram for both resource types with the project scheduled by early start. This produces quite wildly varying resource levels. If there were only one analyst available to the project, he or she would be overloaded during the first two months of the project. One person can work up to 22 days in a month without overtime. To overcome this problem we can try to use the float associated with some of the work elements to smooth the resource

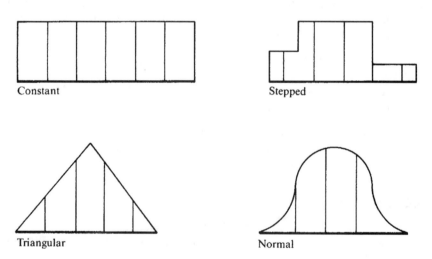

Constant   Stepped

Triangular   Normal

Figure 9.17   Resource profile for an activity

TRIMAGI COMMUNICATIONS BV
ACTIVITY LISTING

PROJECT NAME: CRMO RATIONALIZATION
WORK AREA: MIS DESIGN AND DELIVERY

Acty	Durn	Early	Late	Early	Late	Resource requirement	
		start	start	finish	finish	Analyst	Programmer
	(mths)	(mth)	(mth)	(mth)	(mth)	(days)	(days)
A	3	0	1	3	4	24	—
B	2	0	2	2	4	24	—
C	2	0	2	2	4	16	16
D	1	3	4	4	5	—	12
E	1	0	3	1	4	—	4
F	4	0	0	4	4	16	—
G	1	4	4	5	5	12	8
H	1	5	5	6	6	4	8

Figure 9.18 Activity listing for an IT project

profiles. Figure 9.19(b) shows the bar chart and resource profiles for the project scheduled by late start. This is no better as the analyst is still overloaded, but now in months 3 and 4.

Concentrating on the analyst, Figure 9.19(c) shows a schedule which gives the least variability of the analyst's utilization, giving a maximum level of 24 days in month 3. This can be easily met by overtime. It also illustrates two further points:

– the danger of imposing a rigid resource constraint of 22 days which would delay the project
– the need to encourage the analyst to take his or her annual holiday in months 5 and 6 rather than months 1 to 3.

Alternatively you can take the programmer as priority. Figure 9.19(d) shows the schedule and resource profiles in that case. However, this overloads the analyst again.

9.6 Controlling time

Up to this point, I have explained how to calculate and communicate the schedule. I conclude by discussing how to use the schedule to control the project's duration, which is the primary purpose of setting the schedule. There are four steps in the control process, (Section 8.2):

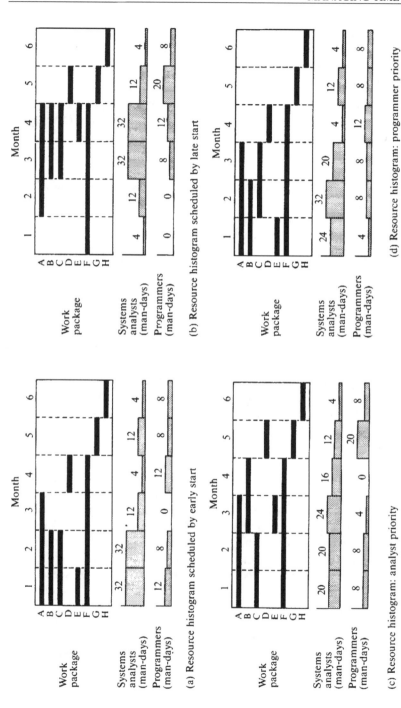

(a) Resource histogram scheduled by early start

(b) Resource histogram scheduled by late start

(c) Resource histogram: analyst priority

(d) Resource histogram: programmer priority

Figure 9.19 Resource smoothing

identified as the critical path. Indeed, if you focus all your management attention on one path, you can guarantee another will determine the duration.

Where delays occur to bulk work, it will have little effect on the remaining float of future activities, until it has been delayed so much that it is itself critical. Indeed resources may be switched from bulk work to critical work to maintain progress on the latter.

In order to determine the impact of any delays on the project, and any proposals for eliminating them, it is necessary to analyse the effect of each on the overall project. This is a repeat of the what-if analysis described above. If the WBS has been well constructed this analysis can often be conducted manually, by analysing the effect of the delay on the work package within which it occurs and then the effect of the work package on the overall project. The milestone plan is a powerful tool for determining whether a work package is critical and its effect on the project. This approach gives greater management control. Alternatively, where there are complex interdependencies and multiple shared resources, the analysis can be performed using the network. This provides a more accurate picture of the effect of changes, but it is difficult to determine the appropriate changes in the first place. The network does provide a valuable support to the manual approach, avoiding oversights.

S-curves

S-curves (Section 8.7) provide a pictorial representation of whether the project is on average, ahead of or behind schedule. The volume variance introduced in that section is another time variance, in addition to the remaining float on critical activities.

9.7 Summary

1. The purpose of scheduling time on a project is:
   - to obtain timely benefits which justify the expenditure
   - to coordinate resource inputs
   - to schedule resource availability
   - to assign priority for resources between projects
   - to meet a specified end date.
2. The schedule specifies the duration, start and finish date, and float of the activities in the project. There are several dates recorded against each activity:
   - early date
   - late date, and float
   - baseline date, and baseline float

  – most likely date, and remaining float
  – actual date, and remaining duration.
3. The schedule can be communicated as:
  – an activity listing
  – bar charts.
4. The duration is calculated by comparing the work content to the number of people available, and allowing for:
  – lost time
  – part-time working
  – interference
  – communication
  – lead times
  – sequencing of tasks within activities.
5. The early and late dates can be calculated from the durations and logical sequence of the activities using a critical path network. The are two types of network:
  – precedence network
  – activity-on-arrow network.
6. Given the initial schedule and resource requirements for each activity, a resource schedule can be calculated showing the requirements for each type of resource with time. This can be smoothed by delaying bulk work to fill peaks and troughs, or by extending the duration of the project. Then resulting schedule is frozen as the baseline.
7. Progress against the schedule can be monitored by:
  – recording progress on the critical or near critical paths
  – recording progress on S-curves.

Reference

1. Morris, P.W.G. and Hough, G.H., *The Anatomy of Major Projects: The reality of project management,* Wiley, 1987.

10
Managing risk

10.1 Introduction

The last five chapters have described methods, tools and techniques for the five functions of project management, managing scope, project organization, quality, cost and time. All five of these require us to make predictions about future performance, and, as we all know, we cannot predict the future. We can only make informed guesses. We have seen several times over the last nine chapters, that the more effort that is put into our estimates (guesses) the more accurate they will be, and the more historical information that can be used in guiding those estimates, the more accurate they will be. However, if we put too much effort into our estimates, we reach a point where the estimate costs more than the impact of the inherent risk. In a repetitive production environment the uncertainty can be reduced to a very low level, and the emphasis of management becomes to eliminate any variations from the status quo, because variations remove certainty and hence reintroduce risk. In a project environment, because of the essential uniqueness of projects, some uncertainty must always remain, and hence the emphasis of management becomes to manage the risk. In my view, the essence of project management is risk management.

In spite of that, six years ago, when I wrote the first edition of this book, risk management was one of the most poorly researched and documented areas of project management. There were books on the management of risk on large projects,[1] but virtually nothing on the essentials of risk management, accessible by all project managers. How that has changed, and now risk management is one of the most well-researched and documented areas,[2,3,4,5] and has been codified into the *project risk analysis and management methodology* (PRAM).[2,3]

In this chapter I describe risk management, as a four-step process. First you identify the risks on your project, and then you assess their impact, by assessing their impact individually and then jointly. Next you develop strategies for reducing the risk, and, finally, you monitor and control the risks as they occur (or not) and the effectiveness of your strategies. The next four sections of this chapter describe these four steps. In the final section I briefly describe the PRAM methodology, and its predecessor SCERT, and relate them to the four-step process described here.

10.2 Identifying risk

I cannot tell you what risks you are likely to encounter on your projects. What I can do is tell you about two ways of categorizing risk, which may help you identify the risks on your projects. Risks can be categorized according to:

– the impact they have
– where control of the risk lies.

Impact of the risk

There are two types of risk under this heading, business risks and insurable risks. Sometimes the word 'risk' is reserved for the second of these, and the first is called 'uncertainty'.

BUSINESS RISKS
These are the risks (or uncertainty) inherent in all our estimates. People tend to treat their project estimates as point-wise correct. However, in reality, our estimates just represent some mid-range value, and they can turn out better or worse than that. (It never ceases to amaze me that in their lives people accept some uncertainty in their estimates of how long things will take, but on their projects they expect their estimates to be exactly correct (Example 10.1).) Business risk is a two-sided risk or uncertainty. Sometimes our projects will turn out better than we expect, when we will make more profit, and sometimes worse, when we will make less profit or even a loss.

I did a series of workshops with a small consultancy who were having a problem with overruns on their assignments. (Over a period of three years, they reduced their overruns from an average of 10 per cent, twice their annual profit, to about 2 per cent). At an early workshop, a director gave a list of overruns. He grouped them by size of overrun in pounds. He started with some nightmares, jobs estimated to cost £20,000, and ending up costing £50,000. His last group were projects with overruns between £1,000 and £2,000, and the last was a project estimated at £200,000 that overran by just over £1,000. I pointed out that the last one only overran by one half of one per cent, and nobody could expect to estimate better than that. He was not pleased by my contribution.

Example 10.1 Uncertainty of estimates

INSURABLE RISKS

These are risks which can only go wrong. There is a hopefully small and random chance that some item of the project will fail. They are called insurable risks, but that is not to say either that an insurance company will want to buy the risk off us, or that we would want them to.

WHY DO PROJECTS FAIL?

I said business risks might turn out better or worse. This concept explains why we need to add the contingency described in Section 8.5, and why projects often fail. The reason for this is as follows. What we estimate is some measure of the mid-range value, usually the most likely out-turn for the work element. The actual out-turn can be better or worse. However, the amount it can be better by is usually constrained, whereas the amount it can be worse is almost limitless, although at what point a bad out-turn becomes an insurable risk is a moot point. Hence the range of expected out-turns is a skew distribution, with more above the most likely than below. There are two other measures of mid-range value, the median, (half the out-turns will be greater than this value and half less), and the mean or average, (if we do the activity a large number of times what will the out-turn be on average). If a distribution is skewed, the median is on the skewed side of the mode (most likely) and the mean on the skewed side of the median. Now the way we estimate our projects is to estimate the cost and duration of the activities, and then say the expected cost is the sum of all the activity costs, and the duration is the sum of the durations along the critical path. What we have said is that the most likely out-turn for the project is the sum of the most likely out-turns. This is incorrect. What we can say is that the expected out-turn for the project is the sum of the average out-turns. This makes the expected out-turn greater than the estimate obtained by adding up the raw estimates, which means our projects will almost certainly fail unless we add a contingency as described in Section 8.5.

You will often come across the so called 1:4:1 formula for estimating durations. This is another mantra of project management, the reason for which is lost in the mists of time. In the early days of project management in the 1950s, and especially for use with the PERT methodology, it was felt that better estimates were obtained by estimating the duration of each activity as:

$$d = (t_o + 4t_m + t_p)/6$$

where d = duration of the activity
t_o = most pessimistic out-turn
t_m = most likely out-turn
t_p = most optimistic out-turn.

The cynics version of this formula is the 1:4:3 formula, (see Example 10.2):

$$d = (t_o + 4t_m + 3t_p)/8$$

As an example of skewed estimating, I use my journey to Henley Management College. I live 40 miles from the college, and the most likely journey time is 55 minutes. I have done the journey in 40 minutes, and so this is the most optimistic. It once took me 135 minutes on a Friday evening, and the delay was due to heavy traffic, but you might call this insurable risk. Apart from that one extreme case, the journey can take up to 105 minutes. If I am teaching at nine o'clock in the morning, I must leave home by quarter past seven to virtually guarantee to be there on time. The journey home on Friday evenings can also take 90 minutes. Hence the most pessimistic journey time is 105 minutes. The distribution is what is called *bimodal*, there are two most likely out-turns, one of 55 minutes corresponding to light traffic, and a lesser one of 90 minutes corresponding to heavy traffic. The median journey time is about 60 minutes and the average about 70 minutes. So if I go to the college every day for a week, how long do I expect to spend in the car during my 10 journeys: 400, 550, 600, 700, 900 or 1050 minutes? Well if I am unlucky and every journey corresponds with crawl-hour (bizarre that we should call it 'rush-hour'), then something like 900 minutes would be an appropriate estimate. But overall most of us would say something like 700 minutes. Yet standard project estimating would give 550 minutes, which we can see is a gross underestimate. Applying the 1:4:1 formula gives 610 minutes for ten journeys and the 1:4:3 formula 720 minutes. The latter is more accurate because the distribution is bimodal. Risk management is trying where possible to time my journey not to correspond with crawl-hour, and so eliminate the upper tail of the distribution.

Example 10.2 Skewed estimating

Control of risk

Risk can also be categorized by where control of the risk lies. Control can be internal or external to the project manager's organization, or legal. Internal risks can be technical or non-technical. External risks can be predictable or unpredictable. Legal risks can fall under the criminal law or civil law, and under the civil law they will fall within the jurisdiction of the law of contract or the law of tort.

INTERNAL RISKS

Internal, technical risks are those arising directly from the technology of the work, or the design, construction or operation of the facility, or the design of the ultimate product. They can arise from changes or from a failure to achieve desired levels of performance. They can be 'business' or 'insurable' risks, although in the latter case the risk is borne by the parent organization, not by an outside insurance company.

Internal, non-technical risks are risks within the control of project managers, or their organizations, which are non-technical in nature. They usually arise from a failure of the project organization or resources (human, material or financial) to achieve their expected performance. They may result in schedule delays, cost over-runs or interruption to cash flow. They are usually 'business' risks.

EXTERNAL RISKS

External, predictable but uncertain risks are risks beyond the control of managers or their organizations. We expect to encounter them, but we do not know to what extent. There is usually data that allow us to determine a norm or average, but the actual impact can be above or below this norm. There are two major types of risk in this category: the first is the activity of markets for raw materials or finished goods, which determines prices, availability and demand; the second is fiscal policies affecting currency, inflation and taxation. However, they also include operational requirements such as maintenance, environmental factors such as the weather, and social impacts – which are all 'business' risks.

External, unpredictable risks are risks beyond the control of managers or their organizations; which are totally unpredictable. They can be listed, but we cannot say which will be encountered on a given project. They arise from the action of government or third parties, acts of God, or from failure to complete the project due to external influences. Government or regulatory intervention can relate to the supply of raw materials or finished good, environmental requirement, design or production standards, or pricing. Whether a change of government at an election falls in this or the following category is a moot point. Actions of third parties can include sabotage or war, and acts of God are natural hazards such as an earthquake, flood, or the sinking of a ship. Failure to complete can arise from the failure of third parties to deliver supporting infrastructure or finance, or their failure through bankruptcy, or a totally inappropriate project design. By their nature, these risks are almost all 'insurable' risks.

TURNING INTERNAL RISKS INTO EXTERNAL RISKS

Before discussing legal risks, I wish to discuss a point arising from this issue of internal and external risk. Standard contracting practice in the UK is to try to dump risk down the contract chain. The client passes risk on to the contractor and the contractor on to the subcontractor. What you sometimes do is take a risk that the client could control and do something about reducing, and convert it into a risk external to the contractor's organization, for which they can do nothing but allow a contingency. The client then chooses a contractor via compulsory competitive tendering, and awards the job to the contractor that bids the least amount, that is the contractor that has allowed the least contingency and is therefore most likely to fail. In Example 10.2, do you award the job of driving me to and from Henley to the contractor that bids 400, 550, 600, 700, 900 or 1050 minutes? If you award the work to the firm that bids 400 minutes, and they go bankrupt when you are only half way home, you have little recourse to cover your losses, and it will cost you another 300 minutes to get the rest of the way home.

There is now a growing tendency to analyse the risk on contracts, and apportion it to those parties best able to control it. This is just good business sense. You can stretch the analogy too far, but in Example 10.2 you could accept that the duration of the journey is client risk and award the job to the contractor that bids the lowest price per minute; or you could allow the contractor to bid a range of prices dependent on traffic densities, and measure the density to determine the price; or you could let the contractor choose the time of the journey, if you have that flexibility. There are a range of options for apportioning the risk rationally. Example 10.3 is an apocryphal story about risk sharing.

Neil Armstrong was being interviewed about the moon landing and was asked what was the most frightening moment; was it as the moon lander came down and might crash; or was it as he stepped off the ladder; or was it when they came to blast off from the moon and the rockets might not be powerful enough. No, he said, the most frightening moment was being on the launch pad at Cape Canaveral, and under him were 2000 components, every single one of which had been bought on minimum price tender! And one of them did fail in 1986.

Example 10.3 Risk sharing

LEGAL RISKS

There are three types of legal risk, risks under the criminal law, risks under the law of contract and risks under the law of tort. (The law of tort is the duty of reasonable care we all have to our fellow citizens. Even where we do not have a contract with somebody, we have a duty to behave responsibly and with reasonable care.) If an employee is killed in an accident at work, you can be prosecuted under the Health and Safety at Work Act or the CDM (Construction Design and Management) Regulations, and fined up to £2000 and sent to jail for two years. You can be sued by his or her estate under the contract of employment or under the law of tort. If a visitor to your site is killed, you can be prosecuted under the criminal law as above, or the law of tort, but you may have had no contract with the individual. This applies to the software industry as much as the engineering industry. There was a lot of conjectural discussion about the computer control system on Sizewell B Nuclear Power Station when it was commissioned. If a failure had occurred, (of which there was never any likelihood), the suppliers would have been liable, under all three sets of legal risks.

Under the criminal law there have been several attempts to bring charges of corporate manslaughter. One such was after the Zeebrugge disaster, although nothing ever came of it. I believe there has been one successful prosecution, although I cannot name the case, but I do know it is very difficult to prove. One person still has to be responsible for the decision that caused the accident, which will not be the case if the accident is due to a series of oversights, as was the case with the Zeebrugge or Bowbell disasters. The current Labour Government is proposing to introduce a charge of corporate killing, which could be based on a general culture of sloppiness and irresponsibility, rather than a single incorrect decision.

In the event of a charge, the case is judged on the basis of what any reasonable professional would have done in the circumstances. Examples 10.4 to 10.7 contain four cases, showing how this might apply. The law is not necessarily fair or logical, as Example 10.6 shows. It just tries to be precise.

Some years ago I was on a course where we were discussing the Health and Safety at Work Act, and one of the delegates said he was responsible for testing the control software for a jet fighter used by the Royal Air Force. He said that in a reasonable amount of time they could test 90 per cent of all the paths through the software, which would represent 99.9 per cent of all the occurrences. However, to test all the paths would take 100 years. His question was what would happen if there was a failure because the control system locked into a path that had not been tested but which had a fault. He was told that he would be judged by what any reasonable professional would have done, and because it was not sensible to test all the paths, he would not be held liable.

Example 10.4 Testing a computer control system

A woman who worked in an asbestos factory in the late 1930s developed asbestos related diseases in the 1980s. She sued her former employers claiming they had been negligent in the containment of asbestos in the factory. They had to be judged by the standards of the 1930s, not the 1980s, but were still judged to have been negligent.

Example 10.5 Seeking damages after 50 years

Children with stunted growth are fed a growth hormone. Up to 1980 this was made from extracts from the brains of dead people. From July 1978, the government knew this could cause CJD, the human equivalent of mad cow disease, but did not replace it with a synthetic alternative until 1980. The families of people who had suffered CJD sued the government. The courts ruled that anyone who had been fed the hormone for the first time on or after 1 July 1978 should receive compensation. Anyone who had received it on 30 June 1978 or earlier could not because the government could not have known there was a problem before then. There was one person who had received it for the first time on about 30 June 1978, and everyone said this is not fair – not fair but scrupulously exact. (The ruling was overturned by the Court of Appeal at the time of writing, and all people suffering CJD can now claim. People not suffering CJD, but who are at risk, want to claim now for the fear they have to live with.)

Example 10.6 The law is not fair, but scrupulously exact

It was suggested to Churchill in early 1945 that the allies might bomb the railway line leading to Auschwitz, and he said it was not worth the risk. People now react in horror that he could have said such a thing, but they are judging by 1990s standards. With the technology of 50 years ago, they were lucky to drop the bomb within two miles of the target. It saved more lives to use the pilot's life to shorten the war than to go on a fool's errand.

Example 10.7 Not judging by today's standards

Techniques for identifying risk
Various techniques can be used to help in the process of identifying risk. Five, which may be used solely or jointly are:

1. *Expert judgement* uses personal intuition and awareness. The use of checklists against the categories identified above can help.
2. *Plan decomposition* shows risks inherent in the interdependency of work. Any event which lies at the start or completion of many activities is a potential risk. These occur at bottlenecks in the network. When analysing the plan, you should also look at all external interfaces, such as external supply, for potential failure of third parties.
3. *Assumption analysis* is win/lose analysis, and focuses on events which might be detrimental, considering both events we want to occur but which may not, and events we do not want to occur but which may. Expert judgement is needed to foresee these events and check for completeness.
4. *Decision drivers* are influences which might determine whether or not certain events may occur, (inside and outside the project). Win/lose

analysis can be used to derive the list of decision drivers. It can be particularly damaging if decisions are made for the wrong reason: political vs technical; marketing vs technical; solution vs problem; short vs long term; new technology vs experience.

5. *Brainstorming* uses social interaction to enhance the above techniques.

Expecting the unexpected

Good project managers learn to be risk aware, to expect failure where they least expect it. This is known as *Sod's law* or *Murphy's law*, sometimes stated as: *if something can go wrong it will; if something can't go wrong, it still will!*

The value of this attitude is that if you expect things to go wrong, you will be on your guard for problems, and will be able to respond quickly to them. The failures may be ones you had predicted, or ones you least expect. If you anticipate problems, and plan appropriate contingency, you will not be disrupted when those problems occur. If the unexpected then also occurs, you will be able to focus your management effort into the areas that might now cause greatest disruption (Example 10.8). This attitude of expecting risks and being ready to respond is sometimes known as *risk thinking*. To some people it comes naturally; others require structured, logical processes of risk identification and analysis to support their response.

In 1983, I managed an area of work on the overhaul of an ammonia plant. We were uprating the steam system, and this required us to run a line between the 50 bar and 30 bar steam mains as shown in Figure 10.1. On the overhaul, we just had to make break-ins into the two mains at each end of the line. These consisted of T-sections, together with an isolation valve. The new line would be run between the two valves once the plant was back on line. The break-in to the 30 bar main was simple. We made an 8 in × 6 in T-section in advance of the overhaul. In the overhaul we just had to cut the line, weld in the T-section, and install the isolation valve. The other break-in, however, carried greater risk. It was to be made in a 12 in line just downstream from the main isolation valve, separating the plant main from the factory main. This valve had not been closed in 12 years, and so we did not know if it would shut tight. If it did not, the job would be more difficult, or even impossible. We put considerable effort into drawing up contingency plans in the event of a partial or full leak of the valve. In the event it shut like a dream. However, when we offered up the T-section at the other end, we found it had been made 6 in × 6 in instead of 8 in × 6 in. We therefore had to make a new T-section in a hurry, and an 8 in pipe of the right pressure rating was not immediately available. That particular job almost extended the duration of the overhaul. However, the time spent planning the other job was not wasted. I knew that so well, I could leave it to run itself and focus my attention on procuring 8 in pipe.

Example 10.8 Expecting the unexpected

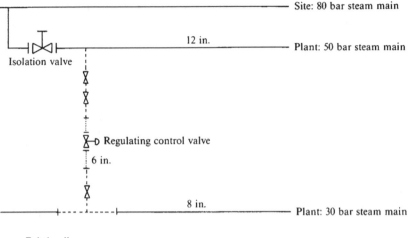

——— Existing line

- - - - Line added or replaced during the shutdown

·········· Line added post shutdown

Figure 10.1   Break-ins to the steam mains of an ammonia plant

10.3 Assessing risk

Having identified possible source of risk to the project, we need to calculate their impact on the project. First we calculate the impact of individual risks, and then determine their combined impact.

The impact of a single risk
The impact of a risk factor depends on its likelihood of occurring and the consequence if it does occur:

Impact of risk = (Likelihood of risk) * (Consequence of risk)

To illustrate this concept, consider the question of whether buildings in the British Isles have earthquake protection. The answer is very few do. Multi-storey office blocks in London do not. The consequence of an earthquake in London of force 7 on the Richter Scale would be severe loss of life. However, the probability of such an earthquake is so small, virtually zero, that it is considered unnecessary to take precautions. However, one type of building which does have earthquake protection is a nuclear power station. The likelihood of an earthquake has not changed, but the consequence is now unacceptably high. The consequence of an earthquake of force 7 in the Heysham area would be that Liverpool is uninhabitable for 10 000 years (or that at least is the public perception). Perhaps we should include the public perception when assessing the consequence of the risk (Example 10.9). Indeed, the assessment of risk is highly irrational (Example 10.10), and so the impact of risk needs to be amended as:

Impact of risk
= (Likelihood of risk) * (Consequence of risk) * (Public perception)

Perhaps the consequence of an earthquake under a nuclear power station would not be as severe as suggested, but the public perception is that it would. In the 1980s, the civil design consultants, Ove Arup and Partners, put considerable effort into designing and testing railway wagons for transporting low level nuclear waste around the country. There were some highly publicized experiments in which a locomotive was slammed into a wagon at 100 miles per hour. In this case, the likelihood of an accident which would result in a release of radiation was small, and the consequence was also small, no immediate deaths, perhaps one or two additional cancer cases resulting in early death several years later. However, this is a highly emotive public issue, and hence the need for indestructible wagons. On the other hand, quite lethal chemicals are transported around in relatively flimsy wagons. In the early 1980s, I worked close to a railway line, along which, twice a day, passed a train towing two wagons filled with cyanide gas. The consequence of a crash involving a leak in the centre of a city would be instant death to thousands of people, but this is not a public issue. A thousand instant deaths from cyanide gas seems to be more acceptable than two lingering deaths from radiation induced cancer.

Example 10.9 Public perception of risk

A classic example of the irrational perception of risk is the BSE scare. First the public behaved irrationally. The number of deaths from new form CJD, which may, just may, be caused by BSE is running at 5 per year, about the same number that die from allergic reaction to peanuts. The BBC went down to the local supermarket to interview an average shopper, smoking a cigarette, with a trolley load of beer, and a car with bald tyres in the car park. 'Are you eating beef?' asked the BBC. 'No', said the shopper, 'it's too dangerous.'

The public seem to have come to their senses, but at the time of writing the government is behaving irrationally. They have just made the selling of a T-bone steak a crime as heinous as the selling of crack cocaine, because it is expected to kill one person every 20 years. The Agriculture Minister appears on the TV and says he is concerned about public health! If he were concerned about public health, he would ban peanuts before a T-bone steak.

Example 10.10 The irrational assessment of risk

Table 10.1 Scaling risk factors

Level	Numeric	Likelihood (%)	Consequence	Perception
High	3	50	P/2	National issue
Medium	2	5	P/20	Local issue
Low	1	0.5	P/200	Company issue
Negligible	0	0.05	P/2000	Not an issue

It used to be common to work out the formulae above numerically. Figures would be chosen for likelihood, consequence and perception, and diligently multiplied together to produce a hit parade of the risks on the project. Perhaps each of likelihood, consequence and perception could be rated high, medium, low or negligible, or on a scale of 0 to 3 (Table 10.1). For each risk you can add the numerics, (effectively adding the logarithms of the numbers), to judge each risk on a scale of 0 to 9. This is silly for two reasons. First, to say a risk of level 6 is worse than one of level 5 and better than one of level 7 is meaningless because the conclusions drawn from the data are more accurate than the estimates on which it is based. Second, it says that the following two risks are the same, one that has a likelihood of 50 per cent but risks 0.5 per cent of the project cost is the same as one with likelihood 0.5 per cent and risks 50 per cent of the project cost. In fact the latter is worse, as it has a much higher spread of potential out-turns. You have to ask which is more important, the expected value of the risk or its predictability, and the latter is probably of more concern.[6]

What is now suggested is to apply the concepts qualitatively rather quantitatively.[7] You still assign to risk parameters a range of values such as those in Table 10.1. You might even have more than three parameters describing your risks. You then produce a table of your risks and their parameters, as Table 10.2, and qualitatively assess the risks. Furthermore, each risk is assessed on a scale with the same number of levels as that assigned to the parameters. In effect, you judge each risk to be high, medium, low or negligible. This avoids somewhat spurious conclusions. Van der Merwe used this approach to remove 10 per cent from the amount Eskom, the Electricity Supply Commission of South Africa, spent annually on the security of its substations.[7]

Combining the impact of several risks

It is a rare project which has only a single source of risk, so to determine the total impact of risk on a project, the elements must be combined. If we

Table 10.2   Qualitative risk assessment

Risk	Parameter 1	Parameter 2	Parameter 3	Parameter 4	Impact
R1	High	Medium	High	High	High
R2	Medium	High	Medium	Low	Medium
R3	Low	Low	Medium	Low	Low

include all possible sources of risk into the model, it will become impossibly complicated, and so we limit our attention to the significant few, the 20 per cent which have 80 per cent of the impact. The work breakdown structure is a key tool in this integration of the risk. In practice there are two approaches:

- a top-down approach, in which key risk factors are identified and assessed at a high level of work breakdown, and managed out of the project
- a bottom-up approach, in which risks are identified at a low level of work breakdown, and an appropriate contingency made to allow for the risk.

THE TOP-DOWN APPROACH

The top-down approach can provide the manager with checklists of potential risk factors based on previous experience, and can help them to determine their relative importance. Furthermore, by identifying the controlling relationships at a high level, it enables the project manager to find ways of eliminating the most severe risks from their projects.[1] The approach is to take a component breakdown for the project, and evolve it down to the integrative level with about 20 elements of the breakdown. The component breakdown chosen will depend on what it is that is expected to create risk. It can be the PBS, WBS, OBS, CBS, or *bill of materials* (BOM), for the facility. You then identify the risk associated with each component, and, critically, the links between the risks: if one risk occurs, does it make another more or less likely. You then concentrate on either eliminating the risk associated with each component, or breaking the links between the risks. If you are successful in breaking the links, you can isolate each risk in the breakdown structure. The reason for limiting yourself to 20 components is that, if you have a sheet of paper describing each risk and each link, you would have 420 sheets of paper. If there are 30 components, you have 930 sheets.

Two tools introduced previously which provide a clear, visual representation of the PBS, WBS and OBS to an appropriate level are the milestone plan (Section 5.4) and the responsibility chart (Section 6.4). The

- set a measure
- record progress
- calculate the variance
- take remedial action.

I describe for now only the first three of these, and the use of S-curves to produce a visual representation of progress. I leave the taking of remedial action to Chapter 12.

SET THE MEASURE

The planned, or baselined, dates set the measure for control of time. It is vital to measure progress against a fixed baseline. If you measure progress against the most recent update of the plan, you lose control. It is not uncommon to come across projects which are always on time because the schedule is updated at every review meeting, and people very quickly forget what the original schedule was; they can remember that the schedule has been updated, but not by how much.

RECORD PROGRESS

Progress is recorded by reporting actual start and finish dates. It is common to measure progress against start and finish dates only, as opposed to trying to assess percentage completion part way through a work element, at a level of the WBS and on a frequency to provide adequate control. Typically, on a project of a year's duration, progress is measured fortnightly against activities of two week's duration, (Section 5.2). Progress is fed up to higher levels of the WBS on a longer frequency.

CALCULATE THE VARIANCE

The variance is calculated either in the form of delays to completion of critical or near-critical work, or as the remaining float of subsequent activities. There is a tenet of project management that you cannot do anything about the past; you can only affect the future. Therefore it is better to focus on the remaining float of subsequent work, or on future delays to the start of critical or near-critical work. Delays to critical or near-critical work have an impact on the remaining float of subsequent work, and when the remaining float of a subsequent work element becomes negative, that extends the forecast completion date of the project. It is important to monitor near-critical work, and not focus solely on the critical path. The mathematical exactitude of the network can produce an undue focus on one area of the project, whereas it may be one of several other near-critical paths which determines the duration of the project, and it was only estimating error that caused one of these to be milestone plan shows the PBS at the strategic level. An interesting outcome of using the milestone plan is you can sometimes find that there is a risk link between two milestones where you have not shown a logic link. This can happen, for instance, where at an early milestone you make certain design assumptions. At a later milestone you find that you cannot meet the design assumptions, and so all milestones dependent on those assumptions are invalid. There is such a link between milestones A2 and O5 in Figure 5.4, for instance. Both assume we know sites 1 and 2, and if that is the case, they are not linked. However, if at A2 it proves impossible to use the chosen sites, then O5 is affected. The responsibility chart shows the OBS, PBS and WBS at the strategic level on one document. It also shows how these are influenced by one element of the CBS, the work content, and by the time scale. It is therefore a very powerful document for top-down risk analysis.

I illustrate the top-down approach with a simple four-work-package project to build a warehouse (Figure 10.2). Assuming end-to-start dependencies only, the duration of the project is seven months. It might be possible to fast track the project by overlapping work packages. However, let us assume that that is impossible on the path A–C–D: it is not possible to buy the steel until the design is finished; and all the steel will arrive at once, so erection cannot begin until the steel has arrived. It is possible to start work on the site, B, before the design is finished, but there is no need, because the duration will be determined by the delivery of the steel.

Now let us consider the risks. Let us assume that the project will start at the beginning of September, after the summer vacation. The risks are as follows:

1. The design of the building may take more or less than three months. From previous experience we may be able to say it will take two, three or four months with the following probabilities:

    – 2 months: 25 per cent
    – 3 months: 50 per cent
    – 4 months: 25 per cent

    Hence it may be finished as early as the end of October, or may stretch to the end of December.

2. The site cannot be prepared if there is snow on the ground. Snow occurs in four months of the year with the following probabilities:

    – December: 25 per cent
    – January: 25 per cent
    – February: 50 per cent
    – March: 25 per cent

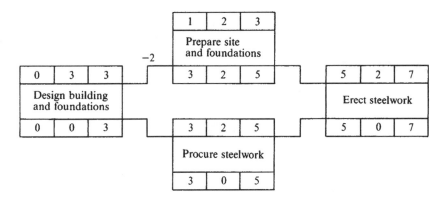

Figure 10.2 Simple precedence network for constructing a warehouse

The duration of this work is dependent on when it starts. If it starts in October, it will take only two months; if it starts in November, it will have the following range of durations (Figure 10.3):

- 2 months: 75 per cent
- 3 months: 19 per cent
- 4 months: 3 per cent
- 5 months: 2 per cent
- 6 months: 1 per cent

There will be similar lists if the work were to start in December or January, but with the probabilities weighted towards longer durations. In some circumstances the preparation of the site will become critical. Now it may be worth while to try to fast track the design of the foundations. If the design could be completed by the end of September, we could eliminate this risk entirely. If it is finished by the end of October, there is a 75 per cent chance of the work being finished on time. If the start of this work is delayed to December, there is only a 50 per cent chance. The choice will depend on the cost of fast tracking the design of the foundations. There will be additional financial charges if this work is completed early, it is unlikely that the cost of the design will be greater *per se*, but there is a risk of rework. In the event, you may actually make the decision on the day, depending on how the design of the steelwork is progressing, and other factors below.
3. There may be two possible suppliers of steelwork: the more expensive one can deliver in one month or two months with equal probability; and the cheaper in two months or three months also with equal probability.

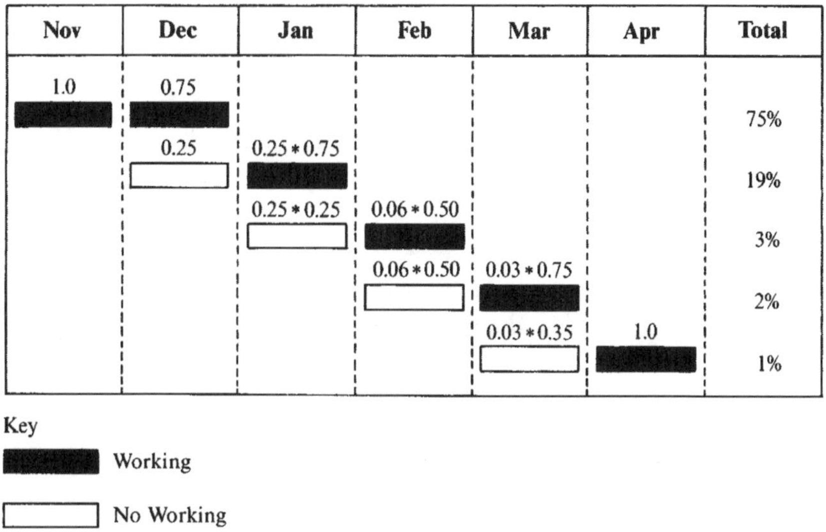

Nov	Dec	Jan	Feb	Mar	Apr	Total
1.0	0.75					75%
	0.25	0.25 * 0.75				19%
		0.25 * 0.25	0.06 * 0.50			3%
			0.06 * 0.50	0.03 * 0.75		2%
				0.03 * 0.35	1.0	1%

Key

■■■■■ Working

☐ No Working

Figure 10.3 Calculating the duration of work package B with November start

The delivery time therefore has the following distribution:

- 1 month: 25 per cent
- 2 months: 50 per cent
- 3 months: 25 per cent

This appears the same as the design. However, the power of the top-down approach is that you can decide what to do on the day, when you know how long the design has taken and how you are progressing with the foundations. To understand this we need to address the fourth risk.

4. This is that the steelwork cannot be erected if there are strong winds, and these occur with the following probability:

- February: 25 per cent
- March: 50 per cent

The duration of this work will also depend on when it starts, as with preparing the site. However, what we can see is that, if the design work finishes at the end of October, it will be better to use the more expensive supplier. There will then be a 50 per cent chance that erection can begin in December and finish in January without any delay, or a 50 per cent chance that it will begin in January, in which case it will finish in February with a 75 per cent chance. This is, of course, dependent on the foundations being ready, and so if it looks as though the steelwork design will be completed early, it will be worth while fast tracking the foundations. On the other hand, if the design takes four months, it would be better to use the cheaper supplier, and just plan to start erecting the steelwork in April, saving on extra cost of the foundations and on having erection fitters stood idle.

This simple case shows that the top-down approach allows you to analyse the interrelationships between elements of risk, and take management decisions based on that analysis and the actual out-turn. Following a top-down approach, you are able to develop additional detail in some areas. In the example above, for instance, you could break the design into a lower level of work breakdown to find out how to fast track the design. Section 4.4 differentiated between fast track and fast build, and it is fast build we should use here to reduce the risk. That requires the design to be broken into smaller packages of work, subject to strict design parameters at the top level.

INFLUENCE DIAGRAMS

Influence diagrams are tools, derived from systems dynamics, that can assist a top-down analysis. They show how risks influence one another; some risks reinforce others ($+$), and some reduce others ($-$). Figure 10.4 is an example of an influence diagram. The power of the technique is to identify loops of influence. 'Vicious cycles' have an even (or zero) number of negative influences, and 'stable cycles' an odd number. In Figure 10.4, loop ADEKLIBA is vicious, and loop ADEGHJIBA is stable. In a 'vicious cycle' an externally imposed influence can be amplified indefinitely.

THE BOTTOM-UP APPROACH

The bottom-up approach analyses risk at a low level.[8] It can identify several critical paths, and calculate a range of outcomes for cost and duration, to enable the project manager to allow appropriate contingency. However, it is essentially a negative approach to risk, as it assumes that risk elements are beyond the control of managers. It does nothing to help the manager to quantify or convey information for developing an appropriate management response to reducing or eliminating risk.

The approach develops a detailed project model, at a low level of breakdown. Variable durations and/or costs are assigned to work elements, as in the above example. However, at a low level it is not possible to calculate the various outcomes manually, as they were above. Instead, we perform a *Monte Carlo* analysis. The project model is analysed many times; 100 to

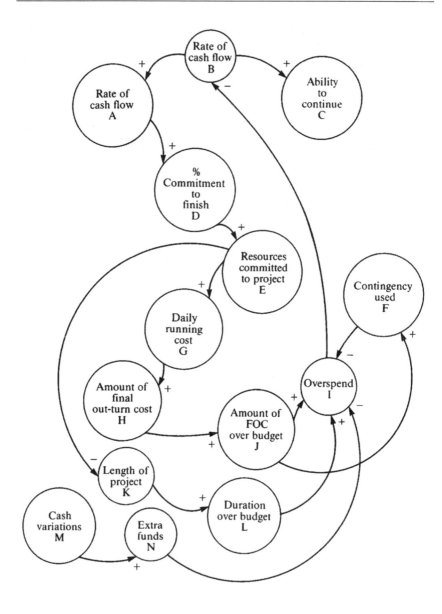

Figure 10.4   Influence diagram

10 000 is typical, depending on the size of the model. Each time, a random number is drawn for each parameter for which there is a range of values, and a value selected accordingly. (This makes the simplifying assumption that the risk elements are unrelated, which may not be the case – see Figure 10.4.) The cost and duration are then calculated using those values, and a range of possible outcomes calculated for the project. Effectively, the project is sampled however many times the analysis is performed. The results of the Monte Carlo analysis are presented as a probability distribution for time, cost, or both. This may be a simple or cumulative distribution. Figure 10.5 shows both distributions for the duration of the warehouse project. For this simple example, the critical path may go through either A–B–D or A–C–D, and the duration can be anything from 6 to 11 months. The likelihood that either or both of the routes will be where the critical paths is:

A–B–D   52 per cent
Both   24 per cent
A–C–D   24 per cent

With a project this small, it is just possible to calculate these numbers by hand: it took me an hour. With anything larger, the figures have to be determined using a Monte Carlo analysis. For the project, the median outcome is 8 months, (half the time the duration will be this or less), and that 90 per cent of the time, the duration will be less than nine months. The most likely duration (the mode) is nine months. If a nine-month duration is acceptable, we may accept these figures. If not, we would need to shorten the project. The critical path shows that the most useful effort may be put

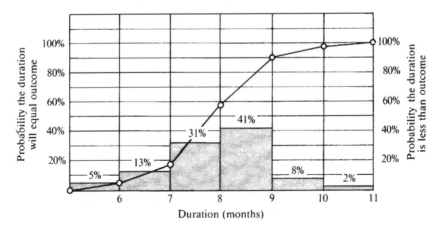

Figure 10.5 Simple and cumulative probability distributions for the duration of the project to build a warehouse

into shortening A–B–D, and that may suggest fast tracking the design of the foundations. However, from this we do not see the effect of the two suppliers. That can only be analysed by the top-down approach.

The owner's view of risk

The quantitative methods described produce a value for the project. However, the true value of the project is not the figure calculated by the project team, using these methods. It is the value the owner puts on the project, and that reflects his or her perception of the risk, and to a certain extent the public's perception as well (if the owner is concerned about public opinion – Example 10.11).

In the early 1980s, NIREX proposed storing medium-level nuclear waste in a redundant mine under ICI's factory at Billingham. It may have been one of the safest proposals for storing such waste. The project would cost ICI nothing (but see Example 10.12), but earn them an income; an attractive project with *no* risk attached. However, ICI would not allow the project to proceed because that was not the way the local community viewed it, and ICI was concerned about local opinion. The ironic thing was ICI used to operate one of the country's largest private nuclear sources on the Billingham site.

Example 10.11 The owner's perception of risk

It is almost certainly incorrect to say that the project described in Example 10.11 would have 'cost ICI nothing'. It was causing a loss of goodwill in the local community, and so the 'cost' was whatever value the company put on that goodwill. Clearly they did not think that 'cost' was worth the returns.

This is part of a wider viewpoint that is gaining credence. The environment itself has a value, and if a project we undertake reduces that value, we should take that into account when assessing the value of a project. In the case described in Example 10.11, that loss of value had a monetary impact in that house prices were falling in Billingham. The cost of the project would therefore not have been borne by ICI, but by the local community.

In this case the loss in value was caused by a fear of anything nuclear. A case in which the environment suffered a real loss in value is the Adriatic coast of Italy. Algae blooms reduced its ability to earn tourist revenues. Economic activity up the Po Valley had caused the blooms. However, the people who received the benefit of that activity did not pay the price. The solution is an environment tax. That can be levied in Italy in the latter case, but should Switzerland pay a tax to Germany for the water flowing down the Rhine? The answer to that question is beyond the scope of this book.

Example 10.12 The value of project opinion and the environment

Communicating the risk analysis

The ultimate purpose of the risk model is to communicate the analysis to all the parties involved:

- to the owner for them to assess its value
- to the champion, so that they can give their support and commitment to the project
- to the project manager so that they can develop their project strategy and perform what-if analysis
- to the integrators, to enable them to manage the risks during implementation
- to people joining the project at a later time, so that they know what assumptions have been made
- to the users, so that they know the commitments they are making.

To be an effective communication tool, the model must be simple, robust, adaptable and complete. Achieving this requires considerable effort. Structuring the model in order to achieve these requirements can take more than half of the total effort of risk analysis.

10.4 Reducing risk

Having identified and assessed the risk, you are in a position to consider ways of reducing it. There are three basic approaches:[9]

- *avoidance*: having identified the risk, you replan to eliminate it
- *deflection*: you try to pass the risk on to someone else
- *contingency*: you take no action in advance of the deviations occurring, other than to draw up contingency plans should they occur.

Pym and Wideman[9] use an analogy of a man being shot at. He can take cover to avoid the bullets; he can deflect or divert the bullets in another direction, allowing them to hit someone else; or he can allow them to hit him, and plan to repair the damage, and hope he has time to do so.

Avoidance

I showed above on the warehouse project, how to avoid the risk of snow holding up the preparation of the foundations by starting the work early enough, so that it is finished before the snow comes. Under avoidance, you change the plan to reduce the risk or eliminate it entirely.

Deflection

There are three ways of deflecting risk:

– *through insurance*: by which it is passed on to a third party
– *through bonding*: by which a security is held against the risk
– *through the contract*: by which it is passed between owner, contractor and subcontractors.

INSURANCE
A third party accepts an insurable risk (Section 10.2) for the payment of a premium, which reflects the impact of the risk, the likelihood combined with the consequence.

BONDING
One or both parties to a contract deposit money into a secure account so that if they or either party defaults the aggrieved party can take the bond in compensation. This is a way of transferring the risk of one party defaulting to that organization.

CONTRACT
Through contracts, the risk is shared between owner, contractor and subcontractors. There are two common principles of contracts:

1. *Risk is assigned to that party most able and best motivated to control it*: There is no point passing risk on to a contractor or subcontractor if they have neither the power nor motivation to control it. The Institution of Civil Engineers is currently revising their standard forms of contract around this principle.[10] There are four styles of contract for different approaches to sharing risk. The selection of an appropriate style will be part of the owner's contract strategies, but is beyond the scope of this book.[11]

2. *Risk is shared with subcontractors if it is within their sphere of control*: To achieve this, back-to-back contracts are used; the clauses in the contract between owner and contractor are included in that between contractor and subcontractors. I have come across instances where the contractor feels squashed between two giants, and accepts quite severe clauses from the owner to win the work, but believes that the subcontractors will not accept them because they do not need the work. This often happens to contractors on defence or public sector projects. The way to avoid this is to try to get the subcontractors to make their contracts directly with the owner, and use the owner's power to pull the supplier into line. The supplier may not need the business from the contractor, but may have a better respect for the owner.

Contingency
The third response to risk is to make an allowance for it, to add a contingency. You can add an allowance to any one of the five system objectives, but typically there are two main approaches:

– make an allowance by increasing the time and/or cost budgets
– plan to change the scope, by drawing up contingency plans should the identified risks occur.

TIME AND/OR COST

You can either add the allowance as a blanket figure, calculated through a bottom-up approach as above, or you can add it work element by work element. Either way, the project manager should maintain at least two estimates, as described in Sections 8.5 and 9.2. These are the raw estimate without contingency, and the estimate with contingency. The former, called the 'baseline', is communicated to the project team for them to work to, and the latter to the owner, for them to provide money and resources. The project manager may also maintain two further estimates, the most likely out-turn, the figure to which they are working, and the current estimate, which is the baseline with some contingency already consumed. The reason for giving the project team the baseline or current estimate as the figure to work to is they will seldom come in under the estimate, and will consume contingency if it is given to them. The reason for communicating the estimate with contingency to the owner is that they want to budget for the maximum likely time and cost.

CONTINGENCY PLANS

These are alternative methods of achieving the milestones, to be used in different circumstances. Contingency plans can be of three types:

1. *Purely after the event*: are plans which are drawn up but enacted only if the risk occurs.
2. *After the event with essential prior action*: are also drawn up and enacted only if the risk occurs. However, some preparation work must be done, such as procurement of long lead items.
3. *Prior action which mitigates the after the event action*: is where a contingency plan is drawn up, but the design of the facility or work methods changed to reduce the cost of implementing the contingency plan. The upfront cost may be increased to reduce the impact of the risk.

The alternative plans may or may not cost more money to implement, though presumably if they cost less it would be better to follow them in the first place. In Example 10.8, we drew up alternative plans should the valve shut tight, shut partially, and not shut at all. The latter plans each would have cost more than the first, which is the one we followed, although the second would have only been marginally more expensive.

It is better to plan to eliminate the risk than to plan how to overcome it, and it is better to plan how to overcome it than to increase the cost and extend the duration to pay for it.

TRIMAGI COMMUNICATIONS BV

RISK ITEM TRACKING FORM   PAGE 1 OF 2

PROJECT: CODE

WORK PACKAGE   CODE

ACTIVITY   CODE

RISK NUMBER: RISK IDENTIFIER

NATURE OF RISK

SOURCE: EU/EP/IT/IN/L   TYPE: BUSINESS/INSURABLE

CATEGORY   CONTRACTUAL/MANAGEMENT/TECHNICAL/PERSONNEL

DESCRIPTION:

IMPACT DATE: LIKELIHOOD   LOW/MEDIUM/HIGH

SUBSIDIARY RISKS

ACTIVITY   RISK IDENTIFIER

ACTIVITY   RISK IDENTIFIER

RISK IMPACT

SEVERITY: VL/L/M/H/VH   SEVERITY SCORE   ...../5

LIKELIHOOD SCORE   ...../3   RISK SCORE   SS * LS = .../15

IMPACT AREA

SCHEDULE:

COST:

PERFORMANCE:

RISK MONITORING

MONTH												
RANK												

Figure 10.6   Risk item tracking form

TRIMAGI COMMUNICATIONS BV		
RISK ITEM TRACKING FORM		PAGE 2 OF 2

CORRECTIVE ACTION · PROPOSED/APPROVED

DESCRIPTION:

RISK REDUCTION COST

RESPONSIBLE MANAGER

REVISED DATE · LIKELIHOOD · LOW/MEDIUM/HIGH

START DATE: · CLOSURE DATE:

REVISED IMPACT

SEVERITY: VL/L/M/H/VH · SEVERITY SCORE ....../5

LIKELIHOOD SCORE ...../3 · RISK SCORE SS * LS = .../15

IMPACT AREA

SCHEDULE:

COST:

PERFORMANCE:

MONTH	ACTION TAKEN	NEXT ACTION	BY WHOM

ISSUE:	DATE:	AUTHOR	APPROVED

Figure 10.6 *(continued)*

10.5 Controlling risk

Having identified ways of reducing risk, you can implement a plan to control the reduction. Figure 7.2, shows four basic steps in control:

- draw up a plan
- monitor progress against the plan
- calculate variances
- take action to overcome variances.

THE RISK MANAGEMENT PLAN

The risk management plan identifies the risks associated with a project, the means by which they have been assessed, and the strategy for their reduction. A risk item tracking form (Figure 10.6) provides a framework for recording the relevant information for each risk. The form, which may be held in a spreadsheet or computer database, describes:

- *why* the risk is significant
- *what* is to be done to reduce it
- *when* the risk will have its impact on the project
- *who* is responsible for resolving the risk
- *how* the reduction will be achieved and how much it will cost.

I have already said that the risk varies throughout the life cycle of the project, and hence the priorities for risk reduction will change. Having each risk recorded on a separate sheet of paper, or recorded in a computer database, allows them to be sorted into appropriate order each month.

MONITORING RISK

The risks are then monitored on a regular basis (weekly, fortnightly, monthly, or at other predetermined intervals) to determine how far each risk has actually been reduced. At each review, the risk tracking forms are sorted into their order of current importance. A list of the most significant lists, usually the 'top-ten', is produced, giving rank this period, rank last period and periods on the list. Figure 10.7 contains an example of a report.

RISK REASSESSMENT

Reassessment should be carried out whenever new risks are identified in the course of risk monitoring. In addition there should be explicit reassessment at key milestones in the project, and at transition between stages. The launch meetings for subsequent stages, Chapter 13, are ideal media for this reassessment. All the above techniques are used for reassessment. It is always easier to improve on an existing plan, but there is the disadvantage that new risks may be ignored.

10.6 The PRAM and SCERT methodologies

The top-down approach to project risk management has now been codified into the project risk analysis and management (PRAM) methodology.[2,3] In this section, the PRAM methodology is summarized to

<table>
<tr><td colspan="5" align="center">**TRIMAGI COMMUNICATIONS BV**
MONTHLY TOP RISK ITEM REPORT</td></tr>
<tr><td colspan="2">PROJECT: CRMO RATIONALIZATION PROJECT
WORK AREA: TECHNOLOGY</td><td colspan="3">MANAGER: RODNEY TURNER
DATE: 26 FEBRUARY 199X</td></tr>
<tr>
<td>RANK
THIS
MONTH</td>
<td>RANK
LAST
MONTH</td>
<td>MONTHS
ON
LIST</td>
<td>RISK ITEM</td>
<td>POTENTIAL
CONSEQUENCE</td>
<td>RISK RESOLUTION
PROGRESS</td>
</tr>
<tr>
<td>1</td><td>4</td><td>2</td>
<td>Replacement for team leader for MIS software development team</td>
<td>Lack of expertise in team. Delay in code production, with likelihood of lower quality – less reliable operation even after testing</td>
<td>Chosen replacement unavailable</td>
</tr>
<tr>
<td>2</td><td>6</td><td>2</td>
<td>Requested changes to user-interface</td>
<td>Now realized may impact h/w–s/w interface definition. If not cleared up at next week's user evaluation of prototype, will delay delivery date</td>
<td>User evaluation of latest prototype set for next week – attendance of some key users still to be confirmed</td>
</tr>
<tr>
<td>3</td><td>2</td><td>5</td>
<td>Resolution of network diagnostic software problems</td>
<td>Delay in completion of software detailed design and coding</td>
<td>New version of diagnostics appears to clear most problems but still to be fully checked</td>
</tr>
<tr>
<td>4</td><td>3</td><td>6</td>
<td>Availability of work-stations for main test phase</td>
<td>Lack of sufficient workstations will restrict progress on testing</td>
<td>Delay in deliveries being discussed with supplier</td>
</tr>
<tr>
<td>5</td><td>5</td><td>3</td>
<td>Testbed interface definitions</td>
<td>If not finalized by end of next month, will delay availability of testbed</td>
<td>Delayed items now being worked on. Review meeting scheduled</td>
</tr>
<tr>
<td>6</td><td>1</td><td>3</td>
<td>Tighter fault tolerance requirements impact on performance</td>
<td>Performance problems could require change to h/w–s/w architecture with major impact on cost and schedule</td>
<td>Latest prototype demonstrates performance within specification</td>
</tr>
<tr>
<td>7</td><td>—</td><td>1</td>
<td>Delay in specification of network data transmission</td>
<td>Could delay availability of hardware subsystems for integration</td>
<td>Meeting scheduled to consider alternatives</td>
</tr>
<tr>
<td>8</td><td>8</td><td>4</td>
<td>Tech author required</td>
<td>Insufficient time for programming staff to produce quality manuals</td>
<td>Requirement with agency</td>
</tr>
<tr>
<td>—</td><td>7</td><td>4</td>
<td>CM assistant required</td>
<td>Inadequate effort for rising CM workload with resulting costly errors</td>
<td>CM assistant joined team full-time</td>
</tr>
<tr>
<td>—</td><td>9</td><td>4</td>
<td>Re-usable database software uncertainties</td>
<td>Potential increase in estimates of coding effort</td>
<td>Uncertainties resolved in latest prototype</td>
</tr>
</table>

Figure 10.7   Monthly top-ten risk items report

show specifically how it achieves the concepts outlined in this chapter. The technique while new, is derived from a previous technique called the synergistic, combinatorial evaluation and review technique (SCERT) which was well documented.[1,11] However, after a decade of further research, the technique has been enhanced, and given a more user-friendly name.

The SCERT methodology (Table 10.3) has three stages and each with two phases.[1,11] The PRAM methodology is now a nine-stage process of risk management (Table 10.4).

Table 10.3 The SCERT methodology

Section	Stage	Phase	Action
Identify, 10.2	Qualitative	Scope	Component breakdown Identify risks Identify responses
Identify, 10.2	Qualitative	Structure	Risks response links Prioritize links
Assess, 10.3	Quantitative	Individual risks	Decide what to quantify Quantify uncertainty
Assess, 10.3	Quantitative	Combine risks	Combine risks
Reduce, 10.4	Manage	Plan response	Identify responses needs Plan responses
Manage, 10.6	Manage	Monitor	Monitor and control

Table 10.4 The PRAM Methodology

Section	Stage
	Define project
As part of project strategy	Focus PRAM
Identify, 10.2	Identify risks
Identify, 10.2	Structure risk
Reduce, 10.4	Allocate ownership
Assess, 10.3	Estimate risks
Assess, 10.3	Evaluate estimates
Reduce, 10.4	Plan responses
Manage, 10.5	Manage risk

10.7 Summary

1. There are five steps in risk management:
   - identify sources of risk
   - determine impact of individual risks
   - assess overall impact of risks
   - determine how the risk can be reduced
   - control the identified risks.
2. There are two types of risk:
   - business risk
   - insurable risk.
3. There are five sources of risk:
   - external – unpredictable
   - external – predictable
   - internal – technical
   - internal – non-technical
   - legal.
4. Techniques for identifying risks include:
   - expert judgement
   - plan decomposition
   - assumption analysis
   - decision drivers analysis
   - group brainstorming.
5. The impact of individual risks is a product of the likelihood they will occur, the consequence if they do occur, and the public perception of that consequence.
6. In assessing the combined effect of several risks, you can use:
   - a top-down approach, a management decision making tool
   - a bottom-up approach, and Monte Carlo analysis
   - influence diagrams.
7. There are three ways of reducing risk:
   - avoidance
   - deflection
   - contingency.
8. Contracts should be drawn up with the policy that risk should be assigned to the party best able and best motivated to control it.
9. There are four steps in controlling risk:
   - draw up a risk management plan consisting of Risk Item Tracking Forms
   - monitor progress against the top ten risks
   - reassess risks at regular intervals, and at key milestones or stage transition
   - take action to overcome any divergence from the plan.

10. The PRAM methodology identifies nine stages of risk management:
   – define and focus
   – identify and structure
   – allocate
   – estimate and evaluate
   – plan and manage.

References

1. Cooper, D.F. and Chapman, C.B., *Risk Analysis for Large Projects: Models, methods and cases*, Wiley, 1987.
2. Chapman, C.B. and Ward, S.C., *Project Risk Management: Processes, techniques and insights*, Wiley, 1997.
3. Simon, P., Hillson, D. and Newland, K., *Project Risk Analysis and Management Guide*, Association for Project Management, 1997.
4. CCTA, *PRINCE 2: Project Management for Business*, The Stationery Office, 1996.
5. Kähkönen, K. and Aarto, K.A. (eds), *Managing Risks in Projects*, Wiley, 1997.
6. Williams, T.M., 'The two dimensionality of project risk', *International Journal of Project Management*, **14** (3), June 1996.
7. Turner, J.R., Editorial, *International Journal of Project Management*, **14** (3), June 1996.
8. Hertz, D.B. and Thomas, H., *Risk Analysis and its Applications*, Wiley, 1983.
9. Pym, D.V. and Wideman, R.M., 'Risk management', in *The Revised Project Management Body of Knowledge*, Project Management Institute, 1987.
10. Institution of Civil Engineers, *The New Engineering Contract*, 2nd edn, ICE, 1995.
11. Turner, J.R. (ed), *The Commercial Project Manager*, McGraw-Hill, 1995.

PART THREE
THE PROJECT MANAGEMENT PROCESS

11

Project definition

11.1 Introduction

Part Two described the methods, tools and techniques for managing the five functions of project management – scope, organization, quality, cost, and time – and the risk inherent in all of them. We shall now turn to the second dimension of project management, the management processes for delivering the project, and describe how the methods, tools and techniques are applied to undertake projects. In Chapter 1, I explained that because projects are transient, they are said to have a *life cycle*, going through several stages of development from germination of the idea, to commissioning of the facility and metamorphosis into a successful operation. During this life cycle, management emphasis changes. The definition of the project evolves in a controlled way, so that the best solution to the owner's requirement is achieved, and money and resources are committed only as uncertainty is reduced. The life cycle followed in this part is the basic one described in Figure 1.5 and Table 1.2. Table 11.1 shows how the four stages are addressed in the three chapters of this part.

Table 11.1   The four-stage life cycle as addressed in this part

Stage	Name	Chapter	Topic
Germination	Proposal and initiation	11	Project definition Feasibility
Growth	Design and appraisal	11	Planning and design Appraisal
Maturity	Execution and control	12	Implementation Measuring progress Forecasting completion Taking action
Metamorphosis	Finalization and close-out	13	Project close-out

In this chapter, I describe 'proposal and initiation' and 'design and appraisal'. I start by describing *project start-up*, which may be used to initiate any stage of a project, even close-out. I then describe proposal and initiation, and explain how to conduct a feasibility study to achieve the objectives of this stage. I then describe design and appraisal, and close this chapter by explaining the use of initiation meetings and the Project Definition Report and Manual as tools to start project definition and record decisions made during that stage and design.

11.2 Project start-up

A project requires the undertaking of a unique task using a novel organization, which must be created from scratch at the start of the project. When new teams are formed, the members take some time to learn how to work together before becoming truly effective. Typically, a team goes through four stages of formation in which its effectiveness first falls and then rises[1] (Figure 11.1):

– *forming*: the team members come together
– *storming*: they find areas of disagreement
– *norming*: they agree principles of cooperation
– *performing*: they achieve the task effectively.

(A fifth stage, *mourning*, when the team is disbanded at the end of the *task*, is introduced in Chapter 17.) A project is subject to time constraints, and so this process of team formation must be undertaken in a structured way to ensure it happens quickly. Furthermore, it may be done at several stages throughout the project management life-cycle, since the team may change from one stage to the next.

The structured approach to creating the project organization is called *project start-up*.[2,3] The term 'project start-up' is used to differentiate from 'project start'; the former is a structured process for team formation; the latter is an action at an instant in time. Fangel[4] draws the analogy with starting the engine of a car, and starting-up the diesel engine in a ship. The former is achieved by flicking the ignition switch, the latter by a structured series of activities, a start-up process, which gives the most efficient and economical operation. The same applies to projects.

This section will clarify the concept of project start-up, and discuss its timing in the project management life cycle. It will describe the objectives of the process, show how these change throughout the life cycle, and review methods of start-up and their effectiveness for achieving the various objectives. It will show that the use of the methods will depend on the type of project, and, finally, it will describe how to schedule the start-up process.

Effectiveness

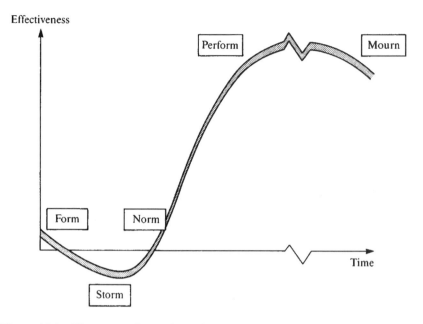

Figure 11.1   The stages of team formation

Initiating projects

It is now widely accepted that a structured start-up process is an essential part of project management.[4] It is necessary, on a unique, novel and transient endeavour, to improve the understanding of the project team of the task they face, and how they are to approach it, and to get them working effectively as a single unit. Research in Austria into benchmarking best practice in project management has shown that the start-up process can take between 1 and 40 days, depending on the size, nature and complexity of the project, with the initial start-up meeting taking between half a day and three days.[5] This process may be undertaken just once on a project, or several times, if there is a significant change in personnel at the start of a stage of the project, or even at the start of work on a milestone.

There has been an increasing need for effective start-up on projects, and this may be due to:

– the increasing complexity of technologies used
– the use of qualified project management earlier in the life cycle
– new patterns of cooperation in projects, including the need for team building and cross-cultural cooperation (Chapter 4)
– a need for increased effectiveness caused by shorter product life cycles

– changes in the way projects are managed, including the use of goal directed approaches,[6] which reinforce the setting of objectives and scope, the use of group methods for building cooperation, and the management of the team through the use of a clear and common mission.

Objectives of project start-up

For a systematic approach to start-up to be successful, the participants must understand what the objectives of the process are at any stage, and must be aware of what specific outputs are needed to achieve the necessary level of understanding. I said above these objectives might be:

– to create a shared vision for the project, by identifying its context, purpose and objectives
– to gain acceptance of the plans, by defining the scope of work, project organization and constraints of quality cost and time
– to get the team functioning, by agreeing its mode of operation and channels of communication
– to refocus the project team on to the purpose of the project, and the method of achieving it.

The first three objectives correspond to Parts One, Two and Three of this book, respectively; the fourth runs throughout. As they move through the stages of a project, the team's understanding of these develops in turn (Figure 1.13). At the start, the emphasis is at the top level, identifying the project's context, developing the shared vision and project strategy. As that is achieved, the emphasis shifts to the second level, developing the project model for the five project management functions, the first dimension of project management. In the third stage, the emphasis changes again into pulling the strands of the project model together, to undertake the work. This is done through the life cycle, the second dimension. Finally, as the facility is commissioned, and handed over to the client, the emphasis changes back to the purpose of the project, the benefit expected from the facility and the product it produces, to ensure that is achieved. Hence, the objectives of project start-up will be different at each stage of the life cycle (Table 11.2), although as you move from one stage to the next, you may review the objectives of the previous stage and look forward to those of the next.

Below each of the four objectives are fifteen subsidiary objectives, Table 11.3. These in turn may influence the emphasis of the work of the project team depending on the type of activity undertaken and decisions taken. The emphasis of the team's work may be:

– *analysis*: of the project's context, previous plans, future tasks and management routines

Table 11.2   Shift of the start-up objectives throughout the life cycle

Objective	Proposal and initiation	Design and appraisal	Execution and control	Finalization and close-out
Context and objectives	Main	Review		Monitor
The project model	Draft	Main	Review	
The management approach		Draft	Main	Review
Commission and handover	Prepare		Draft	Main

Table 11.3   Ten subsidiary management objectives and their effect on the working of the team

Subsidiary objectives	Analyse	Plan	Communicate	Motivate
Context and objectives				
– Impact of context	A		C	M
– Business purpose	A	P		
– Objectives of project		P	C	M
The project model				
– Milestone plan	A	P		
– Responsibility chart		P	C	M
– Detail work plans		P	C	M
– Resource allocation		P	C	M
The management system				
– Management system		P		
– Principles of cooperation			C	M
– Control processes		P	C	
Commission and handover				
– Timely, efficient end		P	C	M
– Disband team		P	C	M
– Hand-over to client		P	C	
– Obtain benefits		P	C	
– Record data	A		C	

– *planning*: of objectives, scope of work, organization and routines
– *communication*: between participants of the results of the analysis and plans
– *motivation*: of participants to carry out work or make decisions.

Table 11.3 relates the emphasis of the team's work to the fifteen subsidiary objectives. When linked to Table 11.2, this shows that during the life cycle the emphasis shifts from analysis and planning to communication and motivation until the end when it switches back to analysis, which probably will match the experience of most people.

Methods of start-up

Another requirement of a systematic approach to project start-up is the use of appropriate methods. There are three standard methods of start-up:

- *project or stage launch workshops*: to develop project plans in a joint team building process
- *start-up or stage review reports*: to collate the results of analysis undertaken during start-up or from a previous stage in accessible form for use during the subsequent stage
- *the use of ad-hoc assistance*: to support and guide the project team.

These three techniques may be used individually or in any combination. The choice depends on several factors. First, the different methods require varying amounts of time, so you must ensure that key team members are willing to devote that time to it. Without it most methods will fail. Secondly, the methods have different efficacy in achieving the objectives in Tables 11.2 and 11.3. Table 11.4 shows the different impact of each method. Thirdly, through project start-up, you should try to build as much historical experience into the project definition as possible, to minimize the uncertainty. You should choose a method which does that for the case in hand. Other methods of start-up include case studies, study tours, social events, education programmes, and other media, such as videos.

Table 11.4   Effectiveness of the techniques for project start-up

Start-up technique	Analyse	Plan	Communicate	Motivate
Launch workshop	High	Medium	High	High
Review report	Low	High	High	Medium
Ad-hoc assistance	Medium	High	Low	Medium

LAUNCH WORKSHOPS

A *launch workshop*: held at the start of proposal and initiation is often called a *Project Definition Workshop*, and at the start of design or execution an *initiation* or *kick-off meeting*. The objectives of the workshop, the agenda and the people invited depend on the stage being launched, and are discussed more fully in Section 11.6.

STAGE REVIEW REPORT

The *Start-up* or *Stage Review Report* is prepared at the end of one stage to launch the next. A report for launching proposal and initiation may be a one- or two-page *Project Scope Statement* (Section 5.4 and Example 5.1). During the feasibility study, this is expanded into a Project Definition

Report or Client Requirements Definition, used to launch design and appraisal. At the end of that stage, a full Project Manual or Project Requirements Definition may be produced in support of the design package, and that used to launch project execution. The contents of each of these reports depend on the stage being reviewed, and are described in Section 11.7.

AD-HOC ASSISTANCE
This may be from:

– internal professionals, such as the Project Support Office
– external consultants
– team members from similar (earlier) projects
– organizational behaviour experts helping manage the team dynamic.

The external professionals can fill one of two roles. They may be there to facilitate the team dynamics, to initiate the storming and the forming. Or they may be invited to bring specific technical expertise relating to the project, to bring experience from having worked on similar, previous projects. The advantage of this method is it provides additional resources with special skills, who may motivate key people. Having someone to share ideas with can be stimulating. A disadvantage is that there can be some confusion over responsibilities, which can lead to wasted effort.

Start-up and the type of project
In Section 1.6, I introduced Turner and Cochrane's goals and methods matrix (Figure 1.15). This defined four types of project. The emphasis of start-up differs for each type (Figure 11.2).

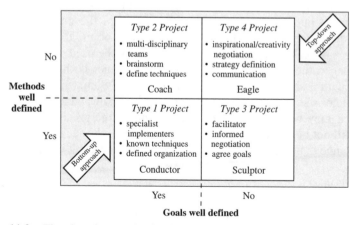

Figure 11.2   The changing emphasis of start-up by type of project

TYPE 1 PROJECTS

The goals and methods of delivery are both well defined, and the team will slip quickly into activity-based planning. These projects will usually be very similar to ones done in the past, (not so unique and novel). The emphasis of start-up will therefore be on briefing the team on the standard techniques. External facilitators who have done similar projects in the past may be used to brief the team. The role of the project manager here is something of a conductor leading the team through the predefined score, but putting his or her own interpretation on it.

TYPE 2 PROJECTS

The goals are well defined, but the methods of achieving them are not. The start-up workshop develops a milestone plan for the project, where the milestones represent the known products. It then develops a responsibility chart to define who is going to take responsibility for determining how to achieve the milestones. The workshop requires a broad cross-section of disciplines to be represented, including all the people who may have a contribution to make on how best to achieve the project. A facilitator may be used to norm the team's behaviour, gaining agreement to the milestones and responsibility chart. The role of the project manager is that of a coach. There is a clear objective of getting the ball in the goal as many times as possible in the next 90 minutes. The coach trains the team in standard plays, but leaves them to put them together as the game unfolds.

TYPE 3 PROJECTS

The goals are not well understood, but the project will follow a standard life cycle, and the definition of the goals will be refined as the project proceeds, using configuration management. The emphasis of start-up will be on agreeing the purpose of the project, the nature of the goals, if not their precise definition, and the life cycle and review points to be followed in reaching a better understanding. A facilitator may be used to help negotiate agreement to these. The role of the project manager is that of a sculptor, starting with a shapeless block of clay or marble. Somewhere in there is a statue. He or she will use standard techniques to cut away the clay or marble. However, they will need to avoid flaws, and so the precise nature of the statue will not be evident until it is finished. (I hope the sculptor is more like Michaelangelo, using an army of apprentices, than a hermit in a garret flat.)

TYPE 4 PROJECTS

Now neither the goals, nor the method of achieving them is known. The emphasis start-up is very much on agreeing the purpose of the project. In the early stages, the team will work on defining first the goals (turning the project into a type 2) and then the methods of achieving them. Planning will be by defining a series of gateways (review points) that the project must pass through before they close forever. A facilitator may again be used to negotiate agreement, and then help with team formation as the project converts to a type 2. The project manager must now take the role of an eagle. He or she must be able to hover above the project and see how it fits into the overall context of the organization, but also be able to identify small problems (a mouse) and go down and deal with them. They must then be able to rise back above the project again, before going down to deal with another mouse.

Scheduling start-up

A schedule of the start-up activities helps to focus attention on the process, and acts as a means of implementing the chosen techniques. The schedule may take the form of a responsibility chart (Figure 11.3), with both a definition of roles and responsibilities, and a time scale. The schedule for starting-up design and appraisal may be included in the Project Definition Report. A comprehensive checklist of items which may be included in the project start-up schedule is suggested by Archibald.[7]

PROJECT RESPONSIBILITY CHART

Project:

X – eXecutes the work
D – takes Decision solely
d – takes decision jointly
P – manages Progress
T – provides Tuition on the job
C – must be Consulted
I – must be Informed
A – available to Advise

Work Cont H/D/W | Period: WEEK 1 2 3 4 5 6 7 8 9 10 11 12 13 14 | Issue/Date: | Approved by:

Companies/Departments/Functions/Type of resource

No. Principle/Milestone name	PROJECT MANAGEMENT TASKS: Environment	Purpose	Objectives	Work breakdown	Responsibilities	Detailed plans	Resource alloc'n	Pm system	Co-operation	Information	PARTICIPANTS: Steering cttee	Project manager	Project office	Participants	Consultants
Project description	○	●	●	●	●						DX	C	C	I	
Definition workshop	○	○	○	○	○	○	○	○	○	○		PX	X	X	T
Draft issue of plan	●	○	○	○	○	●	●	●	●	●	I	PX	X	I	
Meeting with consultants			○		○				○			PX	X	X	A
First issue of plan	●	●	●	●	●	○	○	○	○	○	I	PX	X	I	
Invitations to start-up W/S													X		
Start-up workshop															
· Part 1	●	●	●	●	●	○	○				DX	PX	X	X	T
· Part 2	○	○	○	○	○	●	●	●	●	●	DX	PX	X	X	T
Final editing of plan	●	●	●	●	●	●	●	●	●	●	I	PX	X	I	
Approval of plan	●	●	●	●	●	○	○	○	○	○	D	P	I	I	
Issue of definition report	●	●	●	●	●	●	●	●	●	●	D	PX	X	C	

● Main issue
○ Subsidiary issue

Figure 11.3 Responsibility chart used as a start-up schedule

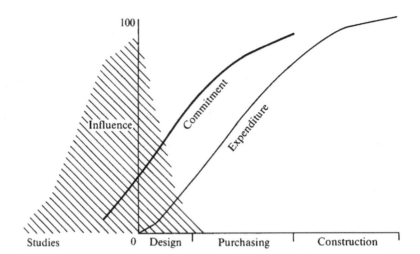

Figure 11.4   The time at which the out-turn cost of a project is set, and the ability to influence it

11.3 Proposal and initiation

The first stage of the life cycle is proposal and initiation, which deals with the definition of the project and its context (Table 11.2). Although the majority of a project's expenditure occurs in execution and control, the greatest influence over cost is during proposal and initiation. Decisions made here have a lasting impact on later expenditure (Figure 11.4). Hence, although only 0.1 per cent of costs may be incurred during proposal and initiation (Table 8.4) perhaps 90 per cent of the expenditure has actually been determined by the end of this stage. The ability to influence costs falls off rapidly during the design stage, so changes made later are impossible to implement without incurring considerable additional cost. This is the relationship between the life cycle and the quality and risk described in Chapters 7 and 10. Proposal and initiation are key to the later success of the project. It is at this stage that we set the bases for the project's success by determining the strategy for its management (Section 4.5). Three of the project management forces which need defining at this point are:

– setting project definition through its objectives and scope
– developing the project model at the integrative level
– defining the project organization.

The project definition
The setting of clear, unambiguous objectives is key to project success. The objectives and initial definition of the scope can be done using the

techniques described in Section 5.4. Section 3.2 described how people can have covert objectives that differ from the project's stated objectives. Even the sponsor can have a hidden agenda. Hence the interpretation of the sponsor's requirement is unlikely to be the subject of unanimous or even objective judgement. This makes even the first step difficult, and means it must be done in a way that leaves little margin for misunderstanding. The Project Definition Workshop (Section 11.6) is a powerful medium for flushing out covert objectives.

The project model at the integrative level
Having defined the project's objectives, we can set constraints for its cost and duration, and the performance of the facility. The purpose indicates parameters for the facility's value and the time window in which it has that value, and from these we determine the maximum cost and latest completion date of the project. The value of the facility depends on the completion date: the later completion, the lower the value (as calculated at the start of the project), as shown in Figure 9.2. The decrease in value represents two things: revenues from the facility having lower present value; and lost revenue if the product has only a limited life. This decrease may allow several build programmes, with a minimum achieved in some optimum time window (Figure 9.1). Three-build programmes were illustrated in Figure 9.2. There may be some indication at this stage whether these times and costs are realistic for achieving the objectives set, but it is not until the feasibility study is completed that you can begin to match the costs to the definition of the work to be done.

The project organization
The owner will consider the source of the resources, whether internal or external contractors, the type of project organization to be adopted (Section 6.3) and a possible project manager. It is better to appoint the project manager early, because that person will be more committed to the project strategy if he or she is involved in determining it. This is a very extensive area, and is best achieved using responsibility charts, (Section 6.4). Remember the process of project organization is one of negotiation, winning people's commitment to the project by demonstrating that it can be of benefit to them.

11.4 Conducting the feasibility study[a]

Much of the above work takes place at the start of proposal and initiation, and leads to the project proposal (the first line in Table 8.4). To initiate the project and so commit resources to systems design, it is necessary to develop the definition further, and refine estimates to the level of the second line in Table 8.4. This is done through a feasibility study. During the feasibility study the range of possible options is examined, and potential issues identified. The aim is to narrow the range of options, provide an assessment of each one remaining, and propose solutions to issues confronting the project. In this section, I describe the objectives of the feasibility study and the factors which should be addressed. I also describe how to set up the study, manage it and bring it to a successful conclusion.

Aims of the feasibility study

Feasibility studies involve time and money, and so it is essential they are well managed. By understanding the aims of the study and the criteria for its success, we can focus our effort. The objectives of the study will be specific to the project, but the following are usually significant:

– exploring all possible options for implementing the project
– achieving a clear understanding of the issues involved
– producing enough information to be able to rank the options
– obtaining a clear picture of the way forward.

THE OPTIONS

As many ideas as possible should be explored. Each option must be thoroughly reviewed to determine whether it can be improved, within the limitations of market and technical conditions. The original specification can act as a guide to the study, but it should not stifle imagination and creativity.

THE ISSUES

The feasibility study must give a clear understanding of the issues. In particular, associated with each option still being considered should be: estimates of costs and revenues; an understanding of the views and objectives of the various sponsors and institutions involved; confirmation of both technical and financial viability; and estimates of the likely economic and financial returns, as described above.

RANKING THE OPTIONS

The study should produce enough information to rank options. The criteria used are based on the strategic factors, described above. Their weighting in the overall ranking of options depends on the sponsor's goals; the public sector will usually give more weight to social and environmental factors than the private sector (Section 2.4).

THE WAY FORWARD

The study should result in a clear idea of future stages. It helps to think of the feasibility study as a funnelling and filtering exercise, directing a wide range of possible ideas into a much narrower range of options, with those which clearly fail to meet objectives sifted out. The study should aim to provide for the next stage – design and appraisal – both a new, refined specification and a work plan. It may also result in a draft plan for the design or execution stages (Example 11.1).

I worked on a three-month feasibility study to assess the efficacy of a new process. We launched the study with a two-week workshop. At the end of the workshop we had a clear objective for the feasibility study, but we had produced no plan, not even at the strategic level, neither for the study nor the year-long systems design stage which followed. The first plan produced was at the end of that year, for the detailed design of the plant.

Example 11.1 Producing a clear definition of the way forward

The factors addressed
The study must provide an understanding of factors influencing success, and assess the advantages and disadvantages of each option to enable them to be ranked. The following factors influence feasibility.

MARKET CONDITIONS
Expectation of returns depends on satisfying demand for the project's product at a certain price level. Usually neither future demand nor future prices can be predicted very accurately. If there is a limited portfolio of potential buyers, or the market is volatile, or demand is price-sensitive (as with commodity products), the project is vulnerable to many adverse circumstances over which the project manager has little influence. However, the existing market environment provides a wealth of information on which to base sales forecasts, establish price structures, understand potential purchasers and consumers, evaluate expected trends in demand and the actions of potential competitors, and learn about the expected quality of the product or service.

SUPPLY CONSIDERATIONS
Existing supply conditions are also important sources of information. The feasibility study should assess the cost, quality and availability of capital equipment, raw materials and labour. Different technical options should also be explored, and specialist technical advice obtained on their feasibility.

FINANCIAL PROSPECTS
The profitability of the project can be analysed by applying economic evaluation techniques (Section 2.4).[8] The financial feasibility also depends on whether the expected return from a project is sufficient to finance debt

and provide shareholders with an adequate return to compensate them for their risk. Financial feasibility is influenced by economic conditions such as interest and exchange rates prevailing when costs are incurred and income received. The approach differs for projects in the private or public sector. The latter often take account of non-monetary benefits and costs, as well as factors such as environmental impact. Shadow prices are used where the market price is considered not to reflect the economic cost or benefit of an input or output of the project. The private sector usually places more weight on purely monetary return, although legislation, tax benefits or subsidy, and public relations considerations may encourage it to place value on non-monetary factors.

Adequate consideration must be given to risk and uncertainty (Chapter 10). Risk and uncertainty cannot be eliminated, but they can be managed and reduced by prudent project design and management, and taken into account in comparison of project options. You should also remember that the shareholders' evaluation of the project, and hence the share price of the company, depends on their assessment of the risk.

Initiating the study

The following five steps are required in setting up a feasibility study.

MANAGEMENT TEAM

Appoint an experienced manager and management team. The make-up depends on the nature of the project. For the feasibility study, it should include technical, financial and marketing expertise, and for larger projects may also have economists, legal and environmental experts, human resources experts, etc. It is essential that a good balance is struck between specialists, as assessment of the options may be biased if one specialism dominates. For example, if technical experts dominate, they may emphasize technically exciting options that may not provide the required financial return. It is often helpful to limit the size of the core management team, as far as the size of the project allows. Compact teams are usually easier to organize and coordinate than larger groups. The manager of the study will usually not be the project manager for subsequent stages. However, it is usually a good idea for the latter to be a member of the management team for the study, and thus have greater ownership and commitment to the results of the study, the decisions made and the strategy set.

SCOPE THE STUDY

Examine the scope of the study to assess the work involved and any constraints imposed (quality, cost, time, etc.). The manager must determine exactly what the decision makers require to guide them in their choice of the project options, and in what form the information is needed. A work plan with the delivery time and content of interim and final reports should as far as possible be agreed in advance with the decision makers. Remember, project management is fractal management; the study needs planning as much as the implementation of the project.

EXTERNAL ADVISERS

Appoint external advisers to supplement the expertise of the core team. It might also be necessary to obtain certain permission and consents, if only on a provisional basis. It would be prudent, for example, to obtain outline planning permission for any construction work envisaged in the project.

PLAN THE STUDY

Draw up a plan for the study, including a milestone plan and responsibility chart. The milestone plan should identify key stages for the study; interim and final reports, meetings, data collection, etc. The plan can highlight different lines of enquiry involved and their interdependence, enabling the different aspects of the study to be coordinated. It should be robust, but sufficiently flexible to cope with any unexpected changes. Adequate allowance should be made for the time required to request and collect data as well as processing and interpreting results.

SCHEDULE THE STUDY

Set the timetable and budget for the study. These must be sufficient to enable options to be properly explored and refined, without endangering the feasibility of the whole project. It is important to budget for an adequate exploration of the options without going to the depth of investigation required for the design and appraisal stage.

The Project Definition Workshop (Section 11.6) can be used to undertake the fourth and fifth steps, as well as developing the initial project definition and strategy.

Managing the study

Once it has been planned, the following are the three main elements to managing the feasibility study

ORGANIZATION

This involves the adoption of a clearly focused but flexible structure based around the milestone plan. The team should be aware of what is expected, and by when. They should understand how they fit into the study framework, and to whom they should report. Hence, roles and responsibilities must be clearly defined. The responsibility chart is the tool which effectively achieves this.

IMPLEMENTATION

This requires efficient communication within the team. The manager should maintain frequent contact with sponsors to ensure the study remains on target, and any change in requirements is identified. The team should maintain good internal communications to ensure delays are reported, to minimize knock-on effects, to avoid duplication, and to confirm all information received has been made available to all members of the team. It is particularly important that good communication is maintained between team members in different fields of expertise to ensure any inter-dependencies are taken into account.

CONTROL

This is the responsibility of the manager who must ensure that milestones are being reached on time, and that the milestones adopted leads to punctual report delivery. Likewise, costs should be monitored to ensure the study remains within budget. Control involves both monitoring of timing and budgets, and rapid and effective corrective action when targets are not met, either by revising targets, or by restructuring present plans within the existing targets. The detail of how work is assigned to people and their progress monitored and controlled, during the feasibility study or any other stage is discussed under execution and control in the next chapters.

Completing the study and transition to the next stage
The feasibility study should act as a springboard for design and appraisal, ensuring it is able to commence in a focused way. The end product should therefore comprise a clear, concise report, the Project Definition Report (Section 11.7), which presents the original specification and objectives, with the conclusions and recommendations for use in the next stage. The report should highlight advantages and disadvantages – cost, revenue, strategic considerations, economic benefits, etc. – for each of the options which deserve further consideration and the proposed solutions to issues confronting the project. Furthermore, the report should indicate sensitivities to variations from the assumed base case.

11.5 Design and appraisal[b]

The second stage of the life cycle is design and appraisal. The primary emphasis in this stage is the development of the project model (Table 11.3). The original outline requirements as expressed by the client in the Project

Definition Report are subjected to more rigorous examination to define exactly what is to be done to achieve the project's objectives. A systems design is developed for the facility, the product it will produce, and the method of building it. This last defines the scope of work for the project at the strategic level (Chapter 5). The project organization is developed at that level, and roles and responsibilities of departments, functions, disciplines, or their managers, are described (Chapter 6). The quality specification, the cost of the project, the time scale and the risk are all planned and estimated at the corresponding level of detail (Chapters 7,8, 9 and 10). From this information we determine whether or not the project is viable and represents a good investment at the accuracy implied by the third line in Table 8.4. This appraisal process is vital, as it is the last chance the sponsor has to decide whether to proceed with the project before committing scarce resources to execution (Figure 11.4). Many of the issues investigated in design are the same as in the feasibility study, but at a lower level of detail. It is not my intention to repeat the discussion of what is investigated, but to focus on special management problems arising in the design and appraisal process.

The design is developed at several levels of the project and stages of the life cycle (Table 11.5), corresponding to different levels of accuracy listed in Table 8.4. It is common to show the life cycle as a serial process, beginning with feasibility and continuing through design and construction, until the facility is commissioned and producing the desired output. Most of the life cycles described in Chapter 1 follow this model. However, the reality of many projects is different. Design in particular is an iterative process, proceeding through these several levels, as our understanding is refined. At each level, the designs must be checked back to the assumptions set in the project's strategy. Even at one level, there may be several iterations, as the

Table 11.5   Life cycle of the design process

Design stage	Design name	Activities
Definition	Customer requirement	Appointment and problem definition Establishment of solution criteria
Feasibility	Functional design	Evolution of alternative solutions
Appraisal	System design	Evaluation of alternatives Selection of preferred solution
Detailed design	Detail design	Detailed design of selected solution
Delivery	As-built design	Manufacture and assembly Facility construction

design proceeds through several formats. In ship-building, the paper design is converted into a plastic model, then into a wooden model from which fabrication jigs are made, before the first vessel of the class is made. The ship is thus made four times before it is completed: once each in paper, plastic and wood, and then the first time in metal. The design process is therefore not a single activity, but a set of activities ranging from the outline requirements to the detail design, and these cover all the stages of the life cycle. The computer industry has developed a spiral model of the life cycle (Section 18.6), which reflects the reality of the design process, and perhaps has applications elsewhere.

The concerns of the project manager during the design process include:

– managing the design process
– managing the urgency
– managing the user
– design, estimation and risk
– managing the appraisal process.

Managing the design process

Design involves the production of information to enable a solution to be selected from a series of options and to allow one scheme to be manufactured or constructed. Information can be in the form of drawings, calculations, computer output, bills of quantities, specifications or fabrications. The target for a good design manager is to produce the right amount of information, using the right people, at the right time, to budget and to the client's satisfaction, while making a profit for their employer. This balance is not easy to achieve. Engineers are notorious for trying to satisfy the client's requirements, while forgetting the need of their own company to make a profit! The application of good project management procedures to the design process can help to ensure the balance is achieved. It can make the process more flexible, allowing the design to proceed efficiently within a framework of gentle control, in which all the designers know what they are doing, why, when it is needed and what to do if the answer they come up with is not the one originally envisaged.

While on paper the application of a project management to the design process may seem to solve all ills, reality is often very different. The project manager not only has to deal with the vagaries of their company's management structure but that of the client and fellow consultants as well. In a busy commercial environment, they rarely have exclusive use of all the experienced designers they require, and so must draw on external resources, competing for the expertise they need. They also often have to deal with heavy pressure from the client to produce action and results. The need for careful planning before quantifiable results are produced is often not understood.

A good design project manager needs to recognize the problems of working in the real world, and be able to tailor their management style to suit the environment. Some projects may be large enough for a task force to be developed with a good working relationship, making communication and management easier. Others may be multi-disciplinary, involving short-term input from many different parts of the company which have to be very highly controlled to ensure that the correct product is produced. Yet other projects may be small with very swift programmes which have to be fitted in between the longer running projects cutting across other deadlines. The busy project manager will normally have to deal with all these types of project at the same time and for different clients.

We saw above that the design process has four key stages (Table 11.5), which apply for each work package within a project as well as for the project as a whole. Prior to starting work on any of the stages, the design project manager should consider how the project will be planned and controlled. There are those who say that design as a creative process cannot be controlled. However, to be of value the facility must be obtained by a certain time (Figure 9.2) and so the process must be managed. Examples 11.2 and 11.3 contain checklists for planning and control of the design process produced by a firm of design consultants. The design manager has to be as much a juggler of resources, costs and time as managers in any manufacturing or production process. In some ways the problem is more complex because the 'product' is unique and can change many times prior to completion. The manager must strike a balance between too much planning and not enough control and too much control and not enough planning, in all aspects of the design process.

PLANNING THE DESIGN PROCESS

P1 Examine the problem carefully with the client and, if possible, with their advisers. Establish what exactly the task is and agree a fee structure for the work, covering various stages of design and taking note of the often highly variable nature of the initial design studies.

The fee arrangement may also include a collateral warranty. This is now commonplace in the construction industry as a result of recent case law on the question of latent liabilities. This must also be recognized and dealt with as a milestone, because the client frequently cannot get funding released for the project from the backers until the document is signed and completed. The time necessary to complete these procedures is often underestimated, which can cause delays.

P2 Establish the basis of a planning network, identifying key milestones to be achieved in design. Plan to do the detailed planning of each phase only when it is necessary, that is on a rolling basis.

P3 Confirm the work breakdown, and identify the packages of design work. Seek to use of the appropriate work-package managers and teams from within your company. Select the right people for the right job, and match personalities to the nature of the task. A careful, meticulous detailer cannot drive a high-pressured fast-track project forward, but should be used to give support to the innovators and strong managers.

P4 Assess time and resource requirements for each phase of design work (at the appropriate time) using your own experience combined with that of the work-package managers.

P5 Check each stage resource allocation against the fee available prior to undertaking the work. If the fee is too small re-evaluate the amount of design proposed, and reduce or delay applying resource or renegotiate the fee arrangement. Aim to do the right amount of work at the right time.

P6 Establish the resources available for each stage are sufficient to meet the programme, using your master design plan as a basis. Introduce contingency allowances at a fairly high level in the plan so that you can control slippage. Try not to build contingency in at each level or else you will never create a workable programme.

P7 Establish, jointly with the department managers in your company, whether your use of their staff (particularly when the project is multi-disciplinary) is compatible with their other commitments and schedule the resources accordingly. Tie this back to the basic network and evaluate any overall effect on the programme. As far as possible smooth out resource peaks to enable easier overall company staff planning, and seek to adjust project priorities to suit. A balance always has to be struck.

P8 Establish work packages, and, if at all possible, write down a brief for the managers as clearly and in as much detail as possible. This is often difficult to achieve, but is very important because it establishes a firm criteria against which success can be measured in each design package. Ensure this brief is a living document, and that it is continually referred to and updated by mutual agreement of the project manager and work-package manager as the design evolves.

P9 Establish the critical path from your network (using rolling-wave planning). In theory your critical path should be determined from the outset by the production of a stable network plan within which variations can take place. In practice, this may not be so easy to achieve as there are usually many unforeseen events which erode your contingency allowance and cause the path to shift. It is, however, always these key activities which dictate whether or not the project is completed on time.

Information and the resources needed are the keys to the well-being of the whole project. It has been suggested that 80 per cent of design problems come from 20 per cent of the activities. However, an over-preoccupation with activities currently identified as critical can also backfire by reducing your awareness of other non-critical areas which can suddenly become critical. A balance has to be achieved and progress on each facet of the network must be regularly monitored and controlled.

Example 11.2 Planning the design process

CONTROLLING THE DESIGN PROCESS

C1 Establish communication systems. Decide which level of designer should talk to which level in the client or consultant teams. Ensure that you are always in the picture as to progress. Ensure that work-package managers are aware of their responsibility to control communication. Only correct, considered information should be released to avoid incorrect action by outside bodies which would destroy confidence in the design team's abilities.

C2 Establish a design review procedure. Regular (fortnightly) design reviews should take place to ensure the whole package is moving towards its target. An open forum in which package managers can discuss problems should be encouraged. People must not to hide major problems but discuss them and seek help before they get out of hand.

C3 Establish a design-checking procedure to interface the review process. Some projects need a full quality assurance (QA) system. This must be identified at the outset to ensure a quality plan is written and implemented incorporating project management systems identified. Some projects (e.g. bridges designed for the Department of Transport) have checking procedures established for each stage. These may include formal checks by other firms.

The checks and consequential alterations must be programmed at each stage of the design, and adequate resources and time allowed. If QA is required, you must remember this is only an aid to sound design office procedures and not a substitute. QA should only help formalize those procedures already being undertaken.

C4 Establish a regular system of meetings to interface the usual client/consultant design team meetings. These meetings may be held instead of or as well as design reviews, depending on the complexity of the job, and should bring together internal design issues and a review of external influences on the design. Following these reviews a short statement of progress addressing key issues and problems should be prepared for issue to the client. Areas where information is required or where instruction is needed should be identified.

C5 As changes occur ensure that the reasons are communicated if appropriate down to the people doing the draughting. There is nothing more demoralizing than facets of the design being repeated when the reason is unclear. Although this may be tedious for the work-package managers, the project manager must encourage the team to keep communication lines open. One must always be conscious of the needs and desires of the individual as well the objectives of the project or else neither will be achieved.

C6 Once the design has begun, check expenditure against forecast costs and fee income regularly. Often delays cause an increase in resources to recover the programme. Delays may require you to move staff from one project to another to avoid overloading one and underresourcing another. While your plan and control systems should allow you to accommodate this, the financial side of your company must not be forgotten. Computerized monthly job cost summaries are out of date before you receive them so ensure you know what the projected cost effects are before they occur.

C7 Changes to the design brief are often made by the client as the design develops. This is a natural part of the design process as the client begins to understand the impact of earlier decisions. While some change should be tolerated, major changes must be controlled, and additional fees sought before embarking on the additional work required. If the client is not aware of the financial implications of the decisions, they will request changes without a second thought, which can rapidly cause your company to make a loss.

C8 Establish which outside bodies (stakeholders) must be consulted, and obtain their approval prior to commencing. These may be statutory bodies, environmental groups, planning authorities, etc. Time to obtain such approvals must be allocated and milestones recognized. You may also require discreet input from the consultant team at regular intervals, and vice versa, depending on the product. You must identify and programme this flow of information as a strategic part of your design process.

Example 11.3 Controlling the design process

Managing the urgency

There is often a tendency to try to shorten the design process to begin work on a project. We saw in Chapter 1 that people tend to jump from perceiving a problem to selecting a solution, or worse to implementing one. They then never truly determine the cause of the problem and the best method of solving it; they just paper over cracks. It is always important to put adequate time and effort into the design process, and the way to ensure this is to have a proper project plan for the design stage, which measures the progress of the design towards completion against a series of milestones. Those people who are keen to begin execution can then follow this plan and progress their work accordingly.

There can also be a tendency to overlap implementation and design to make better use of available skilled resources. This is what was described in Section 4.4 as *fast build, fast track* or *concurrency*, which are associated with increasing risk. The importance of allowing the design stage to take its course cannot be overemphasized. However, we shall now see that the project manager must guard against the opposing risk, namely the desire of the designers to develop the ideal solution or prolong the design period because of the inherent job interest it offers.

Managing the users

Throughout design, designer, client and end user must remain in close dialogue to ensure that the design meets the user's needs. In Chapter 7 we saw that this is the ultimate measure of the quality. However, it is important that the designer and user are not allowed to change the requirements so frequently that no progress is made. Managing the user is vital. The challenge is to ensure essential changes are incorporated, but 'nice to haves' are avoided. Many people suggest freezing user requirements at an early stage. However, that can lead to ineffective solutions, as the process of designing the facility and its product can help to clarify user requirements (Section 19.3). What is actually needed is the application of effective configuration management so that the design moves steadily forward, until a viable design is produced which also meets user's needs.

Managing the appraisal process

Appraisal is the process by which the viability of the project is finally checked before money is committed to its implementation. If the appraisal process results in approval for the project, the sponsor gives authority for the project to proceed and raises finance for it. The appraisal of the project is based on many of the issues identified in the feasibility study, and the methods of analysis outlined in Section 2.4. The project may be compared against quantitative criteria: first that it meets certain minimum investment criteria; and secondly that it compares favourably with other projects competing for the same scarce finance. However, it may also be compared against qualitative criteria, such as its impact on the business, its impact on the environment and its popularity with the stakeholders.

At this stage it is important to perform a thorough analysis of the risk so that appropriate risk reduction measures can be implemented (Chapter 10). It can be useful to appoint an independent team to audit the risk, as the people who have performed the design and undertaken the initial appraisal may be too close to the project to take a dispassionate view. They may be unable to see the obvious risks. The team of auditors may be external consultants, or a separate team of internal designers who have not been involved with the project to date. This issue was also discussed in Section 7.2.

11.6 Initiation, launch and kick-off meetings

Launch workshops were introduced in Section 11.2 as a way of initiating the current stage. Indeed, mini-workshops may be held at the start of work packages, in accordance with the rolling-wave principle. A workshop held at the start of proposal and initiation is called a *Project Definition Workshop*, and at the start of design and appraisal a *design initiation* or *kick-off meeting*. (A similar meeting, a project initiation meeting, may be held at the start of execution and control.) In this section, the objectives, attendees, agenda and timetable of these workshops are described.

Workshop objectives

The main objectives of the workshop are given below:

1. *Gain commitment and build team spirit*: this is the primary objective of a workshop. Many of the others can be achieved by people working alone or meeting in smaller groups. By coming together, they may develop a common understanding, and resolve items of confusion, disagreement or conflict through discussion. If people are briefed after a meeting, (presented with a *fait accompli*), they may nod their heads in agreement, but you often find they do not truly accept what they are told. If people agree to a course of action in a meeting, you usually find they have internalized that agreement, but if they have not, it is difficult for them to avoid their commitments later because several people have heard them make them.

2. *Ratify earlier project definition*: whatever stage is being launched, it is vital for the team to agree what the current level of definition entails, and that it truly represents the user's requirements.

3. *Plan the current stage*: the workshop is used to launch the current stage, and so producing a plan for the stage is key. This should at least consist of a milestone plan and responsibility chart.

4. *Prepare preliminary plans for execution*: it is usually worth while to prepare a draft milestone plan for execution, as this can be a useful basis for the feasibility study or design, even if the subsequent project follows a slightly different course.

5. *Prepare preliminary estimates*: this gives the project team some idea of the expectation of the cost and benefit of the project. Although their subsequent work should not be constrained by the estimates, it can help to set the basic parameters.

6. *Assess risk and develop risk reduction strategies*: Preliminary risk analysis should be undertaken, and risk reduction strategies developed.

7. *Start work promptly*: the workshop should be used to plan the initial work of the current stage, so that the team members can make a prompt start.

8. *Agree a date for reviewing the stage deliverables*: ideally the plan should contain a time scale and budget for the stage. An end date, at least, should be set for completion of the stage, so that it is not left open-ended.

Workshop attendees

The workshops should be attended by key managers, including:

– the project sponsor and champion
– the manager of the current stage
– the manager designate of future stages, especially execution
– key functional managers whose groups are impacted by the project, including technical managers, user managers and resource providers
– a Project Support Office manager
– a facilitator.

The sponsor may attend the Definition Workshop, but not later ones. Possible attendees for a Project Definition Workshop on the CRMO Rationalization Project are given in Example 11.4.

The *sponsor* may be a main board director or regional managing director
The *champion* may be the regional managing director, the operations director, the financial director or the technical director
The *manager of the feasibility study* may be the champion
The *project manager designate* may be the customer services manager, the network manager or the IT manager
Key *functional managers* will include these three, the estates manager, the finance manager, and the sales and marketing manager
There may already be a *Project Support Office* in the IT or networks department, otherwise a field Planning Office could fulfil the role

---

Example 11.4 Project Definition Workshop attendees for the CRMO Rationalization Project

Workshop agenda

A typical agenda for a workshop is:

1. Review the current project definition.
2. Define the objectives of the current stage.
3. Develop solutions and criteria for evaluation.
4. Assess risks and assumptions.
5. Prepare a milestone plan for the current stage.
6. Prepare a responsibility chart against the plan.
7. Estimate work content and durations for the work packages.
8. Schedule the work packages.
9. Assess risk and develop reduction strategies.
10. Prepare initial activity schedules.
11. Prepare a management and control plan.

Most effort goes into the milestone plan and responsibility chart, as that is the most effective use of group working. Sections 5.4 and 6.3 show how to develop them using whiteboards, flip charts, Post-Its and an overhead projector. Involving everyone present around a whiteboard, gains their commitment to the plans produced. Working around a table with pen and paper can isolate members of the team from the working process. Estimates and schedules are best agreed through a process of negotiation immediately after the workshop. The initial activity schedules are prepared so that the team members know what to do immediately following the meeting; it is an initiation meeting (Example 11.1). The management and control plan agrees the approach to be used in managing the project and the mechanisms, priorities and frequency of the control process. It may be the basis of the management approach outlined in the Project Manual.

Workshop timetable
A workshop typically lasts one to four days. I usually allow two hours per item, except items 5 and 6 for which I allow four hours. However, it is important not to stick rigidly to a timetable, but to allow discussion to come to a natural conclusion, as people reach agreement and a common understanding. I sometimes include project management training as part of the timetable, which extends the duration by about a day. I find it useful to schedule a break in the middle of agenda item 5. When developing a milestone plan, people often reach a blank; the plan will just not make sense. However, when left for a while, it just seems to fall into place.

11.7 Project Definition Report and Manual

In Section 11.2, I introduced the Start-up or Stage Review Report, which gathers the results from the work of one stage, and is used to launch the next stage. The report produced at the end of proposal and initiation is called the Project Definition Report, and that at the end of design and appraisal the Project Manual. In this section, I describe the objectives and content of these two reports.

Objectives of the Project Definition Report
The Project Definition Report, sometimes called the Client's Requirements Definition or Statement of User Requirements, gathers the results of the feasibility study into a readily accessible document. It is a handbook for the management, design and execution teams, which defines what the owner expects from the project, and the reasoning behind the chosen options and strategies. This reasoning can always be open to questioning. It is healthy that the teams involved in later stages question earlier decisions. However, by having earlier reasoning recorded, the project teams can avoid repeating

work, and more importantly avoid following previous blind alleys. The Project Definition Report will also be used to launch design and appraisal, and may be the input to a kick-off meeting at the start of that stage. Hence, the objectives of the Project Definition Report are:

– to provide sufficient definition, including costs and benefits, to allow the business to commit resources to design and appraisal
– to provide a basis for design and appraisal
– to provide senior management with an overview of the project's priority alongside day-to-day operations and other projects (both proposed and on-going)
– to communicate the project's requirements throughout the business
– to define the commitment of the business to the project.

Most of these objectives look forward; the report is not produced as a bureaucratic exercise to record the feasibility study, but as a basis for the future stages.

Contents of the Project Definition Report
The suggested contents of the report are:

I *Preface*: outlines the objectives of the document, as described above.
II *Management summary*: a one-page summary for senior managers.
1. *Background*: sets the context within which the project exists, and may describe the purpose of the higher level programme of which the project is a part.
2. *Purpose, scope and objectives*: the reason for undertaking the project, with expected returns, the sort of work needed to achieve that, and the product to be produced by the project in order to achieve the returns.
3. *Work breakdown structure*: initiates work breakdown, stating with areas of work and including a milestone plan. A target schedule may be included.
4. *Project organization*: defines the type of project organization, including:
   – organizational units within the business involved in the project
   – their involvement in different areas of work
   – managerial responsibility for different areas of work
   – the type of project organization to be used
   – the location of project resources
   – the source of the project manager
   – their source and limits of authority
   and describes the responsibilities of key managers and groups in the business, including:
   – project sponsor, champion and manager

– work area and work package managers
– project steering board
– quality assurance board and Project Support Office manager
It may be necessary to include a tentative resource schedule, so the project can be assigned priority. This schedule is derived from high-level assumptions, applied to areas of work or work packages. It should not be based on a detailed definition of work, except in areas of high risk, because that requires an investment in planning resources before the business has agreed to commit it.

5. *Project management system*: defines the tools and techniques for planning and controlling the project, and supporting computer systems. This may include preliminary quality plans and control procedures.

6. *Risks and assumptions*: stated for future reference, and to allow adequate account to be taken in the investment appraisal. This section should record the results of the risk analysis, the risks, their impacts and potential reduction strategies. It is also possible to record solutions discounted, with reasons, to stop future people joining the team from following blindly others previously discounted.

7. *Project budgets*: the initial estimates for the project, and a statement of the maximum amount which can be spent to justify the expected benefits.

8. *Project justification*: an investment appraisal performed using the estimates as they exist, against defined investment criteria. This will justify the commitment of resources to the design and appraisal stage.

9. *Appendices*: contain many of the preliminary plans.

Example 5.1 contains items 1, 2 and part of 3 for the CRMO Rationalization Project. Item 3 may also include a milestone plan, and work-package scope statements, (Example 5.2). Item 4 will be partly descriptive, but may include a responsibility chart. Item 5 may also include responsibility charts, such as that in Figure 6.9, and a recommendation of how to use a computer-based project management information system. Chapter 16 of this book covers the contents of item 5.

The report is typically 10 to 40 pages long, depending on the size and complexity of the project, and its impact on the organization. It is developed throughout proposal and initiation. However, once ratified by senior management at the end of that stage, it should be sacrosanct, and only modified by formal change control.

Objectives of the project manual
The results of design and appraisal are recorded in a Project Manual. This is a definitive document which explains how the owner's requirements set out in the Project Definition Report are to be delivered by describing the

objectives, scope and management strategy for the project as they are defined at the end of the stage. It is used as the briefing document for all people joining the project team in execution and control.

The manual is developed progressively by the project manager from the Project Definition Report throughout design and appraisal. The draft manual is reviewed by the owner and project manager together, until it is signed off at the end of the stage as reflecting their mutual understanding of how the owner's requirements are to be delivered. When the manual is signed off, the project manager must accept responsibility for delivering the project as defined in the manual, and from that point on changes to the manual can only be made through strict change control. The development of the Project Manual, and the master plan it includes, often represents the largest proportion of the project manager's efforts during design after the management of the actual design process itself.

Throughout execution and control, the manual is extended down to the work-package level, as part of the start-up of individual work packages. The manuals at the work-package level must be derived from the Project Manual, but they may highlight the need for modifying the Project Manual.

Contents of the Project Manual

The contents of the manual may include the following items:

1. *Project description and objectives*: summarizes the Project Definition Report, as modified by the design and appraisal process (Example 11.5).
2. *Master project plan*: forms the major part of the manual. The design and appraisal process will result in this master plan for the project. The contents of this plan, which cover the definition of scope, organization, quality, cost and time in the project model, are summarized in Table 1.7.
3. *Management plan*: describes how the project is to be planned, organized, implemented and controlled, although the first two now only need to be done at lower levels of work breakdown.
4. *Performance specification*: defines the required levels of performance of the facility and its product. This is one of the major elements of the quality specification of the project, and will have been developed and refined during the design process.
5. *Functional specification*: explains the technology to be used in the development of the facility, and how that will function to deliver the required output.
6. *Acceptance tests and acceptance criteria*: are derived from the previous two, and are an important part of the manual. They must be defined before work starts for two reasons. First they must be independent. The project team members must not be allowed to develop testing procedures

which match the facility built. Secondly, the project team must know how they are to be judged, if they are to deliver a quality product. In Chapter 7, quality was defined as meeting customer's requirements. These must be defined in advance so that the team members know what their objective is, and they do not produce a product which is either over- or under-specified.

7. *Project constraints*: are derived throughout the first two stages, and so must be recorded for all people joining the project at a later date.

8. *Risks and assumptions*: must also be recorded for two reasons. So people joining the project later know what has been addressed, and so others, especially owners, sponsors financiers and auditors, can see they have been properly addressed and that adequate weight has been given to them.

I had a discussion with managers attending a course at Henley Management College about whether the manual would contain the Definition Report in its entirety, or whether it would be summarized into a single section as a background. We decided on the latter for two reasons. First, it is the job of management to summarize the instructions from the level above when passing them on to the level below, so the next level down can focus on those things which enable them to do their jobs effectively. You inform people on the next level on a need-to-know basis. This does not mean you need to be excessively secretive. You tell the next level enough to motivate them, and make them feel part of the overall management team, without overburdening them with unnecessary information. Secondly, taken to the extreme, you would include the entire corporate plans in the briefing documents to every project.

Example 11.3 Summarizing the Project Definition Report in the Project Manual

11.8 Summary

1. Part Three follows a four-stage cycle:
   - proposal and initiation
   - design and appraisal
   - execution and control
   - finalization and closure.
2. There are four stages of team formation:
   - forming
   - storming
   - norming
   - performing.
3. Project start-up is a structured way to moving the project team quickly

and effectively through these four stages, so as to:
- define the project's context and objectives
- develop the project model
- define the management approach
- commission the facility and hand it over.

4. The methods of project start-up include:
   - stage launch workshops
   - start-up reports
   - ad-hoc assistance.

5. The foundation of the success of the project is secured during the proposal and initiation stage by:
   - setting project objectives and scope
   - developing the project model at the integrative level
   - defining the project organization.

6. A feasibility study is an initial study into the solutions for achieving the objectives and has four objectives:
   - to explore all options
   - to understand all the issues
   - to rank the options
   - to plan the way forward.

7. The feasibility study will address the following issues:
   - market conditions
   - supply considerations
   - financial prospects.

8. The concerns of the manager during the design process include:
   - managing the design process
   - managing the urgency
   - managing the user
   - managing the appraisal process.

9. Appraisal is the process by which the viability of the project is finally checked, and is the last chance to stop the project before significant amounts of money are spent on its delivery.

10. A stage launch workshop may be held with the objectives:
    - to gain commitment and build the team spirit
    - to ratify the project definition as produced in the previous stage
    - to plan the current stage of the project
    - to prepare preliminary plans for the execution stage
    - to prepare preliminary estimates for the project
    - to ensure work starts promptly
    - to agree a date for review of the stage deliverables.

11. A Project Definition Report may be prepared with the objectives:
    - to commit resources to design

- to provide a basis for design
- to set the project's priority
- to inform all those affected by the project
- to gain commitment.

12. The contents of the report may include:
  - background
  - purpose, scope and objectives
  - work breakdown structure
  - project organization
  - project management system
  - risks and assumptions
  - project budgets
  - project justification.

13. The systems design produced during the design and appraisal stage may be summarized in a Project Manual, which may have as its contents:
  - project description and objectives
  - master project plan
  - management plan
  - performance specification
  - technical specification
  - acceptance tests and criteria for acceptance
  - project constraints
  - risks and assumptions.

References

1. Handy, C., *Understanding Organizations*, Penguin, 1986.
2. Fangel, M. (ed.), *Handbook of Project Start-up: How to launch projects effectively*, INTERNET, 1987.
3. Fangel, M., 'The essence of project start-up: the concept, timing, results, methods, schedule and application', in *Handbook of Project Start-up: How to launch projects effectively*, M. Fangel (ed.), INTERNET, 1987.
4. Fangel, M., 'To start or to start-up? – That is the key question of project initiation', *International Journal of Project Management*, **9** (1), 1991.
5. Gareis, R., 'Best project management practice: Results of a research project on project management benchmarking', *Proceedings of Vienna IV, Research workshop within the Project Management Research Network*, R. Gareis and B. Gatzenberger (eds), Wirtschaft Universitet, Wien, November 1997.
6. Andersen, E.S., Grude, K.V., Haug, T. and Turner, J.R., *Goal Directed Project Management*, 2nd edn, Kogan Page, 1995.
7. Archibald, R.D., *Managing High-Technology Programs and Projects*, Wiley, 1976.
8. Turner, J.R. (ed.), *The Commercial Project Manager*, McGraw-Hill, 1995.

Notes

a. Section 11.4 incorporates material from the first edition based on a contribution originally made by Nick Aked and Roger Sharp of Coopers & Lybrand.
b. Section 11.5 incorporates material from the first edition based on contributions made by Mahen Tampoe and David Topping.

12
Project implementation and control

12.1 Introduction

The middle stage of the life cycle is execution and control. During this stage, most of the work to deliver the objectives (build the facility) is undertaken, and thus most of the expenditure made. The stage is started by completion of detailed design. At the previous stage sufficient design (a systems design) has been done to prove the concept and obtain financing. The detail design shows how the work of the project will be implemented, and from this a cost estimate corresponding to the fourth line of Table 8.4 developed. A corresponding project plan is also produced. This plan and design may require three or four times as much effort as the systems design developed at the previous stage, but it is only done after the project has been proved and the finance raised. Once sufficient design has been done, work can begin. If fast-build or fast-track is possible, this may be before detail design is complete. Resources are selected, and they plan the detail work on a rolling-wave basis. Work is authorized by the project manager, and allocated to teams or individuals. As work is done, progress is measured to ensure the desired results are achieved; that is the required facility is delivered within the constraints of quality, cost and time, and that this will achieve the required benefit. If there is a shortfall, appropriate recovery action is taken. This may mean doing nothing because the variances are small, replanning the work to recover the original plan, or revising the plan to accept the current situation. In extremis, it may mean terminating the project, if the original objectives are unobtainable.

In this chapter, I shall describe the management of execution and control. I start by explaining the selection of resources, implementation planning, and the allocation of work. I then describe the requirements for effective control, how to monitor progress and analyse variances to forecast completion of all five project objectives, and how to take action to respond to deviations from the plan. I end the chapter by describing an integrated control cycle. I said in the last chapter that this control cycle applies to the management of feasibility and design and appraisal. It is described here because it is the major emphasis of this stage. I do not describe the detail design process, as it is merely a refinement of what was covered in Chapter 11.

12.2 Resourcing a project

One of the recurrent questions of project management is: 'Do you assign work to people or people to work?'

In one approach – assigning work to people – you form a project team, they decide how best to achieve the project's objectives, and assign the work to the people in the team. The risk is you will find the skills of the people in the team are inappropriate for the work you have to do. In the other approach – assigning people to work – you define the scope of work and then form a project team of appropriate skills. The risk is that the project manager will not be a technical expert, and so will be dictating to experts how they should undertake the task.

To overcome this dilemma, you develop the definition of scope and organization in parallel down the breakdown (Figure 1.13). During proposal and initiation, you define the areas of work, and the functional areas of the organization involved (Sections 11.3, 5.3 and 6.3). During design and appraisal, you work with functional managers, to develop the milestone plan and responsibility chart at the strategic level (Sections 11.5, 5.4 and 6.4). From the responsibility chart, you determine the skill types required and form a team. The team determine how they think the work should be done, and so define the scope at the tactical level. The project manager and work-package manager agree and authorize the work and assign it to the team. Hence, the people to do the work are selected from a resource pool, which is identified by planning the work at the strategic level in the project hierarchy.

The process of resourcing a project includes the following steps:

1. *Identify what is to be achieved*: through the milestone plan.
2. *Identify the skills and skill types required to do the work*: through the responsibility chart. The skills required include technical, craft, professional and functional skills, or managerial knowledge.
3. *Identify the people available*: through discussion with the resource providers. It is important to obtain people with the correct skill. There is a danger, especially with a fixed project team, of selecting somebody to do work because they are available, not because they have the right skills, or that the resource provider may try to provide their least

competent people, and retain their best individuals within their own sphere. You should take account of people's true availability. A person may only be available to a project part time, and be retained for the remainder of their time on their normal duties. In Section 9.3, we saw that someone working nominally full time on a project may do on average only three and a half days work per week throughout a year.

4. *Assess the competence of the people available*: to identify any shortfall in skills. Even after selecting people of the correct skills, it is unlikely there will be a complete match to requirements.

5. *Identify any training required*: to overcome the deficiency in skill levels. Training may be in the form of open or bespoke courses, or on-the-job coaching.

6. *Negotiate with the resource providers*: Throughout this process, you must negotiate with the line managers of the people who will do the work, so that they willingly release their people. If the resource providers will not cooperate, the manager can bring pressure to bear via the sponsor. However, even then they may not cooperate, and block their people working on the project, so it is best to win the resource providers' support. This can be done by gaining their commitment to the project's goals, and by helping them understand how the project is of benefit to them.

7. *Ensure that appropriate facilities and equipment are available*: Facilities may include office space, meeting rooms, security arrangements and transport. Equipment may include computers and other office equipment, computer software, (including word processing, spreadsheets, and project management information systems), telephone, modems and facsimile.

12.3 Implementation planning

Having identified the people to do the work, the team can then define the details of the work to be done and assign work to themselves for execution. The detail work should be planned on a rolling-wave basis, as it is only when you are about to start the work that you have all the information required to plan activities in detail. In this way, you can also allow people to plan their own work. However, I suggested in Section 5.6 that you can create a preliminary activity definition through work-package scope statements for early estimating. In this section, I consider the process of implementation planning, including:

- planning and scheduling the activities to be done
- authorizing the work
- representing the activity schedule
- representing the time schedule.

Planning and scheduling activities

There are five steps in planning and scheduling activities:

1. *Define activities required to reach a milestone*: When selecting activities, the team should choose ones which are controllable, that is they should:
   - *produce a measurable result*: It must be possible to determine when an activity is finished. It is no good dividing a work package into five activities each equal to 20 per cent of the work. In those circumstances the last activity often takes 80 per cent of the effort
   - *have average duration roughly equal to the frequency of review*: See Section 5.2.
2. *Ratify the people involved*: The people to do the work have been chosen as described above. However, once the activities have been defined it may be necessary to review the team to ensure it contains all the necessary skills, and no redundant skills.
3. *Define roles and responsibilities*: The involvement of each of the team members in the activities is then identified. A responsibility chart can be a useful tool for this.
4. *Estimate work content and durations*: The work content and durations are estimated applying the processes used at the work-package level.
5. *Schedule the activities within the work package*: Finally the activities are scheduled within the work package to deliver the milestone on time. This can be done manually, or by building the activities into a nested network, as illustrated in Figure 12.1.

If you adopt rolling-wave planning, estimates of work content and duration at the activity level will be made at a later stage of the project than those at the work-package level, after sanction has been obtained. Some people are uncomfortable with this, fearing that the activity estimates will turn out to be different from – usually higher than – the work-package estimates. What should happen, of course, is that the range of possible out-turns for the total project after activity estimating, should fall within the range after work-package estimating. Table 8.4 shows that the range of accuracy for the project after estimating at the work-package level may be of the order of +10 per cent, and after estimating at the activity level may be +5 per cent. Figures 12.2 (a) and (b) show acceptable activity estimates, and Figures 12.2 (c) and (d) unacceptable activity estimates. Figure 12.2 (d) is unacceptable because overestimating can lead to viable projects being cancelled, or capital being tied up and unavailable to fund other worthwhile projects. If the estimates consistently fall outside the allowable range of those prepared at the work-package level, the estimating data used for the latter needs improving. It is therefore important to feed the results back to the estimators so that they can improve their data.

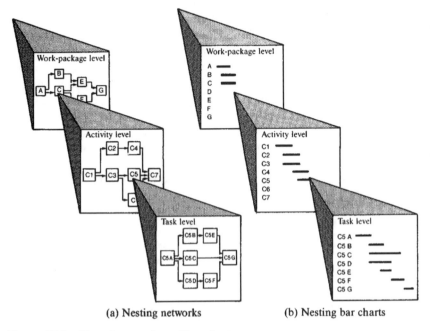

(a) Nesting networks	(b) Nesting bar charts

Figure 12.1   Nested networks and bar charts

If it is not possible to schedule the activities to deliver the milestone on time (subject to Figure 12.2), the delay to the plan must be subjected to change control. The change can be to declare a variance between the current schedule and the baseline, or if the delay is severe to update the baseline.

Authorizing work

The newly created activity schedule is entered into the master plan, and then at appropriate intervals, current work is allocated to individuals to do. Both of these steps must be authorized.

AUTHORIZING INCLUSION IN THE MASTER PLAN

Although the project manager may delegate the creation of the activity plan to the team, he or she must negotiate an agreed estimate with the team, and authorize its inclusion in the master plan because:

– any variances in the estimates as a result of the lower level planning must be agreed
– experts will sometimes plan for a Rolls-Royce solution rather than an adequate solution within the quality constraints, and so the project manager must have an opportunity to ratify the plan
– the experts may sometimes allow themselves excessive contingency.

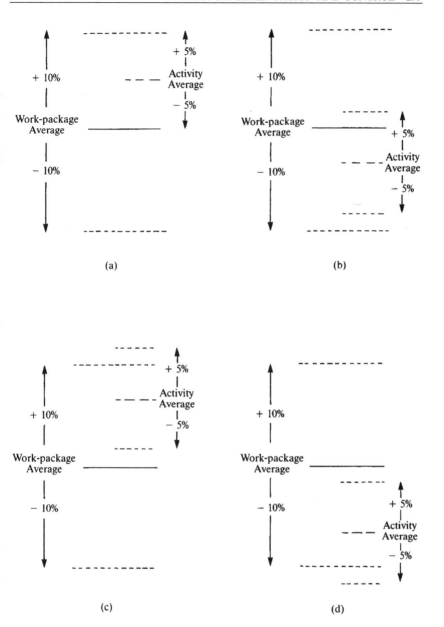

Figure 12.2   Comparison of total project estimates following estimating at the work-package level and activity level

AUTHORIZING ALLOCATION OF WORK

Including the activity schedule in the master plan does not automatically give the project team the authority to do the work at the planned time. The project manager must authorize all work before it is done, often through the issuing of *work-to lists* (see Section 12.4). The project manager may need to re-schedule the work for a variety of reasons:

– it may be dependent on other delayed work
– other resources may need to work in the same space at the same time
– the work may be rearranged as part of a larger recovery plan
– there may be financial or resource constraints.

Representing the activity schedule

There are several ways of representing the activity schedule:

RESPONSIBILITY CHARTS

The responsibility chart provides a complete picture of the schedule of activities which make up a work package. Figure 12.3 shows the activity schedule for milestone P1 in the CRMO Rationalization Project.

ESTIMATING SHEETS

The responsibility chart is an effective tool for representing the people involved, but weak for estimating work content. An estimating sheet, Figure 12.4, can be used for the latter. This is often usefully developed in a spreadsheet, and it:

– lists the activities
– lists the people involved
– breaks the activities into repeated events
– sums the work content of the events to the activities
– spreads the work content between resources
– sums for the work package as a whole
– calculates the duration and cost of the work package.

An estimating sheet only shows the resources represented by an X or C on the responsibility chart. It can be augmented to show start and finish dates for activities. However, it is a tool for calculating the work content and schedule, not for communicating them. A responsibility chart or bar chart is better for that purpose.

NESTED NETWORKS

You can draw a network of the activities which make up a work package. Figure 12.1 (a) illustrates nested networks. If you are using computer tools, the nested network can be included as hammocked networks in the master network, or kept as a separate sub-network linked to the master network.

ACTIVITY SCHEDULE

Project: CRMO RATIONALIZATION
Milestone No./Name: P1: PROJECT DEFINITION
Period: 199X
Issue/Date: A/2 Jan
Approved by: JRT
Activity/Task name:

Companies/Departments/Functions/Type of resource

Key:
X – eXecutes the work
D – takes Decision solely
d – takes decision jointly
P – manages Progress
T – provides Tuition on the job
C – must be Consulted
I – must be Informed
A – available to Advise

No.	Activity/Task	Regional Board	Operations Director	CRMO Managers (2)	CRMO Team Leader	CRMO Staff	Project Manager	Project Support Office	Estates Manager	Network Manager	Networks	IT	Operations	Personnel
	Produce project proposal	C	D	d	dX		PX	A	A	A		A	A	A
	Hold project definition workshop	C	DX	X	X		PX	X	X	X		X		
	Define required benefits	C	D	d	dX		PX		I	I		I	I	I
	Draft project definition report	C	D	d	dX		PX	X	X	X		X		
	Hold project launch workshop		D	X	X		PX	X	X	X		C	A	C
	Finalize milestone plan		D	d	d		PX	X	C	C		C	A	A
	Finalize responsibility chart		D	d	d		PX	X	C	C		C	A	A
	Prepare estimates – time				A		P	X	A	A		A	A	A
	Prepare estimates – cost		A	A	A		P	X	A	A		A	A	A
	Prepare estimates – revenue		A	A	A		P	X	A	A		A	A	A
	Assess project viability		D	d	dX		PX	X	C	C		C	C	C
	Assess risks		D	d	d		PX	X	C	C		C	C	C
	Finalize project definition report	D	d	d	dX		PX	X	X	X		IX		
	Mobilize team		D	d	dX		PX	X			I			

Figure 12.3 Activity Schedule for milestone P1 in the CRMO Rationalization Project

ESTIMATING SHEET		TRIMAGI COMMUNICATIONS BV				02-Jan-9X
PROJECT:	CRMO Rationalization	CODE:	C1	ISSUE:	A	
WORK AREA:	Project	CODE:	C1P	AUTHOR:	LJN	
WORK PACKAGE:	Project Definition	CODE:	C1P1	APPRVD:	JRT	
ACTIVITY:	....	CODE:	....	DATE:	02-Jan-9X	

ACTIVITY/TASK		WORK CONTENT			RESOURCES					9 People
		No of steps	Effort/ step	Total effort	Prjct Mgr	Prjct Offc	CRMO TL	CRMO Mgrs	Ops Direct	Other Mgrs
Number Description			(days)	(days)	1	1	1	2	1	3
1	Produce project proposal	1	4	4	1	2	1			
2	Hold Project Definition Workshop	1	4	4	1	1	1		1	
3	Define required benefits	1	2	2	1		1			
4	Draft Project Definition Report	·1	8	8	2	6				
5	Hold project launch workshop, 1.5 day duration	1	12	12	1.5	1.5	1.5	3		4.5
6	Finalize milestone plan	1	2	2	1	1				
7	Finalize project responsibility chart	1	2	2	1	1				
8	Prepare estimates – time	20	0.1	2		2				
9	Prepare estimates – cost	20	0.1	2		2				
10	Prepare estimates – revenue	1	1	1		1				
11	Assess project viability	1	1	1	1					
12	Assess risks	1	3	3	1	1	1			
13	Finalize Project Definition Report	1	5	5	2	3				
14	Mobilize team	1	3	3	0.5	0.5	0.5			1.5
	SUB-TOTAL:			51	13	22	6	3	1	6
	ALLOWANCE %			10	10	10	10	10	10	10
	TOTAL EFFORT:			56	14	24	7	3	1	7
	UNIT RATE:		£K/day		0.5	0.3	0.3	0.5	0.8	0.5
	COST:		£K		7.15	7.26	1.98	1.65	0.88	3.30

TOTAL EFFORT: 56 DAYS
TOTAL COST: £K 22.22
DURATION: 30 DAYS
TARGET START: 01-Feb-9X
TARGET FINISH: 15-Mar-9X

Figure 12.4   Estimating Sheet representing the activity schedule for milestone P1: *Project Definition* of the CRMO Rationalization Project

NESTED BAR CHARTS

Similarly you can draw a bar chart of the activities which make up a work package. Figure 12.1 (b) illustrates nested bar charts. Responsibility charts at several levels contain nested bar charts. As discussed in Chapter 9, the bar chart is a good communication tool, and as such may be augmented by:

– base line start and finish
– current planned actual start and finish
– estimated work content
– work done to date.

All the above tools conform to the principle of single-page reporting. All the activities which make up a work package are shown together, and alone, on a single page. This can be repeated at lower levels of work breakdown if required.

Representing the time schedule

The activity schedules represent the time schedule at the lowest level of breakdown. The schedule will be represented in many different ways depending on the level of planning and for whom it is being prepared. It is worth while at this point to summarize the different representations (Table 12.1).

12.4 Allocating work

When work is about to be done, it is allocated to the team, often via *work-to lists*. A work-to list is a list of activities to which a person or resource is assigned to work. The activities may be listed by:

1. *Work package*: The person or resource is given the activity schedules for all work packages on which they are working (as a responsibility chart or estimating sheet).

Table 12.1   Representing the time schedule

Level of breakdown	Representation of programme
Integrative level	Project definition report
Strategic level	Milestone plan Project responsibility chart Master network Master bar chart
Detail level	Responsibility chart as activity schedule Work-package estimating sheets Nested network Nested bar chart

2. *Time period*: They are given a listing of the activities to which they are assigned for a given period of time from across all work packages on which they are working. The period is typically the current control period and one or two control periods into the future. That will be six weeks if reviews are held fortnightly. The work-to list contains:
 – all activities started but not finished
 – all activities due to start in the period.

The work-to list may be in the form of a responsibility chart, (Figure 12.3) or output from a computer system (Figure 12.5). It is now quite common for this to be sent from the master plan to the individual's work station electronically, and will subsequently become their time sheet. The work-to list may contain the following information:

 – activity number and name
 – baselined dates and duration
 – current estimate/actual dates and duration
 – estimated work content
 – work to date
 – bar chart of baselined dates
 – bar chart of current estimate/actual dates.

Some people also include float, but I do not agree with this. The team do not need to know the float, and they will invariably consume it. My strongly held views here cause some controversy. Some people say that I do not trust the team, but I am afraid I believe in Parkinson's law: work done expands to fill the time available. I also know that most people are working to tight deadlines on much of their work, and they will put off anything with large float (I do). For this reason, I also do not think people should be given work with a very large float, you should wait until much of the float has disappeared. It is inconsiderate to give busy people non-urgent work, and work which may actually need to change as other work is done. However, I do agree that the team should be told whether work is critical or not. If they need to consume the float, they should negotiate that with the project manager, not assume that the float is there for them to consume by right because it is shown on the work-to list.

At the end of the control period the work-to list will become a *turnaround document*, (Section 12.6), through which the project team report progress. The processes of drawing up the activity schedules, including them in the master plan and issuing work-to lists are shown in the procedure for monitoring and control (Figure 6.9).

The equivalent list for gathering materials on a project is called a *kit-marshalling list*. This lists all the materials required for an activity and the

WORK-TO LIST AND TURN-AROUND DOCUMENT TRIMAGI COMMUNICATIONS BV 15-Feb-9X

PROJECT: CRMO RATIONALIZATION
WORK PACKAGE: PROJECT DEFINITION
REPORT AUTHOR:
APPROVED:
PAGE: 1
PRINT DATE: 15-Feb-9X
REPORT DATE:

ACTIVITY NUMBER	DESCRIPTION	ORG DUR (D)	REM DUR (D)	BASE START	BASE FINISH	SCHED START	SCHED FINISH	ACTUAL START	ACTUAL FINISH	WRK EST (D)	WRK DNE (D)	WRK REM (D)	COMMENTS
P1A	Project Proposal	5.0		01Feb9X	05Feb9X			01Feb9X	05Feb9X	4.0	5.0		
P1B	Definition W'Shop	1.0		10Feb9X	11Feb9X			11Feb9X	11Feb9X	4.0	4.0		
P1C	Define Benefits	5.0		08Feb9X	12Feb9X			08Feb9X	12Feb9X	2.0	2.0		
P1D	Draft Defn Report	10.0	5.0	08Feb9X	19Feb9X		19Feb9X	08Feb9X		8.0	3.0		
P1E	Launch W'Shop	1.5	1.5	23Feb9X	24Feb9X	25Feb9X	26Feb9X			12.0			Workshop Delayed
P1F	Milestone Plan	2.5	2.5	24Feb9X	26Feb9X	01Mar9X	02Mar9X			2.0			
P1G	Resp'ty Chart	2.5	2.5	24Feb9X	26Feb9X	01Mar9X	02Mar9X			2.0			
P1H	Estimate Time	5.0	5.0	24Feb9X	02Mar9X	01Mar9X	05Mar9X			2.0			
P1I	Estimate Costs	5.0	5.0	24Feb9X	02Mar9X	01Mar9X	05Mar9X			2.0			
P1J	Estimate Revenue	5.0	5.0	24Feb9X	02Mar9X	01Mar9X	05Mar9X			1.0			
P1K	Assess Viability	2.5	2.5	03Mar9X	05Mar9X	03Mar9X	05Mar9X			1.0			
P1L	Assess Risks	2.5	2.5	08Mar9X	10Mar9X	08Mar9X	10Mar9X			3.0			
P1M	Final Defn Report	15.0	15.0	22Feb9X	12Mar9X	22Feb9X	12Mar9X			5.0			
P1N	Mobilize Team	2.5	2.5	10Mar9X	12Mar9X	10Mar9X	12Mar9X			3.0			

Figure 12.5 Computer-generated work-to list

date they are required by. If the materials are held in a store, then the list may be issued in the reporting period before that activity, so that the materials can be collected together (marshalled) to a central point, ready for use. If they need to be procured, clearly the list must be issued earlier still. The planning system needs to record the lead time. A computer system can be very useful for this.

12.5 Requirements for effective control

Everything covered up to now has brought us to the point where we are doing work. However, as the work is done we must ensure that we achieve the planned results, and that we deliver the facility to the specification we designed, and within the cost and time at which it was thought to be worth while. Furthermore, as the facility is commissioned, we must ensure it delivers the expected benefits which were used to justify the money spent. We can be sure that this will not occur in a haphazard fashion. The structured process by which we check progress and take action to overcome any deviations from plan is control. There are four essential steps to the control process (Figure 7.2):

1. Plan future work and estimate performance.
2. Monitor and report results.
3. Compare results to the plan and forecast future results.
4. Plan and take effective action to recover the original plan, or to minimize the variance.

The book so far has dealt with the first step. In the remainder of this chapter, we shall deal with the other three steps in turn. Let us start with an explanation of the requirements for effective control. For control to be effective, each step in this four-step process must be effective.

Effective plans

I have discussed the requirements of effective planning throughout the book. In particular, the plans must be comprehensive, and frozen into a baseline to provide a fixed measure for control. If the plans are updated frequently, without the application of strict change control, there will be no measure for control. The project will always be on time, because the plans have just been updated. Team members may develop new activity schedules, but the project manager must authorise them before they are included in the master plan. Work is done against current work-to lists, issued regularly.

Effective reporting

Effective reporting mechanisms (Section 12.6) should satisfy the following requirements:

REPORTS SHOULD BE MADE AGAINST THE PLAN

To ensure that people are interpreting the reports in the same way, they should be made against the plan. In Example 4.4, I described a case in which the project manager and team members were working to different plans. The team members were making verbal reports and reporting satisfactory progress. The project manager could not understand why they were not achieving his milestones. Below, turn-around documents are described as a tool for reporting against the plan.

THERE SHOULD BE DEFINED CRITERIA FOR CONTROL

Likewise it is important to have defined criteria. If people are asked to make ad-hoc reports, they tend to report the good news and hide the bad news. If asked to report against set questions, they will usually answer honestly. If they report dishonestly, it will become obvious at the second or third reporting period. Defined criteria are given in the next section.

THE CONTROL TOOLS SHOULD BE SIMPLE AND FRIENDLY

Team members should spend as little time as possible filling in reports. If submitting reports takes an excessive amount of time, people rightly complain that they are being distracted from productive work (Example 12.1). Simple, friendly tools means single-page reporting nested in the WBS, and reports against the plan, with defined criteria, requiring simple numeric or yes/no answers. Reports are often filed against work-to lists. These are the *turn-around documents* mentioned above. The work-to list contains space for the report, and is returned at the end of the reporting period. The turn-around document may even have expected answers entered.

I used to work on ammonia plant overhauls, each a four-week project. Every day, supervisors came to a one-hour control meeting in the morning, a two-hour meeting in the afternoon, and spent one hour after work completing daily returns. They complained that they should spend more time on the patch motivating their men.

Example 12.1 Simple, friendly tools

REPORTS SHOULD BE MADE AT DEFINED INTERVALS

Just as it is necessary to report against defined criteria, it is also necessary to report at defined intervals. You should not ask people to report only when there is something to discuss. People hate to volunteer failure, so they will not ask for help until it is too late to recover. If people know that they must report both good news and bad at defined intervals, then they will report more freely. The frequency of the reporting period depends on:

- the length of the project
- the stage in the project
- the risk and consequence of failure
- the level of reporting.

At the start of a year-long project, you may report fortnightly at the activity level and six weekly at the milestone level. In areas of high risk you may report more often. Towards the end of the project you may report weekly, or even daily.

REPORTS SHOULD BE DISCUSSED AT FORMAL MEETINGS
To be effective the reports must be made and discussed at formal meetings. Passing the time of day at the coffee machine is part of effective team building, but not of effective control. Formal meetings have an agenda, and a chairman to maintain control. To keep the meetings short and effective, the discussion should also focus on identifying problems, and responsibility for solving them, but the meeting should not attempt to solve the problem.

THE REPORTS SHOULD STIMULATE CREATIVE DISCUSSIONS
To link into the next steps of control the reports must generate creative discussion, so the team can identify where variances are occurring, and possible ways of taking effective timely action.

Effective reviews
Having gathered the data, the team must determine whether the project is behaving as predicted, and if not calculate the size and impact of the variances. The two quantitative measures of progress are cost and time, and so receive significant attention. The team uses the reports to forecast time and cost at completion, and calculates any differences (variances) between these figures and the baseline. It may simply be that work is taking longer and costing more than predicted. Or delays or additional effort may be caused by variances in quality, people failing to fulfil their responsibility, externally imposed delays, or changes in scope. Therefore the variances in time and cost can point to a need to control one or more of the five project management functions. The defined criteria, formal meetings and creative discussions are key to this process.

Effective action
To close the control loop, the team must take effective action to overcome any variances. This may mean revising the plan to reflect the variances, but hopefully it means at least taking timely effective action to stop them getting

worse, and preferably reducing or eliminating them. Effective action requires:

- being able to calculate the impact of any changes in the plan on the project's outcome
- having the resolve to take action.

REPLANNING

This is often called *what-if* analysis. The team calculates the impact of action it may take. The most effective management information is obtained by doing this through plans nested in the WBS (single-page reporting). The impact of a change in one activity on related activities can be analysed at the activity level, and on other work packages at the milestone level. However, in complex situations the what-if analysis may be done with computer systems. To be able to perform this what-if analysis it is vital that the project's plans have been kept up to date.

THE RESOLVE TO TAKE ACTION

This is dependent on managers using their sources of authority, and being able to motivate and persuade their teams. To motivate and persuade the teams, the managers must build their commitment to the common mission, and help them understand how the project will be of benefit to them. Teams are discussed further in Chapter 17. Recovery planning and taking action are discussed in Section 12.7.

12.6 Gathering data and calculating progress

Gathering data

The first step in the control process is to gather data on progress. The criteria for control should be to measure satisfactory progress against the five functions of the project. The data required to control them are given in Table 12.2. These are usually collected at the activity level, but may be collected at the work-package or task levels. When collected at a lower level they can be summarized to report at a higher level. The use of these data in the control process is described in the next section.

I said above that data is most effectively gathered against defined criteria using turn-around documents. These are work-to lists issued at the start of the reporting period and then used at the end of the period to gather data. Many modern computer systems use an individual's time sheet as a work-to list and turn-around document. Turn-around documents provide reports against the plan, defined criteria, and simple, friendly tools. They can also be used as the focus for formal meetings. I find it effective to photocopy the turn-around document on to a transparency, and project it on to a white

Table 12.2   Criteria for control, and required data

Criteria for control	Quantitative data	Qualitative data
Time and Cost	Revised start/finish Actual start/finish Effort to date Effort remaining Other costs to date Other costs remaining	
Quality		Problems encountered
Organization		Responsibility chart kept
Scope		Changes Special problems

board. The team can fill in the document on the board in a group meeting. This process encourages creative discussions to identify any problems, but also enable the meeting to be kept short. Figure 12.6 is a manual turn-around document encompassing the activity schedule from Figure 12.3. Figure 12.7 contains a computer-generated turn-around document. Figure 12.8 is a turn-around document at the milestone level.

Calculating progress

The data gathered are used to calculate progress on all of the five project management functions: time; cost; quality; project organization; scope. In particular, with the first two we try to forecast the final out-turn, the time and cost to completion, as this gives better control than reporting the actual time and cost to date. This concept is part of the forward-looking control of which project managers speak.

Forecasting time to completion

Time is the simplest function to monitor and that is perhaps why it receives the greatest attention. If critical milestones have been delayed, or if the critical path has been delayed (and no other path has become 'more critical'), then it is likely that the project has been delayed by that amount. If the team has maintained an up-to-date network for the project, that can be used to forecast the completion date for the project in exactly the same way it was used to predict the end date initially. The record of effort to date versus effort remaining can also be used to control time, in one of three ways:

– by revising estimates of duration
– by indicating the cause of delays
– through an earned value calculation.

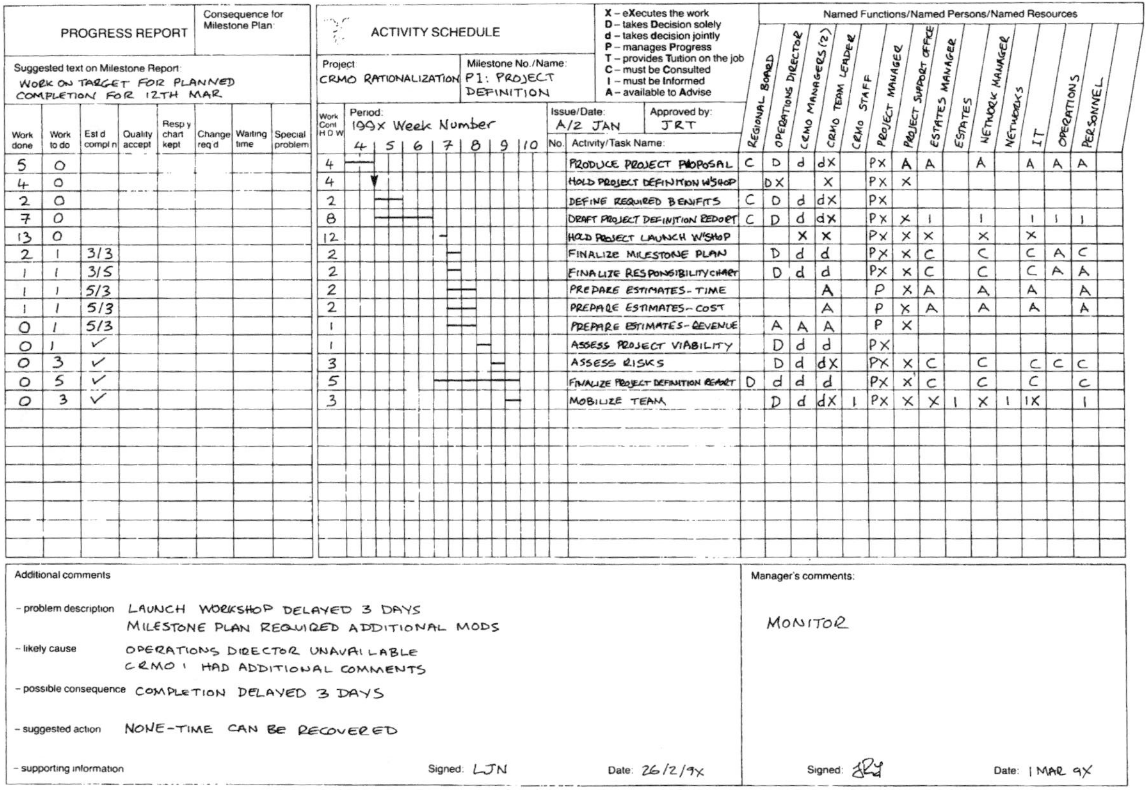

PROGRESS REPORT

Consequence for Milestone Plan:

Suggested text on Milestone Report: WORK ON TARGET FOR PLANNED COMPLETION FOR 12TH MAR

ACTIVITY SCHEDULE

Project: CRMO RATIONALIZATION

Milestone No./Name: P1: PROJECT DEFINITION

X – eXecutes the work
D – takes Decision solely
d – takes decision jointly
P – manages Progress
T – provides Tuition on the job
C – must be Consulted
I – must be Informed
A – available to Advise

Period: 199X Week Number 4 5 6 7 8 9 10

Issue/Date: A/2 JAN

Approved by: JRT

Named Functions/Named Persons/Named Resources

Work done	Work to do	Est'd compl'n	Quality accept	Resp'y chart kept	Change req'd	Waiting time	Special problem	Work Cont HDW	No.	Activity/Task Name	Regional Board	Operations Director	CRMO Managers (2)	CRMO Team Leader	CRMO Staff	Project Manager	Project Support Office	Estates Manager	Estates	Network Manager	Networks	IT	Operations	Personnel
5	0							4		PRODUCE PROJECT PROPOSAL	C	D	d	dX		PX	A	A		A		A	A	A
4	0							4		HOLD PROJECT DEFINITION W'SHOP		DX		X		PX	X							
2	0							2		DEFINE REQUIRED BENEFITS	C	D	d	dX		PX								
7	0							8		DRAFT PROJECT DEFINITION REPORT	C	D	d	dX		PX	X	I		I		I	I	I
13	0							12		HOLD PROJECT LAUNCH W'SHOP			X	X		PX	X	X		X		X		
2	1	3/3						2		FINALIZE MILESTONE PLAN		D	d	d		PX	X	C		C		C	A	C
1	1	3/5						2		FINALIZE RESPONSIBILITY CHART		D	d	d		PX	X	C		C		C	A	A
1	1	5/3						2		PREPARE ESTIMATES - TIME				A		P	X	A		A		A		A
1	1	5/3						2		PREPARE ESTIMATES - COST				A		P	X	A		A		A		A
0	1	5/3						1		PREPARE ESTIMATES - REVENUE		A	A	A		P	X							
0	1	✓						1		ASSESS PROJECT VIABILITY		D	d	d		PX								
0	3	✓						3		ASSESS RISKS		D	d	dX		PX	X	C		C		C	C	C
0	5	✓						5		FINALIZE PROJECT DEFINITION REPORT	D	d	d	d		PX	X	C		C		C		C
0	3	✓						3		MOBILIZE TEAM		D	d	dX	I	PX	X	X	I	X	I	IX		I

Additional comments

- problem description: LAUNCH WORKSHOP DELAYED 3 DAYS
MILESTONE PLAN REQUIRED ADDITIONAL MODS
- likely cause: OPERATIONS DIRECTOR UNAVAILABLE
CRMO 1 HAD ADDITIONAL COMMENTS
- possible consequence: COMPLETION DELAYED 3 DAYS
- suggested action: NONE-TIME CAN BE RECOVERED
- supporting information

Signed: LJN Date: 26/2/9X

Manager's comments: MONITOR

Signed: [signature] Date: 1 MAR 9X

Figure 12.6 Manual turn-around document encompassing the activity schedule

WORK-TO LIST AND TURN-AROUND DOCUMENT						TRIMAGI COMMUNICATIONS BV								15-Feb-9X
PROJECT:		CRMO RATIONALIZATION				REPORT		PAGE:				1		
WORK PACKAGE:		PROJECT DEFINITION				AUTHOR: LJN		PRINT DATE:				15-Feb-9X		
						APPROVED: JRT		REPORT DATE: 26/2/9X						

ACTIVITY NUMBER	DESCRIPTION	ORG DUR (D)	REM DUR (D)	BASE START	BASE FINISH	SCHED START	SCHED FINISH	ACTUAL START	ACTUAL FINISH	WRK EST (D)	WRK DNE (D)	WRK REM (D)	COMMENTS
P1A	Project Proposal	5.0		01Feb9X	05Feb9X			01Feb9X	05Feb9X	4.0	5.0		
P1B	Definition W'Shop	1.0		10Feb9X	11Feb9X			11Feb9X	11Feb9X	4.0	4.0		
P1C	Define Benefits	5.0		08Feb9X	12Feb9X			08Feb9X	12Feb9X	2.0	2.0		
P1D	Draft Defn Report	10.0	5.0	08Feb9X	19Feb9X		~~19Feb9X~~	08Feb9X	24/2/9X	8.0	7 ~~3.0~~	–	
P1E	Launch W'Shop	1.5	1.5	23Feb9X	24Feb9X	~~25Feb9X~~	~~26Feb9X~~	25/2/9X	26/2/9X	12.0	13	–	~~Workshop Delayed~~ Extra Person
P1F	Milestone Plan	2.5	2.5	24Feb9X	26Feb9X	01Mar9X	02Mar9X		3/3/9X(E)	[illegible]	2	1	
P1G	Respbl'ty Chart	2.5	2.5	24Feb9X	26Feb9X	01Mar9X	02Mar9X		3/3/9X(E)	2.0	1	1	
P1H	Estimate Time	5.0	5.0	24Feb9X	02Mar9X	01Mar9X	05Mar9X		5/3/9X(E)	2.0	1	1	
P1I	Estimate Costs	5.0	5.0	24Feb9X	02Mar9X	01Mar9X	05Mar9X		5/3/9X(E)	2.0	1	1	
P1J	Estimate Revenue	5.0	5.0	24Feb9X	02Mar9X	01Mar9X	05Mar9X		5/3/9X(E)	1.0			
P1K	Assess Viability	2.5	2.5	03Mar9X	05Mar9X	03Mar9X	05Mar9X			1.0			
P1L	Assess Risks	2.5	2.5	08Mar9X	10Mar9X	08Mar9X	10Mar9X			3.0			
P1M	Final Defn Report	15.0	15.0	22Feb9X	12Mar9X	22Feb9X	12Mar9X			5.0			
P1N	Mobilize Team	2.5	2.5	10Mar9X	12Mar9X	10Mar9X	12Mar9X			3.0			Completion Expected on Time

Figure 12.7 Computer-generated turn-around document

MILESTONE PLAN				Company: TRIMAGI COMMUNICATIONS BV	Project Manager: SVK		
Project Planned date: P	Operations O	Accommo- dation A	Technology T	Project description: RATIONALIZATION OF THE CUSTOMER REPAIR AND MAINTENANCE ORGANIZATION (CRMO)	Plan Issue: Approved by: Date: A JRT 04 Feb		
				Milestone:	Date: Report:		
01 Jan	(P1)			P1: When the project definition is complete, including benefit criteria milestone plan and responsibility charts.	07 Jan Completed		
01 Feb 01 Mar	(O1)		(T1)	O1: When a plan for communicating the changes to the CRM organization has been agreed. T1: When the technical solution, including appropriate networking and switching technology has been designed and agreed.	04 Feb Plan agreed 04 Mar Completed		
15 Mar	(O2)			O2: When the operational procedure for the CRM offices has been agreed.	18 Mar Completion predicted 22 Mar Awaiting engineering input		
15 Apr 15 Apr	(O3)		(T2)	O3: When the job design and management design is complete and agreed. T2: When the functional specification for the supporting management information system (MIS) has been agreed.	18 Mar Work started where possible 18 Mar Draft functional spec prepared		
1 May	(O4)			O4: When the allocation of staff to the new offices, and recruitment and redeployment requirements, have been defined and agreed.			
1 May		(A1)	(T3)	A1: When the estates plan and roll-out strategy has been defined and agreed. T3: When the technical roll-out strategy has been defined and agreed.			
1 May	(P2)			P2: When the budget for implementation has been determined, and (provisional) financial authority obtained.			
01 Jun 01 Jul	(O5)	(A2)		O5: When the management changes for sites 1 and 2 are in place (first call receipt and first diagnostic centres). A2: When sites 1 and 2 are available.			
15 Jul 15 Jul	(O6)		(T4)	O6: When a minimum number of staff have been recruited and redeployed and their training is complete. T4: When the system is ready for service in sites 1 and 2.			
01 Aug 15 Aug		(A3)	(T5)	A3: When sites 1 and 2 are ready for occupation. T5: When the MIS system has been delivered.			
01 Sep	(O7)			O7: When sites 1 and 2 are operational and procedures implemented.			
01 Oct	(P3)			P3: When a successful intermediate review has been conducted and the roll-out plans revised and agreed.			
01 Mar		(A4)		A4: When the last site is operational with the procedures fully implemented.			
01 Apr	(P4)			P4: When it has been shown through a post-implementation audit that the criteria have been met.			

Figure 12.8   Turn-around document at the milestone level

REVISING ESTIMATES OF DURATION

If there is a consistent estimating error, this will be indicated by a trend.
The estimates of duration can be revised accordingly.

INDICATING THE CAUSE OF DELAYS

Table 12.3 shows four possible outcomes of duration and effort. Both may
be on (or under) budget, in which case all is well. The project may be on
time, but effort over budget, in which case there may be minor estimating
errors, but the team is coping, perhaps by working unplanned overtime.
Estimating errors will be indicated as above. The project may be late, but
no additional effort has been expended. Then the cause of the delay must
have been due to external factors, perhaps other people failing to fulfil their
responsibilities, or late delivery of some materials, or perhaps the project
team have been occupied on work of higher priority (to them). The
qualitative control data (Table 12.2) may help to indicate the cause. If both
time and effort are over budget, then the cause may be serious estimating
errors, rework due to poor quality or rework due to change.

Table 12.3 Determining the cause of delays by comparing of effort and completion dates

Effort	Duration	
	On time	Late
As predicted	No problem	External delays Responsibilities not fulfilled
Over budget	Minor estimating errors Minor changes	Estimating errors Major changes Major quality problems

A trend will indicate the first as described above, and so you will need to monitor effort and duration over several reports. The qualitative control data (Table 12.2) will indicate the second or third cause. You can see from Table 12.3 how the complete set of control data can help initiate discussion over the likely causes of delays and help in their elimination.

EARNED VALUE CALCULATION

The volume variance, calculated as part of the cost control process, will indicate whether the project is on average ahead or behind schedule.

Forecasting cost to completion

The simplistic approach to controlling costs is to compare costs to date to the baseline cost to date. However, I showed in Section 8.7 that this comparison is of little value. If actual cost is less than baseline cost we do not know if the work is underspent, late or even late and overspent. I therefore introduced the concept of *earned value*, or *baseline cost of work complete* (BCWC). This is what was planned to have been spent on the work complete, and so is a measure of the amount of work done for the money spent. With the earned value we can calculate two variances:

Cost variance   = Actual cost − Earned value

Volume variance = Earned value − Baselined cost

These figures can be calculated for the reporting period, or as cumulative figures over all reporting periods to date. The cost variance indicates whether the project is over- or underspent. The volume variance indicates whether it is (on average) early or late. With the variances calculated as shown, a positive cost variance will be unfavourable; the project is overspent, and is therefore likely to turn out over budget. However, a positive volume variance is favourable, the project is (on average) ahead of schedule, and is likely to be completed early. (I say 'on average', because it is possible for a large non-critical item to be early, and a small critical item late, and the project will appear to be ahead of schedule according to the volume variance, but behind according to the network.) The actual cost, earned value and forecast of cost to completion can be calculated from the data gathered as follows:

ACTUAL COST

The actual cost in the period is the sum of the man-hour costs and other costs in the period:

$$\text{Actual cost} = \text{Effort} \times (\text{Man-hour rate}) + \text{Other costs}$$

Obviously if there is more than one resource then the sum over all resources must be used. There is an additional complication when the costs are assumed to be incurred (Section 8.7). It is too late for control purposes when the invoices are paid. In Chapter 8 I described typical assumptions. I would only reinforce here that what is important for control purposes is that actual cost, baselined cost and earned value all incorporate the same assumptions.

EARNED VALUE

This calculation is more complex. For work finished the earned value is clearly the baselined cost of that element of work. For work in progress, some estimate of the percentage completion must be made. This can be done in four ways:

– by summing the percentage completion of work elements at low levels of work breakdown, for instance by adding over the activities in a work package
– by making a visual inspection
– by assuming (at a low level of work breakdown) all work in progress is on average 50 per cent complete
– by using the effort accrued and effort remaining to calculate percentage complete.

Visual inspections are subjective. People usually overestimate percentage completion when using a visual inspection. Indeed, I was told once that in the civil construction industry it is common for a contractor's quantity surveyors to deliberately overestimate percentage completion, to improve the contractor's cash flow. Most of the profit is made by investing money obtained for work which is not yet done. Effort accrued and remaining can be used to calculate percentage complete as follows:

$$\text{Percentage complete} = \frac{(\text{Effort to date})}{(\text{Effort to date} + \text{effort remaining})}$$

The sum of effort to date and remaining are used on the lower line, rather than the original estimate, because that provides a better estimate of percentage complete. You only need consider the case where effort to date is already greater than the original estimate. However, the estimate of effort remaining can be subjective, and may be sometimes obtained by subtracting effort to date from the original estimate (until such time as the former is the greater). Percentage completion can also be calculated by replacing effort by duration in the above formula. The two are the same for a single resource activity. For an activity with internal lead times, or several resources working at different times, effort is needed to give a more accurate answer. When calculating percentage completion at work-package or project level by summing over activities at a lower level, it does not matter too much what assumptions are made at the lower level, because errors cancel out as you sum to higher levels; (as long as there is not a consistent error, such as from deliberate overestimating, which will reinforce at higher levels). Hence, in most cases the 50 per cent assumption for activities in progress is as accurate as you need. Figures 12.9 and 12.10 are a computer-generated cost report for the CRMO Rationalization Project, showing the costs for each work package and the aggregate for the project overall. Figure 12.9 shows the percentage completion of the work packages calculated on the duration, and Figure 12.10 calculated making the 50 per cent assumption.

FORECAST COST TO COMPLETION

This is calculated using the cost variance. The forecast cost to complete of activities is estimated in one of the ways just described. At the project or work-package level it is possible to make one of three simplifying assumptions:

1. All remaining activities will be done at baseline cost:

    Cost at completion = Original estimate + Cost variance to date

2. Over-expenditure will continue at the current rate:

    Cost at completion = Original estimate * (1+% Cost variance to date)
    % Cost variance   = Cost variance/Earned value

3. Some activities in the future will be overspent but it will be possible to make savings in other areas. Using the WBS, a second estimate can be maintained alongside the baselined cost, the current best estimate, and this can be used to forecast the cost to completion.

Figures 12.9 and 12.10 also show the forecast cost to completion. The forecasts are made using the current best estimate.

PROJECT COST REPORT TRIMAGI COMMUNICATIONS BV 31-Aug-9X

PROJECT: CRMO RATIONALIZATION
WORK AREA: —
WORK PACKAGE: —

PAGE: 1
PRINT DATE: 31-Aug-9X
REPORT DATE: 31-Aug-9X

All amounts in (£,000).

WORK PACKAGE NO	DESCRIPTION	ORG DUR (D)	REM DUR (D)	BASE COMPL (%)	PERCT COMPL (%)	BASELINE LABOUR	BASELINE MATL	BASELINE TOTAL	CURRENT EST LABOUR	CURRENT EST MATL	CURRENT EST TOTAL	SCHED COST LABOUR	SCHED COST MATL	SCHED COST TOTAL	EARNED VALUE LABOUR	EARNED VALUE MATL	EARNED VALUE TOTAL	ACTUAL COMMIT LABOUR	ACTUAL COMMIT MATL	ACTUAL COMMIT TOTAL
P1	Project definition	30.0		100.0%	100.0%	11.2	6.4	17.6	11.2	6.4	17.6	11.2	6.4	17.6	11.2	6.4	17.6	11.0	6.3	17.3
T1	Technology design	40.0		100.0%	100.0%	12.8		12.8	12.8	0.0	12.8	12.8	0.0	12.8	12.8	0.0	12.8	12.1	0.0	12.1
O1	Communication plan	5.0		100.0%	100.0%	1.2	2.5	3.7	1.2	2.5	3.7	1.2	2.5	3.7	1.2	2.5	3.7	1.2	2.4	3.6
O2	Operational proc.	15.0		100.0%	100.0%	9.6		9.6	9.6	0.0	9.6	9.6	0.0	9.6	9.6	0.0	9.6	9.8	0.0	9.8
O3	Job/Management desc.	20.0		100.0%	100.0%	12.8		12.8	12.8	0.0	12.8	12.8	0.0	12.8	12.8	0.0	12.8	12.5	0.0	12.5
T2	MIS function spec.	15.0		100.0%	100.0%	4.8		4.8	4.8	0.0	4.8	4.8	0.0	4.8	4.8	0.0	4.8	4.5	0.0	4.5
O4	Staff allocation	15.0		100.0%	100.0%	3.6		3.6	3.6	0.0	3.6	3.6	0.0	3.6	3.6	0.0	3.6	3.7	0.0	3.7
A1	Estates plan	10.0		100.0%	100.0%	1.6		1.6	1.6	0.0	1.6	1.6	0.0	1.6	1.6	0.0	1.6	1.6	0.0	1.6
T3	Technical plan	10.0		100.0%	100.0%	0.8		0.8	0.8	0.0	0.8	0.8	0.0	0.8	0.8	0.0	0.8	0.8	0.0	0.8
P2	Financial approval	15.0		100.0%	100.0%	3.6	1.5	5.1	3.6	1.5	5.1	3.6	1.5	5.1	3.6	1.5	5.1	3.6	1.5	5.1
A2	Sites 1&2 available	15.0		100.0%	100.0%	8.4	6.6	15.0	8.4	6.6	15.0	8.4	6.6	15.0	8.4	6.6	15.0	7.5	6.9	14.4
O5	Management changes	10.0		100.0%	100.0%	2.4		2.4	2.4	0.0	2.4	2.4	0.0	2.4	2.4	0.0	2.4	2.4	0.0	2.4
O6	Redeployment/train	40.0	10.0	100.0%	75.0%	25.6	55.2	80.8	24.4	52.6	77.0	24.4	52.6	77.0	18.3	52.6	70.9	17.9	52.2	70.1
T4	System in sites 1&2	30.0	20.0	100.0%	33.3%	19.2	44.0	63.2	19.2	44.0	63.2	19.2	44.0	63.2	6.4	44.0	50.4	4.5	42.4	46.9
A3	Sites 1&2 ready	15.0	15.0	50.0%	0.0%	8.4	60.0	68.4	9.2	66.0	75.2	4.6	66.0	70.6	0.0	0.0	0.0	0.0	0.0	0.0
T5	MIS delivered	15.0	9.0	50.0%	40.0%	4.8	38.0	42.8	4.8	38.0	42.8	2.4	38.0	40.4	1.9	38.0	39.9	1.6	40.2	41.8
O7	Procedures implem.	10.0	10.0	0.0%	0.0%	1.6		1.6	1.6	0.0	1.6	0.0	0.0	0.0	0.0	0.0	0.0	0.0		0.0
P3	Intermediate rev.	40.0	40.0	0.0%	0.0%	4.0	10.8	14.8	4.0	10.8	14.8	0.0	0.0	0.0	0.0	0.0	0.0	0.0		0.0
A4	Roll-out implem.	80.0	80.0	0.0%	0.0%	64.0	240.0	304.0	70.4	264.0	334.4	0.0	0.0	0.0	0.0	0.0	0.0	0.0		0.0
P4	Benefits obtained	60.0	60.0	0.0%	0.0%	2.4		2.4	2.4	0.0	2.4	0.0	0.0	0.0	0.0	0.0	0.0	0.0		0.0
						202.8	465.0	667.8	208.8	492.4	701.2	123.4	217.6	341.0	99.4	151.6	251.0	94.7	151.9	246.6

Figure 12.9 Cost report using duration to calculate percentage completion

PROJECT COST REPORT

TRIMAGI COMMUNICATIONS BV

31-Aug-9X

PROJECT: CRMO RATIONALIZATION
WORK AREA: —
WORK PACKAGE: —

PAGE: 1
PRINT DATE: 31-Aug-9X
REPORT DATE: 31-Aug-9X

Work Package No	Description	Org Dur (D)	Rem Dur (D)	Base Compl (%)	Perct Compl (%)	Baseline Labour (£000)	Baseline Matl (£000)	Baseline Total (£000)	Current Estimate Total Labour (£000)	Current Estimate Matl (£000)	Current Estimate Total (£000)	Scheduled Cost Total Labour (£000)	Scheduled Cost Matl (£000)	Scheduled Cost Total (£000)	Earned Value Total Labour (£000)	Earned Value Matl (£000)	Earned Value Total (£000)	Actual Commitment Total Labour (£000)	Actual Commitment Matl (£000)	Actual Commitment Total (£000)
P1	Project definition	30.0		100.0%	100.0%	11.2	6.4	17.6	11.2	6.4	17.6	11.2	6.4	17.6	11.2	6.4	17.6	11.0	6.3	17.3
T1	Technology design	40.0		100.0%	100.0%	12.8		12.8	12.8		12.8	12.8		12.8	12.8		12.8	12.1	0.0	12.1
O1	Communication plan	5.0		100.0%	100.0%	1.2	2.5	3.7	1.2	2.5	3.7	1.2	2.5	3.7	1.2	2.5	3.7	1.2	2.4	3.6
O2	Operational proc.	15.0		100.0%	100.0%	9.6		9.6	9.6		9.6	9.6		9.6	9.6		9.6	9.8	0.0	9.8
O3	Job/Management desc.	20.0		100.0%	100.0%	12.8		12.8	12.8		12.8	12.8		12.8	12.8		12.8	12.5	0.0	12.5
T2	MIS function spec.	15.0		100.0%	100.0%	4.8		4.8	4.8		4.8	4.8		4.8	4.8		4.8	4.5	0.0	4.5
O4	Staff allocation	15.0		100.0%	100.0%	3.6		3.6	3.6		3.6	3.6		3.6	3.6		3.6	3.7	0.0	3.7
A1	Estates plan	10.0		100.0%	100.0%	1.6		1.6	1.6		1.6	1.6		1.6	1.6		1.6	1.6	0.0	1.6
T3	Technical plan	10.0		100.0%	100.0%	0.8		0.8	0.8		0.8	0.8		0.8	0.8		0.8	0.8	0.0	0.8
P2	Financial approval	15.0		100.0%	100.0%	3.6	1.5	5.1	3.6	1.5	5.1	3.6	1.5	5.1	3.6	1.5	5.1	3.6	1.5	5.1
A2	Sites 1&2 available	15.0		100.0%	100.0%	8.4	6.6	15.0	8.4	6.6	15.0	8.4	6.6	15.0	8.4	6.6	15.0	7.5	6.9	14.4
O5	Management changes	10.0		100.0%	100.0%	2.4		2.4	2.4		2.4	2.4		2.4	2.4		2.4	2.4	0.0	2.4
O6	Redeployment/train	40.0	10.0	100.0%	75.0%	25.6	55.2	80.8	24.4	52.6	77.0	24.4	52.6	77.0	18.3	52.6	70.9	17.9	52.2	70.1
T4	System in sites 1&2	30.0	20.0	100.0%	33.3%	19.2	44.0	63.2	19.2	44.0	63.2	19.2	44.0	63.2	6.4	44.0	50.4	4.5	42.4	46.9
A3	Sites 1&2 ready	15.0	15.0	50.0%	0.0%	8.4	60.0	68.4	9.2	66.0	75.2	4.6	66.0	70.6	0.0	0.0	0.0	0.0	0.0	0.0
T5	MIS delivered	15.0	9.0	50.0%	40.0%	4.8	38.0	42.8	4.8	38.0	42.8	2.4	38.0	40.4	2.4	38.0	40.4	1.6	40.2	41.8
O7	Procedures implem.	10.0	10.0	0.0%	0.0%	4.0	10.8	14.8	4.0	10.8	14.8	0.0	0.0	0.0	0.0	0.0	0.0	0.0	0.0	0.0
P3	Intermediate rev.	40.0	40.0	0.0%	0.0%	1.6		1.6	1.6		1.6	0.0	0.0	0.0	0.0	0.0	0.0	0.0	0.0	0.0
A4	Roll-out implem.	80.0	80.0	0.0%	0.0%	64.0	240.0	304.0	70.4	264.0	334.4	0.0	0.0	0.0	0.0	0.0	0.0	0.0	0.0	0.0
P4	Benefits obtained	60.0	60.0	0.0%	0.0%	2.4		2.4	2.4		2.4	0.0	0.0	0.0	0.0	0.0	0.0	0.0	0.0	0.0
						202.8	465.0	667.8	208.8	492.4	701.2	123.4	217.6	341.0	97.0	151.6	248.6	94.7	151.9	246.6

Figure 12.10   Cost report assuming work packages in process are 50 per cent complete

S-CURVES

Introduced in Section 8.7, S-curves can be used to represent these concepts graphically (Figure 12.11). This figure also differentiates between the budget estimate and the baseline estimate. The baseline is the measure for control, the budget is the most you expect to spend, and the difference is the contingency. You will often here people referring to budget and baseline as the same thing.

Controlling quality

The data gathered can show where deviations from the specification have occurred. These quality variances may have been identified as part of the quality control process, or may have been noticed by team members. The impact of quality problems on time and cost is indicated by Table 12.3.

Controlling organization

Similarly, the data gathered may indicate where the project organization is not performing as planned. This may specifically be caused by people not fulfilling their roles or responsibilities as agreed in the responsibility chart. Table 12.3 also shows how the control process can indicate the impact of these organizational delays on time and cost.

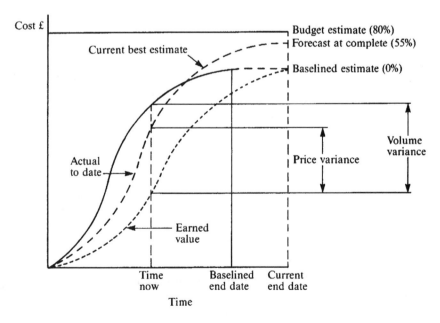

Figure 12.11 Use of S-curves

Controlling scope

Finally, the data gathered can indicate that changes in scope have occurred. These especially will have an impact on the time and cost of a project (Table 12.3). Changes in scope are usually inevitable. However, they should be rigidly controlled, and this requires a change control procedure. Change control is a six-step process:

1. Log the change.
2. Define the change.
3. Assess the impact of the change. Seemingly simple changes can have far-reaching consequences.
4. Calculate the cost of the change. This is not just the direct cost, but the cost of the impact.
5. Define the benefit of the change. This may be financial or non-financial. The latter includes safety.
6. Accept or reject the change based on marginal investment criteria. A return of 40 per cent per annum is possible for marginal criteria, compared to 20 per cent for the project as a whole.

If this procedure is applied rigorously, many changes do not get past step 3. Figure 12.12 is a form to aid this process.

12.7 Taking action[a]

Once we have identified that a project is deviating from the plan, we must take appropriate action. The earlier action is taken the better,[1] because it is then cheaper to recover the project or to abort it should it have proved non-viable. This relationship between project recovery and the life cycle was described earlier in the chapters on risk and quality. In this section I shall describe how to take appropriate action to recover a project.

Recovering a project

The response to the variances can be carefully managed, or unmanaged and reactive. The most effective approach depends on the circumstances. There are cases which demand an immediate response. However, in most cases there is time to reflect and recoup. A structured approach to problem solving (Figure 1.6) is the best means of recovery. Here, I describe a six-step version for planning recovery:

1. *Stop*: regardless of the size of the variance and its impact, everyone should pause. Unfortunately, the most common reaction is to seek an instant remedy. Some common solutions, such as adding more resources or sacking the project manager, may do more harm than good. While this

TRIMAGI COMMUNICATIONS CHANGE CONTROL FORM			
PROJECT: **WORK PACKAGE:** **ACTIVITY:** **ORIGINATOR:**	CRMO RATIONALIZATION............................		
DESCRIPTION OF CHANGE			
IMPACT OF CHANGE			
COST OF CHANGE: £ .... **VALUE OF CHANGE:** £			
	NAME	SIGNATURE	DATE
PROPOSED BY: **CHECKED BY:** **APPROVED BY:**	....	....	....

Figure 12.12   Change control form

reaction is understandable, it is often wrong because of the emotional state of the team. Once I attended a recovery review where the chairman listened to the team, sympathized with them, made no undermining statement and gave them three days off to recover. The result was electric. The team came back remotivated to set things right. The project was back on the rails in very quick time and the product became a bestseller. Keep cool, calm and collected. Remember Dennis Healey's first law of holes: 'If you find yourself in a hole, stop digging.'

2. *Look, listen and learn*: it is important to undertake a thorough review with all team members and the client present. Effective recovery must be based on a clear understanding of the cause of the divergence, and possible ways of overcoming it. Seeking views on what went wrong, and what action the team proposes, is important in rebuilding commitment.

3. *Develop options and select a likely course*: by exploring every avenue and developing a range of solutions. Establish decision criteria so options can be evaluated against an agreed condition. If necessary return to the original financial evaluations, recost and retime each option, air them with the client and then select one which meets the decision criteria.

4. *Win support for the chosen option*: it is important that there is total support from all those involved. There is hard work ahead and uncommitted team members will falter at the first hurdle.

5. *Act*: once the agreed course of action has been accepted every effort must be made to implement it. Deviations from the agreed plan will only add to the confusion and make the situation worse.

6. *Continue to monitor*: the impact of any actions to ensure that they have the desired effect. If not, then the recovery process must be repeated.

Options for action

There are five basic options for taking action:

FIND AN ALTERNATIVE SOLUTION

This is by far the best solution. The plan is recast to recover the projects objectives in a way which has no impact on the quality, cost, time or scope. It may be that two activities were planned sequentially, because they share the same scarce resource. If the first is delayed for other reasons, it may be possible to do the second activity first, and hopefully when it is complete it will then be possible to do the other.

COMPROMISE COST

This means adding additional resource either as overtime or additional people, machines or material to recover the lost time. This is usually the instant reaction to project delays. However, remember the discussion in Section 9.3, describing how to calculate durations: doubling the number of people on a project usually does not double the rate of work. Brooks's law[2] states:

> Adding resource to a late software project makes it later still

The rationale is that the existing people must take time out to bring the new people up to speed.

COMPROMISE TIME

This means allowing the dates to slip. This may be preferable, depending on whether cost or time is the more important constraint on the project. This decision should have been made during the feasibility study, and communicated to the project team as part of the project strategy.

COMPROMISE SCOPE

This means reducing the amount of work done, which in turn means taking less on time to achieve some benefit. Notice I did not say compromising the quality. The latter is very risky once the initial specification has been set, and should therefore be discouraged.

ABORT THE PROJECT

This is a difficult decision. However, it must be taken if the future costs on the project are not justified by the expected benefits. Project teams are often puzzled that their recommendation to terminate a project is ignored; a decision which seems obvious is avoided, and good money is poured after bad, depriving other projects. It takes courage to abort a project. During their lives, projects absorb champions and supporters. Senior people may have become associated with its success and feel if the project fails it may damage their reputation. There is often a feeling that 'with a little more money and a bit of luck the project can be turned round'. The fact is that once an organization makes an emotional commitment to a project it finds it very hard to abandon. Another argument often put forward to support a failing project is that 'as we have already spent so much on it we should finish it'. Unfortunately, this argument is fallacious: future costs must be justified by the expected benefit, no matter how much has been spent so far. If the project's outcome is still important to the organization it may be more effective to abort a project, learn from it and start afresh.

12.8 The control cycle

Building the control processes above into a cycle of monitoring and control can be complex. During a control period you must:

- issue work-to lists
- gather the turn-around documents
- analyse the data
- hold a review meeting
- update the plan

all in time for incorporation into the new work-to lists. Timing these control activities within a control period is a delicate balance between conflicting requirements. If the turn-around documents are gathered too late, changes to the plan cannot be incorporated until the next but one control cycle. If they are gathered too early, the reports will be based on predictions to the end of the control period. Futhermore, if attendance at review meetings is to be compulsory, they should not be scheduled for a Friday or a Monday, which people may take off as a long weekend. Likewise, the meeting at the activity level should be held just before the less frequent meeting at the work-package level. Figure 12.13 shows a procedure for monitoring and control which achieves this balance, while holding reviews fortnightly at the activity level and six weekly at the work-package, or milestone, level. This concept of nesting the reporting cycles is further illustrated in Figure 12.14.

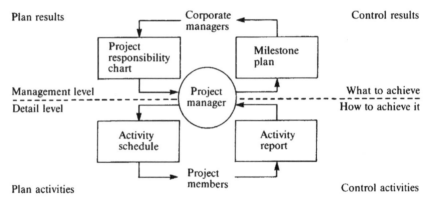

Figure 12.14   Nesting of control cycles in the work breakdown structure

12.9 Summary

1. The process of resourcing a project includes the following steps:
   – identify what is to be achieved
   – identify the skills and skill types required
   – identify the people available
   – assess their competence
   – identify any training required
   – negotiate with the resource provider
   – ensure appropriate project facilities are available.
2. The five steps of activity planning are:
   – define the activities to achieve a milestone or work package
   – ratify the people involved
   – define their roles and responsibilities
   – estimate work-content and durations
   – schedule activities within a work package.

PROJECT RESPONSIBILITY CHART

X – eXecutes the work
D – takes Decision solely
d – takes decision jointly
P – manages Progress
T – provides Tuition on the job
C – must be Consulted
I – must be Informed
A – available to Advise

PROCEDURE FOR PROJECT MONITORING & CONTROL

Project:

Issue/Date: Approved by:

Period: Six Weekly Cycle

No.	Principle/Milestone name	Project Manager	Team Leaders	Project Members	Project Support Office	Steering Committee	Project Sponsor	Companies/Departments/Functions/Type of resource
	Develop milestone plan	PX	X		I	d	D	
	Create high-level network	PX			X			
	Develop new activity schedules	DP	X	X	I			
	Update network	P	C	C	X			
	Issue work-to lists			I	X			
	Do work	P	PX	X	I			
	Return turn-around documents		P	X				
	Activity review meeting	I	PX	X				
	Identify variances (activities)	I	PX	X				
	Plan recovery	DP	X	X				
	Issue activity progress reports	PI	X					
	Review progress against milestones	PX		X	X	I		
	Milestone progress meeting	PX		X	X	X		
	Identify variances (milestones)	PX		X	X	DX		
	Plan recovery	PX	X	X	D			
	Issue milestone progress report	PX	X	X	X	C	I	
	Approve progress						D	

Work Cont. H/D/W: 1 2 3 4 5 6 1

Figure 12.13 Procedure for monitoring and control

3. After creation of the activity schedule, it is entered into the master plan, and at appropriate intervals work is allocated to people. Both these steps must be authorized by the project manager.
4. Activity schedules may be represented by:
   - responsibility charts
   - estimating sheets
   - nested networks
   - nested bar charts.
5. Work is allocated to people via work-to lists, by:
   - time period
   - work package.
6. The four steps in the control cycle are:
   - plan future performance
   - monitor achievement against plan
   - calculate variances and forecast out-turn
   - taking action to overcome variances.
7. For control to be effective, each step in this cycle must be effective. Requirements for effective planning have already been described, and in particular are stated in the five principles of project management at the end of Chapter 4.
8. Requirements for effective reporting include:
   - reports against the plan
   - defined criteria for control
   - simple, friendly tools
   - reporting at defined intervals
   - formal review meetings
   - creative discussions.
9. This can be achieved by gathering data using turn-around documents, which can be used to gather data to control the five objectives:
   - time
   - cost
   - quality
   - organization
   - scope.
10. Time is controlled by recording progress on the critical or near-critical paths, or by comparing the cost of work actually completed to that planned to have been completed. In order to do this, the following progress data is collected:
    - revised start/finish
    - actual start/finish
    - effort to date
    - effort remaining

 – costs to date
 – costs remaining.
11. Cost is controlled by comparing costs incurred to the planned cost of work actually completed. In order to do this, the same data is required. Costs are said to be incurred when the expenditure is committed, not when the invoices are paid, because at that time the plan can still be recovered.
12. S-curves provide a visual representation of progress against both cost and time.
13. When the divergence of achievement from the plan becomes too great, the project must be recovered. The ten-step problem solving cycle can be applied to find the solution to plan recovery. Possible courses of action include:
 – rearranging the plan
 – compromising time
 – compromising cost
 – compromising scope
 – aborting the project.

References

1. Machiavelli, N., *The Prince*, 1514, reprinted, Penguin, 1961, Chapter 3.
2. Brooks, F.P., *The Mythical Man-Month,* Addison-Wesley, 1974.

Note

a. Section 12.7 incorporates material from the first edition based on a contribution originally made by Dr Mahen Tampoe, associate of Henley Management College.

13
Project close-out

13.1 Introduction

The last stage of the life-cycle is finalization and close-out. During the closing stages of a project, the team must maintain their vigilance, to ensure that all the work is completed, and that it is completed in a timely and efficient manner. It is very easy for the good effort of execution and control to be lost, as some team members look forward to the next project, and others become demob happy or demob unhappy. Furthermore, during this stage, the team's focus must switch back to the purpose of the project. During execution and control, the team concentrate on doing the work within time, cost and specification. Now they must remember why they are undertaking the project; they are not doing the work for its own sake, but to achieve business benefit. It is very easy to complete the work within the constraints, and think that is a successful project, while failing to use the facility delivered to obtain the expected benefits which justified the money spent on it. There are a very small number of projects, mainly in information management (IM) where the facility is not utilized at all, and no benefit obtained. However, there are many where it is utilized to less than its full capacity, and the project team often do not see it as their responsibility to ensure that it is. They are more interested in their next project. At this time, the project team must also remember that it may be the closing stage of the project, but it is also the start of the operational life of the facility. Therefore, adequate mechanisms must be put in place to support the facility throughout its life.

As the project comes to an end, the team disbands. If the project is completed efficiently, the team may be run down over some time. As this happens, it is important to ensure that it is done in a caring way. Team members may have made significant contributions, or even sacrifices, to the success of the project. If this is not recognized, at best the project will end on an anticlimax, and at worst it will leave lasting resentment which will roll over into the next project. You must ensure that the team members are given due reward for their contribution, and that the end of the project is marked appropriately.

Finally, there is data to be recorded or lessons learnt for the operation of the facility, or for the design, planning, estimating and management of future projects. Because the team's attention may be focused on completing the task and looking forward to the next project, this often remains undone. Completing records of the last project is a distraction from the next. It also costs money, and it is money spent after the facility has been commissioned. Therefore it provides no immediate benefit, and it is money which can be easily saved, especially if the project is overspent. However, it is precisely when a project is overspent that it is important to find out why that happened, so that the information can be used for the planning and estimating of future projects.

In this chapter, I describe how to bring the project to a timely and efficient completion. I then explain how to hand the facility over to the users, while ensuring that it is fully commissioned to obtain the benefits and that a proper support mechanism is put in place as it moves into its operational phase. I describe how to disband the project team in a caring way, and identify the key data to be recorded at the end of the project, how it is obtained and the purpose for which it is used. This is the second most critical stage of a project. Nobody remembers effective start-up, but everyone remembers ineffective close-out; the consequences are to be seen for a long time.

13.2 Finishing the work

As the project draws to a close, the team must ensure all work is completed in a timely and efficient manner. The following can aid this process:

- producing checklists of outstanding work to ensure all loose ends are tied up
- planning and controlling at lower levels of work breakdown to provide tighter control
- holding more frequent control meetings to ensure that problems are identified and solved sufficiently early
- planning the run-down of the project team as the work runs down to ensure that people are released for other work
- creating a task force with special responsibility for completing outstanding work
- closing contracts with suppliers and subcontractors to ensure that no unnecessary costs are booked
- supporting the project manager by a deputy with finishing skills.

As you approach the end of the project you begin to look at what tasks need to be done to complete outstanding work. Instead of waiting for a fortnight to find out what work has been achieved, you create daily lists of work to be done to complete the facility, hand it over to the client and commission it. This leads naturally to planning at a lower level of workbreakdown, and holding more frequent control meetings. At the end of a project, the risk of delay becomes greater, and so it becomes appropriate to review progress more frequently: weekly, daily or even twice daily. I said in Chapter 5 that whatever the frequency of control, that should be the average duration of activities, and hence you plan against shorter tasks. The checklists are just more detailed plans.

As the project nears its end, you will require fewer resources. This is what gives the S-curve its classic shape. However, to ensure the most efficient completion, you must plan the release of resources in advance. You do not want them turning up one day, and sitting around until you realize they are not needed, because that is inefficient for both the project and the organization as a whole. You must tell people one or two weeks in advance that they will not be required on a certain date. You must also tell the resource providers, so that they can make full use of their people when they are released.

As the teams run down, it becomes essential to combine the members into task forces, to retain natural *hunting* packs. These teams may be of about 6 to 15 people depending on the task at hand. Frame describes task forces created at the end of a project as *surgical teams*.[1] The reasons for this are twofold. People work best in teams of a certain size, and as the number of people reduce, the number of managers must be reduced, with teams merged. It is also natural to give the task forces checklists to complete, rather than spreading the work over disparate groups. Closing contracts with suppliers and subcontractors is another way of planning the run down of the project team (see Example 13.1).

The skills required to finish a project can be different to those required to start it up and run it. Therefore it may be appropriate to change managers in the final stage. However, if this change is to be seamless, the new manager must be a former deputy, who has been involved for some time. This approach was successfully adopted on the construction of the Sainsbury Wing of the National Gallery.

A delegate on a course told me he had been rung up by the accounts department two years after a project had been finished to be told it was overspent. He was asked what was he doing about it. He asked how this could be because the project had finished two years previously, it was underspent then, and no further work had been done. The accounts department said people were still charging their time. The project manager said that there was nothing he could do to stop people charging time, and asked the accounts department why didn't they close the account numbers. They said it was against company policy, and it was his duty to make people stop charging their time! It wouldn't happen to Dilbert.

Example 13.1 Closing account numbers and contracts

13.3 Transferring the product

Key issues in transferring the facility to the users include:

PLANNING FOR THE TRANSITION

There must be a clear understanding of how responsibility for the facility is to transfer from the project manager to the operations manager. This will happen during the commissioning process, which, as we saw above, should be planned at a lower level of work breakdown than its fabrication.

ENSURING THAT THE USERS ACCEPT THE PRODUCT

I spoke in Chapter 6 about involving users in the decision-taking processes. That will win their acceptance of the specification of the facility. At the end of the project the users must be given the opportunity to agree that the facility meets that specification. On a strict contractual relationship, the owner should sign completion certificates to accept the product. When I worked in ICI, the operating works signed completion certificates, even when the plant was built by internal resources.

TRAINING THE USERS IN THE OPERATION OF THE FACILITY

The users will usually not be experts in the operation of the facility. They will therefore require training in its use. This should be planned as part of the project. Indeed, it is probably too late if it is not addressed until close-out. However, it is in this transition stage that much of the training takes place. Training will be in the use of the facility, but may also include simple maintenance procedures. Training can be a significant proportion of the cost of a project. When converting a typewriter factory to robotic manufacture, IBM spent 25 per cent of the budget on training.

ENSURING A DEFINITE CUT-OVER

The planned transition and signed completion certificates should result in a definite cut-over, at which responsibility is transferred, and final payments made (Example 13.2). It is also important from a safety point of view that there is clear ownership at the facility

I conducted an audit in a company which had taken 18 months to complete a contract, but they had not obtained sign-off three years later. The client was always finding fault, and had effectively had three years' free maintenance. At this point, the contractor switched the equipment off, and very quickly agreed a final snagging list and obtained sign-off.

Example 13.2 Signing-off completion certificates

RECORDING THE AS-BUILT DESIGN

To ensure ongoing efficient operation of the project's product, it is important that the as-built design is recorded. This requires the incorporation of all design changes into the final configuration of the product. This is part of the process of configuration management (Chapter 7). This is effectively now a legal requirement, under the CDM regulations. If an accident were to occur because the users were operating a design other than the one built, it would be viewed very seriously by the authorities.

ENSURING CONTINUING SERVICE OR MAINTENANCE OF THE FACILITY

The users may be able to undertake simple service or maintenance, and operating manuals may help them. However, it is usually ineffective, if not impossible, for them to become experts in the technology of the facility, and so it is necessary to ensure appropriate mechanisms are in place to provide back-up. This requires channels of communication between owner and contractor throughout the life of the facility. These channels should be defined as part of the hand-over. In the engineering industry, many contractors make little or no profit from construction of the facility, but large profits from its service. The construction contract is almost a loss leader to win the service contract.

13.4 Obtaining the benefits

Many project managers view their job as finishing when the facility is handed over to the users. However, obtaining the benefit from the project is the final step in the control process, undertaken at the top of the project hierarchy, the integrative level (Figure 1.10). Whether this final step is the responsibility of the project manager or project champion will depend on the circumstances, but it should be agreed as part of the project strategy at the start. It will probably be the champion who will be held accountable if the owner does not receive adequate return on their investment, and so the onus rests on the champion to ensure it happens. There are four steps in any control process (Figure 7.2):

PLAN RESULTS

From the start there must be a clear definition of the project's purpose and the benefits expected from the operation of the facility. This is a clear statement of the criteria by which the project will be judged to be successful, stated as part of the project strategy.

MONITOR ACHIEVEMENT

Following commissioning, the expected benefits must be audited. If the facility is an IS system, you must check whether it is delivering the expected returns. For example, if it is a manufacturing planning system, you must check to see whether the inventory is falling, the work in progress is falling, and the lead times are being reduced, as predicted. Often, after the system is commissioned, no noticeable change is achieved. If the facility is a new product, you must check to see whether the predicted levels of sales are being achieved. If it is a management training programme, you must check to see if there is any noticeable improvement in management performance. (The last of these is the most difficult to check.)

CALCULATE VARIANCES

Determine the cause of any difference between the expected benefits and those obtained. This requires measuring the revenue stream and profitability of the project. The cause may be that the users are not using the product to its full capacity, either deliberately or inadvertently.

TAKE ACTION

Hopefully a small amount of fine tuning of the design of the facility, or a small amount of additional training of users is all that is required to achieve the actual benefit. Projects involve considerable risk, because they are novel and unique, and so it is quite likely that the design carried some small imperfections which can be very easily corrected. Sometimes, improvement will require another project. (That was why the problem-solving cycle (Figure 1.6) was drawn as a circle.)

13.5 Disbanding the team[a]

Over the last three sections, I concentrated on work-related and strategic issues of close-out. However, the team members may face the end with mixed feelings. The cycle of team formation and maintenance (Figure 11.1) showed the team going into mourning at the end of the project, and performance dropping. It can rise as the team look forward to new opportunities, or drop if they face unemployment. This can impact badly on them and the project. It is the task of both line and project managers to manage this emotional response, so that staff are retained and reintroduced into the normal work environment. When considering the motivation of project staff, it must be remembered they belong permanently to the organization and only temporarily to the project. This means that while the project may not need the staff once their contribution has finished, the organization for which they work may value the team members even more because of new skills they learned and may want them for future projects. Retaining project team members is vital, and so the process of disbanding the project team must be managed in a caring way. Key elements in this process include:

PLANNING THE RUN-DOWN OF RESOURCES IN ADVANCE
This, as explained above, is important to achieve an efficient end to the project. It is also important for the motivation of the project team. People feel more motivated to complete their work if they know they are to be transferred immediately to new work. That is only possible if their release has been planned, so that their line managers have been able to plan their future work.

RETURNING RESOURCES PROMPTLY TO THEIR LINE MANAGERS
The organization gets the optimum use of its resources if they are returned promptly to normal duties after completion of the project. Line managers of people seconded to the project are more likely to treat future requests for resources favourably if those people are used efficiently, which means releasing them at the earliest possible opportunity.

END-OF-PROJECT PARTY
The use of 'festivals' is an important motivator on projects. They should be used to mark important project milestones, especially the end of the project. The difficulty is choosing the timing of a party, so that the maximum number of people can come before being dispersed to new jobs, but when they actually having something to celebrate.

DEBRIEFING MEETING
A project close-out meeting can be as important as a launch meeting, as part of the life cycle of the project team. It marks the end of the period of working together, and allows people to show their grief, or frustration, or pleasure at having been a member of the project (Example 13.3).

I worked on the overhaul of ammonia plants in the early 1980s. We held a debriefing meeting after each overhaul. They served a useful purpose of allowing us to let off steam in advance of the next overhaul. For the four weeks of each overhaul, we used to suspend our feelings, to allow work to progress. We would talk to each other bluntly about what work we wanted done, what it would take, and how we felt about having been let down. It was necessary to make progress in the intensity of the overhaul. In the process, feathers got ruffled, but we had to bite our lips and get on with it. At the debriefing meeting, it all came out; we said all the things we had bottled up for four weeks. It was all laid bare, forgiven, and we were ready to start afresh on the next overhaul.

Example 13.2 Releasing frustration at debriefing meetings

REWARDING ACHIEVEMENT

The team members are likely to react favourably to future requests to work for the project manager if their contribution to the project is suitably rewarded and praised. End-of-project festivals are part of that. However, it is equally important that a person's achievement is recognized by those who matter, especially the manager who is to write the individual's annual appraisal, so that the person's contribution to the business can be recognized. An important part of this process is winning the appraising manager's commitment to the project, so that he or she views a contribution to the project as an important achievement during the year.

DISCIPLINING UNDER ACHIEVEMENT

It is also important to discipline poor performance on a project so that good performers do not feel that their effort was in vain and that the poor performers know how to improve in the future. For this latter reason, the disciplining process should be treated positively, guiding people how to perform better in the future. Of course, it might be possible to take corrective action during the project, so the earlier this is done the better.

COUNSELLING ALL STAFF

The fifth stage of team development is mourning, as the project fades into history and the team with it. This is not very good for the ego or self-esteem of the team members who find that overnight they may be reduced to 'has-beens' unless they go immediately to another project or line job. For those who are not so lucky, a counselling session can be of tremendous value. While this may incorporate some of the activities mentioned above, it often encompasses much more. For example:

- it offers a chance for the individual to review career objectives
- it offers scope for skills consolidation in the form of theoretical training to supplement the practical experience
- it shows caring by the organization, which is perhaps the key factor in the whole exercise.

Recalling the case in Example 6.1, perhaps the individuals should have been given counselling well before the end of the two-year period, into planning their re-entry into the line organization. The individuals could then have taken responsibility for their own career development, and perhaps have found opportunities for themselves within the organization where their new skills would have been of great value.

13.6 Post-completion reviews

The control process at the top level of the project hierarchy (Section 12.8) might seem to be the point to stop. However, there is a level in the corporate hierarchy above this (Figures 1.10 and 2.4). We also need to control at this level. The data gathered at this level include:

- as-built design (final configuration)
- a comparison of final costs and benefits for feeding back to the estimating process, and to the selection of future projects
- a record of the technical achievement on the project for feeding back to the design and selection of future projects
- a review of the successes and failures of the project and the lessons learned, for feeding back to the management of future projects.

There are several ways of reviewing the success and failures of projects, but two include debriefing meetings and post-completion audits.

DEBRIEFING MEETINGS
I have already described the role of these in disbanding the project team. It is worth while on most projects to hold a meeting of all people who attended the project launch workshop to review the assumptions made. This meeting may last from two hours to a day depending on the size of the project. On particularly large projects they may amalgamate up from a low level, reversing the cascade of project launch workshops.

POST-COMPLETION AUDITS
On large projects it may also be worth while to conduct a post-completion audit. This is a formal review of the project against a checklist. An audit is often conducted by external consultants. It is also common only to audit

projects which have gone radically wrong. However, better lessons are often learned from successes, so it can be useful to audit projects which have gone well. I describe the holding of audits more fully in Chapter 16.

13.7 Summary

1. The key requirements for effective project close-out are
   - finishing the work
   - transferring the product to the users
   - obtaining the benefits
   - disbanding the team
   - reviewing progress.
2. The work must be finished in a timely, efficient manner. The following can aid this:
   - checklists of outstanding work
   - planning and controlling at lower levels of work breakdown
   - more frequent control meetings
   - planned run-down of the project team
   - use of task forces
   - changing the project manager
   - closing contracts with suppliers.
3. Effective transfer of the product to the users is facilitated by:
   - planning the transition
   - ensuring user acceptance
   - training the users
   - obtaining definite cut-over
   - recording the as-built design
   - ensuring maintenance of the facility.
4. The facility must be commissioned to obtain the required benefit, and this can be controlled by:
   - setting a measure
   - monitoring performance against the measure
   - calculating variances
   - taking action to overcome variances.
5. The project team must be disbanded in an efficient manner, and yet in a way that takes care of their motivational needs. This can be achieved by:
   - planning the run-down
   - returning resources promptly to line managers
   - holding an end-of-project party
   - holding a debriefing meeting
   - rewarding achievement
   - disciplining under achievement

– counselling staff.
6. Post-completion reviews must be held to:
   – record the as-built design
   – compare achievement to plan
   – record technical data
   – learn successes and failures for the future.

Reference

1. Frame, J.D., *Managing Projects in Organizations*, Jossey Bass, 1986.

Note

a. Section 13.5 incorporates material from the first edition based on a contribution originally made by Dr Mahen Tampoe, associate of Henley Management College.

PART FOUR
PROJECT MANAGEMENT PROCEDURES

14
Programme management

14.1 Introduction

There has been an overriding assumption in the last two parts of this book that we were considering a project in isolation. The reality is that the vast majority of projects may take place as part of a programme, or portfolio, of projects. The traditional project management assumption is of the large, isolated project with a dedicated team, in which:

- they deliver well-defined, independent objectives, which provide the full benefit on their own
- they are relatively independent of other projects and operations, with a few minor interfaces
- they have a dedicated team, wholly within the control of the project manager; the manager may desire a larger team, but he or she sets the priorities for the team's work day by day.

In the construction of a building, a fence is put around the construction site. The project will not be dependent on other projects, the only interface with other projects and operations being the connection of services across the boundary. People working on the construction site will be managed by the project manager and will be wholly within his or her control. The majority of projects, however, take place as part of a programme of small- to medium-sized projects (SMPs) in which:

- they deliver mutually interdependent objectives where the full benefit is obtained only when several projects have been completed, (Examples 1.2 and 14.1)
- they are dependent on other projects or operations for elements essential to their completion, such as data, new technologies, or raw materials

– they borrow resources from a central resource pool, and those resources remain within the control of the resource managers; the manager must negotiate release of the resources to the project, and may loose them at little or no notice as the organization's overall priorities change.

I have used the terms small- to medium-sized, large and major projects. It is common to categorize them in this way. However, there is little agreement about what these mean in terms of project value, and there is a wide difference between industries. What constitutes a large information systems project would be considered small in the engineering construction industry. I saw an advertisement for a course which claimed to be about managing 'mega' projects and went on to classify that as projects over £1 million. It is now common to classify the size of projects by the way they use resources and share risks (Figure 14.1). Small- to medium-sized projects are not big enough to justify a dedicated project team, apart from a small core, and therefore borrow resources from a central pool. Large projects have a dedicated team, and can therefore be ring-fenced from the organization. Major projects are too large for one organization to bear the risk on its own, and are therefore usually undertaken by alliances. Perhaps for a private company, a large project will be equal to annual profits, a major project will be ten times greater than that (roughly equal to annual turnover), a medium project will be ten times smaller than a large one, and a small project ten times smaller again.

In the remainder of this chapter I shall focus on small- to medium-sized projects, and the management of a portfolio of such projects. I consider the problem of small projects, and the techniques for managing a portfolio of projects, called *programme management*. I consider the question of whether an organization should adopt a company-wide approach to the management of all its projects, and end by describing the role of a project office in helping to manage a programme. That will lead us on to the use of procedures and systems in the following chapter.

A borough council I worked with was building a new shopping centre, sports complex and car park linked together, with new road access and new services. This was broken into five projects, which now could not be totally ring fenced. The road had an interface with the car park, that with the shopping centre and sports complex, were linked to the services. Furthermore, the full benefit would not be obtained from the shopping centre and the sports complex until the link road and car park were completed.

Example 14.1 Related projects

14.2 The problem of small projects[a]

Small- to medium-sized projects, by definition, compete with other projects for resources from a common, finite resource pool. Within most organizations, there exists a large number of identifiable, smaller projects. Some organizations' operations are entirely based on SMPs. They arise through:

– small companies acting as subcontractors or suppliers to larger ones on several projects
– bespoke manufacturing companies (jobbing shops), making products for several customers
– mass production companies using project methods to introduce new products
– engineering, management and other consultants scheduling expensive staff across several projects
– research institutions undertaking projects for several clients
– organizations managing change, introducing new products or new technology, changing culture, or adopting Total Quality Management.

Often these projects, by themselves, would be less risky than large projects and could be managed effectively without the use of formal project management techniques. However, together in the multi-project environment, they can consume a considerable amount of management effort, because of:

– poor selection and prioritization of resources
– inadequate management and higher overheads
– higher ratio of risk
– a large number of interfaces between the projects.

SELECTION AND PRIORITIZATION
The primary reason for the failure of SMPs is they have inadequate priority for resources, alongside other projects and day-to-day operations. This is true for both organizations undertaking them as internal development projects and as contracts for external clients. Each project is small, and so the individual resource requirement does not appear to be much. However, when too many are taken on, there is insufficient resource to go round, with the result that no projects get completed (Example 2.5). Programmes of projects are the vehicles by which organizations implement their strategy, but many organizations fail to achieve their strategy because they fail to manage the selection process.

POOR MANAGEMENT AND HIGHER MANAGEMENT OVERHEADS

Small- to medium-sized projects are often more complex than they first appear and yet only cursory attention is given to their management. Reasons may be: the benefit is not as obvious as for large projects; smaller organizations do not accept formal project management; project management software is focused on critical path analysis and time management, and not on managing capacity. Also, because of their size, SMPs are often given to more junior managers, whereas the negotiating of priority requires more mature management skills. The cost of management of SMPs can be a very large proportion of the total cost, which increase the pressure for inadequate management.

HIGHER RISK RATIO

On SMPs, risks are more essential than expected. Small- to medium-sized companies managing SMPs can be hit remarkably badly by small risks. In addition, project times are shorter giving higher risk, and making it harder to compensate for overruns. There is less opportunity to recover.

INTERFACES

Small- to medium-sized projects in a portfolio of projects can have a large number of interfaces between them. Often a larger project will be broken into several smaller, subprojects which can be managed independently for most of the time. However, there may be several essential interfaces, where they share technology, information or one project contributes to the work of the other. These interfaces in themselves constitute risks, and so add to the increased riskiness of SMPs when compared to large projects. At times we can be faced with a choice between breaking a larger project into several smaller ones to reduce the risk, but at the same time increasing risk by creating new interfaces, (see Example 14.2).

In the unsuccessful attempt in 1992 to computerize the despatch of ambulances in the London Ambulance Service (LAS), the systems was designed as a single integrated system. In the final failure, the system was brought down almost by the failure of just one line of code, which caused the whole, integrated system to fail. In the successful attempt, three years later, the system was broken into 200 sub-systems, which were delivered and proved separately. This potentially created 40 000 interfaces, increasing the project management problem, but it made the system more robust. The system is now operating successfully.

Example 14.2 Balancing risks in multi-project management

14.3 Programme management

The management of a portfolio of small- to medium-sized projects is known as *programme management*. A programme can be defined as

- a group of projects
- managed together
- for added benefit.

Programme management is the management of a coherent group of projects to deliver additional benefit. The additional benefit can result from:

- the elimination of risk arising from interfaces between the projects
- the successful completion of individual projects through the coherent prioritization of resources
- a reduction in management effort.

Programme management includes the management of interfaces between projects, and the prioritization of resources to enable projects to happen and be completed.

A problem often encountered in programmes is that individual projects lurch from crisis to crisis as priorities are changed, and resources are switched from one project to another. A project starts, and makes some progress, but then loses its resources. Some time later the project starts again, but the total delay is greater than the period the project was without resources because the team take some time to build up momentum again, and they have to repeat some work. They are then switched temporarily to another project, only to return with an even greater delay. The project is on-off on-off, consuming large numbers of resources, but never gets finished (Example 2.5). Thus the tools of programme management are tools to coordinate the projects in a programme and to set priorities between them.

Coordination and impact matrix
The first element of programme management is the coordination of the links and interfaces between projects. The suggested way of managing these interfaces is a five-step process:

1. Identify the links which exist.
2. Group projects into programmes to minimize the links.
3. Determine the impact of the links between projects.
4. Divide the links into major and minor links.
5. Develop plans for managing the major links.

If you compare this five-step process to the risk management process in

Chapter 10 (Table 10.4), you will see that what it does is treat the impacts as risks and manages them accordingly. Ferns[1] proposed the use of an impact matrix to identify and classify the links. He proposed ways of providing a quantitative assessment of the links. As I did in the chapter on risk, I would propose just a qualitative assessment. The responsibility chart can be used as the impact matrix.

Prioritization and master project schedule

Before suggesting a process for prioritizing resources, let us consider some mistakes people make. A common approach is to develop a plan for each project, with its resource requirements, and then combine all the individual project plans into one gigantic programme plan. The computer is then asked to prioritize resources. Now computers are dumb things, and they need to be given a rule. Once given a rule, they will apply it blindly and unquestioningly. One possible rule is to make project A priority 1, project B priority 2, etc. What happens? Project A gets what it needs. Project B gets what it needs from what is left. And project C follows the stop-start stop-start process I described above. Another rule is to give priority by size of float. What happens? Every activity is scheduled 'hard right', that is when it has no float. You cannot abdicate management responsibility to the computer. You must retain management control. You do plan each project, but you must make decisions at a strategic level, and then plan each project within that framework. Thus I propose a six-step process for managing the prioritization of resources across projects in a programme:

1. Develop individual project plans, at the strategic (or milestone) level.
2. Determine the resource requirements and duration of the individual projects at that level.
3. Incorporate each individual project into the rough-cut capacity plan (or master project schedule) as a single element of work, assuming the resource profile and duration calculated at step 2.
4. Assign a priority to each project according to its resource requirements and its contribution to the overall programme objectives.
5. Schedule the individual projects in the MPS, according to their priority, and assign them a time and resource window.
6. Manage individual projects to deliver their objectives within the time and resource window.

This concept of the master project schedule is similar to the master production schedule in manufacturing management. Without it, it is not possible to achieve a balance of resources across several projects of differing priority while allowing them all to make smooth progress, and providing the managers with visibility and control. Resource prioritization in programme management requires a balance of responsibilities between three groups of people: programme directors, project managers and resource managers (Figure 14.1).

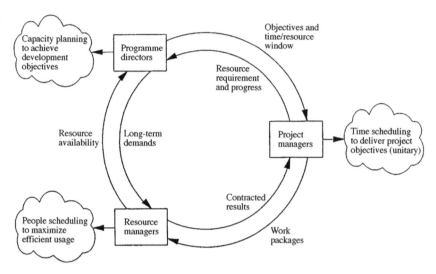

Figure 14.1   Programme management model

Requirements of programme directors

The objectives of the programme directors are to deliver the corporate development objectives within the overall resource constraints of the organization and to predict the future resource requirements. To achieve this, the programme directors use four systems (Figure 14.2).

1. They maintain the corporate plan, which sets two types of objective for the organization: routine objectives, which are fulfilled through campaigns of existing operations, and development objectives, which are achieved through projects. (In bespoke manufacturing companies, or jobbing shops, routine operations also consist of projects for clients.) The individual project objectives are passed to the project managers, who feed back resource requests.
2. The resource requests are entered into the rough-cut capacity plan, or master project schedule, to give a total resource demand for the organization. (This includes the demand from routine operations where they and the projects share common resources.)
3. The resource requirements are compared to the forecasts of availability received from the resource managers. Projects can be moved or stretched to smooth peaks and troughs, or additional resources obtained to fill the

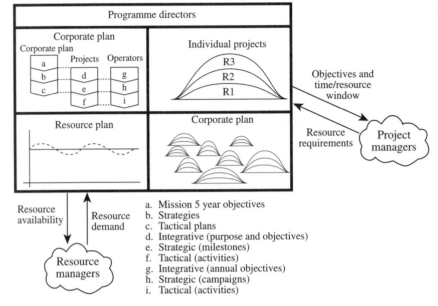

Figure 14.2   Systems for programme directors

peaks. Alternatively peaks can be met by the use of contract staff. The programme directors feed forecasts of future resource requirements to the resource managers.

4. When the resource plan balances, individual projects are assigned a time and resource window (as shown in the top right-hand box of Figure 14.3) which is fed to the project managers.

Requirements of project managers

Project managers must deliver the individual project objectives within the time and resource window assigned by the MPS. To achieve this, project managers use project management systems, including work breakdown structures, networks, bar charts and resource histograms (Figure 14.3).

The resource histogram is used to make the resource demands on the programme directors, and as a way of imposing the time and resource constraints on the individual projects. Multi-disciplinary packages of work are passed via the bar charts to the resource managers, and they complete the work within the agreed time scales to deliver the contracted results (milestones), in accordance with the project manager's plan. Although these resource demands should be within the constraints imposed by the MPS, and the resource managers should thus be able to satisfy them, the work-package plans should be negotiated and agreed with the resource managers

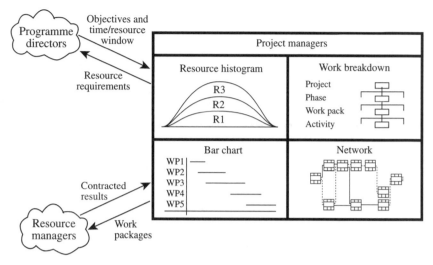

Figure 14.3   Systems for project managers

as far in advance as possible. The reason is that the MPS balances requirements and demands on a time scale of weeks or months, and so the resource managers need to fine tune the requirements on a day-to-day basis (see below).

Requirements of resource managers
The objectives of the resource managers are to deliver the contracted milestones while achieving the most efficient utilization of the available resources. This means achieving, as nearly as possible, continuous working with minimum overlap. To achieve this, the resource managers need four systems (Figure 14.4). They have to:

– compare the work-package plan passed from the project managers to the resource plan used by the programme directors – clearly, if the loop has been properly closed, these should be consistent (within the limits of accuracy)
– they assign work to people to do. It may be assigned to a single discipline via a resource scheduler, or to multi-disciplinary teams via a team scheduler.

Balancing the requirements
Two provisos were made above: the work-package plan and the resource plan must balance, and they must balance within the appropriate limits of accuracy.

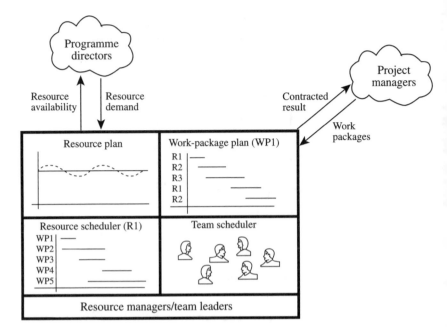

Figure 14.4 Systems for resource managers

1. It appears that resource managers are caught in a pincer between programme directors and project managers, and that they therefore need to ensure that these plans do balance. However, it is the project managers who are seen to fail when projects are not completed, and so it usually falls to them to manage the MPS. Alternatively, it is programme directors who are ultimately seen to fail when they do not deliver the organization's development objectives, and so they must ensure that the balance is achieved. The latter have the greatest influence in terms of ensuring that an adequate system is put in place, but they often delegate its management to project managers.
2. It may be possible to obtain high accuracy within the MPS with a time scale of months. However, the percentage error magnifies as the plan is first broken into individual project plans, and then work-package plans, and ultimately activity plans, with a time scale of weeks, or even days. Thus, even though the plans may nominally balance, there may be quite wild fluctuations day by day. The resource managers must manage these fluctuations to achieve the overall balance.

Programme management information systems needs
The information systems which meets the needs of programme management have three major elements (Figure 14.5) the capacity planner,

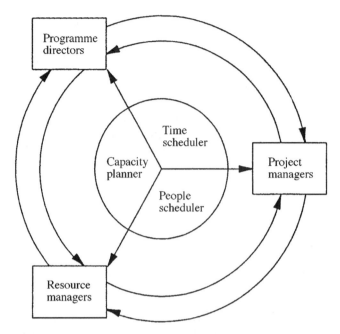

Figure 14.5 Information system for programme management

the time scheduler, and the people scheduler. We will return to systems in Chapter 16, where systems which meet this requirement are described.

14.4 Company-wide project management

It has been perceived wisdom that where an organization is undertaking several projects, it should adopt a common project management approach for all projects in the programme, regardless of the type of project, its size or the type of resource used.[2] The advantages of this are said to be:

– a consistent reporting mechanism can be adopted to give comparable progress reports across all projects in a programme
– resource requirements can be calculated on a consistent basis, facilitating the management of capacity constraints
– people can move between projects without having to relearn the management approach used project by project
– small projects can be used as a training ground for future managers of large projects

An inherent, though often unrecognized, assumption behind this view is that the projects within the programme are fundamentally homogeneous.

However, Payne[3] identified that where projects are inhomogeneous, people reported better results for their projects, and fewer failures, if they tailored their project management procedures to the type of project. He differentiated projects by their size, urgency and skill mix.[4] Elvaristo has focused more on distance. He identified eleven dimensions of distance, although the most common is geographical distance.[5] Table 14.1 shows a classification of projects and programmes with seven types of project/programme over single or multiple sites. He even identified that the route an organization followed through Table 14.1 can influence their choice of procedures. Two organizations operating many projects over many sites might use different procedures depending on whether they first gained experience with a single project over many sites, or a programme on a single site.

Table 14.1 Classification of project with many projects over many sites

Sites	Single project	Many projects	Many programmes
Single	Single project Single site	Single programme Single site	
Many	Single project	One project per site One site per project	One programme per site One site per programme
Many	Many sites	One project per site Each project many sites	Many programmes over many sites

The explanation
Payne's results are fairly easy to explain.

PROJECTS BY SIZE

We should understand why it is necessary to tailor the procedures by size:

1. In the management of SMPs, the main emphasis is on the prioritization of resources across several projects. Small projects also cannot stand the bureaucracy of procedures designed for larger, more complex projects.
2. In the management of large projects, the emphasis is on the coordination of a complex sequence of activities, balancing resources across the activities, but within the control of the project manager, to enable the critical activities to take place in time, and to stop the bulk work becoming resource constrained. Large projects have much greater data management requirements than SMPs. Interestingly, large projects seemed to suffer more than SMPs when common procedures were used, perhaps indicating that all their data management requirements were not met.

3. In the management of major projects, the emphasis is on coordinating the activities of people across several subprojects, and on managing the considerable risk.

PROJECTS BY RESOURCE TYPE

The goals and methods matrix introduced in Section 1.6 explains why projects with different resource types require different procedures:

1. Engineering projects are labelled type 1 projects, and with well-defined goals and methods of achieving those goals lend themselves to activity-based approaches to planning. It is these types of projects that many of the traditional books on project management have been written about, that many of the traditional software products, such as Artemis, have been developed for, and which have a long history of proceduralization in the engineering construction and building industries.

2. Product development projects are labelled type 2 projects. The goals are well understood, but identifying the method of achieving the goals is the main point of the project. These are common in weapons systems development and projects from the electronic manufacturing industries. The early project management procedures developed in the 1950s by the US military were aimed at these types, and more recently goal-directed approaches. Plans for this type of project are best based on a bill of materials (product breakdown structure) based on the known goals; that is a milestone-based approach to planning, where the milestones represent components of the product.

3. Information systems projects are labelled type 3 projects. With the goals poorly defined, the planning approaches tend to be based around the project life cycle; that is a milestone-based approach to planning is adopted, but the milestones now represent completion of life-cycle stages. Methodologies such as PROMPT, PRINCE and PRINCE 2 are aimed at this type of project, as are computer systems such as PMW (see Chapter 15).

4. Type 4 projects tend to be managed as type 2 or type 3 projects depending on their nature. Research projects tend to be managed through the life cycle, whereas organizational change projects tend to be managed through a bill of materials or product-based milestone plan.

If you try to adopt an activity-based approach to managing type 2, 3 or 4 projects, it will increase the likelihood of failure. Thus we see that for projects of different sizes and resource types, we must tailor our project procedures to meet the needs of the individual project types.

The solution

I listed above some presumed benefits for adopting a common approach to the management of all the projects in a programme. Presumably those benefits still remain. Hence, how can we resolve the dilemma of achieving those benefits while still developing a system that meets the needs of the individual project types. The answer is to develop a strategic plan for every project based on the common approach, but allow different projects to adopt different approaches at the detail or tactical level. This means that at the three fundamental levels of planning, the following plans are developed:

INTEGRATIVE LEVEL

A Project Definition Report is developed for all projects, based on a common model. This ensures that all projects are defined in a consistent way, giving a common basis for comparison and prioritization.

STRATEGIC LEVEL

A milestone plan and project responsibility chart are developed for all projects. For types 1 and 2 projects, the milestones represent components of the product, for types 3 and 4 projects, completion of life-cycle stages. This gives a consistent approach for assigning resources and responsibilities, and for tracking and comparing progress. The resource plan is developed at the milestone level.

TACTICAL LEVEL

At this level and below, project planning methods will be chosen based on the nature of the project:

– for small projects, there may be no further levels of planning
– for large projects there may be one or more levels of planning
– for engineering construction and building projects, the lower levels will be developed in some detail at an early stage, based on the known activities to be performed
– for type 2 and 3 projects, the lower level activity plans will be developed on a rolling-wave basis, as early components are delivered, or early life-cycle stages are completed respectively.

Example 14.2 contains an example of the application of this approach to achieve a successful outcome for a project. In the next chapter I describe the use of systems and procedures, and you will see that by adopting the breakdown approach suggested, it is a simple matter to implement this recommendation

---

In Chapter 5 I described a project to build a warehouse in the Regional Health Authority in the UK. The authority was switching from a situation where each hospital bought and stored its supplies to one where the region bought and stored materials centrally. The benefit was a reduction in overall stock holdings, because whereas formerly each hospital was stocked up to peak demand, under the new regime the individual peaks and troughs could be smoothed. The project was divided into 22 subprojects:

- construction of the warehouse (half the £8 million spend) [a type 1 building project]
- creation of the establishment to run the warehouse [a type 2 logistics project]
- writing of the computer systems to operate the warehouse [a type 3 IS project]
- redeployment and training of people (there was a no redundancy policy) [a type 4 personnel project]
- changing the buying function from hospital to region [type 4, organizational change]
- changing the budget from hospital-based to regional-based [type 3, systems]
- implementing in 15 hospitals [type 4 organizational change]
- commissioning the warehouse [type 2, logistics]

There were two project managers, one from the Estates Department, managing the construction of the warehouse, and one from Operations managing the rest of the work. There was also a series of functional team leaders managing each of the subprojects.

Quite by chance, or perhaps because it was the only approach that stood any chance of getting the different project teams to talk, we adopted the planning approach described above. I was invited to run a series of project start-up workshops, to develop plans across all the subprojects. I was engaged by the operational project manager, because having no previous experience of managing projects, he did not know where to begin.

We invited both project managers and all the team leaders to the workshop. The building project manager and IS project team leader refused to come on the grounds that they already had their plans in Artemis and Project Manager Workbench, respectively. We tried to persuade them to come to the start-up workshop, using the argument that although they already had their plans, it might be a good idea to ensure that the other plans were linked into theirs, and vice versa. The IS team leader was persuaded; the building project manager said his plan was published, and the others could determine the links.

At the workshop we developed a milestone plan for all the subprojects, except the building project, and established the links between all the plans. It turned out that the 20 element milestone plan for the IS subproject, although derived from first principles, was a very good summary of the 200 activity plan in PMW. Hence it was very effective at linking that more detailed plan into all the other plans.

A month later we had the first review meeting. We tracked progress against all the milestone plans, and monitored the links between all the subprojects. The buildings project manager rolled his Artemis network along the table top, and everybody stared blankly and asked him what it meant. By the second review meeting he, too, had produced a summary milestone plan of his more detailed network, and from then on, at the monthly review meeting progress of all the subprojects was tracked against the milestone plans.

The building subproject continued to be managed day-by-day against the Artemis plan, the IS subproject against the PMW plan, and all the other subprojects were managed using a paper-based approach. However, progress on all the subprojects was summarized on to the milestone plans, and they were used to compare and track progress at the monthly review meetings. The warehouse was commissioned on time, 15 months after the start-up workshop, with all the subprojects having been completed in phase.

Example 14.2 Tailoring procedures to the type of project

14.5 The Project Support Office

Many project-based organizations use a Project Support Office (PSO) to administer project management routines. It removes some uncertainty from projects if experienced people operate the control procedures. Large to major projects often have a dedicated office comprising people who move from project to project. Smaller projects cannot afford the overhead of a dedicated office, so they share one with projects from related programmes. Often managers of small- to medium-sized projects undertake all the administrative tasks themselves, or share them among people working on the project. What happens is that they do not get done, as the technical work of the project begins to consume all the team's efforts. Hence the services of a PSO can be just as valuable to a small project as to a large one. Indeed, since it will be servicing all the projects of the organization, it can ensure all projects receive adequate priority, only projects for which there are adequate resources are started in the first place, and consistent approaches are used across all projects within the organization. In this section I describe the role of the Project Support Office, and identify the personnel it contains.

Duties of the Project Support Office
The duties of the PSO include:

MAINTAINING THE MASTER PROJECT AND PROGRAMME PLANS
The PSO maintains the master project and programme plans on a central (computer) system:

– for a large project, that will be a stand-alone plan
– for a major project, it may be broken down into subproject plans
– for a programme, the PSO will maintain both a programme plan and individual project plans.

In all cases there must be clearly defined levels of access for different managers. All managers will need to interrogate the plans at all levels.

However, they will only be able to make changes at their level of responsibility. Changes must obviously be within the constraints set at the higher level. If that is impossible, then the approval of the higher level manager must be sought. Sometimes, the ability to make changes is limited to the PSO staff. Managers can only recommend. In this way the integrity of the system is maintained.

MAINTAINING THE COMPANY-WIDE RESOURCE PLAN

The resource aggregation at the project level provides the company-wide resource plan. The PSO can take a company-wide view of the resource availability, and assign resources to individual projects, (within the constraints set by the programme directors). Individual projects are not in a position to do this, unless they have a dedicated resource pool.

PROVIDING RESOURCE DATA TO THE PROJECT INITIATION PROCESS

When the organization is considering whether to initiate a new project, the PSO can compare the resource requirements to projected availability. This information can then be used as part of the feasibility study. The PSO does not have the power to veto a project, it is up to senior management to accept or reject it. However, if there are insufficient resources, senior management must decide whether to stop another project, or buy in resources from outside. That is extremely valuable information. Better not to start a project, than stop it half finished, especially a client contract.

ISSUING WORK-TO LISTS AND KIT-MARSHALLING LISTS

At regular intervals, as agreed with the project managers, or as set by the company's procedures, the PSO will issue work-to lists and kit-marshalling lists (Section 12.4). Giving this work to the PSO ensures that it is done regularly, and that it is done to a consistent style, in a way which people from across the organization can readily understand.

FACILITATING THE CONTROL PROCESS

The PSO can manage the control process, and relieve project staff of some of the bureaucratic processes, allowing the latter to concentrate on the project work. Figure 6.8 is a responsibility chart showing a procedure for this control cycle. The PSO will of course facilitate the control of time, cost, quality, scope, resource usage (organization) and risk. This activity requires the project office to:

– progress, receive and process the turn-around documents
– analyse the consequences of the progress information

– perform the what-if analysis
– revise the plan with the appropriate manager
– reissue work-to lists for the next period.

ISSUING PROGRESS REPORTS

Following on from the control process, the PSO can issue progress reports. These may go to:

– project managers
– programme directors
– other senior managers
– the client.

The reports issued will be defined by a procedures manual. The data gathered in turn-around documents may be used for other purposes, such as:

– pay-roll
– recording of holidays and flexitime
– raising of invoices
– recording project costs for the company's accounting systems.

For the last, it is vital that costs are recorded by the project and sent to the accounts system, and not vice versa. With the latter, information can be received several months after costs are incurred, which is far too late for control. The data can be recorded separately for each system, but then it almost never agrees. The despatch of this data, which may be electronic, will be done by the PSO as part of the reporting process. It is important to review the data before despatch, rather than allowing it to go automatically, to ensure its integrity. However, this can be simplified by building in automatic checks.

OPERATING DOCUMENT CONTROL AND CONFIGURATION MANAGEMENT

Projects can involve the transmittal of a large amount of information. The PSO can coordinate that transmittal. This may include:

1. Keep a library of progress reports for ready access by any (authorized) personnel.
2. Record all correspondence to and from clients and subcontractors. As part of this process, the PSO may include acknowledgement slips, and monitor their return to ensure receipt of the correspondence. Technical personnel can be lax in the recording of correspondence, which can cause problems later if there is a claim. To avoid this, some organizations insist that all outward correspondence goes via the PSO, and a copy of

all inward correspondence is logged there. Since all correspondence becomes part of the contract, the need to log it cannot be stressed enough.

3. Monitor all correspondence between project personnel. On a large project, this can drastically reduce the channels of communication. However, it is more efficient to have a central clearing point for communication on projects with as few as four people. This can be essential if the people have not worked together before, on projects involving tight time scales, and on projects involving research scientists, who do not tend to be very communicative.

4. Maintain the records for quality control and configuration management, to ensure that they are properly completed, before work commences on the next stage. This can also include change control.

5. Monitor the despatch of design information to site or subcontractors, to ensure it is received and the latest information used. I have known of cases where drawings are lost in the post, and, of course, the intended recipients have no way of knowing they should be using new data. Acknowledgement slips solve this problem.

6. Issue management. Issues can arise on a project, which may or may not lead to a change or a claim. The PSO can manage the decision-making process.

PRODUCING EXCEPTION LISTS

As part of the control process, the PSO may produce exception reports. They will produce variance reports at each reporting period, but exception lists will highlight items which have become critical.

PURCHASING AND ADMINISTRATION OF SUBCONTRACTS

Where there is not already a purchasing department within the parent organization, the PSO can take over the procurement function. There is a view that in some project-based organizations a very high proportion of total expenditure on projects is through purchased materials or subcontract labour, and so this function should be within the control of project or programme management.

MAINTAINING THE CLIENT INTERFACE

The PSO may manage the relationship with the client. This includes the issuing of progress reports, the control of communications, and the despatch of invoices. It also involves producing reports against agreed project milestones, and the maintenance of links with opposite numbers in the client organization so that any threats to the contract can be worked through together. The project manager must also maintain close links with their opposite number and the client's sponsor, to help maintain a good working relationship. Contacts with the sponsor and other decision makers can help to ensure continued support for the current contract, which will ease its delivery, and help to win new work.

ACTING AS A CONSCIENCE

Effective project management requires that all the control procedures described are well maintained. Some can become bureaucratic, and distracting for the technical staff. While the project is running smoothly, they can seem unnecessary, and not receive adequate attention. However, if the project does go wrong, then the data and plans are required to plan recovery or defend a claim. It is then too late to start recording the data and maintaining the plans. It must be done from the start. The PSO can relieve project staff of the bureaucratic burden. Because they maintain the plans as their day-to-day duties, they become efficient at it, so the cost of the administrative overhead is less than if project personnel do it. Indeed, the service and support they give can speed up the work of the project. In fulfilling this role, the PSO act as a conscience, because they ensure that the regular reports are filed, and they will not let certain major milestones be met until appropriate documentation is completed.

Personnel of the Project Support Office

The number and skills of people in the PSO depend on their work. Possible personnel include:

PLANNERS

At its simplest, there may be just one or more planners, (called project controllers or planning engineers). They can fulfil all the planning and control functions described above, but not procurement or client liaison.

ADMINISTRATORS

If the document control is particularly complex, then it may be appropriate to include an administrator, clerk or secretary.

COST CONTROLLERS

For larger operations, the cost control function may be split from the remainder. The cost controller is called a cost engineer or project accountant. A cost controller should also maintain links with the estimating function. If the turn-around documents are also used to gather pay-roll data, they may also maintain links with the personnel function.

MATERIALS PLANNERS

Again, for larger operations, or ones with a large material content, it is common to split out the material management function. The materials planners maintain the material and design schedules, and issue the kit-marshalling lists. They also liaise with procurement and stores, and may issue work-to lists to design.

PROCUREMENT CLERKS

When the PSO is fulfilling the procurement function, purchasing, progress and expediting clerks may be included in the staff. There may also be inspectors, and quantity surveyors. The latter will judge performance of subcontractors.

CONTRACT ADMINISTRATORS

When the PSO also manages the client interface, then the staff will include contract administrators or managers.

14.6 Summary

1. A programme is a portfolio of projects managed together to deliver additional benefits. Programme management is the process of coordinating the management of the projects and assigning priorities to them to achieve the benefits.

2. There are five steps to coordinating the projects:
   - identify links
   - group projects into programmes to minimize links
   - determine the impact of links
   - prioritize into major and minor links
   - manage the major links.

3. There are six steps for assigning priorities to projects for resources:
   - plan individual projects
   - calculate individual project's resource requirements
   - place each project into the master project schedule
   - assign each project priority
   - assign it a time and resource window in the MPS
   - manage each project within its window.

4. Tailoring procedures by type of project leads to a more successful outcome. However, there are advantages in achieving some consistency of approach including:
   - a consistent reporting mechanism gives comparable progress reports across all projects

- resource requirements can be calculated on a consistent basis, facilitating the management of capacity constraints
- people can move between projects without having to relearn new management approaches
- small projects can be used as a training ground for future managers of large projects.

5. This can be achieved by having:
   - at the integrative level a Project Definition Report for all projects
   - at the strategic level a milestone plan and responsibility chart for all projects
   - at the tactical level tailored project plans dependent on the type of project.

6. The role of the project support office is to:
   - maintain the master project and programme plans
   - maintain the company-wide resource plan
   - provide resource data to the project initiation process
   - issue work-to lists and kit-marshalling lists
   - facilitate the control process
   - issue progress reports
   - operate document control and configuration management
   - produce exception lists
   - purchase and administration of subcontracts
   - maintain the client interface
   - act as a conscience.

7. The personnel contained in the project support office may be:
   - planners
   - administrators
   - cost controllers
   - materials planners
   - purchasing, progress and expediting
   - contract administration.

References

1. Ferns, D.H., 'Developments in programme management', *International Journal of Project Management*, **9** (3), August 1991.
2. Turner, J.R., 'Company resource planning in the food processing industry', in *Proceedings of the 12th INTERNET International Expert Seminar,* S. Dworatschek (ed.), IPMA, 1988.
3. Payne, J.H. and Turner, J.R., 'Company-wide project management: the planning and control of programmes of projects of different types', *International Journal of Project Management*, **17** (1), February 1999.
4. Payne, J.H., 'The management of multiple, simultaneous projects: a state of the art review', *International Journal of Project Management*, **13** (3), June 1995.

5. Elvaristo, R., 'A typology of project management: emergence and evolution of new forms', *International Journal of Project Management*, to appear in 1999.

Note

a. Section 14.2 incorporates material from the first edition based on a contribution originally made by Deborah Carlton.

15

Project management procedures and systems

15.1 Introduction

I first introduced the concept of project management procedures in Chapter 7, where I said they are an essential element of the quality assurance process. Having well-defined, previously proven, successful ways of managing projects increases the chance of achieving a successful conclusion. However, I did say that the procedures should be used as flexible guidelines, not rigid rules. They should be adapted to the needs of the actual project and to the customer's requirements. In the last chapter, I introduced the need to adopt project management procedures and systems to help manage the projects in a programme. I discussed whether an organization should have a common approach to its procedures or a tailored approach, and showed that the latest research again suggests that the procedures should actually be tailored to the requirements of the particular project.

Similarly, a *project management information system* (PMIS) can be used to help manage the project, and contribute to its quality assurance. Project management information systems were very poorly used in many areas until a few years ago, especially on high-technology projects. On engineering projects, information systems were used to make significant improvements to their management as early as the 1970s, mainly in the management of design information and materials, and in the analysis of risk. However, on high-technology projects, information systems appeared to be used just to play computer games (see Example 15.1). I have left discussion of PMIS until now because, as with teaching children how to do long division before giving them calculators, I think people should learn the principles of project management before using a PMIS. Once a person knows how to manage a project well, they can use a PMIS to make themselves an even better project manager. A bad project manager will use a PMIS to make themselves worse.

In this chapter I shall describe the use of procedures and systems. I shall start by describing procedures and how to develop a procedures manual. I then describe the PRINCE 2 methodology, effectively a standard procedures manual, and what the quality procedure ISO 10 006 says about the use of procedures manuals to achieve quality on projects. I describe the use of project management information systems, the types of package available, how to choose and implement a package, and some of the risks involved.

A delegate on a project management course at Henley Management College in 1989 said he had 20 people on his project team. Three worked in an office and spent all day every day developing plans in one of the more popular systems. No useful information came out of that room, the three people tended not to interact with the other members of the project team, so their plans bore no relation to what was being done. That meant 15 per cent of the project team spent their day playing computer games.

An associate director at Coopers and Lybrand said to me that a managing consultant working for him was doing a job that should have only taken about two weeks. However, every week the managing consultant presented him with a plan developed in the same package that showed where he had slipped a week in the last week. The managing consultant seemed to spend every week updating the plan, and not doing the work. He gave the managing consultant a paper-based reporting tool, and the work was finished in two more weeks.

Example 15.1 The misuse of project management information systems

15.2 Procedures manuals

Having project management procedures is an essential part of quality assurance. Following flexible guidelines which represent previously proven successful ways of delivering projects increases the chance of achieving a successful outcome for your project; redesigning the management process from scratch on every project increases the chance of getting it wrong. Procedures manuals are the medium by which an organization codifies its standard management processes. In this section I describe the purpose of procedures manuals, the essential approach to manuals, and a suggested structure.

Purpose of procedures manuals

There are several reasons why organizations develop procedures manuals:

A GUIDE TO THE MANAGEMENT PROCESSES

Even the most experienced managers may occasionally need to remind themselves of the procedures to be followed in certain circumstances. A procedures manual can serve as a useful *aide-mémoire*.

CONSISTENCY OF APPROACH

It helps in cross-project coordination if all projects within an organization are being managed in a consistent manner.

COMPANY RESOURCE PLANNING

In particular, when calculating the resource requirements of all projects being undertaken by the organization, and setting priorities between them, it is important that the resource requirements of each project are calculated in a consistent manner.

COMMON VOCABULARY

Likewise, it is important when making comparisons between projects, that it is done from a common basis, and that requires a common vocabulary. Lack of understanding of terminology can even create problems within project teams (see Example 15.2).

TRAINING OF NEW STAFF

Project managers often first learn their profession by 'sitting next to Nellie'. Following what they are doing in a procedures manual can help to reinforce their learning. Furthermore, if training courses are structured around the manual, it can serve to remind them of what they learned as they begin to apply it in the working environment.

DEMONSTRATION OF PROCEDURES TO CLIENTS

Often, as part of their terms and conditions of contract, clients demand to see proof of best practice in project management. This is an assurance to the client that the contractor is able to meet the agreed goals (of quality, cost and time). A procedures manual goes some way towards providing that proof.

QUALITY ACCREDITATION

Another way of demonstrating that the organization adheres to best practice is to be accredited against a defined quality standard. These standards are described in the next section.

I worked in a company where the word 'commissioning' was taken by the mechanical engineers to mean M&E trials, by the process engineers as the period following M&E trials during which the process was proved, by the plant operators as the period following process testing in which the first product was produced, and by the software engineers as all of those combined in which the computer control system is tested and proved.

A colleague reports working on a project to construct a petrochemical facility for which there were two project managers, one responsible for the design phase, and one for construction. When asked what they understood by project completion, one said completion of M&E trials, one said operating at 60 per cent nameplate capacity. Both were working to the same day, even though the two dates are at least 15 months apart.

He reports another project to develop a computer system where when asked the same question people gave answers ranging from completion of beta test to the system has operated for twelve months without a problem. Again they were working to the same date even though they were again at least 15 months apart.

On all of these projects, some people were going to judge them to be a success, and some a disaster.

Example 15.2 A common vocabulary

The essential approach

The essential approach to procedures manuals is to describe the processes by which the inputs of a project are converted into outputs. Many people make the mistake of defining how each function or department operates, with projects moving through the functions in a step-wise manner. However, there is overwhelming evidence that this is the inferior approach.[1] Problems that arise are:

- it reinforces demarcations and lack of communication between departments
- some people, especially those who implement procedures under the ISO 9000 series[2] and who also think that procedures should be rigid rules to be followed without exception, use the procedures to avoid doing work at the interface between functions or departments and then to blame project failure on others
- it can cause project development cycles to be slowed because projects are undertaken sequentially, rather than with functions and departments working in parallel, (projects become a relay race rather than a rugby match).

What is more successful is to define the processes through the project life cycle, defining how the organization processes a project as an entity, and defining how the functions or departments contribute to that process. The procedures should have as their core a standard project life cycle for the organization. At that level, the procedures define the inputs and outputs for each stage, with the outputs from one stage becoming the inputs for subsequent stages. Each stage of the life cycle can be broken down into a series of steps, each step with inputs and outputs, showing how the inputs for the stage are converted into outputs. The steps can then be broken into substeps, and so on, through a structured hierarchy or breakdown. The number of levels in the hierarchy will depend on the size of project: small project procedures will not go below the single, life-cycle level; large projects may have three or four levels of procedures. What the procedures must do at each level is define:

- the components of the inputs and outputs, comprising data and information, components of the project plan or reports, quality, risk or other control checks, or deliverables of the project
- what is done at each stage or step of the process
- the contribution of each function or department, or of external contractors or other agencies, to the work of each stage or step.

Some approaches to procedures define two types of input to a step, inputs which are consumed by the step and converted into outputs, and controls which determine the nature of the process. I have never fully understood the difference, and think that sometimes it is either arcane or unclear, and that most of the time it contributes no greater understanding of the process and hence is just sophistry. I do not draw the distinction.

The structure of procedures manuals

In order to achieve these requirements the typical structure of a procedures manual may be:

PART 1 – INTRODUCTION
This explains the structure and purpose of the procedures manual.

PART 2 – PROJECT STRATEGY
This describes the approach to project management to be adopted by the organization, and the basic philosophy on which it is based. It will cover issues such as those described in Chapters 3 and 4. It describes the project model, introduces the stages of the life cycle to be followed (Part Three), and explains why they are adopted. It also explains the need to manage project management functions, and also the need to manage risk.

PART 3 – MANAGEMENT PROCESSES
This describes the procedures to be followed at each stage of the life cycle. The inputs, outputs and their components are listed, and the management processes required to convert the former to the latter are listed sequentially. Example 15.3 presents the contents page of a manual for an information

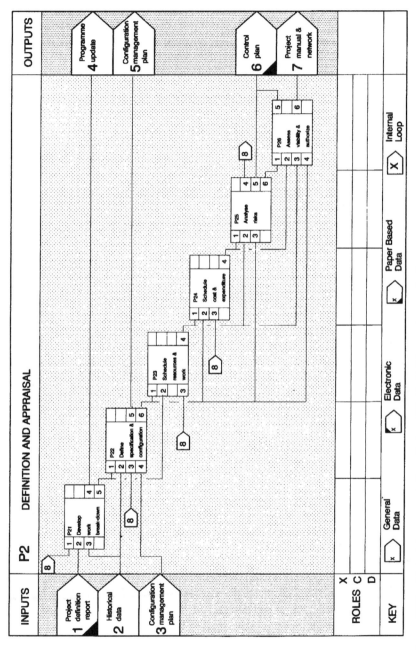

Figure 15.1   Pictorial representation of stage P2: *Definition and appraisal*

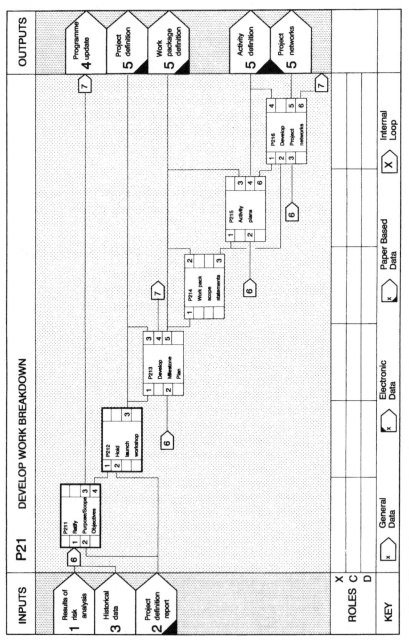

Figure 15.2 Pictorial representation of step P21: *Develop work breakdown*

systems project, which shows that in some areas the breakdown was taken to between one and three levels below the project stage. It is adapted from manuals I have prepared for clients.

In the procedures manuals of Example 15.3, I drew pictorial representations of the processes to achieve each stage or substage in the life cycle. Figures 15.1 and 15.2 are those for successive levels of breakdown. Where there is a lower level of definition, the process is shown as a fine box. Where the process is the lowest level, it is shown as a bold box. Against each bold box were listed the inputs, outputs and steps required to achieve it.

PART 4 – SUPPORTING PROCEDURES

This part explains the administrative procedures used throughout the project. It may describe the method of managing the five objectives – scope, organization, quality, cost and time – or it may explain some administrative procedures, such as programme management, configuration management, risk management, or methods of data collection (including time sheets), or the role of the project support office. Only those important in the particular environment will be necessary.

APPENDICES – BLANK FORMS AND SAMPLES

The inputs and outputs may have standard formats. It will be useful to include the blank forms, and completed examples in the appendix.

TRIMAGI COMMUNICATIONS INFORMATION SYSTEMS DEPARTMENT
Project Management Procedures Manual

CONTENTS

P25 Analyse risks
    P256 Define controls
P26 Assess project viability and authorize
P3 CONTRACT AND PROCUREMENT
    P31 Develop contract and procurement plan
    P36 Make payments
P4 EXECUTION AND CONTROL
    P41 Finalize project model
    P42 Execute and monitor progress
    P43 Control duration
    P44 Control resources and materials
    P45 Control changes
    P46 Update project model
P5 FINALIZATION AND CLOSE-OUT
APPENDICES
A Project planning and control forms
B Supporting electronic databases
C Sample reports
D Staff abbreviations (OBS)
E Resource and material codes (CBS)
F Management codes (WBS)
ADDENDA
1 Current resource and material codes
2 Current management codes

AUTHOR: JRT   ISSUE: A   DATE: 30 APRIL 200X

Example 15.3 Contents page for a procedures manual for an IT project

Tailoring procedures to the requirements of the project

One thing which must be made clear is that procedures should be treated as flexible guidelines, not rigid rules. There are people, I am afraid I call them quality nerds, who say that procedures, especially those implemented under the ISO 9000 series of quality guidelines, once written, must not be changed or the organization will be *'non-compliant'*. Well, there are two things about quality:

– quality is about delivering what is fit for the customer's purpose
– quality is about continuous improvement.

Both of these issues require you to adapt the procedures, project by project, and the second requires you to sit down at the end of every project to see how well you did, and to update the procedures before the next project (see Example 15.4). I also showed in Section 14.4 how different project types and different resource types require different procedures. Hence you must allow some flexibility within your procedures to allow them to be tailored for different project types, particularly by size of project, and different resource types. Further, at the start of every project, the team must sit down and decide how the procedures need to be adapted to deliver a product which meets the customer's needs. It can help to have a procedure to guide this process. Usually the changes required will be minimal, or there will be something extraordinary about the project.

I was asked to bid for project management training at an organization who had just had their major biennial quality audit from one of their major customers. Before the customer had come, they had got out the results of the previous audit, and made sure all the points raised were covered. The customer found 40 exceptions, particularly a lack of structured risk management. But, wailed the company, they picked up on things that were not covered last time, and they then had no interest in risk management. I pointed out that anyone who read the project management literature, on both sides of the Atlantic, would see that risk management is now a major issue, and that methods of risk management have radically improved over the last two years. If they had been tracking the project management literature, they would have be improving their risk management processes.

Example 15.4 Updating the procedures

15.3 The PRINCE 2, ISO 10 006 and the PMBoK

There are several standard project management procedures available, and several project management information systems available give strong guidance on the project management process. Here I describe two of the more common standard procedures, PRINCE 2 and ISO 10 006.[2,3] I also briefly describe the main source document for ISO 10 006, the *Guide to the Project Management Body of Knowledge*, published by the Project Management Institute of North America.[4] None of these, in fact, proscribes the procedures and organization should follow. All three give guidelines as to important issues that need to be covered in organization procedures, but leave it to the organization to actually design their own procedures within the guidelines set.

PRINCE 2

In January 1983, PROMPT II,[5] supported by the CCTA, was adopted as the government's standard for project management, to be used in particular on IS and IT projects in the public sector. In March 1989, after the introduction of a number of new features, the name PRINCE was adopted to differentiate the government version from others. After a major research project, with extensive consultations, PRINCE 2 was launched in October 1996. This incorporated a number of improvements, and was designed to be applicable to a wider range of projects than just IS/IT, although the basic principles of PROMPT have been retained. PRINCE 2 has been designed to meet all the requirements of the international quality standard, ISO 9000, and will subsequently also concur with the project specific standard, ISO 10 006.

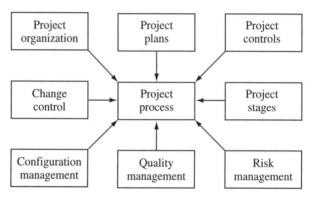

Figure 15.3   The PRINCE 2 components

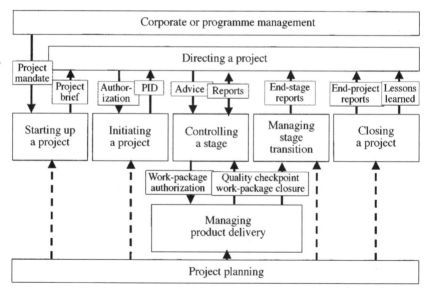

Figure 15.4   The PRINCE 2 project process

PRINCE 2 has as its core a multi-stage project management process, supported by eight components providing standards, techniques and guidelines on key project management support functions (Figure 15.3). The project management process (Figure 15.4) has six components representing the management of the project life cycle:

1. Starting-up a project.
2. Initiating a project.
3. Controlling a stage.
4. Managing product delivery.
5. Managing stage boundaries.
6. Closing a project.

The first two of these are conducted once only at the start of the project, and the sixth once only at the end. The middle three are repeated at each stage of the project. Notice the emphasis on the delivery of a quality product at the completion of each stage and the completion of the project. Notice also the requirement for managing stage boundaries, with both parties on either side of the boundary taking responsibility for the successful handover of the product at that stage. Because PRINCE 2 has been designed by experts to match the requirements of ISO 9000, this is the expert approach to ISO 9000, as suggested above. Figure 15.4 also shows two support elements to the project management process: directing and planning a project. (They say directing, rather than leading or conducting (see Section 1.3).)

As well as emphasizing product quality at the completion of each stage, PRINCE 2 also emphasizes the management of the client/contractor interface, and recognizes almost everybody is a client for some services and a contractor for others. Stakeholders in the project include:

– customers who commissioned the work and will receive the benefit
– users who will operate the product for the customers
– suppliers who provide specialist resources, skills or materials
– subcontractors who provide subproducts or services.

At different stages of the project, these groups will be alternatively client and contractor. Delivery of a quality product and management of the stage boundary requires them to work together in their different roles. PRINCE 2 repeatedly emphasizes that at the handover at the completion of each stage, the customer's business managers must ensure that the business case for the project is still valid as part of the quality control process, and abort the project if necessary. Table 15.1 shows the eight support functions, and their key elements and issues involved, and Table 15.2 identifies its controls.

Table 15.1   The PRINCE 2 support functions

Function	Elements	Issues
Organization	Corporate/programme managers Project board – senior user – executive – senior supplier Project manager Team manager Project assurance – business – user – specialist Project support	Who says what is needed? Who provides budget? Who provides resources? Who authorizes changes? Who manages daily work? Who defines standards?
Plans	Project plan Stage plan Team plan	Used by project board Created at initiation Used by project manager Created end previous stage Used by team manager Created as required
Controls	See Table 15.2	
Stages	Management stages – commit resources – authorize expenditure Technical stages use of specialist skills	Control points, set by project board, beyond which the manager may not proceed without authority
Change		Changes arise from – requests – off-specification – project issues
Configuration	Identification Control Status accounting Verification	
Quality	Internal to the project – customer quality expectation – project quality plan – stage quality plan	

Table 15.1 (*continued*)

Function	Elements	Issues
	In the project's context – ISO 9000, ISO 10 006 – corporate quality policy – quality system – quality assurance	
Risk	Risk analysis – identification – estimation – evaluation Risk management – planning – resourcing – controlling – monitoring	

Table 15.2   PRINCE 2 controls

Control	Objective	Frequency	Made by	For
Initiation Meeting	Approve initiation Stage plan	Start initiation End start-up	Project manager	Project board
Initiation document	Document agreement	End initiation	Project manager	Project board
End-stage assessment	Review status, agree next stage plan	End stage	Project manager	Project board
Checkpoint	Team progress report	Weekly	Team	PM
Highlight	Stage status report	Monthly	Project manager	Project board
Issue	Report change	As required	Anyone	PM
Exception	Predict change	As required	PM	Board
Mid-stage assessment	Review exception plan	After exception report	Project manager	Project board
Tolerance	Allowed change		PM and board	Project manager
Closure report	Confirm project objectives met	End project	Project manager	Project board

Table 15.3   ISO 10,006 recommended project management processes

Process	Description	Clause
STRATEGIC PROCESS		
– Strategic process	Setting direction and managing realization of project processes	5.2
INTERDEPENDENCY MANAGEMENT PROCESSES		
– Initiation and plan development	Evaluating customer and other stakeholder requirements, preparing a project plan and initiating processes.	5.3.1
– Interaction management	Managing interactions during the project	5.3.2
– Change management	Anticipating change and managing it across all processes	5.3.3
– Closure	Closing processes and obtaining feedback	5.3.4
SCOPE-RELATED PROCESSES		
– Concept development	Defining the broad outlines of what the project product will do	5.4.1
– Scope development	Documenting characteristics of the product in measurable terms	5.4.2
– Activity definition	Identifying and documenting activities and steps required to achieve the project objectives	5.4.3
– Activity control	Controlling the actual work carried out in the project	5.4.4
TIME-RELATED PROCESSES		
– Activity dependency planning	Identifying interrelationships and the logical interactions and dependencies among project activities	5.5.1
– Estimation of duration	Estimating the duration of each activity in connection with the specific conditions and with the resources required	5.5.2
– Schedule development	Interrelating project time objectives, activity dependencies and durations for developing general and detailed schedules	5.5.3
– Schedule control	Controlling realization of activities, for confirming the proposed schedule or taking adequate actions to recovering from delays	5.5.4
COST-RELATED PROCESSES		
– Cost estimation	Developing cost estimates for the project	5.6.1
– Budgeting	Using results from cost estimation to produce the project budget	5.6.2
– Cost control	Controlling costs and deviations from the project budget	5.6.3

Table 15.3 (*continued*)

Process	Description	Clause
RESOURCE-RELATED PROCESSES		
– Resource planning	Identifying, estimating, scheduling and allocating resources	5.7.1
– Resource control	Comparing actual usage against resource plans and taking action	5.7.2
PERSONNEL-RELATED PROCESSES		
– Organizational structure definition	Defining project organizational structure to suit the project needs identifying roles and defining authority and responsibility	5.8.1
– Staff allocation	Selecting and assigning sufficient personnel with appropriate competence to suit the project needs	5.8.2
– Team development	Developing individual and team skills and ability to enhance project performance	5.8.3
COMMUNICATION-RELATED PROCESSES		
– Communication planning	Planning the information and communications systems	5.9.1
– Information management	Making necessary information available to project organization members and other stakeholders	5.9.2
– Communication control	Controlling communication in accordance with the planned communication system	5.9.3
RISK-RELATED PROCESSES		
– Risk identification	Determining risks in the project	5.10.1
– Risk estimation	Evaluating the probability of occurrence of risk events and the impact of risk events on the project	5.10.2
– Risk control	Implementing and updating the risk plans	5.10.4
PURCHASING-RELATED PROCESSES		
– Purchasing planning and control	Identifying and controlling what is to be purchased and when	5.11.1
– Documenting requirements	Compiling commercial conditions and technical requirements	5.11.2
– Evaluation of subcontractors	Evaluating and determining which subcontractors should be invited to supply products	5.11.3
– Subcontracting	Issuing invitations to tender, tender evaluation, negotiation, preparation and placing of the subcontract	5.11.4
– Contract control	Ensuring subcontractors' performance meets requirements	5.11.5

ISO 10 006

ISO 10 006, *Quality Management – Guidelines to Quality in Project Management,* describes the essential elements of a project management process in order to deliver a quality result. The introduction to the guidelines says, as I did in Section 7.3, that there are two elements in achieving quality on projects, the quality of the process and the quality of the product. Failure to meet either of these two elements will have a significant impact on the project's product, the project's stakeholders and the project organization. It then emphasizes that the achievement of quality is a management responsibility, with the attitudes and commitment to achieving quality instilled at all levels of the organization. The standard recommends that creation and maintenance of process and product quality requires a structured and systematic approach, which is aimed at ensuring that the customers' and other stakeholders', needs are understood and met. The approach should also take account of the organization's other quality policies. As I have said, the guidelines do not recommend a project management process; all it says are what it recommends as the essential elements of such a process. Table 15.3 contains the recommended elements of the process. Table 15.4 contains other recommended elements of the process contained in other ISO standards.

Table 15.4   Other relevant quality processes

Process	Standard	Clause
Approvals	ISO/IEC Guide 2	
Corrective action	ISO 9004-1:1994	15
	ISO 8402:1994	4.14
Documentation	ISO 9004-1:1994	17
	ISO 8402:1994	3.14
Inspection	ISO 8402:1994	2.15
Preventive action	ISO 8402:1994	4.13
Process control	ISO 9004-1:1994	11
Quality assurance	ISO 8402:1994	3.5
Quality audits	ISO 9004-1:1994	5.4
	ISO 9000-1:1994	4.9
	ISO 10011	4.9.3
Quality improvement	ISO 9004-1:1994	5.6
	ISO 9004-4:1993	
Quality planning	ISO 8402:1994	3.6
Quality system	ISO 8402:1994	3.6
Reviews	ISO 8402:1994	3.9
		3.10
		3.11
Specification and design	ISO 9004-1:1994	8
Traceability	ISO 8402:1994	3.16

Table 15.4   (*continued*)

Process	Standard	Clause
Training	ISO 9004-1:1994	18.1
	ISO 9000-1:1994	6.4
Validation of tools/techniques	ISO 8402:1994	2.18
Verification	ISO 8402:1994	2.17
	ISO 9004-1:1994	12

PMI's PMBoK

ISO 10 006 is derived to a large extent from the *Guide to the Project Management Body of Knowledge* developed by the United States Project Management Institute.[5] This was written as a guideline to the project management knowledge areas that need to be used on all projects, and describes those areas. It is accepted that there may be other knowledge areas in project management, but these do not need to be used on every project. Table 15.5 contains the contents of the guide to the PMBoK.

Table 15.5   Contents of the Guide to the PMBoK

Contents

PROJECT MANAGEMENT FRAMEWORK
1   Introduction
   1.1   Purpose of this document
   1.2   What is a project
   1.3   What is project management
   1.4   Relationships to other management disciplines
   1.5   Related endeavours
2   The project management context
   2.1   Project phases and the project life cycle
   2.2   Project stakeholders
   2.3   Organizational influences
   2.4   Key general management skills
   2.5   Socioeconomic influences
3   Project management processes
   3.1   Project processes
   3.2   Process groups
   3.3   Process interactions
   3.4   Customizing process interactions
PROJECT MANAGEMENT KNOWLEDGE AREAS
4   Project integration management
   4.1   Project plan development
   4.2   Project plan execution
   4.3   Overall change control

Table 15.5 (*continued*)

Contents

15.4 Project management information systems

I have mentioned several times the possibility of using a computer-based project management information system (PMIS). I explained in Chapter 7 how they can help status accounting in configuration management; in Chapter 8 how they can help formulate the cost estimate, and gather cost information to calculate earned value and draw S-curves; in Chapter 9 how they can perform complex time and resource scheduling, and what-if analysis; in Chapter 10 how they can help analyse risk and formulate appropriate contingency plans; in Chapter 12 how they can generate work-to lists and turn-around documents, and gather and analyse control data; and in Chapter 14 how they help manage the data required by programme management. However, I avoided presenting project management as a computer exercise. This was deliberate. The manager must understand and follow the principles of good project management, and the methods, tools and techniques described in this book. Only after mastering the approach, should managers use a computer system to perform some routine processes, to handle the vast quantities of data involved, or to simplify complex analyses. In the remainder of this chapter, I shall describe the use of computer systems in project management. I shall describe the types of system available and their use, how to evaluate and implement systems, and the implications of the use of the systems. I start with the rationale of the use of systems.

I shall occasionally refer to examples of PMIS software. The main system I refer to is Project Manager Workbench, produced in the UK by ABT International, a company of, and formerly part of, Hoskyns and CAP Gemini. Project Manager Workbench (PMW) was first written by ABT, an independent American company. The main reason I refer to PMW is because it is the one with which I am most familiar (I first used the early DOS version in 1984), and it is one of the systems which I think has the best theoretical basis. Almost all systems now run in a Windows 95 or Windows NT environment, although there are still a few available that run on a mainframe. The main trend at the time of writing (in early 1998) is to deliver the system support to project teams over the INTERNET or corporate INTRANET. I was first aware of a company writing its own system in Lotus Notes in 1995, and at the time of writing most of the standard packages are appearing in Java and HTML versions. If I am going to make one prediction about future trends in project management, it is that given the distributed nature of modern project teams, when you come to read this the main vehicle for delivery of PMIS support will be via the corporate INTRANET.

Rationale

Why is there a need for a PMIS? Most organizations have an extensive range of computer-based information systems, accounts, payroll and manufacturing control. It might be argued that these could be adapted to provide control for most projects. However, functionally oriented systems are not appropriate for the management of projects, because they have many unique requirements, including:

INTEGRATION ACROSS THE ORGANIZATION

Projects cut across functional boundaries, whereas most systems are designed in a way which supports the functional hierarchy and hence reinforces demarcations and boundaries between functions.

THE TRANSIENT EVOLVING PROCESS

The PMIS must support the changing control requirements throughout the different stages of the project (see Tables 15.1 to 15.5).

FAST RESPONSE TIMES

Reports need to be produced weekly, whereas other control systems operate on a monthly cycle.

Questions

So what do we require a PMIS to do. Graham[6] suggests we should not ask what data we need to store and manipulate, but instead we should ask what questions PMIS must answer. He suggests that there are three groups of questions, relating, unsurprisingly, to functionality, time, and cost and resources.

QUESTIONS OF OUTCOME

Graham suggests that there are three questions of outcome:

1. *What product will the project deliver?* Which requires configuration management and status accounting information, and product delivery controls as suggested by PRINCE 2.
2. *Will it be successful?* Which requires the identification of stakeholders and their expectations. It also needs market intelligence and information about the competition.
3. *What market segment will it satisfy?* This is related to the second question, but looks at the functionality of the product, the benefits it will supply, and the market segment it is aimed at.

These questions are the most important, because they usually have the greatest impact on the value of the project's product, but they are also the most difficult to gather data on and answer, because they are qualitative rather than quantitative.

QUESTIONS OF SCHEDULE
This of course is the classic question, 'When will it be ready?' Associated questions relate to the delivery of prototypes, the achievement of milestones and of stage reviews.

QUESTIONS OF COST AND RESOURCE
These questions relate to how much money is required, what other resources are required and when. Remember from Chapter 8 that I said that knowing the timing of the expenditure is as important as knowing the total expenditure.

Design of systems
In order to meet these requirements, a system should have two components, the planning system and the control system, and Figure 15.5 shows the former inside the latter. The control system has three major components answering each of the three sets of questions above:

– the client's requirements answering the questions of outcome
– the management system, answering the questions of when, and issuing work-to lists and processing turnaround documents (Chapter 12)
– the resource monitoring systems.

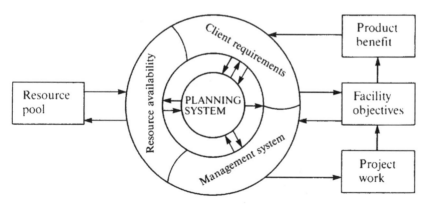

Figure 15.5   The fully integrated PMIS and its links to the context of projects

The planning system may have many components, interfacing with these three control systems. Figure 15.6 shows 16, together with history files. Figure 15.7 shows three major components of a system for programme

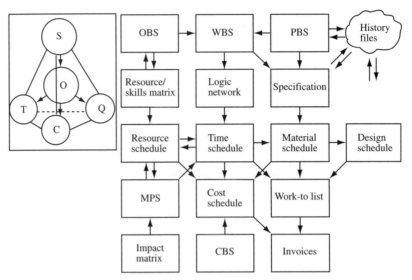

Figure 15.6 Modules contained in the planning systems of an integrated, modular PMIS

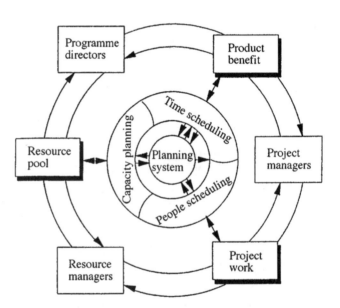

Figure 15.7 Information-systems requirement of programme management

management, the capacity planner, the project management system, and the people and resource scheduler. These three components are in fact all incorporated within the systems proposed in Figures 15.5 and 15.6. ABTI, the providers of Project Workbench take a slightly different approach (Figure 15.8). Their system has a project management system, with capacity planning just done at the highest level of work breakdown, and a people management system. These two systems are joined by their repository, where all the data is held. The project management system is used to plan individual projects and programmes (based as much as possible on historical data). The project information is fed into the repository, which produces work-to lists for individuals. These are presented in the form of predicted time sheets. Individuals then feed in their progress data in the form of completed time sheets, which re-enters the repository and is converted into project progress data. Their repository is able to take project planning data from other systems such as Microsoft Project 98.

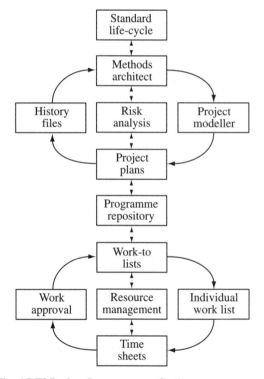

Figure 15.8   The ABTI Project Improvement Cycle

15.5 Types of package

There are several types of project management information system available.

Networking systems

The very simplest systems perform only critical path analysis (CPA). They give you activities, with durations and dependencies, and calculate early dates, late dates and float.

PERT systems

The majority of systems are based on the Programme Evaluation and Review Technique (PERT):

– *Programme*: a networking system calculates the programme or time scales
– *Evaluation*: the system performs what-if analysis to calculate various alternatives
– *Review*: the system tracks progress for monitoring and control purposes.

Some systems calculate and track the time scale only (as the name implies). The more advanced also maintain resource and cost data. Very few perform status accounting, *the most important question to be answered*. The PERT systems come with given data and reporting structures, but the best allow these to be tailored very simply to the users' requirements. The better ones also allow data to be imported and exported to database management systems, such as Microsoft Excel and Access, or Oracle or dBase, and so you can develop additional functionality if you require it. The very best cover almost all of what you require, with the possible exception of design and material management. These systems are designed to be used with small- to medium-sized projects, and programmes of SMPs. Examples are ABTI's Project Workbench, Microsoft Project 98, CA's Super Project Expert, and WS Technology's Open Plan. There are also tailored versions of Artemis which fall into this category. ABTI's Project Workbench and Microsoft Project 98 are the two market leaders.

Cost and resource management systems

These systems are based around the C/SCSC methodology, the central column in Figure 1.4. They do for resource and cost what the PERT systems do for time. However, most now have a link into a networking or PERT system. The two main examples are Cascade produced by Mantix, and WS Technology's Cobra. Obviously ABTI's Repository is performing much of this functionality.

Application generators

These systems come with the ability for the user to develop whatever functionality they want. The system provides core project management functionality, but the user is able to develop additional functionality in the database provided with the system. These systems tend to be used on large, heavy engineering projects where significant data management is required. Artemis is the market leader, which comes with its own database language. Primavera is also a significant player, and is written in Oracle. Open Plan/Cobra are effectively application generators as they are written in dBase and other proprietary database systems. Just to show that the boundaries are disappearing now, because Microsoft Project runs in Access and Excel, you can in effect treat it as an application generator. The main distinction now really is between systems best designed for use on programmes of small- to medium-sized projects and those designed for use with large, heavy engineering projects.

Distributed systems

Since most systems are now designed to run on PCs, they can be run as stand alones, or on a local or wide area network. Anyone who has access to the LAN or WAN, whether directly connected or accessing via a telephone line, can access the programme plan held on the central server. Often, people on remote sites will have a slimmed down version of the system, providing work-to lists and turn-around documents only, whereas the system on the central server, maintained by the Project Support Office will carry the full functionality. There is now a move to systems operating over the INTERNET or in-company INTRANETs. The development of these systems must be the most significant development expected in the late 1990s and early 2000s, but given the significant changes in the systems in the six years since I wrote the first edition of this book, I am not going to look too far into the future.

15.6 Choosing and implementing systems

Figure 15.9 is a procedure (project plan) for implementing a PMIS. (Although the systems have changed beyond recognition in six years, the basic approach is unchanged.) There are essentially four areas of work:

– diagnosis and business planning
– implementation and Improvement projects
– implementation of best practice in project management
– selection and implementation of the system.

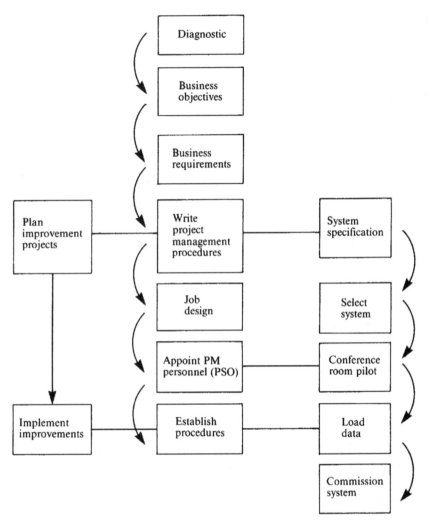

Figure 15.9   Procedure for implementing a PMIS

Diagnosis and business planning

Before you begin to select a system, you must decide its purpose, and how it will be used. There are three steps to this process:

1. *Conduct a diagnostic audit*: This is the vital first step. You must know what you do now, and the strengths and weaknesses of that approach. There are two reasons. Implementing the system will be an opportunity for implementing good project management practice, so you must know

where possible areas of improvement are. However, at the other extreme, you may set yourself an ideal, which is unachievable. It is like asking someone the way to the station, and he says, 'I wouldn't start here!' Unfortunately, you do start here, and so you must know what is a realistic target. The diagnostic audit should be conducted against some definition of good practice, which may form the basis of a procedures manual later.

2. *Set business objectives*: Then, or in parallel, you should define what you want to use the system to achieve. I say in parallel, because it might be worth while to define the ideal, before it is tempered by reality, but the final objectives must be set against the findings of the diagnostic.

3. *Write a statement of requirements*: The SOR is the strategy of how the system will be used, derived from the business objectives. It defines the major stages of managing projects (Part 3). For each stage it defines the purpose and objectives of the stage, the inputs and outputs, and the major processes. The SOR is the document on which the other three areas implementation are based.

Improvement projects

The diagnostic audit may have highlighted some major weaknesses in the practice of project management, and these can be eliminated through improvement projects. These must be planned and implemented like any other organizational development project, according to the principles of this book. The SOR defines the purpose and objectives of the improvement projects. There are three particular improvement projects:

– implementation of project management procedures
– selection and implementation of the PMIS
– training personnel in the procedures and system.

The first two of these are the other two areas of work. The third is common to both.

Project management procedures

I said above that the implementation of an information system can be an opportunity for improving the operation of the business, especially if a packaged solution which represents best practice is used. A PMIS need be no different. The are four steps to this process:

1. *Write a procedures manual*: The procedures manual will be derived from the SOR, and will therefore presumably be based on the procedures followed in the diagnostic audit. (The structure of a manual was described in Section 15.2.)

392 HANDBOOK OF PROJECT-BASED MANAGEMENT

2. *Establish the project management function*: The procedures will imply certain project management roles to be fulfilled. These may be simply project managers, or it may include, project leaders, planners, project accountants and administrators. In the latter case, it may be worth while to establish a Project Support Office (Section 14.5). Job descriptions should be written for all the roles. PRINCE 2 gives guidance on this.

3. *Obtain competent personnel*: The jobs must then be filled. Similar jobs may already exist, with incumbents. They may be able to continue as they are, or they may require some training. Alternatively, it may be necessary to recruit and train new people.

4. *Implementation the procedures*: Implement first on a pilot project. This should be a project which has started, but is less than a third finished. They should then be implemented on all new projects, and those which have reached no more than a certain stage of completion. It is usually not worth while implementing them on projects which are more than two-thirds complete, or have less than six months to run (depending on the size of the projects).

Selecting and implementing the system

This is the *raison d'être* of the whole process, and yet the last thing to be considered. However, that is the right approach. You must make sure that you have good project management practice defined and implemented before you rush into using a PMIS, otherwise its use will become an end in itself. The steps in selecting and implementing the system are:

1. *Design and selection*: Working from the SOR, you develop a functional design, system design and detail design of the PMIS. You choose a shortlist of systems against the functional design. You then do a thorough analysis of the shortlisted systems against the systems design. This analysis requires significant input from the vendors, and so out of fairness to them you should limit your shortlist to two, three or, at most, four systems. Table 15.6 contains a list of possible features and selection criteria of the system. A package is chosen, and bespoke work required to raise it to the requirements of the detailed design is fully defined and quantified.

2. *Conference room pilot*: The system is tested on trial data, and the users familiarize themselves with it, making suggestions as to how it might be improved to meet their needs. You need to be careful, though, to make sure you do not make too many changes and thereby making the system too expensive, or worse still, unusable.

3. *Load the pilot project*: The same pilot project as for implementation of the procedures should be used if possible.

4. *System implementation*: The system will be implemented in parallel with the procedures. The same criteria for selecting projects on which to implement it should be used.

Table 15.6 Possible features and selection criteria of a PMIS

Feature/criteria	Comment
Overall design	User friendliness
Activity/project/programme capacities	
Input features	By network, bar chart, PBS, etc.
Output features	Nature of reports and ability to tailor
Network notation	Precedence every time
Date and calendar formats	
Resources and cost information	
Risk analysis and management	
Hardware requirements	
Size of project	Small/Medium/Large/Major
Robustness of supplier	User base/support offered

15.7 Assumptions and risks

I shall close this chapter by considering some of the assumptions and risks in using a PMIS. The major risks, as I have stated, are that the system will be overly complicated for the need, that people will use a system only because they think that it is an essential part of project management even when it is not necessary, and that the system will take over from reality, what the system is saying will be given more credence than actual events. Even if all these are conquered, there are other issues:

HISTORICAL RECORDS

One use of the systems is to store historical data. Building up a library of past records may help in project auditing, but will certainly help the project manager when planning new projects. They can reuse data on previous, similar work packages, thus saving a lot of time in planning.

JUSTIFYING THE INVESTMENT IN THE SYSTEM

It is difficult to justify the investment in a PMIS, although some research is now being done.[7,8] Because every project is unique, you cannot say whether the project would have been less efficient if the system was not used. It is only if the organization is undertaking several projects you can look to trends. A company I worked with in the food-canning industry implemented a PMIS in its research and development department, and found that productivity of their

R&D staff increased by 6 per cent in two years. Similarly, if a company knows that all its projects are three months late, and it expects an internal rate of return of 25 per cent on its projects, then late completion is loosing it 6 per cent of its spend on projects annually. For every month on average which an organization could reduce the duration of its projects, it could afford to spend 2 per cent of its annual project spend on a PMIS.

PROLIFERATION OF SOFTWARE

There has been phenomenal growth in the number of project management software packages available on the market. There are probably now in excess of 200. This has contributed to the confusion in the market. In addition, the prospective purchaser is not only presented with this vast range of packages, but is also faced the unique range of features which each package offers. It has been suggested that a Pareto principle applies: 90 per cent of the users resort to only 10 per cent of the facilities offered by project management software; and only 10 per cent seem to make use of most functions.[8] But the reason for this may well be poor vendor support or inadequate training.

INADEQUATE TRAINING

Another factor hindering use of the systems is lack of training. In many organizations, information systems are the domain of the IT department. Microcomputers may be beginning to have some impact on their lives. However, their use in project management requires more than self-help, but the number of formal courses in the use of PMISs remains very limited. Furthermore, project managers who have learnt how to use the systems may get very little training beyond their initial introduction, and so will not learn how to use the advanced features of the systems, as described above.

INFORMATION OVERLOAD

Another concern is the amount of information generated by these packages. This is reminiscent of the problems of the early mainframe programmes. However, effective use of the WBS should overcome this difficulty.

15.8 Summary

1. Procedures manuals are an essential part of quality assurance. Their purpose is to provide:
   - a guide to the management process
   - consistency of approach
   - company resource planning
   - common vocabulary

– training of new staff
– demonstration of procedures to clients
– quality accreditation.

2. Procedures manuals show the process of converting inputs to outputs throughout the project management life cycle. In order to do this, the contents should be:
– introduction
– statement of project strategy
– management processes
– supporting procedures
– blank forms and examples.

3. Various standard procedures exist, including PRINCE 2, ISO 10 006 and the PMI *Guide to the PMBoK*. These tend to give advice on the design and contents of procedures rather than offer prescriptive solutions.

4. Project Management Information Systems offer computer support to project management procedures and to data management. The questions that a PMIS must answer are:
– questions of outcome
– questions of schedule
– questions of cost and resource.

5. The essential elements of a PMIS are the planning system and the control system. The planning system holds the data; the control system answers the questions.

6. Types of package available include:
– network systems
– PERT systems
– cost and resource management systems
– application generators.

7. The essential steps in implementing a system are:
– diagnosis and business planning
– implementation of improvement projects
– implementation of best practice in project management
– selection and implementation of the system.

References

1. Turner, J.R. and Peymai, R., 'Organizing for change – the versatile approach', in *The Project Manager as Change Agent*, J.R. Turner, K.V. Grude and L. Thurloway (eds), McGraw-Hill, 1996.
2. A complete list of all the ISO and FDIS procedures relating to quality are given in Table 7.1.
3. CCTA, *PRINCE 2: Project Management for Business*, The Stationery Office, 1996.

4. Duncan, W.R. (ed.), *A Guide to the Project Management Body of Knowledge*, 3rd edn, Project Management Institute, 1996.
5. LBMS, *PROMPT II*, Learmonth and Burchett Management Systems.
6. Graham, R.G., 'Influencing the organization, the power/value of information', in *The Project Manager as Change Agent*, J.R. Turner, K.V. Grude and L. Thurloway (eds), McGraw-Hill, 1996.
7. Ibbs, C.W. and Kwak, Y.-H., *The Benefits of Project Management: Financial and organisational rewards to corporations*, Project Management Institute, 1997.
8. Webster, F., 'Vendor/user dialogue: PM1986 at Montreal', *Project Management Journal*, **18** (3), 1987.

16
Project health checks and audits

16.1 Introduction

I introduced audits in Section 7.3 as a way of controlling the management processes, and checking that they are of sufficient quality to deliver a successful outcome. In this chapter I describe the use of audits and health checks. Audits can be informal, conducted by the project team on themselves, or they can be more formal conducted by people external to the project team, either experts from within the organization or external consultants. The former I call *health checks*, the latter *audits*.

Audits have been used throughout history as a way of ensuring that operations are being conducted in a correct way. There are records of audits conducted in Egypt during the time of the Pharaohs, 4000 years ago. We are most familiar with financial audits, and these are usually conducted in a policing sense, to ensure that businesses are being conducted:

- in the best interests of the shareholders (or creditors)
- in a way which will ensure achievement of the objectives
- in accordance with the law, and without fraudulent activity.

Financial audits must be conducted by independent qualified accountants. Organizations may also conduct detailed reviews of their non-financial activities, or the activities of suppliers or subcontractors, for very similar reasons. These 'audits' may be conducted by internal staff or external consultants, with the objective of ensuring:

- there are no mistakes in the design of the activities
- the work done will deliver the organization's objectives
- activities are undertaken in an efficient way learning from past successes and failures.

Purpose of project audits

Audits are conducted on projects for all these reasons, and they may be conducted at several points throughout a project.

CHECK THAT THE DESIGN IS CORRECT

One of the primary contributing factors to the success of a project is to ensure it is correctly established and designed in the first place (Sections 4.5, 5.3 and Chapter 11). This means that:

– the purpose of the project has been correctly identified
– the objectives set will deliver that purpose
– the facility chosen will achieve those objectives
– the facility is designed in accordance with the inherent assumptions
– the design information used, including any research data, is valid.

An audit conducted at key milestones, especially at the end of proposal and initiation or design and appraisal, can confirm that the project, as designed so far, meets all of these requirements.

ENSURE THE QUALITY OF THE MANAGEMENT PROCESSES

A second major contributor to success is the use of qualified management processes. A project which is well designed, but badly managed, can fail to achieve its purpose. A project which is well designed and well managed is more likely to be successful. An audit can be conducted at any time during a project to determine whether it is being managed in accordance with best practice, and that usually means in accordance with defined procedures, perhaps as set out in a manual. Such an audit is most effective when conducted about one-third of the way into a stage, as the pattern of management has been set by that time, but work is not so far advanced that mistakes cannot be recovered.

LEARN FROM PAST SUCCESS

If a project has gone particularly well, perhaps better than recent projects, then a review can help to identify what was done properly. That can be recorded as a basis for future projects. These reviews are usually best conducted at the end of a project, although it can then be difficult to gain people's commitment as they are keen to move on, as discussed in Section 13.5. However, it is usually easier to get people to review their successes than their failures.

AVOID PAST MISTAKES

Likewise, if a project has gone particularly badly, then it is usually very instructive, perhaps even mandatory, to determine what mistakes were made, so that they can be avoided in the future. However, people can be very defensive in these circumstances (unsurprisingly). My own experience is that there is usually a string of excuses about why this project was unique, and the mistakes would not normally occur, even if the project is one of a series of failures.

Types of project audit

In order to achieve these objectives, three types of project audit are conducted.

PROJECT EVALUATION AUDIT

A project evaluation audit is an independent check of the feasibility or design studies. It is an enforced review of the investment appraisal as it currently stands, and the assumptions on which it is based. It is conducted by independent auditors, often called *red teams*, to see whether they reach the same conclusion as the original design team. The need for this type of audit was described in Section 7.3. The audit covers similar ground as the original feasibility or design study (Chapter 11). The auditors check the validity of the data used in the original studies, and the conclusions drawn from it (Section 11.4). Often the original design team will be over-optimistic, because they have a certain subjective commitment to the project. It is important that the auditors are truly independent, and that they do not share the same commitment to the project, or they may merely repeat the mistakes.

INTERNAL AUDIT

An internal audit, or health check, is a quality control check of the management processes, conducted either by independent auditors, or by the project team, to ensure best practice is being followed, and hence that the project as defined will be delivered to quality, cost and time. (Usually only the design or execution stages will be audited.) When conducted by external consultants, it will be conducted about one-third into the stage. The project team may also make random spot checks on themselves, to ensure that they are maintaining best practice. Such as internal audit, conducted by the project team, we call here a '*health check*'. An audit will cover everything from progress of the work itself, to the procurement and marshalling of materials and resources. The auditors will check:

- the validity of the data being gathered
- how it is being used to generate management reports
- how those reports are being used to take timely and effective action, to ensure that the project meets its quality, cost and time targets.

POST-COMPLETION AUDIT

The successes and failures of a project are reviewed in a post-completion audit. The scope of a post-completion audit may be very similar to an internal audit, but now the auditors are checking past practice with the knowledge, in hindsight, of how the project actually turned out. A post-completion audit may be conducted:

- as an informal review by the project manager and their team
- at a formal debriefing meeting
- 'down the pub'
- as a detailed review by external (independent) consultants.

In this chapter I describe how to conduct audits and health checks. First I describe two health checks, the *projectivity diagnostic* and the *success/ failure diagnostic*. The first checks that the working environment supports project-based working, and the second checks that the project has been established to deliver success in accordance with the principles and strategic approach of Chapter 4. I then describe how to conduct a formal internal or post-completion audit.

16.2 The projectivity diagnostic

In this and the next section, I introduce two diagnostic techniques that the project team can use on themselves to check that the working environment supports project-based management, and to undertake a quality check on the management processes they are using to manage their project. I want to stress that both of these diagnostics are primarily qualitative. The idea is to identify areas of weakness, but also, and more importantly, to identify differences of opinion within the project team in its widest sense. That is:

- differences of opinion between the various groupings and factions in the project team, including sponsors, users, designers and managers
- differences of opinion between the members of these various groupings.

The diagnostic questionnaires ask people to rank their views about various issues on a scale of 1 to 6. We then use simple arithmetic calculations, spreads, variances, means and differences, to highlight where differences of opinion lie, and where weaknesses in the approach to the project or project working within the organization lie. However, these calculations are designed to focus attention, not calculate some answer, like the number 42, which will determine whether or not your project will be successful. Having undertaken the diagnostic exercise, you will want to spend as much time working on determining why differences of opinion exist and then to eliminate them, as you will spend trying to reduce the impact of areas of weakness.

The first is the *projectivity diagnostic* (Table 16.1). This can be conducted at any time to assess the health of project working in the organization, or in the start-up stages of an individual project to induct people into project-based ways of working. I introduced the concept of projectivity in Section 3.5 (Figure 3.4), to represent an organization's ability to achieve its development objectives through project work. Organizations with low projectivity are unable to deliver projects effectively, and therefore consistently fail to achieve their development objectives. The projectivity diagnostic is designed to help you identify how well projects are established, planned, organized, executed and controlled in your organization. More importantly, the projectivity diagnostic checks whether there is a common agreement on these questions by all the people involved in work on your project, on both sides of the projects/operations divide. This diagnostic is designed to help you:

– understand the culture and climate of project work in your organization
– focus on problem areas that need to be dealt with
– identify where improvements can be made to project working in your organization.

There are no right or wrong answers to the questions. For some of you it will be a worry if the responses are not what you expect. For instance, if the majority of people say they cannot clearly see the link between organizational strategy and projects, or if they think there are no established, clear principles and guidelines for project work, then that will be a cause for concern. However, this diagnostic is primarily designed to help you identify areas of agreement and disagreement in your project team (and we mean the project team in its widest sense).

Using the questionnaire
There are 106 questions, grouped into five main problem areas. These are areas identified by Grude[1] as those where projects consistently fail (Section 4.3):

– foundation and infrastructure for project work
– planning and estimating
– organizing and cooperating
– controlling and leading
– executing and obtaining results.

However, when you give people the questionnaire to complete, you may not want to leave the questions grouped, but rather give them a sequential list, in order not to influence their thinking. The questionnaire asks people to rate each question on a scale of 1 to 6, where 1 = false and 6 = true. However, the questions are designed so that sometimes 1 indicates poor performance, and sometimes 6. This is so that people do not get into a routine of ticking every answer 4 to 5, but actually have to think about what the question is asking them. We recommend that you give the questionnaire to a wide variety of people within the organization:

- senior managers representing sponsors, champions and customers
- peer groups representing professional colleagues, resource providers, users and other stakeholders
- project workers, representing designers and implementers
- project managers.

Analysing the results

The results can be analysed in several ways, as follows:

WITHIN GROUPS

When analysing the results within groups, you will want to see whether the group:

- agrees on the organization's performance in all areas
- thinks that the organization's performance falls short in any areas.

These can be broken down, as follows:

1. *Agreement*: In looking to see whether the group agrees on the answers to questions, you will be looking to the spread of answers. I have allowed space for you to record two measures of spread:
   - The spread, S; the difference between the highest and lowest score for the group against that answer
   - The variance, V; calculated as $V = \sum (x - X)^2/N$,
   - where: x is the individual score
     N is the number of people in the group
     X is the mean score for that question, $X = \sum x/N$.
   Recording the answers in a spreadsheet, such as Excel or Lotus 123, will enable you to calculate the mean, spread and variance of the scores easily. I suggest you do not include the X, S and V columns on the questionnaires that you give to the people completing them; they are there to help you analyse the responses. Where there is a high spread, 3 or greater, at least some members of the team disagree about the response to that question. Where there is also a high variance, 2 or greater, there is fundamental disagreement among team members about the answer to the question. (A high spread but low variance indicates that

only one or two members of the team disagree with the majority opinion.) The reason for any disagreement is worth exploring, question by question, and can be made part of the team-building process. I have kept the mathematics simple, because we are interested in qualitative comparisons, not quantitative results or statistics. This is a qualitative exercise; the numbers are just a way of helping to focus attention. You do not need to worry about such things as confidence limits, because they are not relevant here.

2. *Performance*: You can analyse the results to see where they indicate poor performance. We have indicated the polarity, P, of each question, to show which end of the scale in your view indicates good performance (1 or 6). (Again we suggest you do not include this column on the questionnaires you give to the project team for completion.) You can compare the average answer to each question, X, to this polarity and calculate the difference, D, to determine where the team think the organization falls short in performance. A difference of 2 or 3 will indicate below average performance, and 4 to 5 poor performance. The reason why the team think the performance is below average or poor will be more interesting than the fact that they do, and exploring the reason can again be part of the team-building process.

3. *Problem areas*: By calculating the average of the differences, D, for all questions within each of the five problem areas, you can determine which problem areas the group considers are weaknesses of project management within the organization. Because you expect some questions to indicate acceptable performance, an average difference of 2 or 3 will indicate poor performance, and an average difference of 4 or 5 will indicate very poor performance.

BETWEEN GROUPS

You can repeat the comparisons between groups. Primarily, you will inspect the mean answers, X, question by question to see whether one of the groups differs from the other groups. Differences are quite likely between managers, team members, users and so on. Exploring the reasons for differences is more important than the existence of the differences. Similarly, you can inspect the overall results on the problems areas as more of a threat than do the other groups. (Obviously, if all of the groups view one of the questions or one of the problem areas as a threat, then that will be addressed in the comparisons within groups. Here we are only looking for differences between groups.)

Table 16.1 Projectivity diagnostic

No.	Statement	Score	X	S	V	P	D
	*Problem area 1: Foundation and infrastructure for project work*						

No.	Statement	Score	X	S	V	P	D
1.1	It is easy to see the relationship between our project and overall business plans	1 2 3 4 5 6				6	
1.2	We have established sufficiently clear principles and guidelines for project work	1 2 3 4 5 6				6	
1.3	Our principles and guidelines for project work are understood by all involved parties	1 2 3 4 5 6				6	
1.4	Our principles and guidelines for project work are accepted by all involved parties	1 2 3 4 5 6				6	
1.5	In our projects, the client/user roles and responsibilities are defined before start-up	1 2 3 4 5 6				6	
1.6	In our projects, the project team's roles and responsibilities are defined before start-up	1 2 3 4 5 6				6	
1.7	In our projects, the clients/users keep to agreed prioritizations (tasks/time/resources)	1 2 3 4 5 6				6	
1.8	Our project management is not very good at keeping to agreed prioritizations	1 2 3 4 5 6				6	
1.9	In our projects, line managers contribute loyally to decision processes according to their responsibility	1 2 3 4 5 6				6	
1.10	In our projects, line management keep to agreed time limits for decisions	1 2 3 4 5 6				6	
1.11	In our projects, line management quite often reverse decision that have been taken	1 2 3 4 5 6				1	
1.12	In our projects actual resources are committed as part of our planning process without line management being made aware	1 2 3 4 5 6				6	
1.13	Management makes sure that agreed resources for project work are made available at the right time	1 2 3 4 5 6				6	
1.14	Available resources for project work are taken into consideration in our business plans	1 2 3 4 5 6				6	
1.15	Our management plan so that development personnel do not get tied up in maintenance	1 2 3 4 5 6				6	
1.16	Our management plan so personnel are relieved of operational tasks when given project tasks	1 2 3 4 5 6				6	
1. 17	We have sufficient/adequate tools and methods for planning projects	1 2 3 4 5 6				6	
1.18	We have sufficient/adequate tools and methods for organizing projects	1 2 3 4 5 6				6	
1.19	We have sufficient/adequate tools and methods for reporting and controlling progress	1 2 3 4 5 6				6	

Table 16.1   *(continued)*

No.	Statement	Score	X	S	V	P	D
	Problem area 1: Foundation and infrastructure for project work						
1.20	We have sufficient/adequate tools and methods for reporting and controlling quality	1 2 3 4 5 6				6	
1.21	We have sufficient/adequate tools and methods for reporting and controlling time	1 2 3 4 5 6				6	
1.22	We have sufficient/adequate tools and methods for reporting and controlling cost	1 2 3 4 5 6				6	
1.23	We have clear policies/procedures for prioritizing between projects	1 2 3 4 5 6				6	
1.24	We have clear policies/procedures for handling prioritization problems between operational tasks and project tasks	1 2 3 4 5 6				6	
1.25	It happens quite often in our projects that the project team and the clients/users do not have a common understanding of the deliverables	1 2 3 4 5 6				1	
1.26	In our projects, everybody has the necessary knowledge of the procedures/methods/tools we use for project management	1 2 3 4 5 6				6	
1.27	I have the necessary skills to plan and organize projects	1 2 3 4 5 6				6	
1.28	I have the necessary skills to monitor and control projects	1 2 3 4 5 6				6	
1.29	I have the necessary skills to handle people's relationships and resolve conflicts	1 2 3 4 5 6				6	
1.30	Our project procedures/methods/tools are bureaucratic and tedious	1 2 3 4 5 6				1	
1.31	Our project procedures/methods/tools help us obtain commitment from all parties involved	1 2 3 4 5 6				6	
1.32	Our project procedures/methods/tools ensure goal direction and effective use of resources	1 2 3 4 5 6				6	
	Sum						
	Average						

Table 16.1   Projectivity diagnostic (*continued*)

No.	Statement	Score	X	S	V	P	D
	Problem area 2: Planning and estimating						
2.1	Our overall project plans are understandable and give a good overview/description to all relevant parties, not just the specialists	1 2 3 4 5 6				6	
2.2	We make project plans that are too generic	1 2 3 4 5 6				1	
2.3	We make project plans that are much too detailed and activity oriented	1 2 3 4 5 6				1	
2.4	Our plans are tailor-made for the task and focus on what is unique/important for progress	1 2 3 4 5 6				6	
2.5	Our project plans have imbedded quality control	1 2 3 4 5 6				6	
2.6	We have layered planning, where we focus on results and activities separately	1 2 3 4 5 6				6	
2.7	Our plans focus too much on completion date, too little on intermediate results/dates	1 2 3 4 5 6				1	
2.8	We often change our plans during the project	1 2 3 4 5 6				1	
2.9	Our plans always make it easy to control the achievement of intermediate and end results	1 2 3 4 5 6				6	
2.10	Our project plans ensure that we do things in the right sequence, so that we do not have to do things over again	1 2 3 4 5 6				6	
2.11	Our project plans secure effective utilization of resources	1 2 3 4 5 6				6	
2.12	In our project plans, we build quality assurance of the process as well as results	1 2 3 4 5 6				6	
2.13	We have a planning process that stimulates creativity and finding new solutions	1 2 3 4 5 6				6	
2.14	Our planning processes invite involved parties to participate and stimulate communication	1 2 3 4 5 6				6	
2.15	All involved parties are 100 per cent committed to our plans once they are agreed	1 2 3 4 5 6				6	
2.16	We have formalized estimating procedures to ensure maximum quality and commitment	1 2 3 4 5 6				6	
2.17	Our project plans always have a realistic completion date	1 2 3 4 5 6				6	
2.18	Our recourse and cost estimates are unrealistic	1 2 3 4 5 6				1	
2.19	It sometimes happens we change our time and cost estimates because we don't 'like' them	1 2 3 4 5 6				1	
2.20	We often set time and cost estimates too low for 'selling' reasons	1 2 3 4 5 6				1	
2.21	In our projects, goals for individual's work are not precise	1 2 3 4 5 6				1	

Table 16.1   *(continued)*

No.	Statement	Score	X	S	V	P	D
	Problem area 2: Planning and estimating						
2. 22	In project planning, we often over-estimate our own and other people's competence and skills	1 2 3 4 5 6				1	
2.23	In project planning, we often over-estimate our own and other people's available time and capacity	1 2 3 4 5 6				1	
2.24	With us, everybody can participate in estimating and planning their own work	1 2 3 4 5 6				6	
2.25	With us, everybody feels a personal responsibility for their own estimates	1 2 3 4 5 6				6	
2.26	In estimating we often do not account for non-productive time (illness, interruptions, etc.)	1 2 3 4 5 6				6	
2.27	In project planning, we often 'forget' activities	1 2 3 4 5 6				1	
	Sum						
	Average						

Table 16.1 Projectivity diagnostic (*continued*)

No.	Statement	Score	X	S	V	P	D
	Problem area 3: Organizing and cooperating						
3.1	In our projects, the right people are always involved in the right activities	1 2 3 4 5 6				6	
3.2	Key people are often not available for the project at the time when planned	1 2 3 4 5 6				1	
3.3	People on the project are often not motivated	1 2 3 4 5 6				1	
3.4	We lack communication procedures/channels within our projects (all involved parties)	1 2 3 4 5 6				1	
3.5	We lack communication procedures and channel between projects	1 2 3 4 5 6				1	
3.6	In our projects, we have agreed and formalized the flow of information before start-up	1 2 3 4 5 6				6	
3.7	We organize our projects so that we secure effective consulting and hearing processes	1 2 3 4 5 6				6	
3.8	We organize our projects so that we secure effective decision-making processes	1 2 3 4 5 6				6	
3.9	Our way of organizing projects ensures maximum flexibility of human resources	1 2 3 4 5 6				6	
3.10	Nobody complains about lack of information in our projects	1 2 3 4 5 6				6	
3.11	In our projects, everybody knows and accepts their own role and responsibility	1 2 3 4 5 6				6	
3.12	Nobody knows what other people are doing on the project	1 2 3 4 5 6				1	
3.13	We very seldom have conflicts within the team that are the result of bad cooperation	1 2 3 4 5 6				6	
3.14	We seldom have conflicts with clients/users that are the result of bad cooperation	1 2 3 4 5 6				6	
3.15	Our projects are ineffective because too many people/functions are involved	1 2 3 4 5 6				1	
3.16	In our projects, responsibility for tasks and decisions is always connected directly to individuals, so there is no doubt	1 2 3 4 5 6				6	
3.17	We are organized to use the shortest possible route of communication between two persons	1 2 3 4 5 6				6	
3.18	In our projects, the project organization is more a formality than for real cooperation	1 2 3 4 5 6				1	
3.19	We are organized for resolving conflicts when they arise	1 2 3 4 5 6				1	
	Sum						
	Average						

Table 16.1 Projectivity diagnostic (*continued*)

No.	Statement	Score	X	S	V	P	D
	Problem area 4: Controlling and leading						
4.1	In our projects, reporting has no purpose because it is never used for anything	1 2 3 4 5 6				1	
4.2	Reporting is used to watch team members	1 2 3 4 5 6				1	
4.3	Reporting is used in our projects to badger team members	1 2 3 4 5 6				1	
4.4	Reporting in our projects is used to discuss constructively necessary corrective action	1 2 3 4 5 6				6	
4.5	Our project plans are not arranged so that we can report against them for monitoring	1 2 3 4 5 6				1	
4.6	In our company, the project managers do not have the necessary authority	1 2 3 4 5 6				1	
4.7	Project managers are too concerned with details of the technical content of the project	1 2 3 4 5 6				1	
4.8	The project managers are too pedantic	1 2 3 4 5 6				1	
4.9	Project managers will always try to cover up the problems to show a successful façade	1 2 3 4 5 6				1	
4.10	The project managers spend too little time managing the project	1 2 3 4 5 6				1	
4.11	The project managers cannot lead planning processes that result in realistic plans	1 2 3 4 5 6				1	
4.12	The project managers are unable to follow up methodically	1 2 3 4 5 6				1	
4.13	Project managers are unable to inspire others	1 2 3 4 5 6				1	
4.14	In our projects, we have periodical meetings with fixed monitoring procedures that always result in concrete decisions on progress	1 2 3 4 5 6				6	
4.15	By monitoring our plans we are always able to see the need for corrective measures in time	1 2 3 4 5 6				6	
4.16	When we are not able to take corrective action it is always the client/users' fault	1 2 3 4 5 6				1	
	Sum						
	Average						

Table 16.1 Projectivity diagnostic (*continued*)

No.	Statement	Score	X	S	V	P	D
	Problem area 5: Project execution and delivering results						
5.1	Due to our way of working and use of methods we are good at getting people we are not familiar with working together	1 2 3 4 5 6				1	
5.2	In our projects, we use complicated methods too often	1 2 3 4 5 6				1	
5.3	In our organization, everybody has their own way of doing things	1 2 3 4 5 6				1	
5.4	Our projects are often subject to uncontrolled changes of scope, objectives and goals	1 2 3 4 5 6				1	
5.5	Our projects lack formal start-ups	1 2 3 4 5 6				1	
5.6	Our projects lack formal close-outs	1 2 3 4 5 6				1	
5 7	Lack of documentation is a frequent problem	1 2 3 4 5 6				1	
5.8	Insufficient quality control is a problem	1 2 3 4 5 6				1	
5.9	We often deliver an inferior quality result	1 2 3 4 5 6				1	
5.10	Our clients/users often report that they are pleased with the way we conduct our work	1 2 3 4 5 6				6	
5.11	We often deliver a superior quality result	1 2 3 4 5 6				6	
5.12	Our clients/users often report that they are pleased with the results we deliver	1 2 3 4 5 6				6	
	Sum						
	Average						

16.3 The success/failure diagnostic

The second health check is based on the research by Wateridge,[2] into the success or failure of projects, described in Section 4.2. The health check is contained in Table 16.2. There are 85 questions in all, in five parts. The purpose of the five parts is as follows:

- Part 1 helps you identify appropriate success criteria for your project
- Part 2 helps you identify what success factors you should focus on to achieve those criteria
- Part 3 checks you are using appropriate tools and techniques for the management of your project
- Part 4 checks that you have an appropriate range of skills in the project team
- Part 5 helps you identify how well the project is being executed and managed.

The main emphasis again is on checking the consistency of view of all the members of the project team and stakeholders. Indeed, there are no right and wrong answers to part 1. However, once you have identified the agreed success criteria, Table 16.3 helps you identify what success factors ought to be used to deliver those criteria, so that you can check consistency of answers between parts 1 and 2. The diagnostic can be given to a similar range of people as the projectivity diagnostic, and the answers analysed in a similar way.

Table 16.2 Success/failure diagnostic

No.	Statement	Score	X	S	V	P	D
Part 1: Success criteria							
1.1	The success criteria for the project are defined	1 2 3 4 5 6				6	
1.2	The success criteria for the project are agreed	1 2 3 4 5 6				6	
1.3	I believe the success criteria are appropriate	1 2 3 4 5 6				6	
1.4	The project should achieve quality constraints	1 2 3 4 5 6				6	
1.5	The project should be a commercial success	1 2 3 4 5 6				6	
1.6	The users should be happy	1 2 3 4 5 6				6	
1.7	The sponsors should be happy	1 2 3 4 5 6				6	
1.8	The project team should be happy	1 2 3 4 5 6				6	
1.9	The project meets its stated objectives	1 2 3 4 5 6				6	
1.10	The system should achieve its purpose	1 2 3 4 5 6				6	
1.11	The project should be delivered on time	1 2 3 4 5 6				6	
1.12	The project should be delivered within budget	1 2 3 4 5 6				6	
1.13	The project should contribute to the organization's overall business strategy	1 2 3 4 5 6				6	
1.14	There is a clear relationship between the project and business plans and strategies	1 2 3 4 5 6				6	
1.15	The project team do not appreciate the important success criteria	1 2 3 4 5 6				1	
1.16	I am confident the project will be a success	1 2 3 4 5 6				6	
1.17	The project goals are clear to me	1 2 3 4 5 6				6	
1.18	The goals have been explained to the team	1 2 3 4 5 6				6	
1.19	I can explain the benefits of the project	1 2 3 4 5 6				6	
1.20	The project has unrealistic completion date	1 2 3 4 5 6				1	
	Sum						
	Average						

Table 16.2   Success/failure diagnostic (*continued*)

No.	Statement	Score	X	S	V	P	D
	Part 2: Success factors						
2.1	The estimates for the project are realistic	1 2 3 4 5 6				6	
2.2	Project estimates are generally over-optimistic	1 2 3 4 5 6				1	
2.3	Estimates were developed in consultation with the person allocated to the task	1 2 3 4 5 6				6	
2.4	The project has been planned strategically	1 2 3 4 5 6				6	
2.5	The project plans are understandable to all	1 2 3 4 5 6				6	
2.6	The project plans are often changed	1 2 3 4 5 6				1	
2.7	Our plans focus too much on the completion date and not on intermediate results/dates	1 2 3 4 5 6				1	
2.8	The project plan effectively utilizes resources	1 2 3 4 5 6				6	
2.9	I am happy with the plans and estimates	1 2 3 4 5 6				6	
2.10	The project participants are motivated well to achieve the project objectives	1 2 3 4 5 6				6	
2.11	Responsibilities are not well delegated	1 2 3 4 5 6				1	
2.12	The clients/users know their roles and responsibilities	1 2 3 4 5 6				6	
2.13	I am happy with the leadership shown by senior management	1 2 3 4 5 6				6	
2.14	I am happy with the leadership shown by project management	1 2 3 4 5 6				6	
2.15	Communication and consultation channels have been effectively set up	1 2 3 4 5 6				6	
2.16	There is poor communication between the project participants	1 2 3 4 5 6				1	
2.17	The users are involved effectively	1 2 3 4 5 6				6	
2.18	Communication channels are poor	1 2 3 4 5 6				1	
2.19	The project managers do not fully report project status to sponsors/users' project teams	1 2 3 4 5 6				1	
2.20	Corrective measures are always taken in time when the project encounters problems	1 2 3 4 5 6				6	
2.21	All roles and responsibilities are well defined	1 2 3 4 5 6				6	
2.22	All parties are fully committed to the plan	1 2 3 4 5 6				6	
2.23	Resources are available at the right time	1 2 3 4 5 6				6	
2.24	Procedures for handling priorities are adequate	1 2 3 4 5 6				6	
2.25	Quality assurance is not a major aspect of the projects	1 2 3 4 5 6				1	
	Sum						
	Average						

Table 16.2   Success/failure diagnostic (*continued*)

No.	Statement	Score	X	S	V	P	D
	Part 3: Tools, techniques and methodologies						
3.1	The tools, techniques and methods available for planning the project are adequate	1 2 3 4 5 6				6	
3.2	The tools, techniques and methods available for controlling the project are adequate	1 2 3 4 5 6				6	
3.3	The tools, techniques and methods available for organizing the project are adequate	1 2 3 4 5 6				6	
3.4	I agree that the tools, techniques and methods used are appropriate	1 2 3 4 5 6				6	
3.5	The development tools and methods are sufficient for the project	1 2 3 4 5 6				6	
3.6	The management tools and methods are sufficient for the project	1 2 3 4 5 6				6	
3.7	The development tools and methods are poorly applied on the project	1 2 3 4 5 6				1	
3.8	The management tools and methods are poorly applied on the project	1 2 3 4 5 6				1	
3.9	The chosen methodologies stifle creativity during the project	1 2 3 4 5 6				1	
3.10	There are established methods which are to be used	1 2 3 4 5 6				6	
3.11	These established methods are being used on this project	1 2 3 4 5 6				6	
3.12	I believe these methods are appropriate for the project	1 2 3 4 5 6				6	
3.13	There are computer-based tools available for this project	1 2 3 4 5 6				6	
3.14	Computer-based tools are being used effectively	1 2 3 4 5 6				6	
3.15	The project uses methods for assessing and managing risks	1 2 3 4 5 6				6	
	Sum						
	Average						

Table 16.2   Success/failure diagnostic (*continued*)

No.	Statement	Score	X	S	V	P	D
Part 4: Skills							
4.1	There are the necessary skills available to plan the project	1 2 3 4 5 6				6	
4.2	There are the necessary skills available to organize the project	1 2 3 4 5 6				6	
4.3	There are the necessary skills available to control the project	1 2 3 4 5 6				6	
4.4	There are the necessary skills available to develop the system	1 2 3 4 5 6				6	
4.5	Project management are unable to handle fully the human relations aspects	1 2 3 4 5 6				1	
4.6	Conflicts are resolved easily and satisfactorily	1 2 3 4 5 6				6	
4.7	The project plan over-estimates the skills and competences of the team	1 2 3 4 5 6				1	
4.8	Project management is astute in dealing with the politics of the project	1 2 3 4 5 6				6	
4.9	Project management is unable to inspire others	1 2 3 4 5 6				1	
4.10	Project management is good at getting the project team working together	1 2 3 4 5 6				6	
	Sum						
	Average						

Table 16.2 Success/failure diagnostic (*continued*)

No.	Statement	Score	X	S	V	P	D
	Part 5: Execution						
5.1	A life-cycle approach is being applied	1 2 3 4 5 6				6	
5.2	I agree with the life cycle used	1 2 3 4 5 6				6	
5.3	An effective start-up meeting was held for this project	1 2 3 4 5 6				6	
5.4	The right people are allocated to the project	1 2 3 4 5 6				6	
5.5	Project team members are carrying out appropriate activities	1 2 3 4 5 6				6	
5.6	Resources for the project are selected well	1 2 3 4 5 6				6	
5.7	There are no problem areas during the project	1 2 3 4 5 6				6	
5.8	I do not foresee any problem areas on the project	1 2 3 4 5 6				6	
5.9	The management of the project is excellent	1 2 3 4 5 6				6	
5.10	The project team has appropriate members at appropriate times	1 2 3 4 5 6				6	
5.11	The project risks were assessed at the outset of the project	1 2 3 4 5 6				6	
5.12	I believe that the assessments of risks are appropriate	1 2 3 4 5 6				6	
5.13	The project risks are not being managed well	1 2 3 4 5 6				1	
5.14	The deliverables are fully identified	1 2 3 4 5 6				6	
5.15	The deliverables are quality assured constantly	1 2 3 4 5 6				6	
	Sum						
	Average						

Table 16.3   Success factors delivering success criteria

Factors	Criteria								
	Commercial success	Meets user requirement	Meets budget	Happy users	Achieves purpose	Meets time scales	Happy sponsor	Meets quality	Happy team
Leadership	P			S			S		P
Motivation	P			S					P
Planning	P	S	P	S	S	P	S	S	S
Development method	P	S			S			P	
Monitoring	P		P			P			S
Management method									P
Delegation				S					P
Communication		P		P			P		
Clear objectives	S	P			P			S	
User involvement	S	P		P	P		P	P	
Management support	P		P	P		P	P		

Notes: P = primary success factor; S = secondary success factor

16.4 Conducting audits

A formal internal or post-completion audit will be conducted by people external to the project team. They may be experts from the organization or external consultants. An organization may arrange for itself to be checked. An internal audit will be conducted if the project is high risk. A post-completion audit may be undertaken if the project was a disaster. Alternatively, a client organization may arrange for an internal audit to be conducted on a contractor to ensure that they have implemented management approaches which meet the client's requirements. Although the client can sue for poor performance under the contract, sometimes that is a pyrrhic victory, because the contractor is already bankrupt.

There is a seven-step process to conducting an internal or post-completion audit:

1. Conduct interviews.
2. Analyse data.
3. Sample management reports.
4. Compare against a standard of best practice.
5. Repeat steps 1 to 4 as necessary.
6. Identify strengths and weaknesses of the management approach used.
7. Define opportunities for improvement.

CONDUCT INTERVIEWS

How you conduct interviews is a matter of style. You should always have some agenda of topics you wish to cover. Some people prefer to use a questionnaire, either a written one or a list of questions to be asked in a face-to-face interview. They work through the questions in methodical order. My own preference is for face-to-face interviews. I have a list of broad topics I wish to cover, which I explain to the interviewees at the start, but I then allow them to have free rein. Before closing the interview I ensure that all topics have been covered. I find that I learn more this way. Like Agatha Christie's detective, Hercule Poirot, I find that nobody can spin a consistent web of deceit, so if you let them talk, they must eventually tell you the truth. However, if you ask a set of closed questions, it is very easy for them to be economical with the truth. The topics covered should address the standards of good practice which you are using as your basis, as described below.

ANALYSE DATA

You should check the data being used on the project, to determine its validity. The data gathered must be relevant, give a true representation of progress, and be processed in such a way that errors are not introduced. For data which is handled manually, there can be errors of transcription. These are usually unwitting, but they can be deliberate. It is the norm to find that when data is entered manually into several computer systems it does not tally. I once spoke to a project manager in a firm of engineering contractors who said it was common for project accounts and company accounts to differ by up to 5 per cent, which he thought acceptable. To avoid errors of transcription, electronic means of data entry are used now, including bar coding. Furthermore, data may be entered into a single computer system, and distributed to all those where it is needed.

SAMPLE MANAGEMENT REPORTS

Reports used by managers to monitor progress are checked, to ensure that they are relevant and truly representative of progress, and that they enable the manager to spot divergences from the plan easily, so that they can take quick, effective action. The reports may be used by the project manager, work-package managers, or senior managers including the sponsor, champion or steering committee.

COMPARE AGAINST A STANDARD OF BEST PRACTICE

The information gathered about how the project is being managed is compared to a model or standard of best practice. Clearly, while you are conducting the early steps, you bear your model in mind. However, I find it is better to gather the information freely, because you then actually find out what is going on. If you merely ask whether the standard is being followed, it is very easy to miss the gaps, and it is very easy for people to mislead you. The standard of best practice may be a procedures manual used by the organization (Section 15.2), or a diagnostic procedure prepared by a firm of consultants. The standard will be hierarchical, presenting a series of important issues and questions at each stage throughout the life cycle of a project, or against each element of work in a standard work breakdown. This enables the auditor to focus on those areas which are important to the project at hand, rather than wading through a list of irrelevant questions. Figure 16.1 shows a seven-stage life cycle used for auditing contract management[3] (from the contractor's viewpoint), and gives key issues and the important parameters at each stage. Each stage of this life cycle is supported by a series of questions against each parameter. Figure 16.2 shows a work breakdown for auditing project management (from the owners viewpoint), and Example 16.1 gives a further breakdown under planning and budgeting. (This follows the contents of the Project Definition Report presented in Chapter 11.)

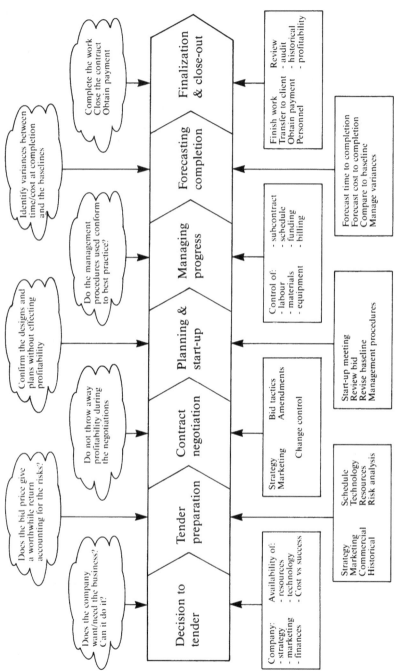

Figure 16.1   Life cycle followed in an audit procedure for contract management

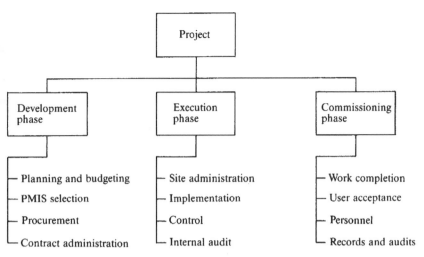

Figure 16.2   Work breakdown used in an audit procedure for project management

REPEAT STEPS 1 TO 4 AS NECESSARY

The comparison may raise further questions about the data, or the management processes used. Alternatively, you may realize that there are things which were not adequately covered during the initial interviews. You may need to return to one or more of steps 1 to 4, until you are satisfied everything has been adequately covered. My style is to conduct a preliminary set of interviews with senior managers to try to establish their views of the problems. As a result of that initial set of interviews, and my experience of similar organizations, I draw up a more detailed audit plan covering selected topics from the audit procedure. I then work through steps 1 to 4 according to that plan. After that first full time through, I typically have 80 per cent of the information I require. One or two more selected interviews may then give me all the information I can reasonably expect to get.

IDENTIFY STRENGTHS AND WEAKNESSES OF THE MANAGEMENT APPROACH

Through comparison of the information gathered with the audit procedure, you can identify strengths and weaknesses of the management approach used on projects in the organization, either on the project being audited or in general. I always believe it is important to identify both strengths and weaknesses, for two reasons:

1. You learn as much by reinforcing strengths as you do by eliminating weaknesses
2. People are more receptive to bad news if you start by giving them good

news. Even when reviewing an utter disaster it can make people feel that not everything they did was wrong

DEFINE OPPORTUNITIES FOR IMPROVEMENT

From the strengths and weaknesses you can identify areas where improvements can be made. Clearly you should aim to eliminate weaknesses. However, the application of the good points may be patchy, and so you can look to widen their scope, or you can find ways of improving their efficiency, and thereby make their application stronger still. Identified opportunities can be implemented via improvement projects (Section 15.6).

TRIMAGI COMMUNICATIONS
INFORMATION SYSTEMS DEPARTMENT
Project Management Audit Procedures

A10   PLANNING AND BUDGETING

A100   Introduction
A101   Undertake feasibility study
A102   Evaluate options
A103   Develop statement of purpose, scope and objectives
A104   Establish key performance criteria
A105   Choose organizational structure
A106   Define design/engineering tasks
A107   Define execution management tasks
A108   Develop milestone plan
A109   Develop responsibility chart
A110   Establish quality assurance procedures
A111   Develop project schedule
A112   Develop project budgets
A113   Obtain project financing
A114   Identify major risks
A115   Select project management system
A116   Establish project administration
A117   Staff Project Support Office
A118   Identify licensing/regulatory requirements

AUTHOR: JRT   ISSUE: A   DATE: 30 APRIL 200X

Example 16.1 Activities under the work package: *Planning and budgeting*

16.5 Summary

1. Project audits will be conducted to:
   – check the design

– ensure appropriate management processes are being used
– learn from previous successes and failures.
2. There are three types of audit:
    – project evaluation audits to check the validity of the design
    – internal audits to check that a project underway is sound
    – post-completion audits, usually to find why a project went wrong.
3. Informal internal audits conducted by the project team on themselves are called *health checks.*
4. There are two types of health check suggested:
    – the projectivity diagnostic, to check the working environment supports project-based management
    – the success/failure diagnostic, to ensure that the project has been established according to the principles of Chapter 4.
5. There are seven steps in conducting an internal or post-completion audit:
    – conduct interviews
    – analyse data
    – sample management reports
    – compare against standard of best practice
    – repeat steps 1 to 4 as necessary
    – identify strengths and weaknesses
    – define opportunities for improvement.

References

1. Andersen, E.S., Grude, K.V., Haug, T. and Turner, J.R., *Goal Directed Project Management*, 2nd edn, Kogan Page, 1995.
2. Wateridge, J.H., 'IT Projects: a basis for success', *International Journal of Project Management,* **13** (3), June 1995.
3. Derby, P., Stirling, D. and Turner, J.R., *The Contract Control Review Guide*, Coopers & Lybrand, 1986.

17

Project managers and their teams

17.1 Introduction

I shall conclude this part about project administration by considering project managers and their teams. These are the mandatory elements of both the project organization and the management procedures and systems; without them, nothing will happen. I have to admit that, with the exception of Chapter 3, all other chapters of this book are fairly clinical in their approach. Even in Chapter 6, where I describe the organization and talk about human resources you might be forgiven for thinking I was talking about androids rather than people. There are three reasons for this. First, to make progress it is necessary to describe an ideal approach. You may quickly recognize in any situation the ideal is not fully achievable, and so must be adapted to suit the circumstances. However, the ideal of best practice always remains a guiding light. Secondly, the way in which the ideal must be adapted is different in every situation; no two projects are identical, remember. I can therefore only describe the ideal, although I hope that by the series of anecdotes I have included I have shown how it was successful in some situations, but less successful in others. Thirdly, I am not an organizational psychologist or sociologist, only a project manager. I cannot give advice beyond my specialism. It is better for you to read specialist books on situational management.[1,2,3]

However, this book would be incomplete without considering project managers and their team. For managers to be able to deliver the project successfully, they must be able to manage the project team, and the individuals within that team. (This is the basis of an approach to management called *Action-Centred Leadership*,[4] Figure 17.1.) Indeed, effective teams are the essence of successful project management.[4,5,6]

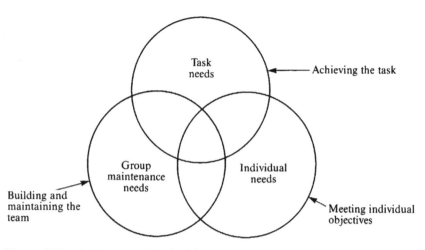

Figure 17.1   Action-centred leadership

I shall define a project team, identify different levels, and explain the processes of team formation and maintenance. I then identify how the manager can judge whether the team is performing effectively, and describe how to motivate the professionals working on a project team. My attention then switches to project managers. I describe their leadership role, and consider what makes an effective project manager, explaining the leadership styles they can adopt and the competencies they require to fulfil their role.

17.2 Project teams, formation and maintenance[a]

In forming the project team, the project manager brings together a group of people and develops among them a perceived common identity, so that they can work together using a set of common values or norms to deliver the project's objectives. Handy[7] says this concept of perceived identity is critical to team formation; without it the group of people remain a collection of random individuals. What sets project teams apart is that a group of people, who may never have worked together before, have to come together quickly and effectively in order to achieve a task which nobody has done before. The novelty, uniqueness, risk and transience are all inherent features of projects, as I showed in Chapter 1. Because the team is novel, it has no perceived identity, *ab initio*, and no set of values or norms to work to. It takes time to develop the identity and norms, which delays achievement of the team's objective. Futhermore, because the objective is novel, and carries considerable risk, it takes time to define, and, if the project is to be successful, this must be done before the team begins work. In this section, I describe the levels of people who make up the project team and the process of team formation and maintenance.

Levels of the project team
In any context, there are three levels of groups[5] (Figure 17.2):

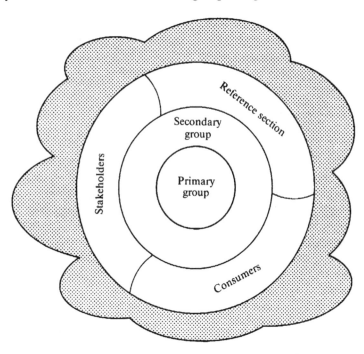

Figure 17.2   Three levels of groups

1. *The primary group*: the set of people who work face to face, and know everyone else in the group. They are the immediate team, or task force. They may work full time on the project for its duration, or be seconded part time. If seconded, then they may be physically seconded to the project office, or they may remain at their normal workplace, but be told that for the duration of their attachment to the project, they will take instructions from the project manager.
2. *The secondary group*: consisting of people who interact with people in the primary group, and contribute directly to their work, but are not part of the task force. In a project environment, these are the functions or disciplines which contribute through the matrix organization. However, they must be treated as part of the larger project team, if it is to be effective.

3. *The tertiary group*: people who have influence over the members of the primary and secondary teams, or who are affected by the work of the project, but have no direct contribution to the work. In Figure 17.2, I have shown the tertiary group split into three parts, those affected by the work of the project, the facility delivered, and the product of the facility, respectively. The first are reference groups, people who have an affect on the members of the primary and secondary groups. They may be family and friends, peer groups or professional bodies. The second group comprises people who live or work in the neighbourhood in which the facility is to be built (NIMBYs), or who will use or operate the facility after it is commissioned, or they may be people whose lives will be irreversibly changed (even made redundant) by the operation of the facility. The final group consists of the consumers, the people who will buy the product produced by the facility. (Sometimes they are the users, but often not.) The expectations of all of these groups of people must be managed if the project is to be successful, as they have a powerful ability to disrupt.

As an example, consider a team conducting an operation. The surgical team is the primary group. The secondary team is the department of the hospital within which it exists, and other departments such as pathology and X-ray. The reference group consists of the College of Surgeons, other surgeons within the hospital, the medical ethics committee and the hospital administration. The users and consumers are the patients and their families.

Team formation and maintenance

The members of a team must identify themselves with the team, and develop a common set of values, or norms, before they can work together effectively as a group. The process of forming a team identity and a set of values takes time. Project teams typically go through five stages of formation called forming, storming, norming, performing, mourning (Figure 11.1).

During these five stages, the teams motivation and effectiveness goes through a cycle in which it first decreases, before increasing to reach a plateau, and then either increasing or decreasing towards the end. The manager's role is to structure the team formation processes in such a way that this plateau is reached as quickly as possible, the effectiveness at the plateau is as high as possible, and the effectiveness is maintained right to the very end of the task.

1. *Forming*: the team comes together with a sense of anticipation and commitment. Their motivation is high at being selected for the project, their effectiveness moderate because they are unsure of each other.

2. *Storming*: as the team begins to work together, they find that they have differences about the best way of achieving the project's objectives, perhaps even differences about its overall aims. They also find that they have different approaches to working on projects. These differences may cause argument, or even conflict, in the team, which causes both the motivation and the effectiveness of the team to fall.

3. *Norming*: hopefully some accommodation is achieved. The team members will begin to reach agreement over these various issues. This will be by a process of negotiation, compromise and finding areas of commonality. As a result of this accommodation, the team begins to develop a sense of identity, and a set of norms or values. These form a basis on which the team members can work together, and effectiveness and motivation begin to increase again towards the plateau. Although norming is important for the ultimate performance of the team, it can have a negative side-effect. If the team norm too well, they can become very introspective, and isolate themselves from the rest of the organization. They work very well together, but produce something the rest of the organization do not want.

4. *Performing*: once performance reaches the plateau, the team can work together effectively for the duration of the project. The manager has a role of maintaining this plateau of performance. For instance, after the team has been together for too long, the members can begin to become complacent, and their effectiveness fall. If this happens the manager may need to change the structure or composition of the team.

5. *Mourning*: as the team reaches the end of its task, one of two things can happen. Either the effectiveness can rise, as the members make one concerted effort to complete the task, or it can fall, as the team members regret the end of the task and the breaking up of the relationships they have formed. The latter will be the case if the future is uncertain. Again, it is the manager's role to ensure that the former rather than the latter happens.

These five stages of team formation mirror the four stages of the project life cycle, although all five can take place within a single project stage. There are several group working techniques which the manager can use to shorten the forming, storming and norming stages, such as the application of the start-up processes described in Chapter 11, and in particular the use of start-up workshops.

Having formed the group, the manager's role is to ensure it continues to operate at the plateau of effectiveness. Over the next two sections I describe the leadership role of the manager, and how to motivate a team of knowledge workers. First the manager must be able to determine just how effective the team really is. On a simple level, this can be assessed by the way in which the team achieves its agreed targets, and by the way in which the individuals' and group's aspirations and motivational needs have been satisfied.[5] The team leader and the line management of the organization must ensure that both corporate and personal objectives are met. If only the corporate goal is met, with time there will be an erosion of morale and effectiveness followed by staff attrition. Often, however, it is only possible to measure achievement of these objectives at the end of the project, when it is too late to take corrective action. Hence, we must also have measures by which to judge the cohesion and strength of a group during the project. Indicators of team effectiveness include:

– *attendance*: low absenteeism, sickness, accident rates, work interruptions, and labour turnover
– *goal clarity*: individual targets are set, understood and achieved; the aims of the group are understood; each member of the team has a clear knowledge of the role of the group
– *high outputs*: commitment to goal achievement, a search for real solutions, analytical, critical problem solving using knowledge and skill, the search for widely tested and supported solutions
– *strong group cohesion*: openness and trust among members, sharing of ideas and knowledge, lively and constructive meetings, shared goal.

17.3 Motivating the project team

How does the manager motivate the members of a team of professional, knowledge workers, to build and maintain their effectiveness and commitment to the project? In the project environment, without the functional hierarchies, distinctions of title, rank, symbols of power and status do not exist, so many factors which are traditionally viewed as providing value to motivate professional staff are no longer available. In the project environment, managers must find new motivational factors which will be valued by their staff.

In this section, I shall recall the features of the project environment which have a significant impact on the motivation of professional staff, and then describe the factors likely to be valued by knowledge workers in the project environment, and which will therefore act as motivators. I also show how the effect of these varies throughout the project life cycle. The conclusion is that people are motivated by the development of their career. However, because they are no longer able to judge that development by their position in a hierarchy, they must measure it by their own growth and learning both within and through the organization. However, money remains a common yardstick by which individuals can measure that growth.

Impact of the project environment on motivation

There are three features of the project environment which have a significant impact on the motivation of personnel (Section 3.4):

MATRIX ORGANIZATION STRUCTURES

Within a matrix organization, people do not have the clear indicators of title, status and rank, as described. They also have reporting lines to two people, a short-term (project) boss, and long-term (functional) boss. Although the project manager tries to motivate the individuals towards the project goals, they often give their primary loyalty to their functional manager. It is that manager who writes their annual appraisal, and has greatest influence over long-term career development. This is exacerbated if annual performance objectives are aligned with the functional hierarchy because projects are of shorter duration than the time scale over which they are set.

FLATTER ORGANIZATION STRUCTURES

With flatter hierarchies being adopted by project organizations, individuals have less opportunity for career advancement, as there are fewer levels to occupy. They spend longer on each level before progressing, which means they have fewer opportunities to measure progress against career milestones (disturbing for a project manager) and are less able to judge how their contribution is viewed by the organization. Words of encouragement are not enough, because individuals can only judge their perceived value by progression, which means promotion.[8] With decision-making processes by-passing the centre (Figure 3.4), individuals may also feel less able to influence their careers, as they no longer have direct contact with senior managers making career decisions. They rely very much on their project managers or their functional managers to act on their behalf on career matters. This feeling of detachment can be heightened if the individual does not entirely understand the direction or strategy of the company, or how their project contributes to it. Having no direct contact with the centre through their work, they will not have the opportunity regularly to question the reasons for strategic decisions, or to suggest alternatives. This can exacerbate all the previous problems if they perceive their manager as the cause of their isolation.

THE TRANSIENT NATURE OF PROJECTS

I showed above how the transient nature of projects means that an individual's annual performance objectives tend to be aligned with their functional responsibilities rather than their project ones. Similarly, because projects only last a short time, they cannot satisfy an individual's long-term development needs in their own right. They can only be a stepping stone. It is the functional hierarchy which provides the focus for the individual's development, and if the individual is to be committed to projects, they must be assigned to projects which they view as fulfilling their development requirements. Furthermore, many people come to work for social reasons.[9] This can be lost in the project environment, and the impact of the second reduced, because people do not stay on a project long enough to develop long-term relationships. However, there are also people who relish the much larger number of contacts the project environment gives them. Such people are able to form new relationships very quickly.

The new motivational factors

A traditional view of motivation is Maslow's *hierarchy of needs*.[9] Maslow proposed that people have five essential needs (higher levels first):

– achievement
– esteem
– belonging
– protection
– sustenance.

People are motivated initially by lower needs. However, as they satisfy one, that reduces in importance, and they become motivated by the next. As their needs move up the list the lower ones lose all effect. Many of the traditional views on motivation are not valid in the project environment. However, Maslow's hierarchy continues to provide a basis for motivational factors. Many people have now passed the point at which belonging is the primary need to be satisfied at work; they satisfy that through their leisure activities. They therefore look to satisfy their needs for esteem and achievement. This is especially true of knowledge workers, and leads to five new factors for effective motivation.[10]

PURPOSE

People must believe in the importance of their work, and that it contributes to the development of the organization. It was shown in Section 3.4 that it is this sense of purpose, and the linking of the work of a project to the mission of the parent organization, which can help overcome the uncertainty of the dual reporting structures in a matrix organization.

PROACTIVITY

As career paths become less clear and predictable, and as senior managers become remote, people want to manage their own career development. Emphasizing the achievement of results, rather than fulfilling roles, and delegating professional integrity through results gives subordinates the opportunity to take responsibility for their own development. Furthermore, allowing people to choose their next project as a reward for good performance on the present one satisfies this need.

PROFIT SHARING

Allowing people to share in the entrepreneurial culture will encourage them to value it. Many organizations now encourage employees to solve their own problems, and to take the initiative to satisfy the customer's requirements, and are allowing employees to share in the rewards. The growing band of freelance workers also shows that many people are taking this initiative into their own hands.

PROGRESSION

As people near the top of Maslow's hierarchy, they become conscious of the need for self-fulfillment. They therefore value the opportunity to increase their learning experiences. Each new project is an opportunity to learn new skills, and thereby increase esteem and self-achievement. However, I said above that in the flatter organization structures, people may have fewer career milestones to measure their progression. The one yardstick they still have is money (or other status symbols such as company cars). These things remain important, not as motivators in their own right, but as measures of achievement.

PROFESSIONAL RECOGNITION

Another measure of achievement is professional recognition. Knowledge workers do not want the anonymity of the bureaucrat, but want to accumulate 'brownie points', to contribute to their esteem and achievement. I said above that in the flatter hierarchies of project-based organizations, managers at the centre may not be in direct contact with professional employees. Line managers must therefore ensure that their subordinates do receive due recognition.

Variation of the motivational factors with life cycle

The efficacy of these five motivators varies throughout the project life cycle (Table 17.1).

Table 17.1   Variation of the motivational factors throughout a three-stage project management life cycle

Factor	Definition	Execution	Close-out
Purpose	High	Low	High
Proactivity	High	Medium	High
Profit sharing	High	Low	High
Progression	High	Low	High
Professional recognition	Medium	Medium	High

DEFINITION

During this stage, the project team try to determine what the project is about, so their focus on its purpose is high. They will try to determine how it can contribute to their development, and so the entrepreneurial spirit will be high. During definition, there will be some opportunity to demonstrate professional skill through problem solving.

EXECUTION

During this stage, the focus switches from the purpose of the project to the work done. The learning opportunities, and chance of profit were set in the definition stage, and there is little chance to influence them during execution. However, through the use of responsibility charts,[11] people can be given responsibility for achieving milestones, and so have some opportunity for demonstrating their professional skill.

CLOSE-OUT

During close-out all five factors come back into focus: the purpose becomes important again during commissioning; people deliver their results and receive their due reward, if the project has been profitable people complete their learning experience, and look forward to the next; they receive their professional recognition. During close-out, individuals can be given career counselling to help manage their careers. Individuals should be helped to define their development needs, plan how they are to be achieved, and to develop networks, internal and external to the organization, to be used in their career progression.

SUMMARY

The five factors have the least combined effect during the execution stage of the project. The manager must therefore look to make the maximum use of the two factors which do have some effect. (*Note*: those factors which have a high ability to motivate, also have a high ability to demotivate if the appropriate action is not taken, or if the project goes badly wrong. If the project has been unsuccessful, then during the close-out stage there can be a rush to get off the project, with the result that work will be left undone.) Through all of this, if both the project manager and line manager understand the expectations and aspirations of the individuals in the team, and take proper account of them, then half the battle is won.

17.4 Leading projects

Much has been written about leadership, some of it by me,[5] but it remains one of the most elusive of topics. Often authors start off by saying they are going to discuss leadership, and end up describing management. I firmly believe leadership is different from management. Somebody can be a good, effective manager, without being an inspirational leader; and yet other people can be inspirational leaders, while being fairly chaotic managers. I read recently an article by Stephen Covey on leadership, and this for the first time said to me what is different between management and leadership. (Unfortunately I have lost the reference.)

In the article, Covey said that there are three elements of leadership, which he called *ethos*, *pathos* and *logos*. Unfortunately the majority of Western managers use only the last of these. They try to persuade their subordinates by the logic of the situation. However, this is not totally effective, without the other two. The effective manager is good on the logos, but to be an inspirational leader, he or she must first convince with ethos and pathos.

1. *Ethos* is the leader's basic value set. The leader must demonstrate to the team that he or she has values and beliefs worth working for. The leader must communicate his or her values to the team, to motivate them to work towards the project's goals.
2. *Pathos* is the leader's relationship with the team. Once the leader has demonstrated to the team inclusive ethical, moral and cultural values, he or she then needs to win their backing and support. Machiavelli[12] says the leader must be respected. He says the leader does not need to be liked, and even said it is best if the leader is respected and not liked. However, he also says it is essential that the leader is not hated, because then mutiny is more likely. Once the leader has convinced the team with his or her value set, and once he or she has developed a relationship with the team, then the team are ready to be persuaded by logic. Without the ethos and the pathos, the logos will flow off the team like water off a duck's back. Logos remains a necessary condition for inspirational leadership, but on its own it is an insufficient condition.

What this might mean for project managers is as follows. *Ethos* can work on several levels. First, the project manager must convince the wider team (primary, secondary and tertiary) of the value of the project to the organization. Secondly, he or she must gain commitment of the team to the overall management approach, and gain support for it as a way to deliver a successful outcome for the organization. Thirdly, the project manager must demonstrate their overall ethical and cultural values, showing an inclusive style that recognizes the contributions of others, and convinces the team that they will be properly rewarded. Then the manager needs to build the *pathos*, that is relationships, between themselves and the project team members, and between the individual members of the team. Both the ethos and the pathos can be achieved through a well-designed start-up process as described in Chapter 11. Once the manager has won support for his or her personal values and values for the project, and once people are working well together as a team, then the team members will be open to persuasion on individual issues that need resolving on the project.

17.5 The effective project manager

Now let us consider what makes an effective project manager. Handy[7] suggests that their are three possible criteria for effective leaders:

- *leadership traits*: effective managers have certain common traits
- *leadership styles*: effective managers adopt certain styles
- *a contingent approach*: effective managers adapt their styles to suit the circumstances.

Traits of effective project managers
There are six traits of effective project managers:[5]

- problem-solving ability and results orientation
- energy and initiative
- self-assured leader
- perspective
- communication
- negotiating ability.

For several years, I have conducted an exercise on courses whereby I ask delegates, individually and in teams, to select 6 traits from a list of 19. There is consistency in the answers, and the results agree with this list. Almost every team has four traits from the list, and many five or six. Handy,[7] in reporting research conducted in the United States into the traits of effective managers in general, says they have the first four of these traits. I once conducted the exercise with a group of managers from the Former Soviet Union. The two teams returned with five traits from this list. The sixth in both cases was technical competence, which is never included by a team of British managers. On discussion, we decided that if the exercise were conducted with German or French managers, then it is likely that technical competence would appear on their list, but it is not something valued by British managers. Conducting the exercise with course delegates has therefore reinforced my view of the six traits of effective project managers.

PROBLEM-SOLVING ABILITY AND RESULTS ORIENTATION

Effective managers are usually of above-average intelligence, and able to solve complex problems, by analysing the current situation and recognizing patterns. Problem solving pervades project management. The achievement of the project's purpose is a problem, as is the completion of each stage of the life cycle. Chapter 1 presented a problem-solving cycle (Figure 1.6) as both a view of the project management life cycle and the management processes within each stage. Furthermore, the control processes is also one of problem solving, planning recovery to overcome variances from the plan. Without a problem-solving ability a project manager would be lost. This ability at problem solving should be coupled with results orientation. The purpose is not to complete work for work's sake, but to achieve the desired ends. The solution to the problems should deliver the planned objectives and defined purpose, not necessarily complete the originally agreed work. *The end justifies the means*[12] or *All's well that ends well.*

ENERGY AND INITIATIVE

The project manager must also have the ability to continue working and managing under considerable pressure and against considerable odds. This requires the manager to be energetic and fit. This energy will be coupled with initiative to see the need for action, and have the resolve to take it. The Russian managers I mentioned above said that this initiative should extend to the management of one's own career as well as the task at hand.

SELF-ASSURED LEADER

Managers must have the self-assurance to know that what they are doing is right. This does not mean they must be extrovert or brash; a manager can be self-effacing while still self-assured. They must take action resolutely, confident in their opinions and judgement. Sometimes it is better to take action, based on incomplete information, being ready to modify the action as new information comes to light, than to dither endlessly looking for the perfect solution. Self-assured managers also delegate readily to their project team, confident in the ability of the team's members, and their own ability to motivate the team. Sometimes, especially in the IT industry, you see good technologists promoted into managerial positions, who are very reluctant to delegate, because they believe, quite rightly, that they can do the work better than anyone else. They work themselves into an early grave, while their team members are idle and consequently demotivated.

PERSPECTIVE

Managers need to be able to look beyond the team, and to see how they fit into the organization as a whole. This need for perspective extends to the project work. The manager must be able to move freely through all three levels of the project hierarchy, and above as well, to understand the detail work of the project and how it will deliver the project's objectives, and to understand how the project's objectives will meet the needs of the parent organization. This ability is known as a *helicopter mind*.

COMMUNICATION

Similarly, the manager must be able to communicate at all levels of the organization, from managing director down to the janitor. They must be the project's ambassador, selling it to senior managers to win their support; they must be able to talk to their peers, functional managers and resource providers to win their cooperation. They must brief and motivate the team; and they must talk to the janitor, because often the latter knows better than anyone how the project is progressing (Example 17.1).

When I was a post-doctoral research fellow, I had an office in one half of a pair of semi-detached houses. We had offices in one house while the other was being renovated. The plan was that when the other was complete we would move into that house, while the one we were currently occupying was renovated. I was due to go to the United States for a month for a combined lecture trip and holiday. About a week before I was due to leave, the janitor, a retired Welsh miner called Frank, asked me when I was going to be away. From the 20th August to the 20th September I said. Frank said that we were due to move into the other house on the 14th September, so it might be worth while for me to put my books in a tea-chest before I left. I said that was a good idea, but decided to check it out first with the administrator of the engineering department. I spoke to his secretary, but she denied any knowledge of the move. So I next asked the builders, but they said they would not be finished until late October or early November. I locked my office door, and went off to the States. When I came back, I found that the door had been forced, and that the move had taken place on 14th September, the very day Frank had predicted. Of course, he had spoken to the University Estates people as they came to survey the work.

Example 17.1 Talking to the janitor

NEGOTIATING ABILITY

In Parts Two and Three the project plan was said to be a contract (Figure 2.6). It is a contract between the project manager (showing what the manager and the team will deliver to the organization), and the project's sponsor (showing the support that person or group will give to enable the project manager to deliver the contracted results). Like all contracts this must be negotiated through bipartite discussions. Project managers rely on their ability to negotiate, because they do not have the direct line authority over their resources as functional managers do. They must win and maintain the commitment and cooperation of other people through their ability to negotiate and persuade.

Styles of effective project managers

Project managers can adopt four styles (Table 17.2).

Table 17.2 Appropriate management styles and team structures at different project stages

Stage	Style	Team
Feasibility	*Laissez-faire*	Egoless
Design	Democratic	Matrix
Implementation	Autocratic	Task hierarchy
Close-out	Bureaucratic	Task force

LAISSEZ-FAIRE

Laissez-faire managers allow the team to manage themselves. They behave like all the other members of the team, and are there to advise if required. This style is appropriate during the early developmental or feasibility stages of a project, or on research projects.

DEMOCRATIC

Democratic managers consult their team, and then decide the best course of action. Note that this style is different from the *laissez-faire* style above, which is almost anarchic, not democratic. This style may be appropriate during the feasibility and planning stages of a project, when you want to encourage people to contribute their ideas.

AUTOCRATIC

Autocratic managers dictate to the team what should be done and how. This style may be appropriate during the execution and close-out stages of a project, when the specification and design of the facility has been decided, real money is being spent, and so early completion is required to achieve the returns.

BUREAUCRATIC

Bureaucratic managers manage through rules and procedures. This style is appropriate on projects with low risk, for which there will be little change, because the bureaucratic manager is unable to respond to change. This means it will also be appropriate during the close-out stages of a project.

TYPES TO BE AVOIDED

In addition, there are styles which should be avoided in project managers. I have already mentioned the technocrat, the person to whom the science is more important than the results, the means more important than the ends. This person searches for the ideal solution, rather than achieving an adequate solution which satisfies the customer's requirements. (There is a saying that the perfect is the enemy of the good.) They are usually unable to delegate, because they have no faith in their project team's ability to achieve the perfect result. Secondly, taken to extreme, the bureaucrat can be ineffective. They pedantically follow procedures, assured in the knowledge that they have done the job correctly, even if not effectively. And, thirdly, the salesperson, who is very good at selling the project, but not at delivering results. All three of these characteristics, technical ability, application of best practice, and the ambassadorial role, are strengths if applied in moderation, but they become weaknesses when applied to excess, and they become more important than delivering the results of the project.

Situational management

Many project managers have a preferred style of management, but research shows they should adapt their style to the stage of the project.[5,13] Different styles are appropriate to different stages of the project, and at those stages different team structures are appropriate (Table 17.2).

During the *feasibility stage*, the research team works under the guidance of the project champion, to gather information about the background to the project, to design a schematic solution, and to gather design information to enable the systems design stage to take place. They will be working very much as equals, contributing their ideas to the effort, and the champion and/or manager will act to facilitate the process. Hence the *laissez-faire* style is appropriate with an egoless team.

In the *design stage*, engineers from different disciplines work together in multi-functional (matrix teams) to produce the overall solution. The manager will want to empower the knowledge workers to contribute their experience to the design process, but must provide firm guidelines as to the overall strategy to be adopted, and the time scales to be met. Hence, a democratic style, which sets firm guidelines and parameters, but empowers the team to work within that is appropriate.

In *implementation*, money is being spent, and the team must work quickly and effectively towards the completion of the project. Hence the project manager must provide quite rigid constraints within which the work should be done. The time for problem solving is over, and the chosen solution must be implemented. No changes ought to be allowed, other than to correct *show-stoppers*, and so the team must be instructed to do the required work. It will often be possible to parcel the work into single-discipline packages, and so the teams can work in a task-based hierarchy.

During *close-out*, the team will reduced in size, and the tidying-up processes will require cross-discipline working again. Hence the smaller groups will work in task forces. Because there will often be hands-on leadership from the project manager during this stage, the team structure is often described as *surgical*.[13] The project manager's own room for manoeuvre will be quite limited now. There will be various essential procedures to be followed during close-out, quality checks, test procedures, etc. Hence the project manager will need to follow various essential checklists in a fairly bureaucratic way.

Not only does the stage of the project impose different management styles, the team itself may look for different management approaches from their managers (Example 17.2).

Silburn interviewed nine project managers, each of whom had two teams.[5] He determined each project manager's natural style, and the style being sought by each of the teams. Usually the manager's natural style matched quite closely the style sought by both of their teams. However, one manger whose natural style was *laissez-faire*, had one team who wanted totally *laissez-faire* management, and another which wanted totally autocratic management. Perhaps the second team was reacting against the manager's natural style. However, the manager had to change his style as he moved between one team and the other.

Example 17.2 Managers' styles, and the styles sought by their teams.

17.6 Summary

1. A project team is a group of people with a perceived identity, who collaborate according to a set of values or norms to achieve the project's objectives.
2. There are three levels of project team, primary, secondary and tertiary groups, and the tertiary group consists of three types: reference groups, users and stakeholders, and consumers.
3. There are five stages of team formation:
   – forming

- storming
- norming
- performing
- mourning.

4. The five factors provide value to knowledge workers, and so can be used to motivate the team throughout the project life cycle. They are:
   - purpose
   - proactivity
   - profit sharing
   - progression
   - professional recognition.

5. The leader inspires through ethos, pathos and logos, not by logos alone.

6. The effective project manager has six traits:
   - intelligence
   - energy
   - self-assuredness
   - perspective
   - communication
   - persuasiveness.

7. The manager can also use one of four styles:
   - democratic
   - autocratic
   - bureaucratic
   - *laissez-faire*.

8. Managers need to adopt a management style appropriate to the stage of the project.

References

1. McGregor, D., *The Human Side of Enterprise*, Penguin, 1960.
2. Argyle, M., *The Social Psychology of Work*, Penguin, 1972.
3. Ribeaux, P. and Poppleton, S.E., *Psychology and Work*, Macmillan, 1978.
4. Adair, J., *Effective Leadership*, Pan, 1983.
5. Turner, J.R., Grude, K.V. and Thurloway, L. (eds) *The Project Manager as Change Agent*, McGraw-Hill, 1996.
6. Tampoe, M., 'Teams: the essence of successful project management', *International Journal of Project Management*, **7** (4), 1989.
7. Handy, C.B., *Understanding Organisations*, Penguin, 1982.
8. Here lies our sovereign lord the King
   Whose promise none relies on
   He never said a foolish thing
   Nor ever did a wise one
   The King's Epitaph (for Charles II, written before his death), John Wilmot, Earl of Rochester, 1647–1680.
9. Maslow, A.H., *Motivation and Personality*, Harper & Row, 1954.

10. Kanter, R.M., 'The new managerial work', *Harvard Business Review*, November 1989.
11. Andersen, E.S., Grude, K.V., Haug, T. and Turner, J.R., *Goal Directed Project Management*, 2nd edn, Kogan Page, 1995.
12. Machiavelli, N., *The Prince*, 1514, reprinted, Penguin, 1961 (Chapter 3).
13. Frame, J.D., *Managing Projects in Organizations*, Jossey-Bass, 1986.

Note

a. Section 17.2 incorporates material from the first edition based on a contribution originally made by Dr Mahen Tampoe.

PART FIVE

APPLICATIONS

18
Applications of project-based management

18.1 Introduction

In this last part of the book, I deal with applications of project-based management, to illustrate the use of project management in different circumstances. I said in Section 14.4, that the approach to project management needed to be adapted to the type of project. In Section 1.6, I introduced the goals and methods matrix, and showed how projects need a different emphasis in their management depending on how well defined are the goals and methods of delivering the goals. In Section 14.4, I primarily concentrated on the size of the project and the type of resource working on the project, although the latter was related back to the goals and methods matrix. I also introduced degrees of distance as a way of classifying projects. In the first edition of this book, I classified projects according to the stage of the product life cycle at which they occur, and according to the industry or sector in which they arose, and devoted a chapter to each. The latter, however, is not a strong determinant of project type, with the resource type, linked to the goals and methods matrix, being more significant.

Hence, what I do here is discuss the product life cycle, and the different types of project that arise at different stages. I then discuss several different types of project, to illustrate different needs and approaches. I consider product development projects, research projects, concurrent engineering, information systems projects and business process re-engineering projects. In Chapter 19, I discuss international projects, and managing projects from different cultures.

18.2 Managing the product life cycle

Several versions of the project life cycle set the project into a wider view of the life cycle of the product the project produces. Wearne[1] proposed a model (Figure 18.1), which is essentially a life cycle of the facility, and is reminiscent of the problem-solving cycle (Figure 1.6). It starts with a survey of demand for the product produced by the facility. That part of the cycle on or within the circumference of the circle describes the life of the facility built by the project. The six steps from study to commissioning relate to the four steps of the life cycle used in Part Three. The next three steps extend the life beyond the project to use of the facility, its maintenance, and monitoring of its performance.

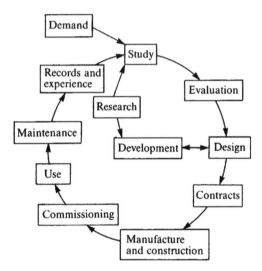

Figure 18.1   Wearne's life cycle for industrial projects

Kerzner[2] proposed a model addressing the life cycle of the product produced by the facility. It is the classic marketing view[3] (Figure 18.2). This is the view of projects filling the planning gap (Figure 2.5 (a)), and draws very little distinction between the project and the product. Some people differentiate between the project and the product life cycles, saying the project is the period up to and including commercialization in Figure 18.2, and the product life is the period from introduction of the product until its decline.[4] The project period can last anything from three months in the electronics industry, to ten years in the pharmaceutical industry, to 200 years for the Channel Tunnel.

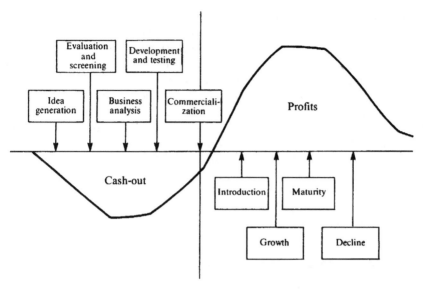

Figure 18.2   Classic marketing view of the life cycle of a product

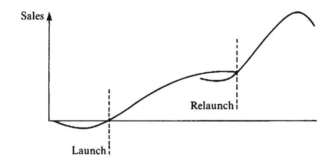

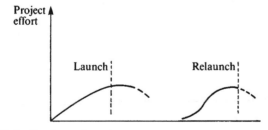

Figure 18.3   Product relaunch

Implied in Figures 18.1 to 18.3 is an assumption that the facility is an engineering plant that will make a product (or perhaps provide a service through its operation, as with the Channel Tunnel). In this book, I have taken a wider view of projects and the facilities they deliver. As well as an engineering plant, the facility may be a computer system, a design, trained managers, a set of procedures. With this view, projects can occur at any step in the product life cycle. There are projects to conduct a marketing survey, research and development projects, and maintenance projects. From the marketing model, there are projects to launch the new product at market introduction, and to relaunch the product at deterioration (Figure 18.3). Projects therefore occur throughout the product life cycle, or at any stage in the strategic development of organizations (see Section 2.2).

In this chapter, I shall examine several types of project arising directly from the product life cycle, which are common for many industries.

18.3 New product development[a]

Let us start with new product development, which in turn can lead to many types of project, including:

– research and development
– product design
– concurrent engineering
– facility design and construction
– product launch.

In this section, we shall describe how organizations create a culture for innovation, the types of organization they adopt for new product development, and how they plan and control the process.

Organization, people and culture

New product development has a key role to play in organizational competitiveness, yet it is one of the most difficult aspects of the company to manage. Organizations which choose in-house development must create a climate which favours innovation. Top management have a key role in this process, to encourage the establishment of a creative environment, which has three key components:

CLIMATE FOR INNOVATION
The innovative climate of an organization and its development policies are inseparable. Product development demands a flexible structure which encourages creativity, entrepreneurship and provides necessary conditions which favour development. However, there can be many pressures within

an organization which act to hinder enterprise, and encourage bureaucratic policies and procedures which constrain change. Many of these were identified in Chapter 3.

INNOVATIVE ORGANIZATION

In order to harness innovation, organizations must be versatile and adaptable in their approach to their circumstances.[5] In essence product development is at its best in organizations which encourage imagination and are organic in nature, rather than those with bureaucratic structures based on routine management processes.

INDIVIDUAL INNOVATION

Whether bureaucratic or organic, organizations consist of people, whose personalities and performance directly affect the success of projects and overall business performance. Thus, organizations need to adopt structures which harness individual innovation. This will be reflected in recruitment and selection procedures, opportunities for development, removal of bureaucratic restraint, and rewards to innovators. It is not possible to prescribe the definitive organizational structure to achieve this; much depends on the company's response to its environment.

Product development organization

In a climate which welcomes creativity, the marketing function has two distinct roles:

1. *Routine, operational marketing tasks*: demanding a structure based on routine activities, planning, coordination of the marketing mix for products which form part of the existing product line.
2. *Novel projects*: requiring less defined structure. New product development projects operate in uncertain conditions, and though planned require freedom from routine organization.

In order to implement in-house product development, the first problem is to find the right organizational format. By nature, innovation is individualistic, requiring each company to develop their own working arrangements. There are several ways in which a business can organize itself for product development

NEW PRODUCT COMMITTEES

These are senior committees meeting on a continual or ad-hoc basis, responsible for coordinating product development. Members are senior functional managers and executives from research, marketing, finance, production, engineering, etc. The principal responsibilities include reviewing and screening proposals, determining policy, planning and coordination. Often the committee is considered to be the coordinating function which ensures the product maintains its momentum and controls the activities of the multi-functional team developing the product.

PRODUCT MANAGERS

Product managers may be given the responsibility for developing new products alongside their routine duties of managing existing product lines. There are several economies associated with this. In addition to monetary benefits, product managers may assume this responsibility as they are sympathetic to the customer requirements and considered to be in the best position to ensure synergy with the existing product portfolio. The disadvantages are that additional management time required may not be forthcoming, nor can the product managers give this unique activity the specialized attention, resources and expertise required while maintaining responsibility for routine activities.

NEW PRODUCT MANAGERS

They are given overall responsibility for product development from planning to implementation. Often the new product manager works alongside existing product managers, but without their operational responsibility, and can thus turn their attention to the creative role and generate practical new product ideas. Although the establishment of a new product manager formalizes the product development role, there are strong links with existing product lines, leading to minor changes, rather than independent, novel or radical innovations.

NEW PRODUCT DEPARTMENTS

These are common in large organizations, take a high profile, working alongside new product managers in generating ideas, and evaluating their feasibility. In contrast to other methods, new product departments place the responsibility with a senior manager. The department provides the umbrella for coordination of various functions for continuous project management. It does not have responsibility for operational duties so may dedicate its efforts to producing quality new products. Sometimes a new product department may be situated within a larger department, such as planning, marketing, research and development, projects or engineering.

VENTURE TEAMS

These are composed of functional specialists working to a closely defined brief, and generally recruited on an ad-hoc basis for a short time. While located in the team, the individuals are removed from day-to-day activities. The team ideally would report to a non-operating executive.

TASK FORCES

These groups are organized on an ad-hoc basis. Members are seconded from operational duties for the duration of a project, or divide their time between routine activities and project work. The aim of task force management is to ensure continued support from the functions throughout a project. As a project reaches the latter stages, task forces may recruit more members with specialist skills.

PROJECT-BASED PRODUCT DEVELOPMENT

Product development involves individuals with specialist skills, from various functions and from managerial levels. The formation of project teams can be effective in solving problems and creating benefits which cannot be achieved in routine ways.[5] However, one particular structure may not be appropriate at all stages of the project. Just as the activity needs to be fluid and flexible, the perfect organization must also adapt to accommodate the different expertise needed throughout the project.

New product planning

The project teams have primary responsibility for the new product planning aspects of the market strategy. The nature of product development creates several planning problems, as projects range from modest expenditure to major investments, combined with indeterminate time constraints incompatible with routine reporting cycles. The diverse activities involved in new product programmes should move through a logical sequence of events. Though considered contrary to flexibility and creativity, development plans are necessary as they help determine critical components of the project. The sequence (project life cycle) suggested by Kotler[3] is often used to illustrate the new product planning process (Figure 18.4).

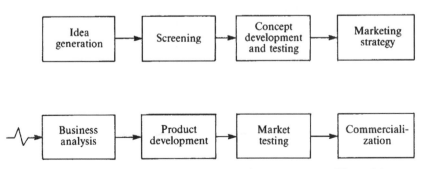

Figure 18.4   New product planning process (project management life cycle)

Plans should be used to enhance rather than hinder the development process. Management should not be limited by this logical progression. The sequence outlined is a guideline to help development, not constrain it. Idea generation, for example, does not always automatically occur as part of the formal planning sequence. Ideas may be initiated by users or employees during normal work (Figure 18.5). Similarly, product development does not always require radical change. Projects may be initiated to modify existing product lines (Figure 18.6). The project may also have several stages running simultaneously (Figure 18.7).

The planning process so far has not established links with business purpose or corporate strategy. Although not part of the routine of the company, project plans should be fully integrated into the strategic plans (Section 2.2). Product development should be complementary to existing products and meet the needs of the product portfolio against market

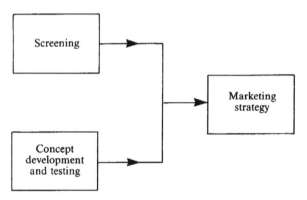

Figure 18.5   Revised sequence for ideas generated by users and employers

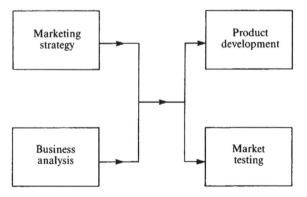

Figure 18.6   Revised sequence for products not requiring radical change

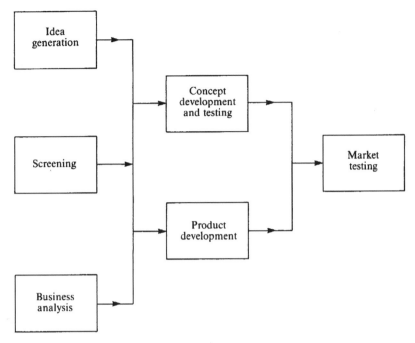

Figure 18.7   Sequence with several simultaneous stages

demands. New products provide an important strategic capability for achieving corporate and business objectives.[6] Strategic issues should direct and influence the new product project in three ways: strategic focus; technical criteria; and market acceptance.[7] Handscome[4] proposes a revised product development planning process which combines strategic focus with the need to combine phases of new product development (Figure 18.8).

Controlling new product development
The control function is an important aspect of product development. The application of marketing control systems to a new product development process reduces the risk. Control processes should therefore be integrated into all aspects of the plan and linked to critical components mentioned earlier. A continuous monitoring programme provides project teams with valuable information which may determine the successful outcome of projects. The key of any system is the extent to which it allows the manager to influence the success or otherwise of the outcome of the venture.[8] Several planning and control techniques may be used to monitor new product projects. Handscome[4] illustrates how these methods may be combined to monitor progress based on project objectives (Figure 18.9).

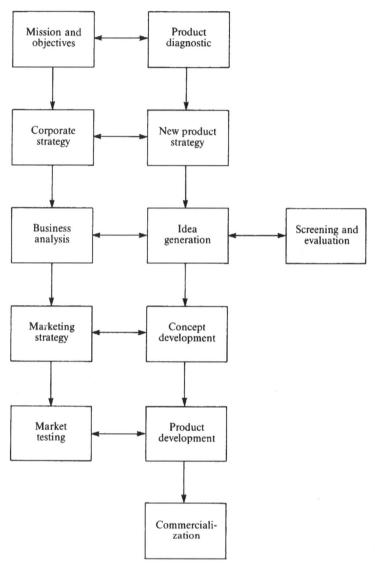

Figure 18.8   Revised planning sequence incorporating strategic focus

18.4 Technological projects[b]

Let us now turn to the management of projects in industrial and technological research and development (R&D). The discussion is relevant to process development as well as to product development. In this section, I focus on those aspects of project management within the R&D context

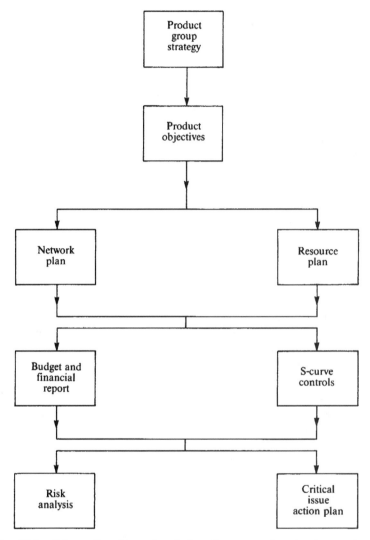

Figure 18.9   Schema for a hierarchy of plans for new product development

which poses specific problems, emphasizing those features, while accepting that most of the principles of project management can be applied in the R&D environment. Well-recognized difficulties of building teams of collaborative scientists, of managing such specialists and of communicating with other functions in the corporation are discussed, together with more positive notes for management. I shall describe what project management means in practice for industrial R&D, so that the non-R&D project manager can understand the requirements when liaising with R&D projects, and R&D managers can put project management principles into the context of their work environment.

The difference between research and development should also be recognized (respectively type 4 projects and type 2 projects in Figure 1.15). Different skills are required for exploratory research than for focused development. The definition of rigid time scale and cost constraints has less relevance in research. However, in the corporate world, research and development are often managed together as one unit, and so to outsiders appear to have similar management issues. In this section, I focus primarily on development, but indicate where generalizations can be made.

Project evaluation and selection

Project selection for research or development can be formal or informal, qualitative or quantitative. Rarely is it clear that a project must be undertaken, and even more rarely clear why that project should be done. There are several choices, and a lack of data allowing rational selection between them. This is one feature of R&D. Even with strong and clear business objectives, the direction of R&D effort often carries a great deal of discretion. There is a lot of guesswork involved in evaluating options, and this may tempt decision makers to rely on gut feel, or do something because it seems interesting or exciting. Hence, there is always some uncertainty in R&D; both in selecting the 'right' projects and in evaluating the chances of success.

One criterion which is often handled badly for the business is time scales. Often the development programme is slowed down, apparently to contain costs. This may have a disastrous effect on the ability of the company to compete in a rapidly changing market, where it is important to be first with a new product, or a swift second with a product modification. Speedy analysis of the risk issues at an early stage can allow more valid selection of major projects for fast tracking.

Important questions for the effectiveness of R&D are: 'Where have the proposals come from?' 'What is the push or pull?' Ideally, communications between marketing, sales, operations and development are close and open enough for productive cross-fertilization to occur, so that market pull and technology push are well balanced. Such open stimulation across functions must be a goal of the technology-based company. Ideas should also come from all levels within the organization, and this only happens if it is encouraged actively and openly, and if mental risk taking is rewarded. There should be some formal or informal flexibility for preliminary evaluation of ideas from outside the formal project control system.

Project evaluation needs to be based on a strong awareness of business objectives and strategy (Section 2.2). A research or development team can only be effective in adding value if it knows where the business is going. This sounds obvious. Unfortunately in practice it is too common for the scientist or engineer to be blissfully unaware of whether or how their activity is contributing to the business. In addition, the industrial R&D organization should have a technology strategy. This should recognize the nature of enabling technologies which are currently the foundation of the business, and emerging technologies which will produce the opportunities or threats in the future. It should provide a consistent statement of how the organization will access the required skills; and how it will use these skills to achieve business results. Surprisingly few organizations have technology strategies which are expressed in these terms to guide project selection. The organization cannot afford to have a prescriptive strategy or approach which imposes blinkers on visionary or radical thinking. Flexibility is an important key, but the strategy should provide the framework on which all decision processes are initially considered. Any decision to break with established guidelines can then be seen for what it is and may indeed prompt reconsideration of the guidelines.

It is clear that some kind of formal evaluation procedure is desirable. This may use an equation in which key parameters are estimated. It should also allow a statement of coherence with, or divergence from, accepted objectives. Even when the decision to proceed with a project can be taken internally in R&D, it is wise to seek support from the operations and marketing functions wherever possible, even for a research project which is a long way from the market place. Research managers are often accused of being insular, and of marching to their own tune, not bothering to communicate with other functions. This works both ways: research managers can be exacerbated by the different languages spoken by functional managers. However, it is a powerful aid to the research manager to have support and understanding from those who will make or sell the product, once successfully developed.

Selection of the project manager

The project manager may or may not be a line manager in the organization. Many R&D organizations operate matrix management systems (see Sections 3.4 and 6.2). Multiple skills are often required for a technology development, and these skill requirements may cross disciplinary boundaries. It is common for physicists, electronics and systems engineers, and bio-technologists to work together on a project. The managers of these teams must be able to coordinate resources whose skills they appreciate but may not understand. They need to be as technically aware as possible, to have a strong sense of the true project objectives, and to have strong people management skills in order to be able to manage diverse individual objectives. In a radical matrix structure, the project manager may not be a line manager, and may have line managers as part of the team. This works well where it is an accepted part of the culture and where the project management line is key to operational success. It is difficult, though, to operate in a more formal, hierarchical organization.

An important feature of the leader in a research project, and to a lesser extent in a development project, is the ability to contribute creatively. Adventurous thinking is required from the team, and this may be reinforced or discouraged by the manager. The manager must be able to use networks of contacts, both internally in the company and externally, to access information and resources, and should have a strong ability to communicate at all levels within the company, and across functional boundaries. The promotion of the excellent scientist to a management position may be disastrous. Creative bench scientists may be lousy managers, so the organization sometimes loses brilliant doers, putting them in positions where they actually do harm if they do not know how to motivate their team. The need to separate rank and role, allowing experienced scientists to continue to contribute to technical development while developing their status and career, is a problem in many organizations.

Project planning

R&D projects are difficult, if not impossible, to plan in detail. The very process of the project is to determine how to achieve the objectives. Therefore you can only plan at the integrative and strategic levels. Indeed, you tend to plan the project to a series of gateways, through which the project must pass by a certain time or fail. Some people say you cannot hurry creativity. That may be the case. But if creativity does not occur by a certain time, to allow the project to pass through the gateway, then it need not occur at all. The plan will use as its starting point schemes which have been produced during proposal and initiation. Ideally the project manager will have been involved in that process and will be familiar with the objectives and rationale. A milestone plan should be developed to indicate intermediate control points against intermediate deliverables, and also the gateways. The planning process may involve some definition of time scales and costs to achieve the milestones. However, these may not be developed from any estimating process, but may just be constraints imposed by market conditions. If milestones are not achieved by a certain date and for a certain cost, the product will not be worth while. Some kind of critical path analysis may be desirable for large projects, which may also require use of project planning software. Project managers learn which packages work best for them in which situations, and selections by different individuals for the same project might vary from a computer-based package, to the simple paper and pencil bar chart. Whatever planning tool is used, and they all have strengths and weaknesses, an issue for effective management is how strictly deadlines and critical paths are treated. The wise handling of plans is perhaps the most demanding skill required of project managers. This may require them to:

– optimize motivation and productivity
– maintain momentum
– control waste
– prevent divergence

but also may require them to allow divergence down a more promising path; or accept delay a promising route suffers an unexpected set-back.

You may say that this is true of any project, but it is most critically needed in R&D, where components of the critical paths may simply not be physically possible to achieve, and other approaches may lead to new unpredictable possibilities. By its very nature, the uncertainty of R&D requires *more* of this skill than most other project types.

Access to information may be an issue for planning and administration. Information systems are required to analyse previous work on similar systems, both inside and outside the company, and to assess the relevance of new ideas. Ideally project managers should have sophisticated data sources at their disposal and should access their networks of informal contacts. From the internal administrative viewpoint, they will need some kind of management information system. This may use sophisticated software or manual paperwork or word of mouth. Working against this is an attitude which pervades the R&D environment, that all paperwork and bureaucracy is a dreadful constraint on creativity.

The planning of the scope time and cost is, of course, only part of the story. Selecting the project team members is another. In many R&D organizations this will be quite simple in that there may only be one person with each of the required skills. This assumes that an analysis of skills required has been done. Often, little consideration is given to this, which means that only the obvious sources of skills are considered. Project launch workshops (discussed in Chapter 11) overcome this, especially if people with a wide range of skills are invited, thereby introducing new views. For a large organization some kind of skills database may be needed. These are rarely well-constructed, and rarely used by project managers, who are more likely to ask for resources from people they have worked with before than from people they do not know. In a large organization a good relational database of skills can be invaluable for strategic skills analysis and rational skills sourcing. These should be well thought out, with key word connections underlying free text skill description, building on technical classifications relevant to the company's market focus.

The team should always include people who will take the product through to the next stages of development (production or marketing), even if they cannot contribute directly to the current technical issues. However, it is sometimes difficult to obtain their commitment. The manager must achieve that by involving them in the planning process.

Research and development scientists often work on several projects at a time. There is some experimental evidence,[9] which suggests that most scientists and engineers are more productive when working on several projects, with peak effectiveness at about three projects. The rationale is that multiple contacts are more stimulating, and that there is less risk of becoming stale or blinkered if tackling several issues. There are, of course, exceptions, and one meets individuals who give their best only in total dedication to one project at a time. Whether it is more appropriate to have a large, self-sufficient project team, or a core team who can call on additional resources as necessary depends on the organization structure and culture.

Building the project team and getting results

A technological R&D team includes people with diverse skills, working across disciplines and several projects. Industrial scientists are usually specialists, often with an academic research career behind them which they still use as the basis for their approach. They are often uncommunicative, preferring to explore ideas alone. This may be for fear of failure, a wish not to share success, or because the culture encourages this, or perhaps because of the kind of people they are. For whatever reasons, many project managers in R&D have trouble building coherent teams, rather than a set of individuals working separately on the same problem. Lack of management skills in the leader exacerbate this. The extent of team working depends very much on the culture of the organization, departments and groups, and on the personalities concerned. Standard management and people development skills are, of course, valid, although they may need targeted interpretation in this culture, as they would in any other (see Chapters 3 and 17). Administration and bureaucracy are almost universally seen as drains and dampeners of creativity. Imposition of unnecessary paperwork of any sort by the project manager may be the worst thing they could do in the eyes of the team!

Communication needs

Communication is a high priority to ensure that new ideas are shared as early as possible. There is also a strong need for communication outside the team. Again, this is true of all project types, but in R&D it is often ignored.

There is a danger that the technical team may not feel that it is necessary to communicate with others until a breakthrough is achieved, or the project is successfully completed. Communication is all important for continuity, validity and congruent relationships, and may be:

– upwards, with senior management
– outwards, with functions who will take the successful development through production and sales
– sideways, with other R&D managers who may not be involved at all.

R&D managers should see information sharing as an important part of their job. This is rarely taken seriously and is the cause of many unhappy endings to otherwise successful projects. The challenge of communicating across language and vocabulary barriers is often disabling, and the onus is really on project managers to put their ideas and results across in English, in a way which is understood by others outside their speciality.

Project review and follow-up
The project must be reviewed regularly, and progress judged against the plan and other initiatives. It follows from the comments made in the last subsection that representatives of other functions should participate, as should senior managers or decision makers, and ideally also one or more scientist with different perspectives or background. One important requirement is that such review processes should not become unwieldy. Although it may be more efficient to hold a series of reviews of all projects in one day, better results are achieved if each is considered separately by fresh minds, unjaded by a series of apparently similar discussions.

When the project has been completed, and the product is moving from research into development and then to manufacture, it is important to have continuity. There should be representatives of the follow-up functions on the project team, and ideally the project manager will continue to be part of the team (if not managing it) in the next stage. They are then the product champion, and so commit themselves more deeply to the programme.

Effectiveness vs efficiency
A theme running through this section is that there is often more concern about efficiency than effectiveness in the management of R&D. Effectiveness is doing the right things, well; efficiency is doing what you have decided to do, as quickly or for as little cost as possible. In order for industrial R&D to add maximum value to the business, it must be effective as well as efficient. Results and business success are not correlated with R&D spend in technology-based companies, nor are they correlated with

productivity (efficiency), unless the objectives are wise. They are correlated with effectiveness, in the sense of flexible and top-quality thinking and appropriate actions. Since projects are the unit of operation for the R&D department, effective project management is the key to ensuring that R&D adds. You should demand flexibility and quality in approach, thinking, communication and practical experimentation. This means that the organization must have coherent, clear objectives which are shared with everyone (a clear mission). It must have a high skill intensity in its resources, and it must invest in their development through wise recruitment and training. The structure and systems of the organization must support innovation, and there should be formal and informal systems to encourage it. Lastly, very nebulous but very important, the culture must be congruent with objectives, standards and expectations, with the working environment supporting these. An attitude which says that we, the team, can win, and leadership which reinforces this expectation, can ensure success against all odds.

18.5 Concurrent engineering[c]

Figures 18.1, 18.2 and 18.4 show the product development process taking place sequentially. Traditionally, product development took place as a relay race: research, followed by development, followed by product engineering and prototyping, followed by production process engineering. Product development processes became artificially extended, not only as it was insisted that one step was finished before the next started, but inevitably there was a delay between one step and the next. Concurrent engineering attempts to overcome the built in delays by running the product development process as a rugby front line, with the steps in parallel. The concept was first adopted in the development of fast-moving consumer goods as early as the late 1970s, but became widely adopted across a range of industries in the 1980s and 1990s. Concurrent engineering is a systematic approach to the integrated concurrent design of products and their related processes, including manufacture and logistics support. This approach is now used in areas other than manufacturing, including construction and business process re-engineering projects. The objectives of concurrent engineering are to achieve:

– decreased product development times and hence earlier time to market
– improved profitability and competitiveness
– greater control of design and development
– reduction in product costs
– improved product quality.

Requirements of concurrent engineering

Several changes are required within the organization and in its approach to projects, in order to allow this to happen:

A CHANGE IN THE ORGANIZATIONAL CULTURE

A shift is needed to the flatter, more flexible approaches of project-based management. There needs to be decentralization of authority, with managers empowered to take decisions without referring them up the line, which builds in delay. However, this environment creates an almost greater requirement for senior management support, to show their faith and support for the product development process.

CROSS-FUNCTIONAL TEAM WORKING

The use of cross-functional teams is inherent to concurrent engineering. It is the only way to achieve the necessary parallel development. This requires people to communicate freely across the functional hierarchy, demonstrating the need for the empowerment and support of managers mentioned above. It also requires teams to work closely with suppliers since their development must take place in parallel. This may require partnering or integrated supply chain management. It also requires advanced contracting methods to allow contracts to be signed with suppliers long before the closure of design.

USE OF TECHNOLOGY

Concurrent engineering only really becomes possible with the use of modern information systems. This includes the use of computer-aided design, engineering and manufacture systems (CAD, CAE and CAM), to aid design integration through shared product and process models and databases. It also requires the use of project management information systems to coordinate the work of the people involved, and to manage the data involved. Configuration management becomes a significant element of concurrent engineering and so the PMIS must be able to perform the status accounting involved.

TECHNIQUES

Concurrent engineering requires the extensive use of iterative working techniques to develop all the aspects of the product, process and logistics design simultaneously.

Risks and pitfalls of concurrent engineering

There are some risks and pitfalls in the concurrent engineering approach:

ATTITUDES OF MIDDLE MANAGEMENT

There may be resistance from middle management. Not only does the cross-functional working threaten their influence within the organization, the process initially increases their costs. Although the increased costs will be repaid through the earlier completion times, managers can see an early fall off in the profitability of their departments, and hence a reduction in their bonus in the early years. When told that the higher costs associated with faster development times will be repaid through increased sales over a three-year period, managers may say that they are only in post for two years, and hence do not get the enhanced payback within their period of tenure of office.[10]

AUTHORIZATION OF THE CONCURRENT ENGINEERING PROJECT

The first problems to be overcome are those of obtaining sanction for the project and for executing it on a concurrent engineering basis. If this has been done before it should not be a problem, otherwise it may be a long, hard battle with all of the organization and departments involved.

The project definition stage is of paramount importance in this respect as it has to satisfy the following major criteria prior to project authorization and major commitment:

1. The product must be within the organization's aims and objectives.
2. The market need for the product must be established beyond doubt.
3. The supply of raw materials must be shown to be secure.
4. The design of the product must be carried out to a sufficient level to establish its feasibility (if necessary including models and/or prototypes).
5. The design of the product manufacturing system and its associated support systems must be evaluated to an acceptable level. They must be within the organization's intended capability.
6. Economic and financial evaluations must show the product to be viable bearing in mind the predicted life cycle, development and production costs.

It is usual during project definition to survey the industry, benchmarking to obtain typical implementation costs for similar products. It may also be possible to use the organization's standard investment appraisal techniques, but these do not always take account of combined development and implementation stages (which are conducted in parallel with concurrent engineering).

The risk associated with authorization of a concurrent engineering project is significant as this is an all-or-nothing approach that commits the organization to prosecute the project to completion. (The only factors to prevent its continuation after authorization would be due to external items such as a dramatic market shift.) In authorizing a concurrent engineering project, senior management must be seen to give both the project and the approach their full support. They are not only authorizing a technical development, they are authorizing radical change and way of life in their organization.

ORGANIZATIONAL AND CULTURAL CHANGE

The adoption of a concurrent engineering policy will inevitably involve significant changes to an organization and its culture. Some of the more important of these may be:

- departmental organization shift to project orientation
- conventional project-oriented organization shift to concurrent project organization
- move out of deep hierarchical structure into shallow, multidiscipline teams
- new organizational reporting structures
- change to business practices and procedures
- establishing long-term customer/supplier relationships and elimination of counter-productive competitive tendering policies
- reorientation of accounting policies away from departments and towards projects.

The importance of these changes will be determined by many factors including:

- the degree of support from senior management
- the existing organization's size and culture
- resistance from established functions
- degree of product novelty and complexity
- difficulties in implementation.

There may be conflict between those who are charged with implementing the concurrent engineering policy and others in the organization. There will almost inevitably be culture clashes between those involved with the concurrent engineering project and those in the rest of the organization (similar to those experienced when projects are set up within functional/departmental-oriented organizations).

MANAGING INTERFACES

There will be many interfaces to be managed including those between:

- management and design
- commercial considerations and design

- suppliers and design
- the various design functions within the concurrent engineering design team
- new product production and support facilities and those of existing products.

Careful selection of the concurrent engineering team, its working procedures and the control facilities employed ensure that these are managed effectively.

TECHNICAL MANAGEMENT

The most important function to control is that of design as this largely determines how a product is to be made or implemented and its associated costs. The designer is often only limited by a relatively few critical constraints, but his work may have great impact on the work of others and on downstream costs. The following aspects of the project are identified at an early date and monitored closely:

- *differentiation*: where there are linkages between highly differentiated departments
- *cross-functional requirements*: where there is a need to take account of the requirements of the other function, particularly those downstream in the development process
- *uncertainty*: where there is a high level of uncertainty in the use, interpretation or content of data
- *intensity and frequency of two-way flow*: where there are major feedback requirements between departments or functions
- *complexity*: where there is a need to liaise between groups because of the complexity of the product or task.

Standardization policies help to ensure conformity, and the extensive use of common electronic data management tools helps to keep all parties working to the same model and standards.

The early development of prototypes and prototype testing is a powerful tool used extensively in concurrent engineering. Its major value is that of identifying and forcing problems out into the open at an early stage. These can then be solved before they become too serious.

COST CONTROL AND RELEASE OF FINANCE

The implementation of concurrent engineering requires a significant departure from conventional financial release and cost control methods as it involves:

- initial release of greater funds on more preliminary information in the early stages

– negotiation of less well-defined contracts with suppliers or contractors who are to assist in the design process
– commitment of greater funding for production facilities at an early stage when parameters are not well defined.

The chief departure from conventional methods is the acceptance of significant financial risk at an early stage and the greater requirement for an effective and continuous cost review procedure that gives early warning of possible cost risk areas. (Bear in mind that the rolling-wave approach to both planning and technical design will have a major impact on the increasing confidence in cost estimates.)

RISK CONTROLS

More stringent risk management procedures are required with concurrent engineering than with conventional developments. In particular, they have to operate across the whole range of project activities, including sales, marketing, personnel, production and support. They are required to impose a consistent risk approach on a continuous basis, covering all items that would otherwise be analysed at major stage reviews. As with conventional developments, they fall into the usual categories of:

– technical risk
– commercial risk
– financial risk
– time risk.

Most of the concurrent engineering techniques and procedures operate with the reduction of risk as a prime motive.

18.6 Information systems projects[d]

As software becomes more complex managers have a greater need to understand its production. Several models of the software life cycle have been developed to aid this process (the need for which is explained in Section 1.5). Many of the models are applicable to other areas of technology, and to R&D projects. The function of a life cycle model is to determine the order in which software development should be undertaken, and to establish transition criteria to progress from one stage to the next (see Section 15.3). Transition criteria include completion criteria for the current stage, and entry criteria for the next. More sophisticated models of software development life cycles have evolved because traditional models discouraged effective approaches to software development such as prototyping and software reuse. This section traces the evolution of the different models, and explains their strengths and weaknesses.

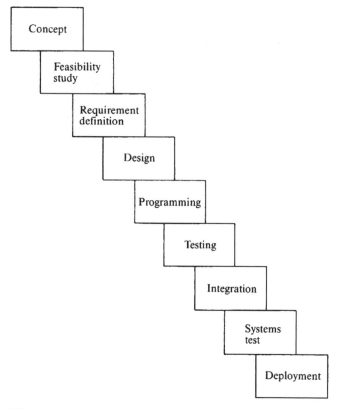

Figure 18.10   The stage-wise model

The code-and-fix model

The earliest model for software development had two, simple stages:

Stage 1: write some code.
Stage 2: fix the problems in the code.

Code was written before requirements were fully defined, design done and test and maintenance procedures described. The strength of this approach was its simplicity, but that is also the source of its weaknesses. There are three main difficulties:

1. *Maintainability*: after a number of fixes the code becomes so poorly structured that subsequent fixes are very expensive. This reinforces the need for design prior to coding.
2. *User requirements*: often the software is a poor match to users needs so it is either rejected or requires extensive redevelopment.

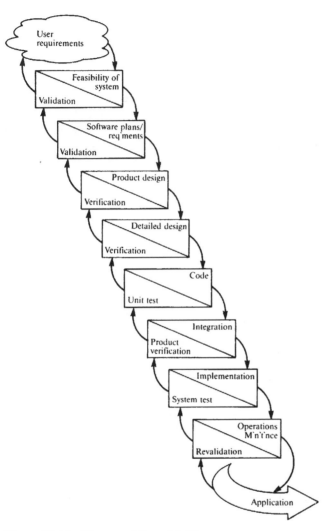

Figure 18.11   The waterfall model (1)

3. *Cost*: code is expensive to fix because of poor preparation for testing and modification. This highlights the need for these stages, as well as planning and preparation for them in early stages.

The stage-wise and waterfall models

Experience on large software systems as early as the mid-1950s led to the recognition of these problems, which resulted in the development of a stage-wise model. This stipulates that software should be developed in successive stages (Figure 18.10). The waterfall model (Figures 18.11 and 18.12), is a refinement of the stage-wise model from the late 1960s. The major enhancement was that it recognized feedback loops between stages, but with a requirement to confine loops back to the previous stage only, to minimize the expensive rework resulting from feedback over several stages. We shall use the second waterfall model (Figure 18.12) to illustrate principles common to many of the life cycles, as it can be easily related to other models, although the specific stages and names vary between models.

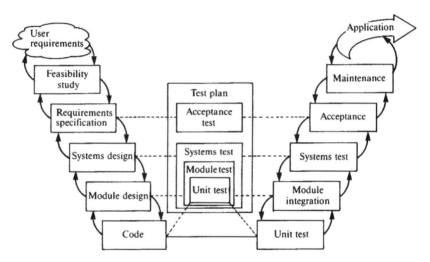

Figure 18.12   The waterfall model (2)

The second waterfall model is characterized by its V shape. Down the left-hand side are stages which derive elements of the system, while up the right-hand side is the delivery of the elements to form the system (Table 18.1). Each stage is defined by its outputs, the deliverable, rather than its constituent activities. A tangible output is the only criterion of progress, the only thing which people can assess objectively. Only in this way can the 95 per cent complete syndrome be avoided. The products of each stage represent points along the development path where there is a clear change of emphasis, where one viewpoint of the design or emerging system is established, and is used as the basis for the next. As such, these intermediate products are natural milestones of the development progression and offer objective visibility of that progression.

Table 18.1   Stages of the software development life cycle

Stage	Description
Feasibility study	Production of verified/validated system architecture based on a design study, including allocation of tasks to staff and machines, milestone plan, responsibility chart, schedules of major activities, and outline quality plan
Requirements specification	Production of complete/validated specification of requirements (functional/non-functional) the system must satisfy. Produced in close liaison with the end user. Means of system acceptance also agreed with end user
Systems design	Production of complete/verified specification of overall architecture, control structure and data structure for the system. Production of draft user manuals, and training and test plans for integration
Module design	Production of detailed designs for each module, together with module test plans. This may actually consist of more than one level of design
Code	Module designs are converted into code units in the target language (such as C, Pascal and FORTRAN)
Unit test	Code units are tested by the programmer. Errors are corrected immediately by the programmer. Once complete, code units are frozen and pass to integration
Module integration (structural testing)	Component units of a module are integrated together, and tested as specified in module test plan. Errors detected are formally documented, and the affected area returns to a stage where the error was introduced
Systems test (functional testing)	Modules are integrated together to form the system, and tested against the system test plan. Errors detected are handled as for module testing
Acceptance test	Client formally witness the exercising of the system against agreed criteria for acceptance
Maintenance	Service life is often grossly underestimated. Software written in the 1960s is still being used. The cost of development can be small compared to maintenance, but the latter is given little consideration.

To provide management control, the concepts of *baseline* and *configuration management* are introduced. The completion of a stage is determined by the satisfactory assessment of the quality of the intermediate products (or deliverables) of that stage. These deliverables then form the baseline for the work in the next stage. Thus the deliverables of the next stage can be verified against the previous baseline as part of configuration management and the quality assessment, before they become the new baseline. Each baseline is documented, and the quality assessment includes reviews of the intermediate products by development personnel, other project and company experts, and usually customer and user personnel. However, there the focus was primarily on baselining time and cost, whereas here it is on quality and scope. For these, you cannot baseline the whole project, only one stage at a time, as the definition of scope and quality evolve throughout the project. This evolution is controlled through configuration management (Section 7.4). It is the documentation and reviews which provide the tangible and objective milestones throughout the entire development process. The waterfall model shows how confidence in the project's progress is built on the successive baselines.

This simplistic description of the life cycle could imply that control of software development can only be achieved by rigorous control of the staging, so that no stage is considered complete until all prescribed documents have been completed to specified standards, and no stage can be started until all its input documents are complete (giving non-overlapping stages). Although the intended rigour of such an approach is commendable, it is unrealistic on a large development project. It is not intended that the life cycle should be interpreted in such a simplistic way.

The strengths of the waterfall model are that it overcomes the problems in the code-and-fix model. However, its great weakness is its emphasis on fully elaborated documentation as completion criteria for early stages. This is effective only for some specialist classes of software, such as compilers and operating systems. It does not work well for the majority of software, for example user applications and especially those involving interactive interfaces. Document-driven standards have pushed many projects to write elaborate specifications of poorly understood user interfaces and decision support functions, which have resulted in the design and development of large amounts of unusable code.

The spiral model

The spiral model[11] (Figure 18.13), which is still evolving, can accommodate all the previous models as special cases. The radial dimension represents the cumulative cost of undertaking the work to date. The angular dimension represents the progress of each cycle of the spiral. The model reflects the concept that each cycle involves a progression through a repeated sequence of steps for each portion of the product, and for each elaboration from overall concept document to coding of each individual program. Each loop of the spiral passes through four quadrants:

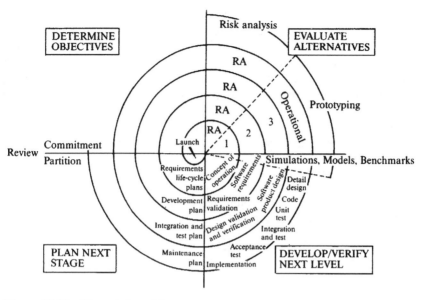

Figure 18.13   The spiral model

– determine objectives, alternatives and constraints
– evaluate alternatives, identify and resolve risks
– develop and verify the next level of product
– plan the next stage.

DETERMINE OBJECTIVES, ALTERNATIVES AND CONSTRAINTS
After planning and launching, each cycle begins with identification of:

– objectives of this portion of the product being set, including performance, functionality, ability to accommodate change, etc.
– alternative means of delivering this portion of the product, including alternative designs, reuse, or buying in
– the constraints imposed on final deliverable by the various alternatives, including cost, schedule, interfaces, etc.

EVALUATE, IDENTIFY AND RESOLVE RISKS
The next step is to evaluate the alternatives against the objectives and constraints. Frequently this process identifies areas of uncertainty which are significant sources of risk. If so, this stage should involve the formulation of a cost effective strategy for resolving the sources of risk.

DEVELOP AND VERIFY THE NEXT LEVEL OF PRODUCT

Once the risks are evaluated, the next stage is determined by the relative importance of remaining risks. This risk-driven basis of the spiral model, allows the model to accommodate any appropriate mixture of different approaches to software development including specification-oriented, prototype-oriented, simulation-oriented, transformation-oriented, etc. The appropriate mixed strategy is chosen by considering the relative magnitude of the program risks, and the relative effectiveness of the various approaches to resolving risk.

PLAN THE NEXT STAGE

This completes the cycle. An important feature of the spiral model, as with others, is that each cycle is completed by a review involving the primary parties concerned with the product.

Management and the spiral model

There are four key points:

INITIATING AND TERMINATING THE SPIRAL

The spiral is initiated by the hypothesis that a particular operational objective can be improved by a software solution. The spiral evolves as a series of tests of this hypothesis. If at any time the hypothesis fails, the spiral is terminated. Otherwise it terminates with the installation of new or modified software.

FEATURES OF THE SPIRAL MODEL

The model has three essential features:

1. It fosters the development of specifications which need not be uniform, exhaustive or formal. They defer detailed elaboration of low-risk software elements, and avoid unnecessary breakages in their design until the high-risk elements of the design are stabilized. (This is rolling-wave design, and developing work breakdown to a lower level in areas of high risk at an earlier stage.)
2. It incorporates prototyping as a risk reduction option at any stage of development. Prototyping and the reuse of risk analysis were previously used in going from detailed design to code.
3. It accommodates reworking or a return to earlier stages as more attractive alternatives are identified, or as new risk issues need resolution.

EVALUATION

The main advantage of the spiral model is that its range of options accommodates the good features of existing software, while its risk-driven approach avoids many difficulties. Other advantages include:

- it focuses early attention on options reusing existing software
- it accommodates evolution, growth and changes of the product
- it provides a mechanism for incorporating software quality objectives into product development
- it eliminates errors and unattractive alternatives early
- it identifies the required amount of each resource
- it uses the same approach for software development, software enhancement, or maintenance
- it provides a viable framework for integrated hardware and software system development.

However, the model is still evolving, and there are three areas which must be addressed before it can be called a mature, universal model:
1. *Matching to contract software*: the model works well on internal development projects, but needs further work for contact software. Its adaptability makes it inappropriate for fixed-price contracts.
2. *Relying on risk assessment expertise*: the spiral model places a great deal of reliance on the ability of software developers to identify and manage sources of project risk.
3. *Need for the further elaboration of the stages of the model*: the steps of the model need further elaboration to ensure all software developers are operating in a consistent manner. This includes detailed specification of deliverables and procedures, guidelines and checklists to identify the most likely sources of project risk, and techniques for the most effective resolution of risk.

RISK MANAGEMENT
Efforts to apply and refine the model have focused on creating a discipline of software risk management (Chapter 10). A top-ten list of software risk items[12] (Table 18.2), is one result of this activity. Another is the risk management approach (Section 10.6).

The problems of real life
Unfortunately, software development is not quite as simplistic as these models might imply:

- exploratory work on subsequent stages, including costing, can be required before the current stage is complete – for example design investigation is almost invariably required before it can be stated that the user requirement can be achieved within a realistic budget
- problems encountered in later stages may require reworking of earlier stages – failure to recognize this leads to earlier documentation becoming inaccurate and misleading

– the users' requirements may not remain stable throughout a protracted development process – it is then necessary to consider changed requirements and consequential changes in later stages.

Table 18.2   A prioritized top-ten list of software risk items

Risk item	Risk management technique
Personnel shortfalls	Staff with top talent: team/morale building: cross training prescheduling key people
Unrealistic schedules and budgets	Detailed/checked cost and duration estimates; design to cost; incremental development; reuse of software; requirements scrubbing
Developing wrong functionality	Organization/mission analysis; ops concept formulation; user surveys; prototyping. early user manuals
Developing wrong user interface	Task analysis; prototyping; scenarios; user profiles (functionality, style, workload)
Gold plating	Requirements scrubbing; prototyping; cost-benefit analysis; design to cost; value engineering
Continuing changes to requirements	High change threshold; information hiding; incremental development (defer changes to later increment)
Shortfalls in procured components	Benchmarking; inspection; expediting; reference checking; quality auditing; compatibility analysis
Shortfalls in subcontracted tasks	Reference checking; preaward audits; fixed price contracts; competitive design/prototyping; team building
Shortfalls in real-time performance	Simulation; benchmarking; modelling; prototyping; instrumentation; tuning
Straining the capabilities of computer science	Technical analysis; cost-benefit analysis; prototyping; reference checking

It is therefore important that the life cycle is not rigidly imposed. In reality, there are no clearly defined breakpoints between the stages. Equally, all the stages are composed of several substages or packages of work. However, once this is recognized, it leads not to the conclusion that the life-cycle model must be discarded, but it represents a valuable model of what is involved in the technical work of software development. The biggest single problem in the software cycle is the communication across the boundary from one stage to the next. At each stage there can be a degradation of the definition of the users' requirements. Quality assurance (Section 7.3), and configuration management (Section 7.4), play a crucial role in managing this flow of information.

Resourcing the life cycle

Many of the names of stages in the life cycle are similar to resource types working in software development. This results in each type becoming primarily associated with a stage: systems analysts with design, programmers with coding. You will hear IT people referring to the work of each resource types as an 'activity', and then they confuse the 'activity' of the resource with the work of the stage. Then resource types are not assigned to the project until the work of the stage with which they are associated is about to begin. The result is that items with long lead times are ignored by earlier resource types, resources have no time to prepare before starting, and resources cannot complete their input within the time allotted. In reality, most resource types should work throughout the project. Where the work of one resource type overlaps with a stage, that defines a work package. Early work packages are in suppcrt of the design process, and in preparation for the stage in which the resource is primarily involved. Later work packages are in support of implementation.

18.7 Business process re-engineering projects

Business process re-engineering or organizational change projects carry the added complexity that people's working lives are being radically changed, and that can lead to resistance. Key lessons arise from the study of organizational change projects:[12]

1. Define a clear and explicit strategy for the change, to which the improvement projects can easily be linked. This strategy needs to spell out what the organization is moving from and where it is moving to. It also needs to define the main thrusts of the change (quality, simplification, employee involvement, new technology, etc.), which will provide the key elements of the change.
2. Define strategic objectives for each change project, and show how these interrelate. Manage the interdependencies involved.
3. Define the key issues involved:
   – at the strategic level
   – for each of the main thrusts of change
   – project-by-project.
4. Use workshops to share the outputs from change projects, and to test options and plans.
5. Use cross-functional teams to collect and analyse data, and to generate and test options.
6. Build ownership for the change projects by soliciting input from a variety of sources.

7. Manage stakeholders explicitly at each stage of the improvement project.
8. Ensure all outputs from projects are defined, and that these mesh with assumed inputs to other improvement projects.
9. Allow for the possibility of emergent projects crystallizing (like the structure project), rather than resisting change in project definition at all costs.
10. Analyse and evaluate the difficulty of change projects in terms of:
   – scope and complexity
   – duration
   – 'iceberg issues' (especially behavioural resistance)
   – fluid outcomes.

It is also recognized that people undergo a cycle of emotional response to the change process. Table 18.3 shows the cycle and the attitudes encountered. There is no point trying to ignore this cycle. It will occur, and you will have a more successful outcome if you manage the cycle than if you try to pretend it will not occur.

Table 18.3   Emotional response to extreme change

Stage	Response
Stability	Management communicates their vision, the need for change and the consequences
Immobilization denial	People are taken by surprise. Their reaction is anxiety and confusion. People defend themselves against what they see as a threat to their life or livelihood: – 'They can't mean me!' – 'Is that what we get for years of loyalty!' – 'Management is overreacting; it can't be that bad!'
Anger	Openly displayed anger towards management emerges. People try to take control, through their power base in the organization, through trade unions, etc. Alliances are formed; efforts to divide management are made; all means to reverse the situation. Management must persistently argue the case, and not indulge in personal warfare.
Bargaining	People begin to aim for a modified solution. All kinds of remedies will be proposed in order to try to reduce the impact of the change: – 'If we take a cut in salary?' – 'If we increase our productivity?' Management must be steadfast and stick to reality
Depression	Frustration and a feeling of having lost spreads. People find it difficult to work and organizational paralysis sets in.

Table 18.3   (*continued*)

Stage	Response
Testing	The individual and the organization start working with alternative exit strategies to try to facilitate the individual's transition: – 'Did you say I could have six months' pay while looking for a new job?' – 'Being paid through a year's MBA programme would help the transition.' Management helps to find realistic alternatives
Acceptance	Individuals and the organization deal realistically with the situation. They may not like it but they accept it. Management gives recognition and support towards future plans New stability is achieved.

18.8 Summary

1. Projects can be classified in many ways. Different types of projects require a different approach or emphasis to their management.
2. In addition to traditional projects to deliver and commission a facility, projects can conduct:
   – marketing surveys and product development
   – research and development
   – maintenance and decommissioning.
3. New product development can lead to many projects:
   – research and development
   – product design and prototyping
   – facility design and delivery
   – product launch.
4. New product development can be managed through:
   – new product committees
   – product managers
   – new product managers
   – new product departments
   – venture teams
   – task forces.
5. The stages of the product development life cycle include:
   – idea generation and screening
   – concept development and testing
   – marketing strategy
   – business analysis

- product development
- market testing
- commercialization.

6. Selection of R&D projects should be against the corporate strategy, in particular a technology strategy which will recognize the enabling technologies of the future and how the company will exploit them.

7. The project manager should be chosen for their ability as a leader and communicator, and not for their technical expertise. Communication must be upwards, outwards and sideways.

8. R&D projects cannot be planned in detail, so must be planned against key milestones (important intermediate deliverables), with time and cost constraints set by the market requirements. Skills types must be chosen systematically and creatively.

9. An organization must be effective in achieving its R&D objectives. It is no good to achieve nothing efficiently.

10. Concurrent engineering is used to overlap stages in the product development cycle, to speed up the delivery of new products.

11. Concurrent engineering requires the adoption of new project management practices, including:
    - a change in organizational culture
    - cross-functional team working
    - use of new technology, information systems and other new techniques.

12. There are risks and pitfalls associated with concurrent engineering, including:
    - attitudes of middle management
    - authorization of the project
    - organizational and cultural change
    - managing interfaces
    - technical management
    - cost and risk controls and release of finance.

13. There are four types of model of the life cycle for software development projects:
    - code-and-fix models
    - stage-wise models
    - waterfall models
    - spiral models.

14. Stages in all the models are identified not by the work done, but by the deliverables, or intermediate products, in which they result. The control process focuses on the quality of these deliverables.

15. Spiral models, which can incorporate the others as special cases, view the project as moving repeatedly through four quadrants:

– plan the forthcoming stage
– determine objectives, alternatives, constraints
– evaluate alternatives, and identify and resolve risks
– develop and verify the next level product
– plan the forthcoming stage.
16. The management of business process re-engineering projects requires the careful management of the response of the people affected.

References

1. Wearne, S.H., *Principles of Engineering Organisation*, Edward Arnold, 1973.
2. Kerzner, H., *Project Management: A systems approach to planning, scheduling and controlling*, Van Nostrand Reinhold, 1984.
3. Kotler, P., *Marketing Management: analysis, planning and control*, Prentice-Hall, 1988.
4. Handscome, R., *The Product Management Handbook*, McGraw-Hill, 1989.
5. Foxall, G., *Corporate Innovation, Marketing and Strategy*, Croom Helm, 1984.
6. Craven, D.W., *Strategic Marketing*, Irwin, 1985.
7. Buell, V.P., *Marketing Management: A strategic planning approach*, McGraw-Hill, 1968.
8. McDonald, M.H.B., *Marketing Plans: How to prepare them, how to use them*, Heinemann, 1984.
9. Pelz, D.C. and Andrews, F.M., *Scientists in Organizations: Productive climates for research and development*, Institute for Social Research, 1976.
10. Toney, F., 'Good results yield . . . resistance: Proving that project management pays is met with denial in one Fortune 500 company', *Project Management Network*, October 1996.
11. Boehm, B.W., 'A spiral model of software development and enhancement', *Computer*, May, 61–72, The Institute of Electrical and Electronic Engineers, 1988.
12. Turner, J.R., Grude, K.V. and Thurloway, L. (eds), *The Project Manager as Change Agent*, McGraw-Hill, 1996.

Notes

a. Section 18.3 incorporates material from the first edition based on a contribution originally made by Dr Susan Foreman of Henley Management College.
b. Section 18.4 incorporates material from the first edition based on a contribution originally made by Dr Janice Light and Professor Gordon Edge.
c. Section 18.5 incorporates material based on research done by Michael Hougham. In using his research, I have sometimes incorporated his text.
d. Section 18.6 incorporates material from the first edition based on a contribution originally made by Anne French.

19
International projects

19.1 Introduction[a]

Another categorization of projects is international projects, that is projects involving parties from two or more countries. These projects have problems very specific to themselves, but particularly the problem of cultural fit. Indeed, as we shall see, the term 'international projects' can involve a multitude of different types of projects with a range of features. In this chapter, I consider the different types of international project and their management and characteristics. I then list common problems associated with their management and describe how to overcome them. I explain the issue of cultural fit, and describe work done by Hofstede, and what it says about the approach of different nationalities to the management of projects. I also describe the tensions that can arise on projects in developing nations, especially between a donor and recipient country. I then explain how to manage and win international projects.

19.2 Types of international project

International projects come in many forms and may include the following:

Projects in your own country for a foreign client

There are many reasons why a foreign client may want to make an inward investment into your own country. They may want to develop new markets, make use of local expertise or labour, or gain access to raw materials. In this case, you will have the familiarity of working in your own environment, within your own legal system, and with familiar subcontractors. The main difficulty will arise from working with a client of a different culture with an unfamiliar way of doing business. It will be important to understand their different approaches and to try to accommodate them. You may expect that, because they are working on your own home ground, the client will be making an attempt to respect your local culture and ways of working.

However, it can still be valuable to understand their culture, so that you can understand their ways of working, and not unwittingly offend them. The exception can be working with Americans, in which case you can expect them to expect you to adapt yourself to their culture entirely (see Example 19.1).

While running a course in Malta, I spoke to a Maltese who had just completed an assignment with the US Navy in Naples. He had been employed as a consultant, but effectively worked as an employee of the US Navy. He said that he had been told that he would be sacked if he accepted so much as a cup of coffee from a contractor as that could be interpreted as a bribe, and he certainly was forbidden to pay anything that could be interpreted as a bribe. He said it was virtually impossible to work in Naples without lubricating the wheels with 'commissions', and a contractor would be deeply offended if you refused a cup of coffee.

Example 19.1   The foreign client respecting the local culture

Projects in your own country using foreign contractors

You may use a foreign contractor because you need to buy expertise not available in your own country, or because to do so would be cheaper than to use local alternatives, or because you are to a certain extent compelled to do so by European or other international competition laws. As a contractor working for a foreign client you may be required to use a subcontractor nominated by the client. The problems are again mainly ones of different cultures and ways of working. Now you may expect even more that the supplier will respect your way of doing business, especially if they want to break into your local market. However, it can still be valuable to understand their approaches just to avoid any misunderstandings (see Example 19.2).

I once spoke to an American partner of Andersen Consulting. He told me that when they were sending a consultant to an assignment in a mainland European country, the consultant was sent on a two-week language and cultural awareness course. However, if they were being sent to Britain, they were not sent on such a course, but he felt they should be. English and American English are different, and sometimes quite significantly so. (You tell the English to walk on the pavement, and they will walk on what the Americans call the sidewalk; you tell Americans to walk on the pavement, they will walk down the middle of the road on what the English call tarmac). On a recent visit to the United States, I often found myself asking a question as a rhetorical question and finding it interpreted as a statement by my hosts. (I have the same problem in the Netherlands, but not in France.) I commented on this to one of my hosts, and she said she found it very arrogant to ask a question by stating what I thought to be the answer, yet it is normal behaviour in England and France.

Example 19.2 Working as a contractor overseas

Projects in a foreign country for which you are the client

The reasons why you may want to make an inward investment into another country are stated above. Now we will be working in a different business environment and legal system to which we will almost certainly have to adapt. We may expect our suppliers to respect our cultural traditions, and as the client we may have some influence in that respect. However, it may still be necessary to understand local traditions, just because we are in the minority, and because we may unwittingly cause offence as implied in Example 19.1. (See also Example 19.3.)

Under US federal law, US companies are forbidden to give bribes anywhere in the world. Under German federal law, German companies are forbidden to give bribes in Germany. But if they are operating in a part of the world where offering 'commission' is part of standard business practice, then they are allowed to pay it, and it is treated as an allowable business expense for tax purposes in Germany. Many employees of American companies have told me that when working overseas, one of the reasons for forming joint ventures is to pass the bribes via the joint venture partner.

Example 19.3 Respecting local traditions vs expecting your traditions to be respected

Working as a contractor for a foreign client in their country

You may have been employed for your expertise, you may have been used because your own government provided aid, and required that a certain element of the contract should be procured in your country. The aid may even have been in the form of services rather than cash. As well as problems of cultural differences, risks you may encounter include:

- the financial risks and credibility stakes may be high
- as the client is employing you for your expertise, they may not know very much about the project and the scope may not be well defined
- because of this lack of knowledge the client may not have full confidence in the project
- the project management and interfaces with the client may well be executed in a foreign language
- the client may have a significantly different cultural background and not be confident in your project management techniques
- with fewer shared cultural and commercial assumptions, the chances of a damaging misunderstanding arising are much greater.

A solution to many of these problems is to include local nationals into your project team. This has the benefit of enabling you to avoid many of the language, cultural and social difficulties, as well as opening doors for you in the country within which you are working. Under normal circumstances you will be expected to work within local traditions (see Examples 19.1, 19.2 and 19.3). The exception is aid projects, where as a representative of the donor country you may have greater expectations of the locals conforming to your ways of working. However, this is often not the case (see Example 19.4).

The Jamaica Maritime Training Institute Project lasted for more than 13 years with Norwegian aid money. The project was originally planned for three years. However, as the project neared its original end date, local job opportunities for the Jamaican staff were limited. Hence, they had no desire to complete the project. This was well understood by the local authorities. The prevailing prognosis, after 13 years of project work, is that at least another five to seven years of work are needed before the original goal, as it was formulated, could be reached. This does not even include the development of a counterpart staff professional enough to take over all necessary administrative and technical responsibilities!

Example 19.4 A foreign aid 'failure'

Projects in a country for clients also alien to the country

This is likely to be for a multinational company used to operating world-wide. Such a company is likely to be fully aware of most of the related problems. When it decides to proceed with an international project it is usually after stringent research and development studies and most of the main potential pitfalls have been addressed. A typical example of such a project might be the building of a refinery for an international oil company in the Middle East. Characteristics of such projects might be:

- well defined project scope
- stringent contractual and funding conditions
- the client will closely monitor all aspects of the project in an extremely professional way
- the client may well insist on various aspects of the project being carried out in a very prescribed way and may require you to utilize some of its existing facilities
- the law applying to contracts may be that of the country where most of the work is to be executed. This could cause difficulty when operating in countries with significantly different cultures.

The client will most likely have a much better appreciation of the overall context and factors affecting the potential success or failure of the project than you will. It is therefore essential that you talk to them at all times, maintain their confidence and use their expertise.

Multinational joint ventures

This type of project is often the most difficult to execute, not from the technical viewpoint, but from the complexity of dealing with a number of different national bodies each with its own aims and priorities. A good example of such a project is the development and production of the high-speed trains for the Channel Tunnel which was undertaken by an international team on behalf of the British, French and Belgian railway authorities. Features of these projects include:

– complex multinational contractual and funding arrangements
– multinational project teams
– relatively poor project definition at the outset
– a requirement to observe and maintain national interests
– the project may be spread out over a wide geographical area if each participating nation expects to execute its own share of the work
– good communications are of paramount importance.

With this type of project it is essential that the organization structure is set up correctly and implemented right from the start. Lines of responsibility, authorities and demarcations must be clearly understood at all levels. A good principle is to ensure that truly multinational teams are established in each major work location. This provides an informal communication facility between nations and, among other advantages, helps to avoid cultural and language problems.

19.3 The problems of international projects

Having considered some of the types of international project, we can identify some of the problems that arise in their management.

Culture

The main problem is one of culture. Our approach to personal relationships, our approach to doing business and our approach to project management are determined by our basic mental programming. The lily pond model (Figure 19.1) illustrates that our behaviour is the visual representation of our attitudes and beliefs, which is determined by our values and basic programming, which in turn is based on our unquestioned assumptions about what is right and wrong. Hofstede[1] identified that our assumptions are based on our family, education, linguistic, gender, social, regional, religious and ethnic backgrounds, and these influence our behaviour as individuals, in groups and as professionals. In working on international projects we need to understand the approaches of different cultures, to be able to work with people and predict behaviours, and not to give and take offence. The next section deals with this in greater detail.

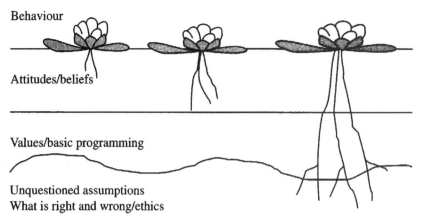

Figure 19.1 Lilly-pond model

Distance

The second most significant problems arise from the degrees of distance. The most obvious dimension of distance is geographic remoteness, but there can be other dimensions of distance as well:

- *time zone*: it can be easier for someone in Britain to work with someone in South Africa, and someone in New York to work with someone in Argentina than people in New York and Britain to work together, because of overlapping working hours in the first two cases
- *organizational behaviour*: in some organizations that encourage individualistic behaviour or strongly functional working, even people working in adjacent offices can be remote from each other (see Example 19.5); new people joining an organization (or a new joint venture) must learn the language, jargon and ways of working before they can work effectively (see Example 19.6)
- *language and culture*: these also cause degrees of distance, as discussed above (see Figure 19.2)
- *professions*: each comes with its own jargon and mental models, which can cause as much remoteness as language and culture.

Modern technology, such as e-mail, fax, video conferencing, satellite telephones and Internet and Intranet are helping to eliminate some of these degrees of difference and reinforce others (see Example 19.5 again). Indeed, some people are turning modern technology into an opportunity, achieving 24-hour working on design projects, with people working in India, London and California sharing a common database. Firms from Europe and North America are also having design work,

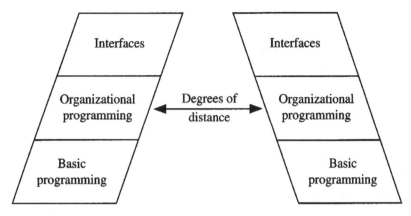

Figure 19.2   Degrees of cultural distance

computer programming and even secretarial services provided from India, where wage rates are low, but productivity and quality are high.

At Henley Management College, there is something of a ritual of morning and afternoon coffee. It can be a useful way of networking within the organization, and asking someone a question as an alternative to telephoning them or sending a memo or e-mail. A visiting academic from North America commented on this, and said that in his university he did not see most of his colleagues from one day to the next. He came in at 8.30 in the morning, went straight to his office, came out only to give lectures or go to the library, and went home at 5.00 in the evening or even later. Academic research assessment techniques which reward individual performance greater than team performance reinforce this behaviour.

Example 19.5   Organizational remoteness (1)

My sister-in-law, on joining the consultants McKinsey, was handed four typed pages of acronyms and told to learn them by the next day or she would not be able to work effectively.

Example 19.6   Organizational remoteness (2)

Organization, management and communication
International projects often require more complicated organization structures in order to deal with a number of factors including:

– collaboration with joint venture partners
– special requirements from funding agencies

– national interests, and the requirement to use local labour and suppliers
– local administrative requirements
– providing facilities for expatriate personnel.

Productivity and logistics

The need to use local labour, transportation or storage facilities can cause difficulty. Working abroad you may employ local labour for non-specialized functions, as it will be cheaper. Sometimes, especially when working for the government, it may be a contractual requirement to make a given percentage of the costs sourced locally. The productivity of local labour may be lower. There is a rule of thumb that the lower the wage rates of a country, the lower the productivity, sometimes such that unit labour costs are higher. (One major exception is India where productivity rates tend to be as high as in Western countries.) You also need to be aware of local working patterns (see Example 19.7). Another difficulty can be local social security and employment legislation (see Example 19.8). To cope with this it can be a good idea to employ all local labour through a local joint venture partner.

I ran a three-day course in Egypt. I asked the local organizers what working patterns I should have during the day, and they said whatever I normally did in the United Kingdom. On the first day we started at 0900 and broke for lunch at 12.30, returning at 13.30. The audience were asleep for most of the afternoon. I asked what the problem was and they said that their normal day was to start at 0700 and work for seven hours until 1400. They would then have lunch followed by a siesta in the heat of the day. We did that on days two and three of the course.

Example 19.7 Local working hours

Someone on a course at Henley Management College had worked on a project to build a new airport in Nairobi. At the end of the four-year project it was found that under Kenyan employment law it was almost impossible to sack someone if you had employed them for more than 12 months continuously – difficult if you are working on a transient project.

Example 19.8 Local employment law

Local legislation and regulation

Finally, work in a country often has to be done under the law of that country, including laws covering:

– contract
– business

- employment
- health and safety
- environmental protection and planning.

For this reason it can often be critical to employ a local agent who can ensure that you meet all the local requirements. In the Middle East, having a local agent is in itself a necessity, to guide you through local business practices and to pay appropriate 'commissions'.

19.4 Cultural difference

Cultural is the most significant problem on international projects. In this section I consider dimensions of cultural difference, how this impacts on project management and how to manage cultural difference.

Dimensions of cultural difference

There have been many studies into the nature of cultural difference. I consider first the work of Hofstede, and then attitudes to time and what needs defining.

HOFSTEDE

Hofstede[1] identified four parameters of cultural difference:

- *power distance*: the extent to which the less powerful person in a society accepts inequality in power and considers it as normal
- *individualism*: the extent to which individuals primarily look after their own interest and the interest of their immediate family (husband, wife, children)
- *masculinity*: the extent to which the biological existence of two sexes is used to define different roles for men and women
- *uncertainty avoidance*: the extent to which people are nervous of situations they consider to be unstructured, unpredictable or unclear, and the extent to which they try to avoid such situations by adopting strict codes of behaviour and a belief in absolute truths.

He surveyed 27 countries from 10 regions. Some of his findings are plotted in Figures 19.3 and 19.4 (regions and countries are represented by the codes shown in Table 19.1). In Figure 19.3 developing countries and Western countries form two district groups. The former are in the first quadrant, implying a greater respect for authority and society than in Western countries. In Figure 19.4 there is no pattern meaning that 'masculinity/femininity' and 'uncertainty avoidance' are unrelated to national wealth.

Table 19.1   Country ranking of fitness for project management

Rank	Country	Code	Initiation score	Planning score	Execution score	Termination score	Total score
1	Germany	GER	6.10	2.17	2.17	2.49	12..93
2	Italy	ITA	5.56	3.86	3.86	2.43	15.71
3	France	FRA	5.10	4.80	4.80	3.61	18.31
4	USA	USA	5.23	5.03	5.03	4.28	19.57
5	Netherlands	NGT	5.89	4.66	4.66	4.44	19.65
6	Norway	NOR	6.70	4.28	4.28	5.09	20.35
7	Gt Britain	GBR	5.45	5.12	5.12	5.26	20.95
8	Arab Countries	AR	5.48	5.11	5.11	6.49	22.19
9	East Africa	EAF	6.07	4.57	4.57	7.13	22.38
10	Sweden	SWE	6.57	5.17	5.17	6.41	23.32
11	Denmark	DEN	7.18	5.15	5.15	6.44	23.92
12	Japan	JAP	8.10	5.48	5.48	5.62	24.68
13	Thailand	THA	7.43	5.16	5.16	7.43	25.18
14	West Africa	WAF	6.74	5.91	5.91	8.21	26.77
15	Philippines	PHI	5.59	6.80	6.80	8.73	27.92
16	Yugoslavia	YUG	8.17	6.58	6.58	7.67	29.00
17	Malaysia	MAL	6.07	7.93	7.93	10.04	31.97

ATTITUDES TO TIME

We all know stories about Latins being free with time and Germans punctual. Attitudes to time reveal different mental programming. Germans believe events are controlled by planning and respecting deadlines. Things have to be ordered. Time is something tangible – it is limited and can be wasted and lost. Keeping people waiting is personally insulting, it implies they are not busy and are therefore unimportant. In this environment, a project leader meets few problems stressing the importance of missed deadlines. Plans are carefully thought out and followed. In other parts of the world, the Middle East and Japan, time is seen through much longer lenses. It flows organically, and things come together at appropriate moments. This view does not discount persistence in effort and thriftiness with resources. Emphasis is placed on doing things at once, particularly on getting relationships established. Doing things as they arise means interruptions which derail forward plans. Deadlines are seen as movable because it is more important to ensure that relevant issues are attended to when they occur so that continuity is maintained. Imagine, then, the confusion when a Japanese company, attempting to establish a project with a US organization, feels that a meeting to sort out how to proceed is urgent. They try to arrange it for two days' time but are told that senior American executives do not have time in their busy schedules within the next two months! The Japanese believe the Americans are not taking them and the relationship seriously.

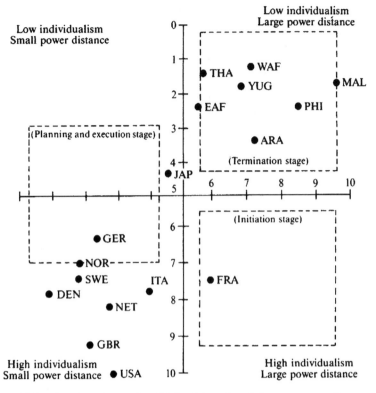

Figure 19.3 Country plot against Hofstede's cultural factors *power distance* and *individualism* against assumed preferred behavioural attitude scores within each project stage. *Source*: Hofstede, 1991

The Americans think the Japanese do not realize how busy they are running other aspects of their business.

WHAT NEEDS DEFINING

Some cultures like everything spelt out in detail, assuming that unless things are stated they become woolly and a source of disputes. This aspect of multi-cultural working causes the most obvious difficulties around contracts. This view is adversarial, concentrating on areas that *may* cause dispute. A different perspective is to focus on the common interest at the centre of most projects. Building sufficient contractual infrastructure to provide shape and a way of working is thought to be important. The conflicts of interest are expected to be worked out as they occur to meet the specific circumstances. The aim is to build and preserve a relationship that will realize the project's purpose. The English project manager, brought up

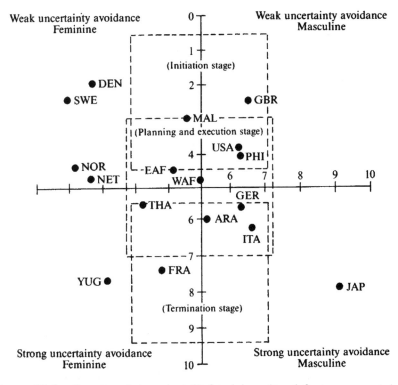

Figure 19.4   Country plot against Hofstede's cultural factors *uncertainty avoidance* and *masculinity* against assumed preferred behavioural attitude scores within each project stage. *Source*: Hofstede, 1991

in the adversarial tradition can expect a pragmatic approach to contracting when working with Swiss or French partners in a project. It does not mean that they are commercially careless or not astute business people.

Cultural profile of project managers

We sometimes assume project management is a discipline with universal rules, applied uniformly worldwide. This assumption views project management as a systems science, with mechanistic systems, applied universally. Project management really is a social science (some people even describe it as an art), which will be applied differently by different cultures. Jessen[2] proposed that the requirements for power difference, individualism and uncertainty avoidance varied throughout the life cycle of a project. He surveyed 60 projects from three continents, and deduced the level of each required at each of four stages of the life cycle (Table 19.2 and

Figures 19.3 and 19.4). (Masculinity he assigned a median score throughout since it appeared to have no affect on performance.)

Table 19.2 Preferred cultural approach, and assumed attitude scores, at each stage of the project life cycle

Trait	Feasibility	Design	Execution	Close-out
Power distance	High (7.5)	Low (2.5)	Low (2.5)	High (7.5)
Individualism	High (7.5)	Medium (5.0)	Medium (5.0)	Low (2.5)
Masculinity	Medium (5.0)	Medium (5.0)	Medium (5.0)	Medium (5.0)
Uncertainty avoidance	Low (2.5)	Medium (5.0)	Medium (5.0)	High (7.5)

1. During initiation, *power distance* should be high, as this is when the manager must give priority to the requirements and direction of top management (or the client). *Individualism* should also be high, as there is a need for creativity and innovative thinking during this stage; *uncertainty avoidance* should be low, as feasibility demands the ability to think in new directions and uncover new solutions, which often means risk, change and unpredictability.
2. During planning and execution the picture changes. *Power distance* should be low, as the people who do the work should also be responsible for planning and executing it. The main purpose of planning and execution is to ensure that the prescribed goals will be achieved and the project team are the best people to decide the method of achieving it.
3. During close-out attitudes should change again. *Power distance* should be high, as evaluation of the work done and results obtained are the responsibility of top management, because they are able to evaluate the work objectively, and also because they are able to view the project in its wider context. *Individualism* should be low for the same reason. *Uncertainty avoidance* should be high, as the termination of the project needs to be a well-structured process (Chapter 13), ending with the achievement of the project's objectives and ensuing benefits. Furthermore, the project team may feel insecure about the future, and so the manager should aim to maximize their security.

Doing a least squares fit of a country's Hofstede scores to the requirements for effective project management derived from his survey, he deduced a country's performance at each stage of the project life cycle and overall (Table 19.1).

The results show that project management is typically a Western approach to problem solving. It is probably also not surprising that Germany is top of the list; their very systematic industrial approach could well have been the model for the initial development of project management in the United States in the early 1950s. Arab countries and East Africa are also in the upper half of the list, showing either an in-built ability in these cultures to use the project approach, or a very strong and perhaps forced implementation of project management in these countries by Western cultures, which may have directly affected their behaviour.

Most European countries fit into the accepted mould for project management, having the right structural tools for systematic planning, organizing and executing projects. They have self-confidence (high individualism) for taking on challenging tasks and doing them independently (low power distance), and accepting and fighting risks (low uncertainty avoidance). Their weakness occurs during start-up and termination, when it is necessary to ensure that the organization is doing the right projects, and ensuring that the completion of the project results in the required benefits.

Scandinavian countries, which often regard project management as typifying their cultures, score fairly low. They are well known for managing nearly everything through projects, with the result that organizations have far more projects than they have resources to handle them, and large files of projects almost never terminated.

The United States, which invented the concept of project management 50 years ago, scores well in both diagrams, but their small power distance, and their high acceptance of risk, expressed as weak uncertainty avoidance, could result in weak project termination, implying unnecessary time and cost overruns.

Japan seems not to fit the project profile particularly well in any diagram, having too strong an uncertainty avoidance, and lacking a profile that triggers project initiation, planning and execution. As we know this has not prevented powerful industrial development in that country. It is probably also not so remarkable that the project approach is less used in Japan. Instead they prefer approaches such as production programming and quality circles which fit more with their cultural preferences, and are the backbones of their success.

Developing countries score fairly low on many of the described project management features. Indeed, these are the same factors for which they are often criticized by Western aid providers. However, they score fairly well on project initiation, and they have a good balance between femininity and masculinity. Futhermore, their balanced uncertainty avoidance is a great advantage during project planning and execution. Here their fit is much better than, for instance, the Scandinavian countries.

Finally, we can match in project performance between pairs of countries. This provides interesting comparisons. For instance, the United States and

Great Britain get very high score values in Africa, the Middle East and South East Asia, and, surprisingly, the host country also acts as teaching agent with their greater ability at project initiation. It is also surprising that the Scandinavian countries, which in Hofstede's analysis came out with very much the same cultural profile, seem to behave quite differently when compared on the different project phases. Norway, for instance, performs very well at project planning and execution in East Africa, while Sweden seems to be much better off in the Middle East. Hence, contrary to the common belief that the Western-oriented techniques of project management are just straightforward procedures that anyone can learn and implement, there are considerable cross-cultural problems in pursuing the approach in non-Western countries. Usually, insufficient focus is given to the fact that project management is not just a technique; it is an attitude of mind. Project management originated in Western countries, and its popularity has been steadily growing, but the outcomes have not always been in line with the expectations, particularly in developing countries. Traditionally this has been explained as a weakness in the local human resources, and the remedy being more training in the different mechanics of project execution, often in a Western setting. However, the reason for poor project performance may well be a weak understanding of local needs by Western countries, particularly needs beyond the project scope which are hard to articulate and define in Western terminology. Futhermore, many Western cultures are weak in both the project initiation and the project termination phases, due to their individualistic attitudes towards authority, risk and challenge, and quality of life. In summary, in spite of its increasing popularity and widespread appeal, the many pros and cons of the project approach should be given serious consideration before implementing it. In particular, the following two issues should be addressed:

1. The project concept is based on a limited resource effort, laid out in a stages development. Each stage has its own distinguishing characteristics requiring a unique attitude; from the creative, strategy-oriented and holistic approach in the early stages, to the very formal, tightly controlled and administrative-oriented performance necessary towards the end of the project.

2. Even though the project approach originated in Western cultures, these cultures are not necessarily the best ones for staffing and directing all stages of a project's phases, particularly in developing countries. It could be quite educational for Western cultures to honour alternative approaches to problem solving and execution, particularly where other cultural attitudes in fact present the better project performance.

The project leader's role in managing differences

Faced with such a bewildering array of factors, all conspiring to reduce project performance, project managers might be forgiven for wanting to cut and run! However, there is a range of strategies emerging that companies and project managers can employ in order to realize the full synergistic potential of cross-boundary project teams.

PROJECT MANAGER SELECTION

Too often we find wholly unsuitable project managers are dumped into complex situations. No one has taken care to think about which sort of person and experience is best suited to making a success of these complex roles. Before managing such projects, project managers should have had experience working in different organizations, managing a range of disciplines and, ideally, having lived and worked in more than one country, preferably as a member of project teams (see Example 19.9).

I worked with a company where the head of Estimating wanted to try his hand at project management. The only project he managed was in Israel, and the project was 100 per cent overspent.

Example 19.9 Project manager selection

AWARENESS OF OWN PROGRAMMING

It is sometimes a surprise to project leaders to realize that to work in a multi-cultural environment they need to be aware of their own mental programming. If the project leader is from the company and country owning the project, the automatic assumption is that things will be done 'our' way. One challenge for a project leader is to balance and evolve the demands of the interface between their 'home' organization, the client organization and culture, and team members. Companies who work internationally find that to be successful they have to modify their own thinking and working practices. Cross-cultural working is a two-way street, not colonization.

AWARENESS OF OTHERS' CULTURAL PROGRAMME

Working in multi-cultural environments requires the project leader to appreciate that things will be done, seen and understood differently. Project leaders need to be curious, not shocked, and should demonstrate interest in finding out and understanding different people's world views. They need to respect values leading to behaviours alien to them, but important to the individuals and society to which they belong. Assuming things will be done 'our way' only pushes differences underground so that they become embedded blockages. This easily creates an atmosphere of winners and losers which can prejudice effective delivery.

LEADERSHIP AND MEMBERSHIP OF PROJECT MULTI-CULTURAL TEAMS

For teams to work effectively, the roles and responsibilities of the leader and team members, both individually and collectively, must always be agreed upon. If the team is composed of people from different cultures, the expectations of leadership and membership differ. Clarifying the degrees of equality, responsibility and accountability expected of the leader and members is fundamental. So team start-up and team building is vital for success. The activities well known in team-building events will be just as important, but extra dimensions need to be added for international teams. There are three dimensions that have to be orchestrated to achieve high performance:

– ability to discuss and respect established ways of working
– awareness of own cultural programming
– awareness of others' cultural programming.

ABILITY TO DISCUSS AND RESPECT ESTABLISHED WAYS OF WORKING

This means building a team culture where cross-cultural issues are openly discussed, so that appropriate ways are found to integrate all needs. In addition to formal team-building sessions, informal contacts between team members, suppliers, clients and other stakeholders establish and nurture networks, and create links that accelerate mutual understanding, curiosity and mutual respect. In low definition cultures, informal relationships and getting to know individuals are considered more important than formal relationships (see Example 19.10).

An English project manager commissioning a chemical plant in Latin America recognized that he and his family would have to spend a lot of time getting to know local dignitaries, suppliers, politicians and government officials if he was to be able to set up and hand the plant over. He explained that when at home he rarely saw anybody from work. He was keen on his garden and being with his family. However, he realized that his new job would place a whole new set of responsibilities on him and his family in a new culture. Social activities connected with work had to be undertaken.

Example 19.10 Respecting local ways of working

ACCELERATE PERSONAL NETWORK DEVELOPMENT

The development of good personal relationships between people who have shared experiences is one of the most potent ways a project manager can influence project performance. However, companies in long-term joint ventures can also influence the wider networks through frequent job interchange, personal mobility, lateral career moves, interorganization conferences, meetings and training courses. The more the webs of relationships between the organizations intertwine the better. This must be done not only at the top, but at all levels of the organizations concerned. IBM call this 'entanglement'.

LANGUAGE

Decide early on a common working language. Provide accelerated language training for all those whose first language is not the chosen language. Work hard on those for whom it is the first language to modify the way they speak. They must think as if it were a foreign language and should talk slowly, enunciate clearly and avoid slang or jargon. Simultaneously, however, find ways to make it easier for those who are learning by translating key documents into several languages and by having a newsletter in more than one language.

CROSS-BORDER COACHES

Identify people across the organization who have an awareness of the dimensions of difference and use them as coaches or mentors to the project team, either on training courses or available to advise less experienced people about how to operate effectively in such environments. Such coaches can be supplemented by more formal cultural briefings about different countries that are increasingly available from specialist organizations.

COMMUNICATIONS INFRASTRUCTURE

New communications technologies are powerful tools for project managers, but they frequently fail to live up to their promise. The key lesson is not to fall into the trap of believing that e-mail, electronic and video conferencing, groupware and other technologies get people communicating. The personal relationships and networks need to be built in part first, and then the technologies can help dramatically to develop these networks further. Get the basics in place at the beginning: good telephones, several fax links and a good directory of who is who, what they do and how they can be contacted. Supplement these with project start-up workshops, where all the key players get to meet each other personally and work together, and you will have rapidly created the basic technical and interpersonal infrastructure you need. Out of this, the need and scope for more sophisticated methods will emerge more clearly.

19.5 Projects in developing countries

Projects in developing countries often involve additional problems to those discussed above. The projects are often funded by governments or international aid agencies rather than by the normal commercial sources. They also have different criteria for success or failure. Similarly, because the benefits of the projects are not necessarily to be enjoyed by those funding it, conflict is likely to arise between those directing or managing the project and other interested parties. This is particularly acute where cultural differences in approach to management techniques have an important part to play. We consider problems arising from:

– lack of infrastructure
– differing perceptions of host and donor countries.

Lack of infrastructure

Problems with lack of infrastructure can be more serious than one might expect. We take for granted the availability of everyday facilities and commodities. In developing countries you cannot afford to take anything for granted, and you cannot expect to buy your way out of trouble if the item you need does not exist in the locality. This may give the following impact on your operations:

PROCUREMENT
The availability of bulk materials and consumable items which would normally be bought locally has to be researched carefully. You should not assume that adequate supplies of everyday raw materials, such as aggregate, cement and water, will be available to you or your contractors when you need them.

CONTRACTING
Items which you would normally delegate to the contractor to supply have to be procured by you, requiring you to make more detailed materials take-offs, and putting you at considerably more risk for claims from contractors for late deliveries of materials.

TRANSPORT AND COMMUNICATIONS
Some projects in developing countries make heavy demands on local transport facilities. Although practical in an advanced country, special planning would be required to store and make phased deliveries in a developing country.

DOMESTIC ACCOMMODATION, CANTEEN AND RECREATION FACILITIES
It may require a significant effort to provide these to a suitable international standard. The living conditions of the expatriate in a developing country

require special attention. It is normal for long hours to be worked, and there is often very little to do during rest periods. The enemy then is boredom, particularly when the climate is not very agreeable and the project location is remote. This applies to everyone in the project team and particularly to the spouses and families.

UTILITIES

The provision of power, water (potable and for construction purposes) and industrial gases may add considerably to the cost of your operation.

SERVICES

The availability of adequate medical facilities, laundry, schools, shops, etc. all have to be considered when mounting an operation in a developing country.

IMPORT RESTRICTIONS

Developing countries place import restrictions on many commodities, sometimes to protect their own industry and sometimes to save valuable currency. Whatever the reason, this type of problem is likely to hit you when you least expect it. It may be that the project manager is unable to import his or her Range Rover or, more seriously, you may have to make do with an inferior local product at a critical stage.

RESTRICTIONS ON WORK PERMITS

For many reasons the authorities in developing countries place restrictions on who they will allow to work in their country. Having secured permission to enter the country, delays may still occur before a work permit is issued. This places a considerable administrative workload on the project. Applications for work permits usually have to be endorsed by the foreign national who is sponsoring the project. This often gives a client the right to dictate the numbers of personnel and the individual that you can employ, even although such a right is not written into your contract.

Differences of perception

Projects are undertaken in developing nations for three conflicting reasons:

– as a vehicle for economic development
– to provide employment
– as a tool for management development.

At first sight, the first two may seem to be compatible; the first creates the second. However, the first requires the project to provide a good financial return for the investors, and that requires the right products to be produced at the lowest cost, which often leads to the use of capital-intensive, high technology. However, for the recipient nation it may be socially, economically and culturally desirable to use labour-intensive processes to create employment for growing populations, conserve foreign reserves and protect the cultural heritage. The project itself also provides employment, as described in Example 19.4, which works against its early, efficient completion. The need of developing nations to use projects as a vehicle for management development works against both the other objectives. Donor nations would like to use their own experienced managers, but the developing countries must use projects to create efficient, wise management.

Different view of the owner

The donor country views itself as sponsor, and primary decision taker; the recipient country view themselves as owner, and the donor country as merely a funding agency. They may even view the donor country's desire to be primary decision taker as neo-colonialism. However, a greater problem than these is the cultural differences between the two countries, which may mean they take a radically different approach to managing projects. The donor nation often tries to impose its approach, because it has greater experience of project management. That may not be appropriate in the cultural environment of the recipient nation, and indeed it is the latter who is best able to decide what is best. It also conflicts with the recipient nation's need to develop its own managers.

The problem of organization

I have shown that certain organizational structures and planning procedures seem to support effective project management better than others, and certain information and communications systems seem to be more effective at achieving objectives which satisfy both the project and the parent organization. Effective project management has all four stages of the life cycle under the control of one company or organization. This enables the company to set the basic rules for developing the right type of project organization, with particular emphasis on convincing all levels of management of the advantages of, and the necessities for, proper project management. The problem which project managers often face is that even though their role is far more than that of a middle manger in a traditional, functional organization, this is seldom fully recognized by higher levels of management. Project managers find themselves under constant pressure to deliver results, but ones which require extensive internal cooperation and high level approval. Projects by nature demand change, and often senior management initially accept the importance of these changes, but when the execution of the project requires them to change their traditional roles, they refuse to cooperate because they find the new situation threatening.

This is particularly prevalent in developing countries. Too many projects have been initiated with the best of intentions from all parties involved, but have faltered because the project manager, or senior management, have not established a workable organization with adequate definition of responsibility combined with proper lines of communication. In environments where the participants have different values, different frames of references, different standards and cultural norms, and even different languages, these problems can be quickly magnified.

The problem of efficiency

The importance of understanding cultural difference in performing projects in developing countries is well known, but the practical implications are not widely recognized. The main reason is a problem of measurement. While money, goods and labour are readily measured, the change in cultural factors such as motivation, communication and leadership performance are far more difficult to assess. However, without understanding how to develop metrics for the latter, the former is very difficult to influence. Since it is generally assumed that a sound society should be effective, that is function according to its objectives, the purpose of administration must be to ensure that higher performance and effectiveness is obtained to achieve these objectives.

Effectiveness is a term used when describing private and public activities, but it is not easy to define (Sections 1.2 and 18.4). Productivity is easier to observe, defined as the quantitative relation between outcome of production against use of resource. The output is either goods or services, specified in terms of quantity or measurable quality. The use of resources can be expressed as work, services, raw materials, equipment, plants and financial resources, measured in financial terms.

In the West, productivity is widely accepted as a central factor in fuelling economic growth, creating surpluses for increased living standards and combating inflation. However, it must be given a simple, commonly understood measurement if it is to be evaluated as a factor for economic growth; its measurement must be good enough to establish wage and income distribution policies, determine cost and price levels, and identify investment and training needs in particular sectors. The more complex an environment, as in development projects, the more difficult it is to attribute productivity measures to particular projects, as they can often mean different things to different people in different contexts.

Since high productivity can only exist in a supportive environment, project strategies in developing countries must ensure conditions exist for productive development. One shortcoming in the teams of both the donor and recipient countries may be an inability to mobilize, allocate and manage financial, material and human resources against mutually acceptable productivity measures. The West's models promote planned structural changes and procedural effectiveness. However, this can lead to fatal misconceptions about what should constitute measures of success in cultures different from their own, and to a consistent failure to check whether local capacities match the requirements for execution.

The problem of close-out

In developing countries, it is often difficult to say how people working on a project will be employed after it is completed. In organizations and cultures where projects are part of well-defined strategies, this is less a problem since the parent organization can usually cater for the released manpower from recently completed projects. However, this is not the case for development projects taking place in developing countries, where the end objective may in fact be unclear, and where the parent organization does not really exist within the country, but is imported from the funding country. In these situations, the staff are only employed for the duration of the project itself, and there is no parent organization to return to on completion of it. The problem is exacerbated if the economy of the country is weak and so there are only a limited number of job opportunities, which is generally the case in developing countries. Indeed, this is true even in Western countries at times of high unemployment.

19.6 Managing international projects

In describing the management of international projects, it is worth while to consider two further issues:

– the selection of the overseas project team
– the selection of an international partner.

The overseas project team

The character of any team is determined by the quality of its senior personnel. This is especially true of the international project where individuals are thrown together more closely and there is less scope for toleration of personalities who do not fit in. A good project team does not just happen. It is achieved by hard work, particularly by the project manager, and this work has to be done before the overseas team is mobilized. The selection of the project team itself also requires careful consideration. Factors which should be taken into account when selecting personnel include:

ABILITY TO WORK WELL WITH OTHERS

This is probably the most important characteristic. The turnover on international projects is caused more by poor interpersonal relationships than by deficiencies in technical skills. Character deficiencies are more serious in the close confines of the international project than they are in the home office (see Example 19.9).

PRIOR EXPERIENCE ON OVERSEAS APPOINTMENTS

This is always a good pointer, but check with previous employers or managers. The person you are considering may be the one person who did not fit in with the rest of the team.

STABILITY UNDER PRESSURE AND ABILITY TO COPE

There are many pressures on the expatriate staff member and his other family while working overseas. These include:

- working and making decisions on the spot with limited support
- coming to terms with different working patterns and practices of other foreign nationals
- overcoming language barriers
- domestic pressure from the family due either to working abroad with single status or to the family themselves trying to come to terms with the problems of living abroad.

VERSATILITY

The overseas team requires personnel who are able to cope with every situation which may confront them, be it the breakdown of a much-used computer system or the emergency repair of a broken down car under hazardous conditions. You have to have personnel skilled in their own technical disciplines, but it pays to look for hidden talent as well!

PATIENCE AND DIPLOMACY

Overseas personnel at all levels have to have interpersonal skills and be able to relate to the nationals in their host country.

PROFESSIONAL EXPATRIATES

These are people who spend a high proportion of their lives working on major overseas contracts for a variety of clients. They can bring a vast range of experience to a project team not only in a technical sense, but also in such important areas as knowledge of local customs, how to get things done and general environmental awareness.

The international partner

Many problems of overseas working can be overcome by working with partners experienced in the countries concerned, especially choosing a local partner. In order to be confident of the relationship, you need to be careful in partner selection. Issues important in choosing a partner include:

NATURE OF THE COMPANY

Since your fortunes are linked to how well partners do their job and respond to the unpredictable, a clear-sighted view is needed of their reliability in the face of risks. There should therefore be a thorough review of their financial strength, backing, track record in the technology and markets, and their strengths and weaknesses. This is especially important with new partners.

RELATIONSHIP WITH GOVERNMENT

Since most overseas projects involve export credit guarantees, overseas aid, or other financial aspects impinging on government relationships, the effectiveness of a partner's relationships with its own government could be crucial. For particularly large or controversial projects, it may be necessary to create contacts between national governments, in which case it is vital to have good links established at both company and government level.

ATTITUDE TO RISK

Risk on international projects include normal contractual risks such as bid and performance bonds, penalties, damages, but also major additional risks such as climatic conditions, delays and damage in port and freight handling, and security of storage. The most important interface with partners is their readiness to tolerate the extra cost of responding to these risks. An essential prerequisite to agreeing the scope of shared work, is to define roles and responsibilities clearly, and to be sure of the channels of communications on solving joint problems. The awkward issues lie in ensuring precise monitoring and identification of problems early enough for joint management decisions.

MARKET AND LOGISTICS CAPABILITY

In the context of the market, the partner's competence in handling an international project should complement and be integrated with one's own, so that actions to clients, authorities, local interests and government agencies are consistent and tactfully effective.

19.7 Summary

1. International projects may include:
   - projects in your own country for a foreign client
   - projects in your own country using foreign contractors
   - projects in a foreign country for which you are client
   - working as a contractor for a client in their home country
   - projects in a foreign country for clients also alien to that country
   - multinational joint ventures.
2. Problems on international projects are created by:
   - culture
   - degrees of distance
   - organization, management and communication
   - productivity and logistics
   - local legislation and regulation.
3. Dimensions of cultural difference include:
   - uncertainty avoidance
   - power distance
   - individualism
   - masculinity
   - role of time
   - consideration of detail.
4. In order to manage these differences, managers need to:
   - select an appropriate project manager
   - be aware of the programming of themselves and others
   - use appropriate leadership styles
   - discuss and respect established ways of working
   - accelerate personal network development
   - use appropriate language
   - use cross-border coaches
   - develop a communications infrastructure.
5. Additional problems of projects in developing nations include:
   - lack of infrastructure
   - different objectives
   - different view of the owner
   - the problem of organization
   - the problem of efficiency
   - the problem of close-out.
6. In putting together a management approach for international projects, you need to:
   - choose appropriate staff
   - choose an appropriate local partner.

References

1. Hofstede, G., *Cultures and Organizations: Software of the mind*, McGraw-Hill, 1991.
2. Jessen, S.-A., 'Some reflections on project performance in developing countries', in *Proceedings of the 9th World Congress on Project Management*, D. Gower (ed.), IPMA, 1988.

Note

a. Research for this chapter was undertaken by (in alphabetical order): Chris Benjamin, Wendy Briner, Colin Hastings, Mike Hougham and Svein-Arse Jessen. In using their research, I have sometimes drawn heavily on their text.

20
Epilogue

In Chapter 4, I described pitfalls in project management, common management mistakes (as opposed to risks inherent in the work). From them, I derived five principles of good project management. I end by summarizing the five principles, and presenting the inverse of the pitfalls as profiles of success.

20.1 Principles of project management

The five principles of good project management are:

1. Manage through structured work or product breakdown
2. Focus on results
3. Balance objectives through the breakdown structure
4. Negotiate a contract between the parties involved
5. Adopt clear and simple management reporting structures.

1. *Manage through structured work or product breakdown*
   - to delegate responsibility
   - to define the scope
   - to isolate risk
   - to isolate changes.
2. *Focus on results*: what to achieve, not how to do it:
   - to control scope
   - to give a flexible, but robust plan (using rolling-wave planning).
3. *Balance objectives through the breakdown structure*
   - between areas of technology
   - between technology and culture (people, systems and organization).
4. *Negotiate a contract between the parties involved*: all planning is a process of negotiation:
   - between the owner and contractor

- between the project team members
- through bipartite discussion
- by trading benefits for contributions.

5. *Adopt clear and simple management reporting structures*: use single page reporting, nested through the breakdown structure, to give:
- visibility
- clarity
- commitment.

20.2 Profiles for success

Profiles come under four headings:

1. Foundation.
2. Planning.
3. Organizing and implementing.
4. Controlling.

1. *Foundations*:
   - align the project with the business
   - gain the commitment of your boss and involved managers
   - create shared vision, a sense of mission.
2. *Planning*:
   - use multiple levels, through a breakdown structure
   - use simple friendly tools, one sheet per level
   - encourage creativity by delegating to experts through results
   - estimate realistically.
3. *Organizing and implementing*:
   - negotiate resource availability
   - agree cooperation
   - define management responsibility
   - gain commitment of resource providers through the shared mission
   - define channels of communication.
4. *Control*:
   - integrate plans and reports
   - formalize the review process, through
     - defined intervals
     - defined agenda
     - defined criteria
     - and controlled attendance
   - use your sources of authority as a project manager.

Subject index

No index references are given to end of chapter summaries. The end of chapter summaries are themselves an alternative form of index.

Author and source index

Authors and their affiliations, books, journals, and other sources

Proprietary methodolgoies, software and suppliers

Project index

Examples and companies

Types and industries

Locations